W9-ALK-939

FALLIN' UP

MY STORY

TABOO

WITH **STEVE DENNIS**

A TOUCHSTONE BOOK
PUBLISHED BY SIMON & SCHUSTER

NEW YORK   LONDON   TORONTO   SYDNEY

Touchstone
A Division of Simon & Schuster, Inc.
1230 Avenue of the Americas
New York, NY 10020

All photos not otherwise credited are from the author's personal collection.

First Touchstone hardcover edition February 2011

For information about special discounts for bulk purchases, please contact Simon & Schuster
Special Sales at 1-866-506-1949 or business@simonandschuster.com.

The Simon & Schuster Speakers Bureau can bring authors to your live event.
For more information or to book an event contact the Simon & Schuster Speakers
Bureau at 1-866-248-3049 or visit our website at www.simonspeakers.com.

Designed by Ruth Lee-Mui

Manufactured in the United States of America

10 9 8 7 6 5 4 3 2 1

ISBN 978-1-4391-9206-1
ISBN 978-1-4391-9209-2 (ebook)

For Nanny—for your love, in your memory.

If one advances confidently in the direction of one's dreams, and endeavors to live the life which one has imagined, one will meet with a success unexpected in common hours.

—Henry David Thoreau

CONTENTS

CONTENTS

When I was young, somewhere between boyhood and adulthood, Nanny Aurora hung a dream catcher above my bed. She would read me a story, then tuck me in, kiss me on the cheek and wish me good dreams. I didn't know back then what this Native American charm meant. I now believe it was there to catch my dreams before others crushed them.

When I was twenty-three, and somewhere between chasing my dreams and making them a reality, my grandmother passed away and joined the man she spoke with every day: God. I didn't know back then what her death meant. I now believe that she passed on to become the angel who saved me from myself; to stop me from taking a wrecking ball to the very dream she helped build.

By the time I'm an old man, I believe I'll come to an even deeper understanding of my life—the reasons, the purpose and the meaning of the paths I took. Between now and then, I'll sit with my children and read them this story as a Gomez family legacy. I will read it to them as part—I hope—inspiration and part cautionary tale. And the overriding message will be as simple as a lyric: "Dream big, find a way, make it happen. Just don't mess it up when you get there."

Because God doesn't always give second chances.

Not unless you're *really* lucky and walk with angels.

And, believe me, I was one of the lucky ones, performing and dancing with a dream catcher called Nanny whose wings helped me fly and, more important, allowed me to remain midair, soaring.

PREFACE

I come to my senses in that place they call "rock bottom."

I stare through the prison bars and assess the shit I'm in. It takes only a few seconds to realize that shit doesn't get much deeper than this, and I feel framed by my own stupidity: the architect of the dream turned kamikaze pilot.

That crazy duality would have made up the wording on my gravestone had grace not saved me from death.

Instead, I get to consider the epitaph on my career, if not my life: the unknown wording that the Black Eyed Peas management and record label are no doubt already discussing with the stonemason.

I'm busted. It's over . . . it's all over, I tell myself.

I sit with my back against the stone-cold wall, aching. The drugs that raced through my bloodstream have worn off, and this feels like the steepest and darkest comedown yet.

In the seconds before coming to, I hadn't known where I was or what was happening; suspended in oblivion. I instantly want to rewind and trap those seconds in a jar and seal them—and me—into some crude, homemade snowglobe. But, as is usual with retribution, there is no escaping the reality of my own making.

My head feels heavy and mechanical, my mouth is so dry that it feels like I've got a dozen cotton balls stuffed under my tongue, and the sense of dread is building into a quiet panic.

I'm sitting on a cement bench in a dirty police cell, and my wrists still remember the sensation of being cuffed even if my mind is still piecing together the fragmented details. Gray walls surround me on three sides. On my right, there are floor-to-ceiling prison bars caging me off from the corridor leading to the sheriff's office.

I hear voices. Faint sounds of formal activity.

Then laughter.

Are they laughing at me?

Did I hear them say "Black Eyed Peas?"

What are they saying?

What are they saying about me?

Paranoia is a bitch when drugs leave it embedded in your head.

My muscles tense and shiver. My heart races. This one muscle is probably as confused as I am with my lifestyle: racing with excitement in the high, sinking with anxiety on the down. And each time, it never really knows how close it is to death. But the rest of my body seems well aware of its proximity to the abyss, because everything inside feels like it is turning to jelly and about to erupt and cover the walls in shit. Even being in my own skin feels claustrophobic.

Now I know how my cat feels when I put her in that carry cage before taking her to the vet. Her wide eyes always tell me that she doesn't know what the hell is going on either, and I'm suddenly empathizing with her.

My white hoodie feels like a straitjacket, and my legs are bouncing in the black Jordan basketball shorts I'd put on in a hurry before leaving home. I slip my feet into my flip-flops and stare at the cement wall facing me. There's nothing to look at except dents, grime and peeling paint.

As for fixtures and fittings, there is the one bench and a sink in the corner. I'm grateful for the absence of a mirror because I don't want to confirm how hellish I look: ghostly pale with dark bags haunting the eyes, skin covered with acne bumps, cheeks so gaunt that I look like the masked one in the movie *Scream*. I've seen this face hundreds of times staring back at me in the bathroom mirror at home when giving myself a pull-yourself-together pep talk.

"C'mon son, you're going to stop," I'd quietly urge my reflection, "tomorrow, you'll be sober."

Or the lie that says "After this one, I'm not going to do this shit no more."

Maybe each time I walked out of the bathroom, my reflection still stood there in the same spot, laughing.

The emptiness of the cell reminds me of my first apartment in Hollywood. Only this joint is cleaner—it doesn't have cockroaches crawling out of every crevice like my old place did.

Shit, I can't slide back to those days again. Come too far.

I start pacing, my flip-flops shuffling and popping on the floor, spitting a pathetic rhythm.

"I fucked up," I murmur, "Biggest fuck-up EVER!" I shout.

The stone walls echo it back to me just in case I missed it the first time.

At times like this as a kid, when bad shit happened, I'd escape into my imagination and block everything out. But even the wild and crazy dreamer has to wake one day and *this* is my wake-up call, delivered in the late afternoon of Tuesday, March 27, 2007.

This day will change my life.

This arrest—for rear-ending some poor woman on the freeway while off my head on a mad concoction of drugs—registers high on the Richter scale of wake-ups. They say that life gives you a few chances to work it out for yourself before conspiring to bring about the rock-bottom downfall; the final warning before the endgame. I guess this is where the lessons start being learned.

Outside the cell, my name is scribbled in chalk: "Gomez." No need for Jimmy. Or, as Mom would correct me. "It's JAIME (that's 'Hi-meh," the Spanish pronunciation) YOUR REAL NAME IS HI-MEH!!"

Not that it matters. Shame doesn't address you on first-name terms.

The date of birth on my arrest sheet will reveal my age to be thirty-one, with a subtext that mocks: "Should know better." Especially for a man soon to be married and a father of one who not long ago looked into the eyes of the woman he loves—like, *really* loves to her core—and vowed: "I'll change. Things will be different."

"Yeah right," I imagine my girl, Jaymie, saying (that's "Jaymie"— pronounced as it sounds).

There's no mention anywhere of my stage name: Taboo. It's like the officer told me when they slammed me inside: "That counts for nothing. Here, you're the same as everyone else, dude."

The irony is another kick in the nuts. I've spent all my life working my ass off to be something other than "the same as everyone else," trying to escape an ordinary life and break the mold. I was never settling for the just-earn-a-steady-wage life. I longed to be a performer. That is all I had ever wanted since the age of five, and I had made it happen.

In 1995, the dream was birthed. I was no longer just Jimmy Gomez from Rosemead, California. I became Taboo, one of the founding Black Eyed Peas. Our journey had been exploding since 2001, taking us from a small underground group in Los Angeles to a stratosphere we have at times struggled to believe. Police cells are awful places to realize how blessed you have been.

Just six weeks before ending up here, we won Best Pop Performance at the 49th Grammy Awards for "My Humps," adding to the two Golden Gramophones won in 2005 and 2006. That same night in 2007, we'd announced the Lifetime Achievement Award given to Booker T. & the M.G.'s, and I opened the golden envelope and called out Mary J. Blige as the winner of Best R&B Album for

Breakthrough. On Hollywood's surface, life could not have seemed sweeter. But demons lurk beneath that glossy exterior, and they are never satisfied with mere achievements and happiness. Inner demons want your dream just as much as you do—but they just want it realized so they can fuck it all up. I am the Hollywood cliché. The textbook example of someone ill-equipped for the success he wished for.

In my mind, I place these two L.A. scenes side by side: the Grammy night with the Peas and Mary J. Blige, and this shame, experienced alone, inside the City of Industry police station in the San Gabriel Valley. All my pretend masks of rock-star status lie smashed on the cell floor, and the exposure makes me feel like a fraud.

A police officer arrives at the bars. He points at an empty cup and tells me they asked me to pee in it for a urine sample, but I was incapable; so many drugs in my system that even my pipes weren't working.

"We're going to need you to do a blood test," he says.

I look behind him, down the corridor, and see a clock. It's 4 p.m. Shit.

My acting coach Carry Anderson and film agent Sara Ramaker will be going nuts.

I'm never going to make my scheduled appointment.

"This is a big one . . . could be good for you," Sara had said just days before.

Today was the big meeting with producers to discuss a small part in the movie *The Bucket List,* starring Jack Nicholson and Morgan Freeman. I was up for the role of Manny the mechanic—something else now lying in pieces.

It is eight hours since I was arrested, and the officer reminds me how he saved me from a beating earlier. I try to put the jagged pieces of my memory together. I ask how.

"You wouldn't stop rapping, and you were sharing a cell with two gang members," he says. "They were screaming for you to shut up. We had to move you into another cell for your own safety."

Oh shit. I remember now.

"Yeah," he adds, "you kept rapping and saying you were from the Black Eyed Peas."

He smiles as he says this, like he knows it will hurt.

My humiliation is complete. I feel disgusted at being me. The officer stands there staring at me, indifferent to my crisis. He must be immune to seeing so much regret unravel in here.

I've now convinced myself that I have no career left to return to.

I want to pull off my head and throw it against the wall. I want to suspend it from the ceiling like a piñata and smash it with a baseball bat so that all the self-saboteur's madness lies in chunks on the floor.

PREFACE

"Oh," says the officer before leaving, "and you better know that the paparazzi are waiting for you outside." And he walks off.

I lean against the wall and await some formalities: for the $15,000 bail to be posted by management, for my blood to be taken and for the customary mug shot that I know will end up on TMZ—and it does.

As I wait, my guilt projects this montage of images and people onto the facing wall: there's Jaymie going out of her mind, wondering why I never arrived home; there's Josh, my teenage son from a previous relationship, looking frightened and bewildered, wondering what has become of his dad; there's Will, Apl, and Fergie, shaking their heads and asking "What were you thinking, dude?"

I then picture my stepfather Julio sighing and tutting with unsurprised disappointment as he says aloud: "Ayyyyy, Hi-meh."

Just like he always did.

And then there's the face of Nanny Aurora—my late maternal grandma, my second mom, best friend, confidante, chief cheerleader, inspiration, and the boulder for me to lean into and step up from. We'd visualized me making it in the music industry since I was a boy. This one thought of her is enough to calm me in the moment. I think of her and disappear into those childhood days as a form of comfort blanket.

I'm six years old and we're at El Mercado, the teeming indoor market of the Mexican-American community in East L.A. My feet have picked up dirt from shuffling across the diamond-shaped tiles, and the smell of leather won't leave my nose. I'm sitting in a booth with Nanny—the same black and tan booth we claim each Sunday, week in, week out, to secure the best seats in the house—inside the second-floor El Tarasco restaurant, sitting atop the warren of market stalls. Nanny's seated opposite me, her white-as-snow hair tied up and bundled into a scarf, her shoulders covered by a black shawl.

My feet barely touch the floor and I'm mesmerized by the wonder on her face as I spoon a bowl of soup to my mouth, never taking my eyes off her as she looks sideways to the empty dance floor, expectant. She's so . . . excited. It makes me excited. She's brought us here for a mutual weekly treat to watch a Mexican musical ensemble, the mariachis.

These guys are my kings. Grandma loves Freddy Fender, Elvis Presley— and El Mercado's mariachis. They bring Western Mexico to East L.A. We are die- hard fans: boarding the RTD bus each week, each Sunday afternoon, to reach this venue between Lorena and 1st Street, and getting there early to find our seat before the lunch-time rush senses the entertainment is about to begin. Then out they come—an ensemble made up of a violinist, a guitarist, a trumpeter and a lead vo- calist, performing on a wooden dance floor as a stage, with a terracotta wall as the backdrop. There is nothing more emblematic of Mexican music than the sounds of the mariachi, with songs serenading the woman. Grandma's foot is tapping the moment the first guitar string vibrates, as they dance in their wide-brimmed hats and somehow sing with fixed grins on their faces. She catches me staring up at her.

"Look at them, Jim," she says.

She always calls me Jim, never Jaime. Always the English version, not the Spanish. Never "Hi-meh."

The mariachis' outfits are dazzling, glittering with silver and shining studs and buttons. Their energy is contagious, and I watch them work the crowd and work hard, earning their applause. Faces once miserable from long hours at tough jobs are now beaming just like Grandma's. The place is rocking. People are getting up and dancing. Strangers are coming together. Grandma is clapping to the beat. I start giggling and clapping, soup now slurped and finished.

"If you want to dance and entertain like them, Jim, you can," said Nanny, leaning in. "Do you want to dance one day?"

I nod my head, fast.

She points out every aspect of their costume as they perform: the stitch-work, the meticulously shiny buttons, the pristine whiteness of their boots, how everything shimmers and matches, how they move in synch, how rehearsed they are. It's all about detail, detail, detail. I don't know it at the time, but she's train-ing my mind and fueling my dream. Detail in the look, detail in the execution. My unconscious child's mind considers my first lesson in entertainment well and truly locked in.

I skip out of El Mercado, energized by the performance we never tired of seeing. Nanny makes me think—makes me believe—that, one day, I could be a performer, far better than the mariachis. The dreams we would go on to weave went far and beyond El Tarasco restaurant.

"One day, you could be climbing steps onto a stage before the world. Believe that, Jim. Believe it."

Nanny exposed me early on to music, dance and entertainment, and showed me what to notice. Even though the Black Eyed Peas was another world from the mariachis, no one could have been prouder when the first shoots of suc-cess started to sprout before her death in 1996.

"Way to go, Jim!" she'd shout, "Way to go, Jim!"

In the confines of the cell I have earned, I start to cry, holding my head in my hands.

My own shame is worse than anything anyone else can heap on me.

Then, before this guilt crushes me, it's as if her spirit hits me with her wooden hairbrush. She only ever disciplined me once with that brush—when I

PREFACE

became too hyper as she combed my hair. But if I ever needed a good whack from her, it was now.

Nanny was proud of her Native American heritage as well as her Mexican roots. She was part Shoshone, and encouraged me to embrace the "warrior spirit" that was, she said, forever in my blood. Under Shoshone law, a defeated warrior has to leave his tribe forever. Legend demanded it.

This thought jolts me. Am I headed for exile?

When your tribe is the Black Eyed Peas, when you've got a family full of so much love, and when you've worked so damn hard to manifest a dream, there is no defeat. Except for self-defeat.

Even within all the deserved guilt I feel, I stand, feeling empowered, like I'm psyching myself up before a concert.

Don't let this beat you, I keep saying, repeating it like a mantra.

Don't let this beat you, I keep hearing, as if it is someone else's voice.

In that moment, I knew I had to rewire my entire thinking.

I make a silent vow to myself: I might now appear like the pathetic celebrity archetype who was given the world and threw it away, but it will not break me.

It's not over . . . it's not over, I tell myself.

Shoshones admire strength, wisdom and power in the spirit, not the weakness, ignorance and futility of the human ego.

I roll up the right sleeve of my hoodie and there's the reminder: a tattoo from Australia 2002, seared in ink into my skin in Chinese and Japanese characters, spelling it out for me: "Spirit Warrior."

Get it together. Get in touch with that warrior spirit.

You've fallen, Tab, that's all. Get back up. Put back the pieces.

When I'm finally sober, the police allow me to retrieve my Range Rover Sport. On the drive home, there is only one question repeating in my mind: "How did it come to this?"

FALLIN'
UP

LEAVING DOG TOWN

We all say we're misfits in the Black Eyed Peas, and I really was born one. I've often imagined the looks on everyone's faces when I arrived into the world on July 14, 1975, shortly after one o'clock on a baking Los Angeles afternoon. There I was waiting to burst onto life's stage as this eagerly awaited, dark-skinned Mexican-American boy with Native American ancestry, and then I arrived . . . as light-skinned as could be.

"Oh look, he's as white as a coconut!" were the first words that greeted my birth, spoken by my father, Jimmy.

With parents who were both dark and with Shoshone blood running thick on Mom's side, this was not the shade of baby that had been ordered.

Uncle Louie, my mom's brother, arrived in the room, took one look at me and said: "He looks like a long white rat!"

Mom said she was just grateful I came out fast.

I'm not saying I was a disappointment. I'm just saying that I was breaking the mold from the moment I came out of the gate. It should, therefore, have come as no surprise to anyone that a) I grew up feeling a bit of an outcast, and b) there was a good chance I'd follow through and be a nonconformist. From day one, it was clear that I wasn't going to fulfill anyone's expectations of me.

Nanny got it: she would later tell me that she knew I was going to be different from that first minute. But in her accepting eyes, "different" in a good way. I guess even then she could tell I wasn't going to be your average pea in a pod.

I was born at East Los Angeles Doctors Hospital, directly off Whittier Boulevard—a seemingly never-ending street that today is crammed with markets and dollar stores but which was once a cruising capital for the young *chavalos* in their low-riders on the Eastside in the 60s, as immortalized by a seven-piece Chicano group called Thee Midniters. Not much came out of East L.A. back then beyond their 1965 hit *"Whittier Boulevard,"* which led to them being referred to as "the local Beatles," though I doubt John Lennon and Paul McCartney sweated it too much.

At the baby shower a few weeks before my birth, my mom couldn't stop dancing. She heard music and just had to start moving.

"Laura!!" everyone said—Laura was short for Aurora—"you're going to have the baby if you're not careful!"

"But I can't stop dancing. I need to dance!" she told them.

And she danced and danced, and everyone laughed, for about two hours solid.

Mom says she knew I was going to be a handful then and there. It's good to know that, even in the womb, I was injecting the Black Eyed Peas vibe, jumping around, rocking it, getting everyone on their feet. Mom said it was like that for the last three months of her pregnancy.

That's why I like to think I started dancing even before my life truly began.

I also like to think that I gave Mom fair warning.

If you met me in the street and you knew nothing about the Black Eyed Peas and asked my name and where I was born, the reply could mislead you. I'd give you my birth name: Jaime Luis Gomez. I'd tell you where I first grew up: a Mexican-American community in East L.A. That would probably surprise you, because you might, as many do, mistake me for an Asian. If I told you the projects I grew up in and you knew the Eastside, I'd catch that look in your eye and I'd say, yeah, that's right—the neighborhood nicknamed after a street gang called Dog Town. These are the stamps of my identity, about as informative as markings in a passport. They tell you nothing about who I am or what my story is, and what it further explains to me, looking back, is why I never felt I belonged from day one. Don't get me wrong: no one is prouder than I am of my Mexican-American roots, but these are merely my roots and national identity. This information doesn't completely define me.

Mr. Callaham, my sophomore English teacher, once said every story needs a good beginning, middle and end. I remember him saying that. It must have been one of the few times I was listening and not daydreaming my way through class.

The thing is, I didn't much like the story that was laid out for me: the Latino who should understand his place in the world, stay loyal to the 'hood, get "a

real job" and do the nine to five thing. I didn't see a good beginning, middle or end in that.

What you've got to understand is that in my community, there was the story you were handed at birth—a carbon copy of the one issued to everyone else around you; a future of limitations that asks the dreamer that dares to be different: "What makes you think you're so special?" I think that I was born with something of that Indian warrior spirit that Nanny talked about, providing me with a defiance that refused to respect pre-established boundaries. To me, you've got to be willing to smash your way out of any ice block that's encased you. You've got to be willing to break out and be as original as you want to be, become the person you have the potential to be, as opposed to being the person others expect you *should* be. It is about ripping up the hopeless story and rewriting the dreamer's script. Something innate within me knew this from being a boy.

There is a quote that me and my homie and best friend David Lara often remind each other of: "Those who abandoned their dreams will always discourage the dreams of others."

I learned from an early age that few people tell you what is really possible, except for free spirits like Nanny. Because, if you become the one who does make it happen, then it reminds others of their own limitations and what they, maybe, could have done, but didn't choose to. Find any tight community and then find the dreamer within it—and there'll always be a gang of naysayers pissing on his or her parade.

That is why there is much more to me than where I come from. Because it is what was invisible—the determination, the belief, the perseverance—that shaped my story, and for those people who stonewalled me with doubt or never believed where I was headed, only one silent reply ran through my mind: *Oh, you don't think so? Okay, just watch me.*

My mom, Aurora Sifuentes, and dad, Jimmy Gomez, met at a Mexican market on the Eastside. Mom was out shopping with Nanny, Aurora senior, when their paths crossed. It probably says a lot that I don't know much more about the romantic part. Mom was a twenty-year-old student, securing qualifications that would ultimately get her a job as an official with the Los Angeles Unified School District, and Dad was a twenty-three-year-old mechanic. He'd previously had a relationship with a woman named Esther that produced a son—my half-brother Eddie who is four years older than me. I don't know the details of that messy story other than Eddie ended up staying with Dad.

Mom and Dad fell in love, got married and she was pregnant with me at twenty-two, but the honeymoon period didn't last long because, as Mom would tell me, there were two sides to my father. His better side was the kindhearted, affectionate gentleman. His bad side was the drinker, and, when this side kicked in, the good-looking charmer fell away and exposed the flawed man. He wasn't a bad man, but alcohol sadly changed him. He would later get his act together, but not before it was too late as far as Mom was concerned.

Apparently, he performed a drunken dance called the "Pepe Stomp." Basically, it involved nothing more technical than him stomping his feet on the spot, getting faster and faster. There was this one time when he lost his balance and fell backward into the playpen that was set up for my arrival. He crashed into it and was rolling around drunk. I wasn't even born yet and Mom was already worried for my welfare. The final straw came during an argument when he picked up a bicycle and threw it at her when she was far into her pregnancy. The bike didn't hit her, but almost flattened my half-brother Eddie who stood there wailing over his near-miss with this two-wheeled projectile. Mom was smart enough and strong enough to get out soon after.

That is why I don't know my dad. He was at my birth and hovered around the edges for a bit, but he was one of those dads on paper and by blood, not by deed. He had next to nothing to do with raising me. Mom used to laugh that his favorite song was "Daddy's Home" by Shep & The Limelites. Not bad for an absent dad.

I admire Mom for having the courage to make a new start and choose the life of a single parent. In many ways, it would have been easier to stay, but she took the tougher choice and a part-time job in a toy store near downtown L.A. She was no foreigner to hardship. In her childhood, home had once been a garage converted into a makeshift studio, shared with Uncle Louie and Nanny.

Nanny's name was Aurora Acosta when she married Luis Sifuentes. I know nothing more about Granddad other than that he was always suited and booted, and he left her at an early stage of their marriage. I never have understood why I was named after the two most unreliable men in the lives of the two ladies who raised me: Jaime and Luis. Maybe I was intended to be the improved version of both men?

Mom always said I was handsome "like your father" but I personally thought he was on the ugly side, so I never thanked her for that. I had his nose, ears and name, but the similarities ended there. I'm tall, he is short. He is dark-skinned, I am light. I have ambition, he did not.

Nanny remained on amicable terms with Granddad, but, back in her day, a single mother of two standing on her own two feet was as good as marooned, so it was a good thing she was a survivor.

Her first priority was getting a roof over their heads, and she knew some friends who had garage space.

"I don't have much money, but I'll rent it from you," she offered.

"And do what with it?" they asked.

"Turn it into a home," said Nanny. And so this spot—no bigger than a den—was where the family lived for a bit, complete with heaters, furniture, and a small portable television, and she made it as comfortable as she could afford.

When it came to "new" clothes, Nanny made them out of whatever fabrics she could beg, borrow or find. She struggled big-time to support her children, but she'd take no heroine's credit. "All that matters is family," she once told me, "and the rest will take care of itself."

I don't think she needed a man after Granddad because there was only one man she ever trusted after that—and His name was God. The fact that she ultimately managed to buy her own home when her kids had grown up and moved out speaks volumes for the faith she had, and the impossible situation she turned around.

With that definition of what struggle really feels like, it is easy to see why Mom thought it was no big deal going it alone. But she wasn't alone. She had me. And those next five years were to be the happiest time we would share. It was just me and her versus the rest of the world.

I could not see horizons as a child.

Everywhere I looked, there were walls, fences and gates hemming us in, and the great concrete slab of L.A. County Jail stood six floors high and all ugly-looking in the distance, about a mile down the road. I lived within a concrete jungle within the concrete metropolis of Los Angeles; a part of the city that the tourist bureau doesn't promote; a poor vicinity that is a world away from Sunset Boulevard, Melrose Avenue, Beverly Hills, and the beaches.

The neighborhood—*el barrio*—was one of government tract housing built in 1942 for low-income Mexican-American families. "The projects," they called it. The official name was the William Mead Housing Project, and it housed four hundred fifty cookie-cutters that stood back to back in bleak uniformity; two- and three-story brick blocks painted tan-red with a thick white-painted band separating each floor. The number and color of the front door were the only marks that set each unit apart. I swear that even the palm trees and triangular washing lines were in the same spot outside each block.

It was not a place where dreams were made, and life was tough because of all the unemployment, drugs, and crime. People's lives seemed as cookie-cuttered as the housing units, and options were limited. But however bleak life seemed to the outsider, there was a strong sense of family, community, and the value of sticking together.

Home was a first-floor corner unit at the end of one of the oblong blocks of small-ass apartments. It was nothing more than a studio apartment with a grilled front door, and Mom and I were two out of an estimated 1,500 residents on site, bounded by the county jail on one side and the Los Angeles River on the other. The river ultimately fed into the Pacific Ocean at Long Beach, but that's the only idyllic-sounding fact I can bring from the 'hood.

This first home was a special place because it represented the world I shared exclusively with Mom. The walls were all white and there was enough room for one red floral-print sofa that clashed with the yellow hard-backed chairs at the round wooden dining table. We shared one bed and had one black-and-white television set. The front door opened onto a balcony that, when I was pretending to be a soldier or warrior, became my look-out post on the world, under the spotlight of the California sun.

Nanny Aurora was a constant visitor, coming over on the bus from her place in South Central L.A., and all three of us would sit outside on that balcony, eating Nutty Buddy ice-cream drumsticks that she brought as a regular treat. Not a week passed without Nanny visiting, or else we got on the bus to visit her. The mother-daughter bond was fierce, and I, as the favorite son and grandson, was the lucky kid who got all the love and attention in the middle.

One floor below the balcony, there was a worn and scorched patch of grass. Scorched by the sun and worn by the wheels of my red Big Wheel bike. This patch was both my playground and stage as Mom busied herself upstairs, keeping watch as she listened to her disco vinyl collection of the Bee Gees, Donna Summer, and Chic. She was a bit of a disco queen, and if ever I hear Chic's "Le Freak" or Lipps Inc.'s "Funkytown," it always sends me back to blazing hot days playing outside my first home.

I spent my earliest years running around kicking a football and riding my Big Wheel on the surrounding paths, feet in the air, pretending to be "CHiPS" on highway patrol. Mom often sent me out in costume: as a warrior, a pirate, or a bad-ass *luchador*—a masked Mexican wrestler. She stuffed my shirt with padding and gave me a towel for a cape, and I pulled off some killer moves to win the *campeonato*—the championship—by nailing key matches with imaginary opponents. I was always pretending to be someone or something on that grassy "stage" because there was no affording the hi-tech Atari console and its alluring game cartridges.

I look back now and see how basic life was, but we didn't grow up wanting or grasping for anything. We were the have-nots who didn't know what it was to have. It was the same for all of the lower-income families, and we killed the hours by playing ball and making our own fun inside pretend worlds.

I played alone a lot of the time. I saw Eddie now and again, as Dad drifted in and out for the first two years of my life, fighting to be allowed back in, but always coming up against Mom's wise blockade.

As boys, there was one thing our young eyes couldn't miss: the monster-sized graffiti on every wall. I grew up reading the words DOGTOWN on the end of

each block, on stone walls and garages. These black-sprayed letters stood taller than me, and this one phrase became the adopted name for the housing project. I didn't grow up saying I lived at William Mead. I grew up saying I lived at "Dog Town," without first knowing what it meant. Until one day, my curiosity got the better of me as I walked back from preschool, called Head-Start, with Mom.

"What is Dog Town?" I asked.

She stopped and made me take a good, hard look at a group of young men hanging in the parking lot. Their car engines were idling with sunroofs open and music blaring; the distant sound of the Miracles, Smokey Robinson, and the Originals.

These dudes leaned against the rear bumpers or sat on the hoods, smoking. They wore plain tees or wife-beaters with perfectly creased pants, and some wore bandanas wrapped around their mouths like surgical masks. But if one thing stood out, it was their bald heads with necks covered in tattoos that also covered their backs and arms. Now and again, you'd see an older person sporting tattooed teardrops running from one eye. Like a crying clown. I didn't know until later in life that each "tear" equaled a life taken, marking out these dudes as killers.

"Those people over there," Mom started to explain, with her head next to mine, her hands on both my shoulders. "You must always steer clear, Jaime. Never be in that area."

Another time she told me, "That is not our life . . . that is not us."

That was my introduction to the *cholos*—Mexican gangsters—and the street gang culture of L.A., issued as a steer-clear warning.

"Dog Town" is the name and calling card of one of the countless criminal street gangs that give Los Angeles the unwanted label of "gang capital of America." The slogans and graffiti are tagged everywhere to remind everyone whose turf they are on—not to be confused with a stretch of beach in Venice known as skateboarders' Dogtown. Each morning, I was confronted with this street-gang reminder when I came out the front door, walked down the center steps between units and stepped into the courtyard. There, screaming in my face from another unit's gable-end, was DOGTOWN.

Street legend says this gang name came into play in the 1940s, so called because of an old dog pound in nearby Ann Street. Stray dogs used to run wild and attack people, so a price was put on stray dogs' heads, leading to the area's teens capturing these snarling dogs and claiming the reward. But this also led to family pets being kidnapped for the bounty money, and these kids earned notoriety as local hoodlums. In response, they set up the Dog Town gang.

So the story goes.

Things had progressed beyond prices on dogs' heads by the time I was a boy. Now, there was a price on *people's* heads, and gang members were packing it with blades and guns. If my childhood was an album cover, you'd paint the picture of me in the foreground as a boy running around and getting grass stains on my knees by playing football or riding my Big Wheel. But, in the background, something sinister and dark was always going down.

Mom kept instilling her fear-loaded warnings because she knew—more than I did at the time—that the law of averages said there was a 95% probability that I'd grow up to be a *cholo*, one of them. Each child in my community was so susceptible, given life's disillusionment. Gang life was in the DNA of the community, and Mom feared those outside influences.

Mom never let me forget what the life of a *cholo* represented. Her constant warnings must have seeped in on some level because I grew wary of these people hanging around on the streets. It was like she'd planted a bad dream in my head with images of jails, people dying, and people crying.

My uncle Cate, Dad's brother, was murdered, and my aunt Minnie, Dad's sister, was the first person to die in the family from a drug overdose. Too much heroin, I was told. One murder and one drug overdose, minus the gory detail, is the sum total of my knowledge about the horrors that no one really spoke about.

Then there was my Aunt China. She wasn't a gangster but she had huge respect in East L.A. neighborhoods because she was a stand-up, no-nonsense, boisterous woman who took no shit from anyone.

The name Gomez had an element of notoriety attached because of the family's toughness.

My impression is that Dad thought he was tougher than he was: there was the image he had of himself, and there was the sad truth exposed when he was drinking. As a result, I grew up regarding him as a bit of a joke, to be honest.

What was no laughing matter was the Primera Flatz gang, which ruled the 'hood. In its heyday, it had an estimated 350 members who'd leave their calling card on walls with the giant initials "PF from AV" for Aliso Village. The one hundred twenty–strong Dog Town gang was one of its affiliated subgroups, just two out of around seven hundred twenty gangs and a total of 39,000 members spread throughout the whole city, according to estimated figures issued by the LAPD in 2007.

I would say about 60% of our 'hood was gangsters.

Street gangs in the 70s were not as organized as they are today. Back then, there were a lot of turf battles, gang fights and rumbles between members armed with knives, chains and bats, and only the odd handgun. Today, the profits and weapons have escalated into some serious shit, where the gangsters on the streets are equipped with semi-automatic weapons and their bosses—the Mexican Mafia—are running empires from inside prison.

These days, L.A.'s judges are giving city attorneys the power to set curfews and put gang members in jail if they are found loitering in the streets, or pos-

sessing weapons and tools for spraying graffiti. Dog Town was covered by one of these injunctions in 2007 as part of a campaign to clean up the northeast of L.A. But back in the day, gangs pretty much had the run of the streets with their own form of martial law. It was the law of the neighborhood that came first, and federal laws came second. It was lawless in many ways, even if the cops would disagree. Kids grew up learning to be streetwise from an early age. The first lessons in life were pretty simple: never rat anyone out, never snitch, and never backstab your neighbor. Hold your head high, stare everyone down, stand your ground. Understand that, and the neighborhood will have your back. Know where you belong, and you'll always be protected. Everyone looked after everyone in a tribal sense, and I think Mom felt both comfortable and uncomfortable within this environment. She accepted that gangs were part of our community but she didn't want me getting sucked in.

I often went to sleep hearing bedlam in the parking lot, and the sound of sirens wailing. And there was always one ever-present but weird smell that hung in the air. This scent of childhood was everywhere—morning, noon and night—and I now know that it was the constant clouds of smoked weed, wafting out of homes. That same heavy scent that wafts around music festivals or backstage at concert venues.

The whole gang scene was not my thing. I never was enticed by it.

Mom did everything in her power and limited income to keep our heads above water. I wouldn't say that we lived below the poverty line, but we lived basic, hand to mouth. I helped where I could, running up to the store with our weekly food stamps to get groceries, and, in the summer, lining up for the government-issued "summer lunches" in the projects. For these lunches, each unit received a weekly book of tickets. Each stub was good for one brown paper bag that contained a sandwich, one carton of milk, a bag of potato chips, and an apple. It was our government-issued gourmet meal, as far as I was concerned.

Mom worked her ass off as a student and at the toy store, putting in as many hours as possible to provide for us and afford the best toys—at discount— for Christmas. She always wanted to better our lives, she said.

Discounted toys were a perk of her job, and she got me some incredible stuff. I remember the typewriter, the new bike, the "CHiPS" uniform with helmet, handcuffs, and police badge, the GI Joe, the telephone, the board games. You name it, she got it. I saw how hard she worked and how I was the center of her world. It sounds selfish, but, as a kid, that's all I wanted. It is because of her self-sacrifices back then that I love her to death today.

These toys kept me entertained a lot of the time. In fact, I only really had one playmate, and that was a sweet girl called Penny, the daughter of my babysitter Lola who lived in the unit opposite. Whenever Mom studied or worked, Lola took me under her wing. I'll never forget Penny's high-pitched voice and dark pigtails. She stuck to me like glue.

"JIMMY!!!!" she'd scream from below the balcony, calling me to the railing. "You coming out to play?"

It's fair to say that she probably was my first crush, because we were inseparable for a spell. In our pretend worlds on that grassy stage, she'd be the princess to my prince, or the parade girl in the wrestler's ring when I was the *luchador.* Without Penny—and my soft toy dog Cleto—it would have been a pretty lonely childhood.

There was a man called "Roadie" who lived in the same block as Penny. He was this big, heavy-set black man, a rare sight in our Mexican community, and he was the kindest, gentlest soul. He hoarded baskets full of candy. That's why we called him "The Candyman."

Whatever other deals might have been going down in the projects, there was only one supplier that mattered, and that was Roadie with his candy and Bazooka gum. Apparently, he bought candy in bulk, then sold it off to parents and us kids for ten cents a bag, much cheaper than the stores. It was like having Willy Wonka on our doorstep. You name it, he had it. I was too young to comprehend matters of race at the time, but it somehow registered with me that he was different-looking. But he was like the friendliest of uncles, all smiles, warm and embracing. At some level, that imprinted me with the message that all black people were cool like Roadie.

His candy was almost as good as the "chip-chips" Mom made most mornings for breakfast. We used to invent names for different meals, and "chip-chips" was the random label for her specialty: fried tortilla shells with eggs. When I smelled that dish frying, I'd race to the table and sit there, knife and fork at the ready. I looked forward to these breakfasts because it was the one time in the day that I got to sit down with Mom and have her undivided attention. Then, at the end of the day, she'd always read me a bedtime story, holding me in her arms. Or, sometimes, she'd take my action figures or stuffed animals and make up voices in their character, using role-play to wish me goodnight. The start of a day and the end of a day were my happiest times, and there was nothing more comforting than feeling the bed dip when she climbed into bed.

"Mom's here . . . I can sleep now," I would tell myself.

"Love you, Jaime," she'd say, thinking I was asleep.

Life was perfect then. Nothing and no one could come between us.

At least, that's what my innocence told me.

Shortly before my sixth birthday, this man called "El Amigo" walked into our life, and he picked up my world in both hands and turned it upside down.

I was too young to figure that Mom maybe needed attention and love

from a source other than me, so I never saw this thunderbolt coming. I suspect she felt guilty, too, because when Julio Arevalo walked through the door, she played down his importance by always using the *el amigo* reference—nothing more than a friend.

So El Amigo is a friend, I accepted at first. Okay.

Wow, he's here a lot for a friend, I thought over the coming weeks.

Oh, now you're going out at night with him more and more, I soon realized.

Mom never used the word "boyfriend" or bothered to have one of those mother-son chats that explained everything. He just walked into our life and was invited to stay, and I was left to figure out the rest.

It was all very black and white to me: I wanted to be with Mom but this strange man, who seemed a bit weird and false around me, had stolen time and attention that was mine.

Then everyone started mentioning how happy Mom looked.

So, okay, this man makes her happy, I thought.

She was smiling. She was laughing.

That's a good thing, I thought.

But I still stared at Julio and wished he'd disappear into a cloud of smoke. I imagined having magic powers that would zap him away, and return things to how they used to be.

Julio worked in the airplane manufacturing industry. "Julio helps build planes!" Mom said, as if that would impress me. It didn't.

He was your average-looking dude: slim, with big black hair and matching moustache. I can see him now, slouched in that armchair, cracking open a beer.

I guess he tried his best with me, playing at the role of surrogate dad, but I wasn't feeling it. I was resistant for a long time. I just looked at him and thought: *Who is this guy? He's not my dad. He's not my uncle. So why's he here?*

It didn't take long before dramatic changes happened.

Nanny started arriving in the late afternoon to be babysitter for the evening. Then the announcement was made that we were moving in with Nanny, and that is when we left Dog Town. We left behind the projects and moved the few miles to South Central L.A. I said good-bye to Penny and Roadie, and was transplanted to what felt like a whole new world.

At first, I thought it was meant to be a temporary stay, but as things turned out, South Central became my home from the ages of five to seven. And even after then, I would still return to Nanny's and spend three months living with her every summer, without fail.

In moving to South Central, I went from a 100% Mexican-American community to one that was mixed, where Mexican-Americans were the minority. It was 70% African-American, 30% Mexican. I was vaguely aware of this difference from visiting Nanny, but it was only through living there that I fully appreciated what that meant. One very good thing was that it was in South Central L.A. that my ears first started hearing the distant sounds of hip-hop. And it seemed ideal that I was now living with my two favorite ladies. But then Mom started to spend more time staying over at Julio's place in South Gate. That meant fewer shared breakfasts and fewer bedtime stories.

Then I saw suitcases being packed—Mom's, not mine.

Then she left for Mexico on a vacation. What she didn't say was how long she'd be gone. When she left, the wrench hit me as an ache. Nanny tried to reassure me.

"It's just you and me now!" she said. "We'll have fun together!"

Mom disappeared to Julio's hometown of Morelia, the capital of the state of Michoacán to visit his family. Each hour she was gone felt like a day, and each day felt like a week. By the end of week one, I was crying myself to sleep. I guess these inexplicable absences always feel like a catastrophe when you're a kid; and hours always seem longer in childhood than they ever do in adulthood. But this wrench was understandable: she had never before traveled outside the United States and we had never before been separated. With Mom gone from my side, it honestly felt like the end of the world, especially because I felt that this new man in her life was supplanting me.

In the end, she was only gone about three weeks, but that is a lifetime when you are a kid. Her eventual return was treated as no big deal, and things soon returned to as they were before she left.

Until she sat me down and told me she was pregnant.

As she broke this news, with Nanny looking on, I pretended to listen, but all I was thinking was *"You want another kid? Why? What's wrong with me?"*

At that age, I guess you really do think the world revolves around you, and I think every child is jealous of anyone cutting in on him and his mother. It steals attention. As I saw it, in comes this guy and stands between me and Mom, and now I've got to contend with another one of me arriving on the scene? If I couldn't have Eddie as a brother, I didn't want anyone else.

Mom seemed to spend most of the pregnancy bedridden at Nanny's. It really took a toll on her body, and she was constantly weak and fatigued. I kept asking why this thing in her stomach was making her so sick. There was always some adult explanation, but all I could focus on was her cries and groans. I'd sit on the edge of her bed, unable to leave her side, willing her to get better.

Her misery ended when my new sister, Celeste, was finally born on November 15, 1981. I was seven years old.

Our sibling relations didn't get off to the best of starts when I took my first look at her, wrapped in a bundle in Mom's arms in the hospital, and observed: "Why is our baby so ugly?"

"Jaime! That's your sister—she's beautiful!" Mom laughed.

"But, Mom! She's ugly . . . can't you get another one?"

I will never forget that sharp dig of jealousy, and I think that's when I started sticking even closer to Nanny.

Please understand, no one worked harder, or gave me more love, than Mom. But these big changes in our life were tough for me. And this was my first hard lesson: that when things are going great, it won't last, that when someone loves you, they can leave without you—don't count on them always being there. These were the mental imprints.

But even at a young age, I had a flair for keeping it positive. And one very positive outcome of these otherwise unhappy changes was being with Nanny—the single person most responsible for redirecting the course of my life.

DREAMING BIG

Much of my childhood was erratic: living with Mom, and then living together with Nanny; living in a Latino 'hood, then living in a mixed-race community; hearing nothing but the rhythm of Spanish music, then feeling the pulse of hip-hop. I didn't even know what my proper name was: Mom called me Jaime—pronounced the Spanish way—but Nanny said don't worry about it, Jim is cool.

Within the inconsistencies that made my childhood feel pretty rootless, I listened mostly to Nanny because, under her wing in South Central L.A., she became my guide—in both education and life.

She was a teacher in every sense of the word. She taught English as a second language to the Mexican kids at 66th Street Elementary, the same school where my education began, so education was a big deal in her home and Nanny immediately began to influence me with her positive outlook on life. I always say she was was my first music manager because she taught me all about self-belief.

She stepped into the vacuum left by Dad, and instead of putting a baseball bat in my hand, she put a dream in my grip and educated me in the ways of performance. She was a teacher, father, and second mother all rolled into one.

Nanny instantly became my sympathizer and chief supporter. I thank God every day for her influences, and I can picture her vividly as she was back then: a sturdy woman with a shock of white hair, and owl-like, light-framed glasses with tinted lenses that dominated her gentle face. By her side, at all times, was a purse that smelled of perfume. In that purse, she always kept gum or breath mints. That might explain my obsession for always wanting to have fresh breath!

She wore a silk scarf or black shawl, and was the most thoughtful, kind-hearted soul you could meet. She was the essence of a lady, but didn't mind getting her hands dirty, either. Since Granddad walked out, she learned to be self-sufficient and never called on a handyman without trying to crack the problem first. I remember most her soft-spoken voice. It was never once jarring, even on the rare occasions when she raised it.

She was a live wire and was genuinely gung-ho about life. I don't think I ever saw her beaten by circumstances, and I never heard her whine. By comparison, Mom was a bit more downbeat and withdrawn, and always seemed wrapped in worry or tension.

Nanny loved dancing, and nothing stopped her natural exuberance. For a time, she walked with a cane because she'd suffered a broken foot in a car accident, but whenever the music started, she threw that cane to one side and got her boogie on. She was keen to show off her "sock hops" and the jitterbug. A bit of pain and inconvenience was not going to stand in her way.

I am convinced that love of dance is her biggest legacy to me. She always said she saw the dancer in me, telling me that I had rhythm. It didn't seem to matter what music was playing or what age I was, I found the beat and moved to it, with Nanny applauding and encouraging me the whole way.

"Dance, Jim!! The world is yours—dream big," she would shout.

The more she told me I had rhythm, the more my enthusiasm fired. The more she encouraged me, the more she made me believe that I had a certain something. I don't know about metaphysics or manifesting. All I know is that this true lady awakened my dreams and made me unafraid to entertain them, and this is what I'll drill into my own kids: the spirit of dreaming endlessly. Make your dreams vast and limitless, and then run with whatever talent God has given you.

Nanny encouraged me to focus on the future from an early age. As inspiration, she took me to see the mariachis at El Mercado or the Million Dollar Theater in downtown where Mexican artists performed. On countless days, we returned home and put on our own "show" as she led me toward a future I don't think either of us could have imagined. But we imagined a stage nonetheless:

Nanny's the MC and I'm the act. She's front of house, and I'm waiting in the wings.

"Ladies and gentlemen," she announces, getting into it, "all the way from Los Angeles, California . . ."

As she bigs me up, I'm tucked around the corner of the doorway between her living room and kitchen, thinking that all dressing rooms must have wood-paneled walls and thick, Merlot-red carpet.

". . . please give it up for . . . Jimmmm . . . GOMEZ!!"

I hear my name and step out. Cue music. She places the needle on the record, there's a dusty crackle of the vinyl, and then some Elvis Presley number starts up. I'm dancing around, rocking out to the King, improvising—free-styling like an amateur but running with the beat for a breathless three minutes.

Nanny's hands are the only ones clapping, but I hear an entire auditorium. She's only one person sitting on the edge of an armchair, but I see lights and hundreds of faces.

She's clapping on the beat, urging me along. "Way to go Jim! Way to go Jim!" and I hear an entire audience screaming my name.

I turn it on some more, giving it every move I've got until the song ends.

Nanny is beaming with approval: "You'll be a dancer one day, Jim!"

She gives me a big hug

"You think so, Nanny? Really?"

She nods her head and claps her hands. "Yes! Yes!" and then she'd be into the kitchen, fetching me a bag of candy as a treat, and I bask in her approval.

My childhood is a box full of memories like that.

When she was cooking in the kitchen, she'd pretend it was a restaurant called Los Amigos and we had to get meals ready. She was the chef. I was her assistant.

At other times, I was the detective and she my female partner. Or I was an attorney, armed with a briefcase, and she my client. Or I was a sailor, kitted out in full uniform, or a pirate wearing an eyepatch and wielding a sword. A childhood full of costume changes.

Nanny's humble home was a magical place, because it was always full of warmth, fun, imagination, and the spirit of entertainment. Within her world, I was the boy Max in *Where the Wild Things Are,* and Nanny was the friendliest "wild thing." As a result, we both escaped into my imagination all the time. Life seemed a happier place somehow, when locked in there together.

Nanny lived in a duplex right across the street from 66th Street Elementary. That meant I could leave home at 8:25 a.m. and be behind my desk by 8:30 a.m. From her front window, looking across East 67th Street where she lived, I could see the school entrance, the monster trash cans, and the cafeteria windows. There was a market on the street corner where we'd always go for supplies, and, at the other end of the street, a big car showroom that sold repaired cars.

I was a dreamer at school more than anywhere. It was daydreaming that made education bearable. From boy to teenager, Nanny always checked my marks and reminded me of the importance of a sound education, but I was never going to

shine academically. I was more the fly in the classroom, buzzing around, unable to sit still. Throughout my school years, I'd stop buzzing around only for English and art—anything that had to do with creativity—but, nine times out of ten, I'd be away in another world. Until, that is, I felt the sting of a slap across the head and heard the word "Gomez!"

In whatever school, and whatever age, I was one of those shy kids who was a bit withdrawn, a bit of a loner. The downside of being a dreamer is the isolation that comes with being lost in your own head. I probably spent more time in my own company than I did with groups of friends or peers, and I kept watching the clock and looking out the window, forever eager to bolt out those doors, cross the street and be back with Nanny.

Her place was my haven. It was cramped and basic, and it got cold because she couldn't afford heating bills. Southern California can chill the bones in the winter months, so Nanny opened all the interior doors and warmed the house by turning on the oven and leaving its door agape—letting the heat drift through the kitchen and into the small living room, the one bedroom we shared, and the tiny bathroom. Her German shepherd dog, Lady, always slept close by.

There were three places where Nanny lived: at the stove, cooking her fried chicken special or macaroni and cheese, baking amazing yellow cake with chocolate frosting; the bathtub, where I'd join her washing our clothes by hand; and the armchair where she'd sit and watch me perform. This is also where she prayed, without fail.

She prayed each night before bed and then woke at 5 a.m. to put on a pot of coffee before sitting in her armchair to read the Bible, saying a prayer as the day began. I wasn't the kind of kid who asked a lot of questions. I was more the observer who watched and learned. I got up one day to see what she was doing, standing sleepily at the doorway in my pajamas. They say every performer goes "into the zone" before going onstage, and Nanny did the same as she prayed, in an almost meditative state. She was at one with God. All was hushed quiet—the kind of quiet you don't dare interrupt. She was in her moment, Bible resting on lap, mug of coffee steaming on a side table, lost in prayer.

I became convinced that Nanny's home was some earthly outpost for God, because of all the symbols and religious ornaments everywhere. Bad spirits would never have visited our place—the presence of Him was too great. She also burned sage, honoring an ancient Native American tradition to keep out evil spirits and negative energy. And there was a dream catcher hung above her bed, to the right where she slept—another Native American tradition. With my head on the pillow before lights out, I stared at this feathered web dangling from the ceiling and trusted its powers.

If it was good enough for Nanny, it was good enough for me.

One day, I asked what it was meant to do. She told me it was there to catch and ward off bad dreams, only allowing the good dreams through. That probably explains why, after reading me a chapter of "Peter Pan" or "Sleepy Hollow," she'd wish me good dreams before sleep.

The Virgin Mary stood guard above the door between the living room and kitchen, in the form of a three-foot-high painting. In Mexican culture, the Mother of Jesus plays a pivotal role, signifying the strength of a woman taking care of her children; the mother who says there is no need to be afraid because she is there to protect them. In our culture, the Virgin Mary is Our Lady of Guadalupe—a revered Catholic icon.

The miraculous story of this apparition is one of the first lessons I learned as a kid. The event of December 12, 1531, is seared into Spanish Catholic minds. When Nanny recounted the story, it was as absorbing as listening to the tale of Peter Pan. I've never been able to tell it as well, but the short version is that a peasant called Juan Diego saw a vision of a lady, a teenage girl, surrounded by light, as he walked the slopes of the Hill of Tepeyac en route to Mexico City. This Lady told him to build a church at the spot where she appeared. As she spoke, Juan Diego recognized her as the Virgin Mary, and he rushed back to tell his local bishop of this revelation. The peasant was sent back to get this apparition to prove her claim. The Lady instructed Juan to gather flowers. Even though it was winter, he found some Castilian roses. He gathered them, and the Lady arranged them on his laid-out cloak. Juan Diego carried this bundle back to the bishop and presented the roses. And that's when they both saw it—the miracle image of Our Lady of Guadalupe imprinted into the cloth of the peasant's cloak; an image showing her standing in prayer, wearing a crown of twelve stars, bathed in sunlight, and standing on a crescent moon carried by an angel.

That was the proof they asked to see, and that's why the shrine of Our Lady of Guadalupe in Monterrey, Mexico, is the most-visited Catholic pilgrimage destination in the world. In December 2009, six million people paid homage to mark the day. In 1992, Pope John Paul II dedicated a chapel to her memory within St. Peter's Basilica in the Vatican.

Our weekly pilgrimage in L.A. wasn't as impressive. Nanny paid her respects every Sunday at the shrine at the far side of the car park outside El Mercado before we went to buy groceries and watch the mariachis.

There, Our Lady of Guadalupe is framed within an arch at the back of a brick-walled building. At her feet, the Mexican community laid a garden of flowers and lit candles in prayer. I always approached this spectacle in awe, and couldn't believe how many flickering candles and colorful flowers there were. Each week, Nanny added to the collection, and prayed.

She stood in front of the shrine, with Our Lady of Guadalupe looking down on her. I always stood a few steps behind, never really knowing what to

do other than be quiet. Nanny was so still, head bowed, eyes closed and hands clasped to her chest in prayer.

What are you thinking? I always wondered, looking up at her. *What are your prayers?*

She only ever told me she was speaking to "Baby Jesus' Mom," and that's all I needed to know. What *she* didn't know was that as she looked up to Our Lady of Guadalupe, I kept my gaze on *her,* equally as entranced. In my eyes, Nanny was bigger and better than the Virgin Mary. No one was stronger and no one protected me more.

This was all part of an unbreakable Sunday ritual.

Nanny got up and prayed. We went to morning mass at Olvera Street Church, and she prayed. We visited the shrine, and she prayed. She went to bed, and prayed. It was like her Sundays were one constant prayer—punctuated by one small window of entertainment, courtesy of the mariachis.

One Sunday, on the walk back to the RTD bus home, Nanny and I were chatting about Our Lady of Guadalupe, and how important she was.

"Nanny," I said, "I will protect you. If anyone ever tried to harm you, I'd protect you."

Not that she needed protection, and certainly not from a six-year-old boy. She was the type of grandma who wasn't afraid of taking the bus home at ten o'clock at night in a bad neighborhood. Fearless, she was. But I told myself that I'd always be there for her.

"I know you'd protect me," she said, humoring me.

"I'd kick anyone who came at you. I would!" I told her.

She looked down at me, smiled and ruffled my hair.

Little did I know that some weeks later, I'd get the chance to prove myself.

We were at a downtown bus stop, waiting for the RTD off 7th Street and Spring. It was mid-afternoon and we were standing around, not saying much. Then, from nowhere, this guy darts in and grabs her purse. He didn't drop her and she didn't let go, and they're both tugging at this purse.

Nanny was defiant, struggling with all her strength.

I was paralyzed.

She started screaming and yelling.

I stood there, rooted to the spot.

Nanny struggled and struggled. There she was, this sixty-year-old woman, and this twenty-odd-year-old mugger was getting nowhere. He eventually gave in, let go, and ran off empty-handed.

On the bus ride home, not much was said. I was still replaying it in my head and I bet Nanny was pretty shook up, even if she didn't show it. She broke the silence by turning to me and joking: "Jimmy, I thought you were going to kick him this way and that way and protect me! Where were you?"

"I'm sorry, Nanny. I—I—I . . ."

She gave me the biggest squeeze. I knew Nanny was a tough one, but she was a superhero that day. Like I said, Our Lady of Guadalupe had nothing on her.

Nanny did this as she taught me about life—her actions spoke for her: *So, you think I'm homeless with two kids? Boom! Give me that garage and I'll turn it into a home. Do the impossible. So you don't think I can dance with this cane? Boom! There goes the cane—you watch me dance. Do the impossible. So you think you can mug me in broad daylight? Boom! I'll fight back and win. Do the impossible.*

Back at the house, I thought we'd both had our fill of reality for one day.

Outside, in the backyard, was the brown rusty shell of a decrepit Chevy Dodge truck. Its wheels were as rooted into the ground as the weeds around it, and a trailer packed with old tires was tied to its back. This corner of the driveway looked like a junkyard. The truck was a ghost of a vehicle. It had no engine, no windows, two worn-out seats and a steering wheel. "This is your truck, Jim," Nanny said when I moved in. "Take it wherever you want."

I often sat inside with Lady the dog, taking myself on "drives across the country" when Nanny was in the kitchen. Then she'd come out and join me, getting in the passenger seat, and we'd both pretend to be farmers taking stuff to the market.

On this particular day, all three of us—Grandma, me and Lady—climbed aboard. I turned the keys and my voice imitated a choking, starting engine.

"Where you want to go, Nanny?" I asked.

"Anywhere, Jim," she said, "Just drive."

In moving to South Central L.A., I had swapped one gangland turf for another. I was now in the heart of hostilities between two of the most notorious, most violent gangs going: the Crips and the Bloods. Some serious shit was waged between these two, particularly back then: drug trafficking, extortion, robbery and murder.

Of course, I wasn't aware of much in those days. All I knew was that the Crips wore blue and carried a blue rag or a handkerchief.

And the Bloods wore red.

I lived in a Crips-ruled area, meaning the graffiti on the wall read CRIPS instead of DOGTOWN, and it didn't take long to get handed a lesson about what colors *not* to wear.

I walked into a liquor store wearing a red St Louis Cardinals hat. I was seven, but I knew no better, and age was no defense. As I walked through the main

entrance, someone flipped the hat off my head. "Yo, you can't wear that dead hat here!"

"Why not? I like the Cardinals," I said, with an innocence that now makes me cringe.

"You're in a Crips 'hood—you don't wear red around here!"

I never did wear red again. I did as I was told, but I never felt the appeal of gang lifestyle. I didn't seek a reputation on the street. That seemed pointless. I wanted to build a reputation as a performer. That is where the hope was.

Before turning eight, I moved out of Nanny's to be with Mom and my new sister Celeste in Julio's apartment in South Gate. I didn't want to leave South Central L.A., but I had no choice. Mom decided she wanted to live as a family with Julio. After almost three years in Nanny's haven, I had to return to a foreign world.

As we moved in, Julio's old roommate, a Pakistani man named Jamal, moved out, so it all felt forced and I felt squeezed in. I moved into a family setup that I couldn't associate with, and Mom couldn't give me 100% anymore since she now had Celeste and Julio to also worry about. Consequently, it was never home to me. Nanny's place was home. Julio's place—and that's how I referred to it—felt cold and functional. I had also been returned to a predominantly Mexican-American community in South Gate and a new school in Otis Street Elementary. But my heart and soul stayed with Nanny. I longed for those three months each summer when I got to return to South Central L.A., and I enjoyed those summers from the age of seven to fifteen.

In my first summer back with Nanny, I found that Uncle Louie had moved in with his two daughters, my cousins Jez and Darleen, because he had fallen on hard times. He had been living from check to check after coming out of the U.S. Marines and he had to retreat home to get himself together. My cousins slept in Nanny's bed, Uncle Louie slept on a pull-down bed in the living room, and the couch became my bed for those twelve weeks that I stayed. As cramped as things were, I enjoyed it because there was always activity and constant chatter. Now *this* felt like family—and it guaranteed an audience of four for my "performances."

If I ever had any kind of father figure in life, it was my Uncle Louie.

He was the coolest uncle, because he was into basketball, and we watched videos and talked about music and his dope tennis shoes. When at Nanny's, we stayed up late and listened to Zapp and Roger, Slick Rick, Too Short and Public Enemy. If it wasn't for Uncle Louie, my ears wouldn't have first pricked up to the kind of music that the black community listened to.

The thing I remember most about Uncle Louie is his shoes, because he was always shining them. Polished like a mirror, in a spillover discipline from his days as a Marine. He sat there at night, applying polish with a cloth and rubbing up a shine with a toothbrush. That's one thing I noticed about him: everything had to be neat and in order. Even if his life wasn't.

He got around on a ten-speed pedal bicycle. He had a few of them out back in the yard, and he used to do them up and make them look pretty flash. One day, he left the house all neat and tidy, and cycled away on one of them. A few hours later, he walked back through the door all bloody and beaten up. Nanny fussed and cleaned him up, and I remember sitting there, frightened by his mashed-up face.

Apparently, he'd cycled to a store, and they took his bike, took his cash, and beat him up. Violence scared me. That might explain why I had been no good at protecting Nanny at the bus stop. Fights, crime, and confrontation paralyzed me.

Nanny didn't allow us to think too much about fear or stuff like that. She kept the focus on fun, and with three kids around the place, she was in her element as chief entertainer. She was all about taking Christmas to the next level, sending us on hunts around the house at Easter and keeping us occupied and happy during holidays. On birthdays, she'd stand on a chair, hands behind her back, and gather us around.

"READY?"

We'd be at her feet, looking up, begging like puppies. Uncle Louie would be giggling already, well ahead of the excitement.

"Okay . . . one . . . two . . . three . . . PIPILOOYA!" And she'd throw her hands in the air and these dollar bills and coins would come raining down. That was her thing—creating fun and connecting with us kids.

What I liked about South Central L.A. was that the Mexican-American kids that I saw had no problem hanging with African-American kids. Everyone was like "it's good . . . we're cool," and hostility had no place to go.

Other things also registered. Black kids started talking to me like a brother, regardless of my skin color. I was embraced, accepted and treated as one of them, and *it felt good.* I saw their fashion and instantly thought it cooler than anything I'd ever seen or worn. And their music sang to me: the streets came alive with the arrival of West Coast hip-hop, and something about these beats flicked a switch inside. I heard talk about Run-D.M.C., Afrika Bambaataa, and the Sugarhill Gang. I heard people rapping and rhyming, and the whole vibe oozed coolness.

I watched as kids brought out ghetto blasters, threw down sections of cardboard and started spinning, gliding, popping and ticking like robots, freaking out on their backs, heads, hands, and feet. This dance art form is called b-boying. Or breaking. The "b" in b-boying stands for "break," because when hip-hop first started, these dancers used to dance during the breaks in the song as the DJs worked the turntables. B-boys are what the media would later label as "break dancers."

B-boys would "break" in the playground or street, magnetizing circles of crowds. That a dancer from the streets could attract such a buzz seemed like the coolest thing in the world. I told myself then and there that I wanted to be able to do that. But not just do it, master it. Forget BMX, basketball, football or baseball. I'd found my craze. I'd found my new friend for life.

The man who fueled this obsession was Boogaloo Shrimp, aka dancer and actor Michael Chambers. I was nine when he starred as "Turbo" in the movie *Breakin'* (and its sequel *Electric Boogaloo*). That movie showcased the art of b-boying, with him popping, breaking, and free-styling all over, and he was the sickest dancer I'd seen. I bought the video to watch this pioneer of West Coast hip-hop so I could mimic his moves. All I seemed to do was press play, pause, rewind . . . play, pause, rewind . . . and practice, practice, practice. Boogaloo was the dancer who inspired Michael Jackson to moonwalk, and he was a phenomenon in his own right, too.

Everyone spoke about that first movie of his, and suddenly b-boying was the new craze. At this time, the hip-hop culture was emerging from underground and was beginning to dominate communities on both the West and East coasts of America. What started out as DJs spinning beats in underground clubs was now a scene that was spilling onto the streets, with dudes spitting out rhymes and b-boys freestyling to the beat.

I don't think it's an accident that the hip-hop culture took off in minority areas where life is hard and violence regular. It sprang up as an outlet to give the voiceless a voice, and meaninglessness some meaning. If rock 'n' roll let the middle classes find their voices and scream, then hip-hop let people from the projects find their voices and express themselves. And it wasn't about being Mexican-American or African-American or Asian-American. The hip-hop I would know was about one nation, one people. Puerto Ricans enjoyed hip-hop just as much as African-Americans on the East Coast. Its inclusiveness was contagious.

I had known I wanted to be a performer of some kind since the age of five. Now, around the age of nine, the detailed picture was coming into focus.

I think that is what happens as a kid—dreams are constructed in stages. First, there is the imagination that builds the fantasy. If that fantasy hangs around long enough, it becomes a sort of vague dream. That notion then becomes a fixation, something the spirit latches onto before the child wakes up. And then—sometime in adolescence—you become the committed dreamer if the passion has endured.

No one would become more committed than me. As a boy, something about the imagery, style and sound spoke to me, the outsider, and invited me in. Once inside, I wanted to barricade the doors and lock myself in.

Because I was home.

BREAKIN' OUT

Hip-hop was my genie's lamp.

Even misfits can have moments when everything falls into place, and this discovery was one of them; when something hit home so deep that, even as a boy, it *just made sense*. Age nine, this "knowing" was disguised as jump-out-of-my-skin excitement. As a Black Eyed Pea, this knowing is the joy I savor each and every time I step out on stage with Will, Apl and Fergie.

Think about having zero sense of touch, sight and sound, and then, one day, you discover them all in unison and realize you can express yourself for the first time. That's the best way I can describe what finding dance and hip-hop felt like.

There will always be better, more technically perfect dancers, but when I'm ready to rock a place, my self-confidence is sick, and the emotional and physical release is volcanic. In that mode, I *feel* unbeatable. Before any performance—both in the early days and during the 2010 E.N.D. world tour—there is something inside me that just wants to erupt.

Minutes before going on stage, all this anxiousness and adrenaline is pulsing, like my entire body is amped to a thousand thumping speakers. It is a build-up that tells me that I'm ready to kill it, smoke it, slay it.

Then the crowd is bouncing and it's on and . . . euphoria; a nirvana in which both you and the crowd lose yourselves and meet somewhere in the middle of a transcendent energy that bonds fans with group. All Pea-bodies riding the same wave.

There is no better buzz than the one that comes with performing, and I experienced the first embryonic rushes of these electric sensations as a kid, as if my body was tuning into the future.

Before I even entered double digits in age, I was impatient for the stage, desperate to prove what I knew inside. All this pent-up energy meant I could never sit still, so I poured it into endless practice. But when you're itching for a start, there's also a whole load of frustration that builds, and school life felt like one of those overly long television commercials that get in the way and stop the action. My real education was on the streets and through hip-hop, and couldn't be found in textbooks or classrooms.

When I was twelve, sitting in my bedroom one night, I tried to express this frustration on paper. It wasn't the attempt of a budding poet, more the first stab of a budding rapper. I remember staring at the moon, thinking that's what Nanny told me to shoot for. I remember thinking it was dark, and I remember hearing crickets making their noise in the night heat. This rap/poem today reads like the basic language of an adolescent diary but it went like this:

> *Moons in the horizon*
> *Surprisin' that my sun's not risin'*
> *Crickets' chirps are tremendously loud*
> *And here I sit on this lonely dark cloud*

That's the first poem/rap I ever put down, and I'd spend hours toying with wordplay, stringing sentences together, bouncing words together. It's not much in and of itself, obviously, but it was a start.

I probably spent no more than a total of twelve full days with my brother Eddie in my first nine years, but both Mom and my absent dad rose above their differences to recognize the brotherly bond. Eddie and me could have walked side by side as best friends through life, but our lives would turn out very different.

I was the long skinny white rat and he was the little fat kid. "Big-boned," Mom said. He loved to eat. He was like the German kid in *Charlie and the Chocolate Factory,* always wanting more and stuffing his face. One time, Mom got so frustrated with him asking for seconds that she took away his plate and put the whole cooking pot in front of him. Eddie ate it up quicker than a hungry dog.

I grew up truly loving this kid. I even loved his black-rimmed glasses with bottle-top lenses that matched his round face.

Our affinity was rooted in my infancy. Apparently, when I'd learned to stand in my playpen, we used to play this game where I'd throw all my toys over the top and he'd pick them up, gather them together and toss them back in. Then

I'd throw them all out again—and we'd go on and on like this for ages, with me giggling in amusement. We played ball together on the rare occasions I was allowed to visit Dad's. All I can really remember about those visits was Dad sitting in his chair, doing a crossword. He'd serve us glasses of lemonade which we weren't allowed to drink until after we'd finished our meals. I could have told Dad that even the fizzy gas wouldn't have stopped Eddie finishing off his plate.

As more distance developed between Mom and Dad, Eddie became more distant, too. All I remember is the fact that Dad's $75-a-month child support checks dried up and the phone stopped ringing to arrange visits with Eddie. I was crushed because my whole thing at that age was about seeing him.

I knew that our next visit was likely to be our last because Mom had prepared me. We stuck together like glue that afternoon. We were happy in our oblivion, enjoying the present moment like kids do. The last thing Eddie did for me was hand over a parting gift: his prized toy robot—all blue, red and silver and standing about two feet high. It was a super-robot Tranzor-Z and was as high-tech as anything we'd owned. Eddie said he was giving it to me so that I wouldn't forget him. It was one of those matter-of-fact farewells that kids don't really understand. I watched him walk off with Dad, and this robot became my playmate for a bit. Eddie then dropped off my radar.

I wouldn't see him again for another twenty years.

Shortly before my ninth birthday, we moved from Julio's apartment in South Gate to the community of Cudahy—a city district named after a meat-packing baron. It is the second-smallest city in Los Angeles County, and yet, they say, one of the most densely populated, mainly by Latinos.

When I think of my time in Cudahy, I think of tension because there is no worse feeling than finding a "fit" within the hip-hop culture, then going home to feel like the misfit in the family.

I felt like an imposition in Julio's eyes, and it was his energy that seemed to dominate the place. Inevitably, I acted out my resentment and the more I took it out on Mom for inviting this setup into our lives, the more we fought, and the more confused I felt. In the outside world, something felt ill-fitting about being in Cudahy, too. I'd returned to a world where Spanish music reigned again. I looked around and thought *Where are my black friends?* and *Where's the hip-hop?* There had been so much diversity in South Central L.A. Now I was immersed in a humongous Mexican community.

What hit me hardest was hearing the word "nigger" for the first time. I've always been particularly sensitive to words, and this one word made me cringe. I couldn't associate with the hatred of its delivery or why everyone bitched against black people. I listened to this shit and thought *You have no idea* but I didn't say anything out of fear—the fear of being called out as a race traitor and a sellout.

Taking a stand like that would have to wait till later.

There were "race rules" that were as backward and dumb as they were hard and fixed: don't talk with black people, don't hang out with black people, and don't date black girls.

It was like being an alien in my own land because I viewed the world through different—and open—eyes. It was real simple for me. My eyes had seen and appreciated another culture. I saw love. I heard real music. I saw dancing. I saw friendship. I saw brothers.

I didn't see color.

And I didn't see all the trouble this would cause me farther down the road.

For my ninth birthday, there was a knock on the door.

Mom let me answer, knowing the surprise that would greet me: a professional crew of b-boys bedecked in red and black, with a ghetto blaster balanced on one of their shoulders. These dudes looked so fresh, wearing bandanas, parachute pants, spikes, black gloves, and berets with pins in them. One guy even had these flashing glasses which, to me, represented the coolest gadget in the world.

"Happy Birthday, Jaime Gomez!" they announced, before leading me—like some starstruck kid—outside into the sun-soaked driveway. With the movies *Beat Street* and *Breakin'* still the rage, it was as good as if Boogaloo Shrimp had turned up on my doorstep.

Mom had set it up with a local radio station after seeing something in one of the newspapers that advertised special b-boy surprises, sending crews to private homes for 30-minute gigs.

I watched in awe with Mom. This was on a different level to anything I'd seen being tried in the streets. I watched every move as intensely as any student would his master. There was a fluidity and momentum that took my breath away. These boys busted moves so fast that it looked like all their limbs were spinning into the air, as fast as rotating helicopter blades. This was a true art form of dance in motion.

At the end, I saw Mom place a roll of dollars in their hand.

Wow—you can get paid for this, I thought.

From that moment on, there was no stopping me. There was no sitting around in front of television anymore. That became a waste of precious time. I focused on becoming a b-boy. Mom helped me buy the gear because she saw what it meant to me, and I went all-out and had the African medallion, the zipper pants, the fat shoelaces, the baggy jeans, the b-boy hats, the fisherman's cap, the big jackets. Mom laughed when I tried it all on, making fun of the size-50 pants.

"Are you meant to look like a clown?" she asked.

"It's the style, Mom!"

I'd be out there, doing it, about five hours a day. I couldn't wait for class to end so I could practice. It was hard shit trying to be a b-boy. There was so much to learn before I could even think about mastering technique. There was the "six step" "up-rocking," "flares," "c-stepping," "air-trax," "freezes," "backspins," "knee-spins," "head-spins," the "1990s" (spinning on one hand) and the "2000s" (spinning on two hands), the "turtle," "hand glides" and the "windmill," to name a few.

I started learning how to "pop" first—using the arms, robotic-style. I'd master popping in the bedroom mirror, the bathroom mirror and any shop window reflection. I'd practice for hours to nail the rhythm of how my body was going to move, concentrating on just one tick of a hand or wrist movement. I wouldn't move on until I had mastered it to perfection. Then, I moved on to mastering the ground-work, spinning on my back.

When Mom was at work, I'd pull down all the mirrors—about six of them—and place them in a circle in the living room, allowing me to watch myself from every angle as I went through every move.

There was this one time when she came home early.

"Jaime! What are you doing!" she yelled, standing at the door.

I flipped up. "I'm breaking, Mom."

"The only thing you're going to break is my mirrors. PUT THEM BACK . . . NOW!"

It would take Mom a few years before she understood my passion.

By the age of eleven, we moved—again—to another largely Latino community: the city of Rosemead.

My new school, Janson Elementary, prided itself on its Henry Ford motto: *"Coming together is a beginning, keeping together is progress, working together is success."*

I decided to put this "working together" promise to the test after recognizing the upside of being the new kid on the block, especially the kid armed with the fresh dance moves. I spotted the opportunity to make an impression and answer the eternal question that followed me throughout childhood. "Who's the new guy?"

The school Christmas assembly was being planned and I wanted to make an impact. Dancing was the one thing that didn't make me feel shy, and when you've found that key, that tool that cracks open the shell, you want to run with it.

I grabbed my moment when teacher Miss Rasmason was organizing the sixth grade's class performance at a Christmas concert. Everyone set their minds to singing a Christmas carol, and my heart sank.

That's not cool, I thought.

Undeterred, I stuck my hand in the air.

"Yes, Jaime?"

"Miss, can I dance during our bit?"

That took her by surprise. She nodded. "Sure, Jaime, what kind of dancing?"

"B-boying, Miss—you know, break dancing," I said.

All Latino heads turned around and locked onto me. The girls snickered and the boys scoffed. But Miss Rasmason was still nodding. Uneasily, but definitely nodding. She pointed out that it would be a challenge doing hip-hop to "Walking In a Winter Wonderland."

"I'll just do my thing, Miss," I said.

We struck a compromise. I'd sing along to "Walking In a Winter Wonderland" with the rest of them but we would insert a break and I'd play my own beat and dance to it. Admittedly, it was hardly Run-D.M.C. or Boogaloo Shrimp territory, but it was a chance to prove myself.

The big day came and the whole school—pupils, parents and teachers—were there. The Christmas classic started up, and the choir sang: *"Sleigh bells ring . . . are you listenin'/In the lane . . . snow is glistenin'/A beautiful sight/We're happy tonight . . ."*

And then, halfway through and after the chorus, it stopped and my segment kicked in. I'd brought in my ghetto blaster and decided to play some old-school East Coast hip-hop, Whodini's "Freaks Come Out at Night" I remember feeling so in charge of the moment; of *knowing* I was doing good. The choir was all still and silent behind me, and there was me doing my thing, throwing down some crazy routine.

At the end, as I was standing in front of the stage, between the choir and the applause, I noticed the looks on the faces of the teachers, not the kids. I saw wide smiles, raised eyebrows and hands clapping, enthusiastically.

I looked back at the seated pupils and saw the girls thinking "That was cool" and the boys thinking "Whatever, dude." But I didn't care. I'd bagged the teachers. I'd bagged some major approval for the first time in my young life. Not one disappointed look to be found.

So now when people asked "Who is this kid?" I was suddenly the kid who could dance. I'd gone from nerd to the dude with street cred in one performance. Now *that*—as a kid—was dope.

Rosemead, in the San Gabriel Valley, represented my fourth move before turning twelve. This erratic path had passed me around: 66th Street Elementary to Otis Street Elementary to Park Avenue Elementary to Janson Elementary. And then Rosemead High.

I always seemed to be having a suitcase packed, saying good-bye to one set of people and having to start over with new friends. This nomadic life trained me not to bother with other kids too much because something always told me "I can't get used to this because we're only going to move again." I attached myself to no one.

The good thing about Rosemead is that we would settle and *not* move again, and shifting sands cemented into firm foundations. That's why I nowadays call it home—my true home.

"Where you from?" someone asks.

"Rosemead," I say, proudly.

That's right—one of the Black Eyed Peas. From Rosemead.

I'll never stop feeling proud when I say that.

I was proud of the new house, too. Julio must have been doing well building his planes, because he'd managed to buy the property from his brother and park a Mercedes in the garage. This house represented success to me—a step up in the world. It wasn't the projects, or a duplex or an apartment, but a house with three bedrooms, two bathrooms, a den and a humongous backyard. I wasn't sharing a bed or sleeping on the couch. I had a single bed and a big room of my own. The house even came with its own bar in the den, and Julio stocked it with his liquor. He also kept a wooden bong, kept from his hippie days, stashed in one of the cupboards. It would take a few more years before I'd realize that this *wasn't* a musical instrument.

It didn't matter that the house stood beside the 10 freeway, leaving us caught within the day and night drone of traffic noise. We opened the front door and looked across the road to a great slab of a wall, behind which was the eight-lane freeway. The San Gabriel Mountains were to the north, and you couldn't miss the electric giant of Edison International, which also made Rosemead its home.

What was outside didn't concern me. All I was bothered about was plastering the walls with my inspiration: posters of my heroes, Bruce Lee and Michael Jordan. In different ways, these two icons captured what the warrior spirit is all about: never hearing of defeat, never hearing the word "no," embracing a dedication that turned practice into perfection.

Lee mastered his martial arts technique to a point where he created his own signature style. He took basic kung fu and transformed it into a more flexible art called Jeet Kune Do. Then he became an actor who, because of his popularity, changed perceptions of Asian-Americans in the West; he was the Asian underdog who became the American hero; the first ethnic superhero on television. His entire attitude said: "Okay, I'm a little guy. I don't look much. But I have charisma and I'll kick your ass if you mess with me."

I often imagined what powered Michael Jordan when he was a kid growing up in Brooklyn. He'd set his sights on being a basketball player, but was rejected as a sophomore for being too short. He responded by growing four inches and proving his worth, and the rest is history. He had a finesse and a focus for

each ball he slammed through the basket. As he would later say when inducted into the Basketball Hall of Fame: "Limits, like fears, are often just an illusion."

Lee and Jordan were also about *precision:* precision timing, precision with craft, precision with their execution. And in both cases, they had dreams that no one could stop, and they only achieved them by mastering their skills and technique. It was their examples that gave me a leg up within my own inspirations and dreams.

I'd lock myself away and get inspired by the acrobatic moves of the Nicholas Brothers, the Mop Tops, and the Soul Bros. In fact, one of the best mix tapes I made during junior high included all the above plus Michael Jackson's "Baby Be Mine" and Prince's "When Doves Cry." Two classics.

I listened to Michael Jackson—visualizing Boogaloo Shrimp—for hours to practice my footwork floating, gliding and sliding moves.

I never sat in silence as a kid. There was always music playing somewhere. Music that would get people up and moving. I'd be forever making mix tapes from the radio station KDAY on 1580 AM. It made me itch to perform, and it was during one of my three-month summer stays at Nanny's that I put on my first "show."

Nanny and I got the bus to Uncle John's house in the San Fernando Valley and gathered a small crowd of friends and relatives. There must have been about twenty people in the front room that day, and Nanny had made sure that each of them paid an "admission fee" of one dollar each. The looks on all their faces, and the pride in Nanny's, told me that I surprised the family that day. It was like "He's one of us but he's dancing like a black dude!" And they paid me for the privilege. The sum total of twenty dollars was my first fee as a performer.

Through all this, I remained a dreamer.

I covered textbooks with unconscious streams of thought, killing the hours from morning till lunchtime, and from lunchtime till end of school.

Once, I covered the front of the red Spanish book *Hola.*

"Jaime Gomez!" announced a horrified Miss Chrisanti one day. "This is vandalism!"

But she didn't understand my creativity. "I'm learning how to rap, Miss . . . it's art, Miss!"

I had to pay twice for defacing school property. But it was as I tagged and defaced the book on the second occasion that I started playing with the word "Tab."

What's a "Tab?" I wondered.

"Hey, put it on my Tab" or "A Tab of acid" or "Tab the soda."

Then "Tab" became "Taboo." *Like the 1970s porn movie,* I thought.

Illicit. Sexy. Out of bounds.

I looked at the word and liked the way the "T" and the "b" jumped up from the other low-lying letters; two tall buildings sprouting up from low-lying units. The "T" and the "b" reaching higher. The word itself just looked . . . fresh.

I pondered some more what "taboo" meant. Off-limits. Unspeakable. Something forbidden. Something non-conformist.

I wrote it out in capital letters. Suddenly, the book cover now became a wall for my ink graffiti: "TABOO" in light lettering and then "**TABOO**" in block capitals. My hand was now some kind of laser, writing as fast as I thought.

"TAB-OOOOOO."

"TA-B-BOY."

"TAB-007."

I started signing my name feverishly, like I'd been asked to sign dozens of autographs in one mad minute. This "vandalism" cost me another ten bucks, but it seemed a small price to pay for what would become the right stage name.

So yeah, that's how I came to calling myself Taboo.

The name stuck throughout my teenage years and people thought it was cool. What wasn't considered cool were my choices in life, and I would learn all about the literal meaning of the word "taboo," and the consequences that would soon hit home.

STRICTLY TABOO

I was Rosemead High School's equivalent to Mumbles out of *Happy Feet.* In the same way that no one had ever heard of a tap-dancing penguin in the 2006 movie, no one in Rosemead had ever heard of a Mexican b-boy. I was the hip-hop kid in a community where there was no such thing as hip-hop kids.

"Yo, you think you can free-style? Really? Don't be ridiculous!" was a common reaction.

Not even Mom and Julio took it seriously. I think they viewed my passion as a hobby I'd outgrow. I can't blame them, because one look at my hip-hop clothes or ninja-inspired outfits told the lie that I was still playing dress-up, like the days in Dog Town. It's hard to convey serious intent as a kid, because, as that kid, you don't even realize the destiny you're running with. But passion is passion at whatever age, and, for a good five years, I'd pretty much rewound and replayed every move, style and technique.

Ask Tiger Woods what he did with a golf club as a kid or Michael Jordan with a basketball or Andre Agassi with a tennis ball. It was the same for me with b-boying. I was dancing good and killing the floor; so good that everybody started sitting up and taking note. I'd proved my worth in South Central L.A., but my dancing really flourished in the largely Latino area of Rosemead, where there was only a small pocket of black kids in the community. My skills won their acceptance and friendship, but the flip side also meant that—in the eyes of the Latinos—I had crossed the racial divide. There was a notable racial separation at Rosemead High.

It wasn't quite a race war, but Mexicans stuck with Mexicans, Asians with Asians, and African-Americans with African-Americans. Just like the prisons.

"Acting like a black dude" and making friends with black kids was therefore perceived as me selling out and swapping sides. But in *my* eyes, it was never about sides. It was only about one thing: proving myself as a b-boy.

But none of that creative reasoning mattered. I had broken the taboo of hanging with black friends. The bagging that followed had the same, sad ring to it:

"Yo, why you gotta dance like a black dude, homes?"

Or "Here comes the wannabe nigger."

Or "Hey, homes, why you doing that chino shit?"

I heard it in the corridors, the playground, the school bus and on the walk home.

I was *expected* to be the Mexican homie who wore Ben Davis or Dickey gangster pants and Cortez Nikes. Or I was supposed to dress like a jock or one of those disco biscuits. Instead, I wore MC Hammer pants, polka-dot shirts, Heavy-D shoes and the African medallion.

I wasn't deliberately making a statement. It just felt more like me, and the upshot was that I looked different by fashioning a look inspired by the hip-hop culture.

When you're born light-skinned "like a white coconut," or when you've always arrived as the new boy at school, or when you've been the Latino mixing it in an African-American community from an early age, there's no such thing as being afraid of looking different.

But certain "looks" were like uniforms that set races apart, and I was seen as the kid wearing the wrong uniform, hanging with the wrong people. But I wasn't going to cave in to peer pressure and start conforming. If my name's Taboo, I'll embrace the taboo, I told myself. I found steel in that bravado. Masks matter just as much in everyday life as they do on stage.

I made my own decisions. Including the decision to affiliate myself with four or five black friends who were outnumbered within Rosemead High. There were only five black kids who were as isolated in number as I felt by choice. These guys—Courtney, Eclipse, Phoenix, Terence, and Antwon—were my homies more than anyone else. It seemed an easy choice to hang with kindred spirits who shared the same vibe and thirst for creativity as wannabe performers.

Because of Mom's aversion to me taking down the mirrors to rehearse, we spent a lot of time rehearsing at different homes, but our main stomping ground was the house of Phoenix—aka Joey Jordan—because he lived two blocks from school, and it became a convenient rally point. It seemed his mom was always away, and she was cool with us using the crib to get our practice on. We also went to Antwon's house, using his garage, in South El Monte.

Wherever we were, it was *Groundhog Day:* we'd watch dance videos, listen to new music, try out new routines, and smoke mad weed which had filtered into our possession. We then killed the fridge's contents, and I'm pretty convinced that when Phoenix's mom came home, she must have thought bears had raided the fridge. Those were good times, and I doubt I'd have become such an accomplished dancer had it not been for the support and creativity of these adopted brothers. Being around them helped set my bar high.

Together, we pushed each other to the next level. There was a lot of love and soul within that group. We were tight and loyal and needed to be because my affiliation with them meant that the Mexican kids started hating on me.

I found scrawled insults on my locker door: "Wannabe Nigger," "Traitor," "Judas," and "Stick With Your Own Kind." In the restrooms, my name was written out large as "Jaime Gomez" . . . with a thick black line through it. They'd also write "Hyme-dog Gomez" in big letters. I never understood what that meant and never had the nuts to ask.

Each morning, I walked to school with anxiety, wondering what shit would greet me. Wondering where the next round of abuse was heading from. I was treated as an outcast, and was being publicly excommunicated. I didn't talk to Mom about it, or Nanny. The number-one rule on the streets is to never snitch, and I knew Mom would have been straight down there, trying to find out who was punking me.

I had a lot of time to deal with this shit on my own because I was a latch-key kid—carrying around the front door key as a pendant on my necklace—who let himself in after school around 3:30 p.m., cracked open a soda, turned up the beats and waited for Mom and Julio to walk through the door around 7:30–8 p.m.

My sister Celeste was always with Terry, the babysitter who lived down the street. She took care of all the kids in the neighborhood, but something in me preferred being home alone. In that thinking time, I figured that the locker slogans would fade away, but that would turn out to be wishful thinking.

I'd previously been aware of racial tensions as overtones, but now I felt serious hostility. Personally, I couldn't understand it, because the only discriminating factor in my mind was whether someone had talent or not. Maybe it was the naïveté of my youth, not comprehending that race mattered so deeply to others. But if it was naïveté, then it was the by-product of me mixing it with different creeds in South Central L.A.

In Rosemead, the Latino way of thinking ran in the opposite direction to my instincts that automatically counted everyone as friends. My crew were into music, dancing, and creativity. On the other hand, many Latino kids wanted to hang out, get faded and smoke cigarettes. There seemed nothing productive about that. And maybe—because of Mom's early warnings—I saw a street-gang future that made me swim harder against the tide.

Either way, I didn't feel the shame or embarrassment that the heads in my neighborhood wanted me to feel.

I'm not saying it wasn't intimidating to be singled out for the heavy treatment, but I wasn't going to show them I was scared. If I had one strength as a kid, it was putting my head down and listening to no one but me.

Something in life has always pulled me in the right direction—something magnetic. I was drawn to Nanny, drawn to dancing, drawn to my black friends, drawn to opportunity, and it's that magnetic theme which runs through my story. It would later pull me toward bad influences, too, and that's a story for later. But this theme is what led me, as a Black Eyed Pea, to call my registered company "Tab Magnetic," because of the magnetic forces at play in my life; because there is something magnetic about destiny.

At fourteen, my confidence—in terms of dance anyway—was also magnetic. My skills were so polished that I could take out anybody who stepped in my way. When you feel that empowered, there's always going to be the moment when you want to prove it to a larger audience. I call it my Karate Kid moment.

Lunchtimes at Rosemead High were when "dance lunches" were held outside in the school courtyard. Some guy acting as DJ brought out the school's sound system, and rocked the crowd as other high school juniors danced in the middle of a circle thick with spectators. It was in one of those circles that I first came across an older group of Mexicans who went by the name Z-Crew. They dressed all GQ-style; a look that was all about skinny Z Cavaricci pants with the pleats, high waists, belt and buckles, and paisley-patterned silk shirts. They were your pretty, boy-band type who thought dressing fancy looked cool. Their dance style was all boy-band fancy, too—very New Kids on the Block.

I had watched them for a week or two, telling myself that they were dancing in the past, and I could dance in the future.

There I was, the freshman standing on the sidelines, dressed really fresh with tie-dyed baggy pants, a mesh beanie, a crazy tie-dyed jacket and a medallion, looking like I'd wandered off the Jungle Brothers tour bus. I kept watching the Z-Crew with their over-rehearsed choreography and it was really wack. Then this voice inside me ignored the age gap and started whispering: "You can take 'em . . . you can murder 'em."

So I jumped in—me as one versus the Z-Crew as four.

The crowd cheered my audacity as the under-sized little kid in baggy pants taking on his elders, calling them out. I executed moves no one had really seen before except on the big screen. I rocked it: spinning on one knee, popping, gliding and busting some fancy footwork. Everything I did tore a new asshole in every single one of the Z-Crew. I was so lost in the moment that I didn't notice that they had scooted off the floor and merged into the crowd. The crowd kept cheering and giving me props for destroying it.

When the beats stopped, I stood there, out of breath but elated. The underdog had pulled the card of the high-school juniors. It was then, as the crowd split, that I heard the shout "Trash the freshman!"

The Z-Crew and its boys wanted to slam me in a nearby trash can for showing them up. They charged and I started running—and that's when Mr. Dunaway turned up, with impeccable timing, and they scattered.

I had broken another taboo and declared dancing war—and it wouldn't be the first time that Mr. Dunaway would have to save my ass.

Karish was my first girlfriend, and represented the breaking of another taboo: the one that said "Never date a black girl."

I was hooked from the first class we shared; hooked on the first hallucinogenic substance that life ever offered me—that drug called puppy love. It made me believe all the standard delusions of a boy's virgin experience: kidding myself that she was the love of my life and the girl I'd end up marrying. She would be my girlfriend for the next three years, which is why she finds a place in this story.

We spent a lot of time at her mom's place—first in El Monte and then Rowland Heights. I remember sitting with Karish and telling her all about my dreams, imagining a future that I felt sure would make me even more cool in her eyes.

How something sounds matters.

Music matters.

Sound is the oxygen we breathe, and music is the blood in our veins.

You think about what sound is, and then think what the world would be like without a single sound; without music—how dumb, mute, barren and black-and-white our lives would be. Sounds merge to make music, with different instruments, beats, notes, effects and frequencies. And music becomes musicality—connecting with us on the deepest, most intimate level, making us feel better, keeping us company, bringing us alive, helping us remember, making us jump around, lulling us to sleep, calling us to action. It is the one bridge which spans every single possible emotion, and it is a fact of life that every single human being around the world ingests music to feel good. It is the most intimate medium that connects strangers. As Bono once told Will: "Music puts us in their ears and in their heads."

When the Peas are making music, we see colors. It is almost a psychedelic experience. If we were able to see sound, we think we'd see color, because each song carries a certain energy and aura.

So as Will comes up with a beat, a sound, a chorus, we all focus on the music and envision a color; seeing the hues that fire in our head. Do it. Listen. When a sound hits your ears, what's the frequency? Is it vibrating high, to bring you up? Or vibrating low, to bring somberness? When you hear, what do you see? Is it light or is it dark? Is it red, because it's hot, steamy and sexy? Or blue because it evokes darkness, sadness, or a deep reflection?

Take some Black Eyed Peas songs as examples.

"I Gotta Feeling": it's red because it's uplifting, radiant, firing the body. We actually say it's a rainbow; a party of colors.

"Where Is the Love?": it's blue and gray because it's sadness seeking hope, creating emotion with all that talk of the KKK and the CIA . . . people dying, people crying.

"Meet Me Halfway": it's pink because it's soft, it's about love, it's girlie.

"Imma Be": it's gold and silver because it's regal, and robotic futuristic.

This approach is an understanding we all share, and it's Will that implanted this vision and made us see music this way.

For me, from a young age, music—and especially hip-hop—was a rush that took over my body and tapped into my soul, firing electrons that made me want to wild out. It releases a feeling beyond serotonin and beyond endorphins. It's beyond drugs. I can be feeling sick, tired, or blue, and then music and performing bring me up. It really does feel like an electric charge, firing colors in my head.

And even the sounds of childhood made me feel good: the music thumping out of street ghetto blasters, the music of De La Soul or MC Hammer. The sound of a good melody. The soothing sound of Nanny's voice.

But there was one sound which I loathed: the sound of instructions.

Anything wrapped in that barking, instructional tone reminds me to this day of my stepfather's voice, as well as another sound which grated in childhood— the sound of my birth name.

Mom and Julio insisted on pronouncing "Jaime" the Spanish way. I heard Hi-meh and heard a thousand fingernails being scratched down a chalkboard.

"Hi-meh, get me a beer!"

"Hi-meh, take out the trash!"

"Hi-meh, go water the grass!"

Mom hated me being called Jimmy. "Your name is Jaime," she'd say, "not Jimmy."

I knew why it jarred. Because Dad was "Jimmy," and she wanted no reminders. But "Jimmy" was the identity I had associated with since the age of five. Acoustically, it was soothing on the ear and full of fun and pleasantness; a constant reminder of Nanny's voice.

The sound of "Hi-meh" speaks of parental authority and the coldness of Julio from childhood days. It also echoes Mom's warnings about street gangs when, during my teenage years, she said: "Jaime, if you see trouble, you run. You hear me, Jaime—you run!"

So I hear "Hi-meh," and I want to run.

You can imagine it's a bit of a mindfuck to have two names as a kid. If I'd have been a dog, I'd have run around in confused circles. But each night, before lights out, I quietly reminded myself: "You are Jimmy and you will be a performer!" I'd say it over and over. Just for the sake of clarity.

All you need to know today is that Jimmy is my name, and Jimmy is who I am. Call me "Hi-meh" and the hairs of my neck will bristle. Call me Jim or Jimmy, and we're good.

It didn't matter what Julio called me. The tension was always going to blow. It didn't help that every time I wouldn't do something, or every time we butted heads, he'd yell and jab his index finger into my chest to ram home his point.

"Hi-meh" . . . JAB . . . "when are you going to . . ."

"Hi-meh" . . . JAB . . . "have you . . ."

He once overheard me telling Mom how I was going to be a performer one day, and he scoffed out loud. "You'll never make it, Jaime! Get real. I was in a band, too, and I never made it, so what makes you think you can, huh?"

This man shitted on my parade every day. Every time I saw him, he was shaking his head and tutting and I'd think "Damn dude, what did I do *now*?"

I never asked anything of Julio or approached him for comfort. It's like he had this force-field around him that repelled me. He was a hard kind of guy, both inside and outside the house—the direct opposite of me. Yet, with Celeste, he was the kindest, warmest, best father a girl could ask for.

I felt like the black sheep in the family, and, in response, I took it out on Mom. Cleaning my room became my way of making a point because it allowed me to crash about and rant. I'd say the things that kids say to wound, and then, as punishment, I'd get handed more instructions, chores and jabs from Julio. I self-created the teenager's vicious circle.

It all came to a head during a big screaming match when he jabbed me once too often. I pushed him back. He shoved me. And the whole thing ignited in the living room. A near-decade of resentment exploded and we started swinging at each other. Mom screamed for us to stop, and she jumped in the middle with a broom to separate us. When the dust settled, she said she couldn't cope with the tension anymore.

"I need you to go stay with your Nanny," she said.

I loved being back with Nanny and Uncle Louie. When I arrived, Nanny instantly knew what was needed: a dose of fun.

"C'mon, Jim, we're off to the recreation center," she said.

This one recreation center was attached to the retirement home where my grandfather lived. He was sick with polio, and there was a gathering for one of his birthdays. He and Nanny had remained on amicable terms despite him leaving the marriage. God taught her all about forgiveness.

I think a chief reason she visited was because of the opportunity it provided to dance with me at the small gatherings they held. We danced the salsa and the jitterbug. She loved Ritchie Valens and once his music started, there was no stopping her. Not many kids went dancing with their grandma, because it wasn't cool, but it was never about being cool. It was about being happy and spending time with Nanny—she kept up with all my moves! That's what I was saying about music earlier: it can bring people alive. It restored Nanny's youth.

If I ever became deflated because of the domestic setup with Julio, Nanny breathed fresh belief and encouragement into me. She permitted my dreams by believing in them. After two months, I returned home to Julio's and an uneasy peace. Only this time, I brought back something Nanny insisted I keep.

It was a gift, she said.

I knew its importance from the moment she placed it in my hand.

And that's when I hung her dream catcher above my bed "to catch my dreams before others crushed them."

"Don't you stop believing, Jim!" she said on my final day, giving me a big hug.

That's the thing about the sound of someone's voice who believes in you. It's like music. Because it's always guaranteed to make you feel good.

If home life was like walking on eggshells, school life became a minefield.

There's nothing more intimidating for a fourteen-year-old when, on that walk to school, all you can think about is one group—Z-Crew—gunning for you. Abuse was guaranteed every day, and I suspected a full-out assault was imminent. It was a question of learning how to dodge it.

They hung around the perimeter walls and corridors, and I just walked by, watching my own back. I knew they'd try to grab me when alone.

What had made matters worse was that my b-boy skills had got noticed by seniors who were jocks and they started taking me under their wing. These guys—Kevin Brackens, Jack Phan and Pat Ahing—were the sporty types who also loved music.

Together with my black friends, we formed a crew, and the dance lunches turned into face-offs between us and the Z-Crew.

We kicked their asses every time. Which exacerbated my traitor status. I was dancing with the enemy, competing against—and then defeating—my own. Huge disrespect, they said.

One of the chief assholes was a guy named Alex. He was a tall, dorky-looking dude with a long nose, and his henchman was this big guy named Hurley, who was as wide as a freeway.

These two jerks looked mean even if they did dance like clowns, and it was inevitable they were going to catch up with me, and the shit was going to hit the fan.

I'll never forget when it finally did. I was walking to class when Hurley stepped out and barged into me, shoving me into Alex. He took a swing. I ducked, and then this mini-mob rushed at me, pushing me around in the middle of this melee. That's when I heard the voices of two teachers shouting. Mr. Dunaway, together with Mr. Morgan, had saved my ass again from a beating.

Nanny reassured me that it was only jealousy, but it didn't matter. What mattered to me was answering them back—by rising stronger. Let my feet and moves do the talking. And sweet revenge lay a few years down the road.

Flash forward to the Black Eyed Peas years, and I was asked to sponsor a football team called The Rosemead Rebels. I'd paid $5,000 so they could have new uniforms and helmets and look the shit. There was a ceremony and photo shoot, and I walked up, introduced as "Taboo from the Black Eyed Peas."

And who happens to be the coach of the Rosemead Rebels? Alex. It was one of those rewarding moments that life dishes up.

Everyone shook my hand and thanked me for all my support, including Alex.

I couldn't resist the childhood reminder: "Hey, do you remember being such an asshole to me at school?"

"Hey, we were kids! I love your music, man."

"It's all cool," I said.

But in my head I was thinking *Yeah, bow down—kiss my Converses and juggle these nuts!* because it was a sweet payoff to a chapter of my childhood, and a reminder that life is all about the long game. The underdog always bides his time. What matters is patience and self-belief. You tap out to no one. And, for me, the best place to take that belief was the arena of a "battle."

SOUL CHILDREN

Imagine a circle of people standing two or three deep, forming a human arena, like one of those crowds in a schoolyard when some dudes are having a rumble. Picture that, but instead of fists flying in the middle, there are dance crews busting their moves; hip-hop gladiators throwing down the gauntlet.

Now imagine that circle mutating into five other circles, all breaking out under the same roof: a school gymnasium, a community center, an underground club. The music is banging and these pockets of circles are bouncing as a free-styling MC stands in the center, spitting out verses off the top of his head, rapping into a mic held tight to his lips; and b-boys are calling out their opponents, cross-stepping, flipping, spinning to some crazy beat.

This is "battling"—MC versus MC, dancer versus dancer—and this scene was my social preoccupation from the age of fourteen.

These venues became echoing pits of nonstop music and dance, and I couldn't stay away from its trance. It was my first addiction in life.

This is where you earned your name, won your stripes and built your street cred, as each dancer or MC entered a circle and threw down his skills, leaving the crowd as judges. Whoever was handed the loudest cheer, won.

In this fight for respect and supremacy, battles broke out most week nights and weekends up and down the East and West coasts. In L.A., crews rocked up from all over the city: West Covina, South Central L.A., Pasadena, Venice, Downtown, Glendale, and Crenshaw.

Each new battle tested my skills, and I improved with each experience, pitching into L.A. venues such as the Armory, Masonic temples, Mission, and even Marilyn's in Pasadena. Word spread around school about backyard battles, or battles in parking lots, or battles in an arcade at Tilt inside the Montebello shopping mall. Such was the craze of the era.

I'd keep my ear to the ground and go anywhere and everywhere, getting the bus or relying on Mom whenever she had the time to drive me across town. If you wanted to find me outside of school between the ages of fourteen and fifteen, all you had to do was scout the nearest battle. A regular venue was always the parking lot of the In-N-Out Burger joint—across the street from Rosemead High— but I was looking to take things to the next level.

That higher level was an all-ages hip-hop/funk club event called Ballistyx, held at a club called Whisky A Go-Go, on Sunset Boulevard, across the street from the Viper Room. I first stepped into that club with Eclipse, both of us eager with wonder. Musical archives could have foretold me that only good things happen at the Whisky: a club so steeped in musical legend that you could get drunk on its history. It played its part in showcasing and launching great careers and acts: Alice Cooper, the Doors, Frank Zappa's Mothers of Invention, Chicago, Motley Crüe. Over the decades, musical trends had lined up in the street and passed through the same single side-door we rushed through, from rock 'n' roll to punk to heavy metal. By our time, all booths and seating from the "good old days" had been removed, leaving a whole dance floor open for battling.

Ballistyx Battles were held on Thursday nights between seven o'clock and eleven o'clock, courtesy of actor-turned-club promoter David Faustino, better known as Bud Bundy from *Married With Children.*

There were two perks to this weekly event: it provided a venue for those kids who wanted to indulge in dance, and it allowed us to stay out late, beyond eleven. This whole hip-hop arena of intensity was personally transformative because when immersed within its energy, I didn't feel shy, insecure or intimidated. It was like I'd left those cloaks at the doorway and swapped them for the performer's cape. I became a different person: confident, believing, assured in my skills. I'd always been lazy as a kid, especially at school or around the house. But when it came to dancing-stroke-performing, you might as well have put a rocket up my ass. I had the willpower to be a performer. I didn't have the willpower for much else.

I hovered on the circle's edge, awaiting to kill it. My focus was pinpoint. I psyched myself up like a boxer in his corner, waiting for the bell to sound.

I'd imagine Nanny as the coach in my head: *"Way to go, Jim!"*

Then I'd envision Bruce Lee, all ninja-style before a martial arts tournament.

When I stepped in to serve up my rival, the beat instinctively told my body what to do.

I won first time out, and the cheers I received made me feel like I'd just hit a home run for the Cardinals. Of course, I got defeated, too, but that only made me strive harder next time.

Before long, I was knocking down most challengers, and it made me puff out my chest and stand a little taller in life.

Once I made my solo point, me, Phoenix, Eclipse, and Courtney formed a dance crew called Divine Tribal Brothers. I've still got video footage of me and Phoenix killing a battle in a school gymnasium in Baldwin Park; there we're murdering the dance floor with crazy routines; two skinny kids in baggy jeans and tent-sized tees, and me in my fisherman's hat. I watch that video now and again and see the determination on our faces. That footage acts as a constant reminder of how far I've come.

Five of us would pack into Mom's white Sentra with her at the wheel, then we'd head to wherever the battle was. She'd come back to pick us up about three hours later. I'm not sure she really understood what went on inside until, one time at Ballistyx, she arrived early and started talking to the man on the door. She looked into the distance, scanned the floor and saw a commotion shielded by a wall of people encircling something or someone. What she never realized was that it was nearly always me in the center of that commotion, performing my ass off. She'd tell you today that she never thought anything would come of it; that she thought I was wasting my time. Mom was always waiting for me to land "a real job."

Around this time, I received a phone call from Phoenix's friend John Trochez who told me about this young cat Polo Molina, who represented a Pasadena rapper called Ron Johnson. He was holding auditions for dancers for one of Ron's shows at Universal Studios, North Hollywood, so John had dropped in a good word for us.

Polo Molina is a hustler and a fast talker. He was roughly the same age as we were, but he was clearly a manager-type with growing connections. Besides Ron Johnson, he managed a small solo act named Little E, who was a twelve-year-old MC with a big future. This kid also happened to be his nephew.

John Trochez organized our impromptu audition at his house in the San Gabriel Valley. Me and Phoenix walked into this living room, thinking this was our big moment. I can't say that an audition in someone's living room, standing on a wooden floor, was my idea of how the big break would look, but we were happy to take our chance.

The doorbell went and in walked Polo, wearing casual gear that included a red top, beige shorts, white socks, a green baseball cap and a pair of Doc

Martens. He was also sporting a black eye from a fight the previous night. Everything about this guy said he meant business.

"C'mon then, let's see what you guys got," he said, and he sat back, arms spread out in a "T" across the back of the sofa.

We did our thing. He watched intently.

When the music stopped, we were left standing there, a little awkward in the silence. Polo nodded his head, looked at John, and John raised his eyebrows. Then Polo nodded and said we were in. Our heads nearly hit the chandelier because we jumped that high.

While Phoenix spoke with John, Polo pulled me to one side and, as cool as a cat, said: "There's something special about you two. I'm going to take that and do something with it . . ."

I now wanted to jump through the ceiling.

". . . and what I'm going to do is blow you up and make you famous," he added. I'll never forget him for those words. They are carved into my mind with tattoo ink, dated as the moment when someone *believed* in me other than Nanny. I had been longing to hear that independent recognition: ". . . there's something special about you . . ."

So Polo brought us on board to be a part of Ron Johnson's dancers for the Kiss FM event put on by DJ Hollywood Hamilton at the Universal Amphitheater. When the only stages you've ever known have been club floors and school gymnasiums, that famous amphitheater was some prize. Me and Phoenix ditched battling for a month and rehearsed a routine every day at Polo's house in Pasadena. We knew our moves so well that we could've done them with our eyes closed.

Then life dealt its first lesson with the kind of disappointment that leaves you feeling like a filleted fish. Ron Johnson was shooting some interracial love story movie called *Zebra Head* in Detroit and filming had overrun. He had to cancel his segment at the Universal gig, and our first big opportunity fell through the cracks.

But if Polo is great for one thing, it is his motivation and keeping it on the up and up. "There'll be other chances, other performances," he said.

The first notion of belonging to a musical group—not just a dance crew— came after meeting fellow Latino David Lara, someone else who felt more at home with his black brothers than his Mexican-American peers. This homie from Rosemead High would turn out to be my biggest friend and ally, and we've been brothers ever since. He's a brother from another mother, not by blood, but our alliance was, and remains, as strong as any brotherhood out there.

Today, David is a constant shadow as my day-to-day manager; one of those sounding boards which will throw back to me an honest opinion, whether I like it or not. He is my true *compadre*, and I'd go as far to say that he has proved as much a guide and support to me in life as Nanny.

It was Karish's idea that we meet, because she'd got to know him during choir class after he'd arrived as the new boy in his sophomore year. He was two years younger than me, but I knew he was one of us the moment he started to speak with the black kid lingo. He wasn't just an outsider, he was another misfit from a Mexican community.

I had found him sitting alone in the library, looking awkward in this big, black Charles Barkley jacket, so I walked up and made the introduction. Today, David—or Deja as I call him—will tell you that I was this confident cat who swaggered up like I was the Prince of Persia or something.

"Yo, I hear you can kill it on the singing tip," I said to Deja, because Karish had already told me that he could sing his ass off.

Deja sipped his drink, and nodded his head like someone with nothing to prove.

I felt like an idiot when his full story emerged: he'd arrived at Rosemead High after transferring out of the Hollywood High School of Performing Arts, where the singer Brandy was also a student. That school was the big game, and nearly all its students already had agents and managers, so Deja was clearly a heavy hitter.

A few weeks later, he confirmed his incredible talent at Rosemead High's Disney-themed Christmas concert, when he stepped up with a solo spot, singing "A Dream Is A Wish Your Heart Makes" from *Cinderella*.

And. He. Killed. It.

I'm like "Wow—this quiet mothafucka *can* sing!"

One of the best voices I'd heard. If I could do a mix tape of the past and the present, I would line up Deja with Fergie in a ballad. He can come up with some crazy melodies that blow me away.

I hit it off with Deja not just because he could sing but because his experiences as a Latino mirrored mine. In fact, the reason he'd transferred out of Hollywood High was because he was mercilessly bullied for "singing like a black dude, hanging with the black kids and walking around like someone whose shit didn't stink"—his tormentors' words, not mine.

He must have been getting some real heavy shit for him to walk away from a school like that. It also explained why, when we first met, he told everyone the lie that he'd arrived from New York and not Alhambra, a city district of L.A. Informed by his experiences at Hollywood High, he thought people would accept him—and his hip-hop lingo—more easily if he said he was from the East Coast.

Deja was quiet and smart. He was someone who read books and could speak articulately. But he was also a fellow dreamer, and we'd often sit and imagine the future together, visualizing the day we'd make it in the music industry.

"We'll be on tour one day. We will," he always said.

He'd sing. I'd rap. He'd write. I'd freestyle. And all that energy, fueled by the other boys in our crew, made us collectively believe that *something* was possible. You don't need to see the horizon to know it's out there. You just need to keep driving toward it.

But I don't think Deja thanked me when I used him as my cameraman, videotaping my routines in the backyard. Like most vocalists, he had little patience for the technique I obsessed over.

"Dude, this is boring . . . why are we doing this?" he moaned, holding the camera steady.

"I've got to get this right . . . just keep filming," I said, excitedly.

My obsession with endless practice never did drop off. I'd drag him outside for two hours at a time, making sure he kept a steady hand so that I could watch the footage and then analyze and fine-tune every move.

Just when Deja thought we were done, I'd call out another move. His patience had to be infinite, bearing in mind what I made him endure because he heard it all:

Okay, just let me nail the Atomic Drop.
Or let me do the Cabbage Patch again.
Or if I could do the Running Man . . . or the Roger Rabbit . . . or the Robo Cop.
How can I freak it?
Oh, okay. . . . now let's do the House Dance.
Now let me practice my popping and ticking . . .
Deja, are you getting all this?

With Deja singing, and Eclipse starting to rap more, we made the decision to turn our dance crew into a rap group. So Divine Tribal Brothers morphed into United Soul Children with me, Phoenix, Eclipse and Insane as dance-rappers, and Deja as lead singer. It was like an early version of Black Eyed Peas but with a male lead vocalist.

It helped that Deja had a driver's license, meaning that he provided wheels with the occasional loan of his Uncle John's Mitsubishi. We'd turn it up loud in the car, and free-style to our destination's end, getting a little light-headed on the Ganesh beedies we smoked—these skinny little tobacco-leaf cigarettes we'd buy from Indian markets.

When they ran out, we smoked cinnamon sticks.

Eclipse, aka Greg Pritchett, was someone who was always dreaming up a thousand ideas and concepts for raps. The creative juices always flowed with him around. He was this slim-fit, eccentric dude with a deep, booming voice, and he sported cool dreds. Now, this guy could dance and, if I'm honest, I felt more in tune when dancing alongside him in a battle. He was more the stop-and-go robotic-style dancer that better complemented my smoother, fluid go-with-it style.

Don't get me wrong, Phoenix, aka Joey Jordan, could dance, too, but he had a taller, skinnier frame so he was all arms and legs, jabbing his elbows and punching his feet. A dancing flamingo. If anything, he should have been a stand-up comedian, because he had a stash of funny jokes and a razor-sharp tongue. Take him on, and he'd cut you down.

Insane, aka Antwon Tanner, was a pretty boy from Chicago, and all the students and teachers loved him. He was a rapper who couldn't dance for shit, but he was more "Insane" by name than "insane" by nature. He was a funny cat and great lyricist, too.

The first rap we all wrote together was called "When We Come" with lyrics that boasted how our presence on stage would make every other crew drop to their knees: *"When Insane comes, all the crews drop/When Eclipse comes, all the crews drop/When Taboo comes, all the crews drop/When Deja comes, all the crews drop . . ."*

And then came my first verse that I kicked and performed, from 1991: *"Well it's Taboo, chilling with my crew/So make way, coz I am coming through/And what I come to do is rock a hype show/And when I grab the mic, the crowd yells 'Ho'/Mic check A, mic check B/Here comes The, capital T/Don't forget the O's coz everyone knows/Anything goes when it's straight from the soul."*

We entered the annual talent contest at Rosemead High with that song, as well as a rap version of James Brown's "Make It Funky" for which Deja came up with a dope melody. We threw in some proper lighting and a smoke machine (as advised by Deja), and our three-minute performance ultimately killed it.

We should have taken first place in the contest but lost out to some Mickey Mouse cheerleaders who performed some okeydoke shit. We had to settle for third place, winning $30 each. Ask any of us at that time, we all thought the $120 prize money was the start of great riches to come.

We'd gone from dancing to battling to performing, and there was a shared will that was intent on making it. Whatever "making it" meant. But that's probably why me and Deja made a pact: "If one of us makes it, we come back for the other."

I'm surprised we didn't write that pact on a wall somewhere. We seemed to write everything else on the walls of Rosemead and El Monte.

We didn't just belong to a dance crew, we were part of a tagging crew as well—another underbelly of the youth subculture within Los Angeles.

Tagging is the street art of writing on walls, and we tagged just as much as we danced: on bus stops, buses, mailboxes, windows, fences, walls, concrete pillars and bridges. If it was flat and bare, it was considered a blank canvas worthy

of our art. And "art" is what we called it, because "art" is what it was. Graffiti was seriously beautiful to me. The cops would define it as crime and vandalism, but try telling that to someone like British street artist Banksy. His work was born out of an underground scene in Bristol, southwest England. Our work was born out of the underground scene in L.A. It's art because it's a spontaneous collaboration of artistic and musical minds.

And let's face it, it hasn't done Banksy any harm. In 2007, two of his graffiti pieces sold at Sotheby's auction house in London for $55,000 and $46,000.

What price "vandalism?"

I'm not glorifying anything, but I'm also not writing a thesis on the distinctions between what is art and what is vandalism. This is just my childhood, and you can pretty much dissect it into two halves: time spent battling and rehearsing, and time spent tagging.

In my eyes, graffiti was one of the four elements of the hip-hop culture: graffiti, DJing, MCing and b-boying. That's why I embraced it. I don't know what motivated Banksy, but I do know he started out like us, in a tagging crew—Bristol's DryBreadZ Crew (DBZ). The crew to which we belonged was the Still Kicking Ass Crew (SKA)—and those initials broke out in bubble lettering all over the area, sprayed with Krylon paint aerosols, detailed with markers.

What you've got to understand is that our minds weren't set on damage or destruction, but on creativity and presentation. It wasn't about defacing property. It was about bringing life to soulless brick, concrete, and glass.

This is how an entire youth culture expressed itself when I was a kid. No different than cavemen in the Stone Age or student revolts in the 60s and 70s. Likewise, hip-hop culture gave its people a voice on the street, through the mouthpiece of graffiti. Still Kicking Ass was a massive crew of taggers with hundreds of members, and we each adopted street nicknames: Eclipse was "Ekces," Phoenix was "Dox" and I was "Dalas."

Why Dalas? Because I liked the look of the word after I'd played around with letters. Just as with "Taboo," I liked the big first letter and the rising middle letter. That's what fascinated me about words—how the letters looked, how they connected.

We carried around a palette of artist's tools: Mean Streak permanent markers, Krylon spray paint, Diamond Scribes, Pilot markets, Magnum markers, thin-line markers. In all colors of the rainbow.

I was constantly manipulating and reshaping a word; dressing it with symbols, quirky trademarks, and filling in backgrounds, and then turning it into block lettering, bubble lettering, 3-D lettering. I'd get lost in my own tagging jungle, dismantling and rebuilding one word, then switching around letters, all in the pursuit of my own style, stamp and originality with whatever crazy, lavish lettering I could dream up.

I obsessed about the smallest detail—even telling myself that the *smoothness* of a word mattered; the smooth flow of letters when joined, with letters always slanting slightly to the right. If it flowed, it felt connected. If the letters were connected, the word felt right. Once the graffiti bug bites you, it's in your blood every time you write.

Even today, the tagging influence remains with me. I'll be in hotel rooms with the Peas and someone will pick up a menu or a phone directory and say: "Tab! Can you stop tagging everything?" Because I had already been there, unconsciously tagging my name, my wife's name, the group's name. Whatever I'm talking about on the phone, I'm tagging it.

"Dude," said Deja one day last year during the E.N.D. tour, "I'm looking to order some food off the menu and all I can see is TABOO written a thousand different ways!"

The main thing is that these days I've curbed my enthusiasm and my tagging is restricted to menus, phone directories and tableside notepads. I don't want hotel and venue managers, or chauffeurs or pilots, getting worried. I boxed up my serious tools years ago.

It was a close shave with the law that made me stop.

As a teenager, I went solo tagging one evening on Rosemead Boulevard, on the bridge that crossed the 10 freeway that ran parallel to my street address. I was tagging an entire roll call—writing everyone's names—and was deep in concentration, wearing a hoodie, when all of a sudden I heard the police sirens sound twice behind me.

I spun around and saw the blue and red lights of one of the cop cars coming toward me. I threw my marker, jumped the bridge onto the grassy embankment and ran the entire length of the freeway, arriving home panting like a thirsty dog.

I told Mom some guys had started chasing me. Which wasn't exactly a lie.

I stuck with the rest of the crew after that, and it was when we were on the bus one evening that we met another tagger, a Latino kid by the name of Mooky. It was through Mooky that we would discover all about the small world of battling and tagging, and the serendipity of meeting certain people. That's what I like about life. You meet some random cat on a bus and you think "He's cool." Then, some ways down the road, he's the guy who ends up making the crucial introduction that would change your life.

It was one evening in 1992 that a battling crew called Tribal Nation stopped me in my tracks with skills that removed me from any kind of self-congratulation.

I'd gone to the Whisky with Eclipse, and you always knew when some-

thing special was going down because of the size of the crowd around one circle, and one guy was clearly dancing up a storm.

I wandered over and watched an eccentric-looking black dude rapping like a madman, one hand on the mic, one hand twisting his tight dreds. He had this wide-eyed intensity that made it look like he was in some kind of trance. The speed at which he rapped was something I'd never heard before. It was incredible. No other MC had a chance against that whirlwind. This fresh sixteen-year-old owned the floor and had more energy than the whole club combined. He was as colorful as his socks were loud, and as brilliant as anything I'd seen on the street, in videos, or in battles.

That's my first memory of first seeing will.i.am—then known as WilloneX.

In another corner was the other half of Tribal Nation: a crazy, exotic-looking Filipino dude dancing better than I had ever seen anyone dance in there; flipping out and breaking with a bunch of keys jangling on his belt buckle. This kid danced like he had volts running through him; he got all acrobatic, executing precision backflips and somersaults. He could flip in an arch from the palms of his hands to the balls of his feet, and vice versa. I had seen gymnasts with less agility.

And that is my first memory of apl.de.ap.

These guys dressed sharp, too: both sported dreds twisted tight to the scalp, and both suited up in thrift-store vintage clothing with 1970s jackets, turtlenecks, polyester pants and crazy workman boots. If I'd known what "star quality" meant back then, I'd have attached that label to them both.

I just remember watching them and thinking "Damn, who are these cats?"

We didn't get talking straightaway. That would come later. We just flashed across each other's radars, making ourselves known. Tribal Nation and Divine Tribal Brothers—maintained as the battling element of our group—eyed up our respective talents from across the floor, without ever engaging. It was almost a standoff, like two real tribes checking each other out from across the plains.

I then spotted the guy from the bus, Mooky—the third strand of Tribal Nation. He hailed from the San Gabriel Valley but always traveled to hang with Will and Apl. One week later, he was the one to suggest we should all hook up. Mooky had been best friends with Will since they were eight years old and he felt we would get along.

Will and Apl later told me that they spotted me "doing something special" in my thrift clothes and beret and wondered "Who's the dancer?"

"He's kind of scary looking . . . but his dancing is dope," Apl had said.

That still makes me smile, because the scary look was partly by design. All that mattered was getting noticed.

Back home, Mom and Julio started noticing how much time I was investing in battling. I think they grew more and more concerned for my future.

Why else did I start hearing noises about "Why don't you start looking for a part-time job?" or "One day, you're going to have to get a real job!"

But that's all it was to me—just noise.

At age sixteen, I started taking martial arts lessons with Deja. Basically, I took it up not to become the tough guy, but because I wanted to incorporate the same crazy ninja moves into my dance routines. Martial arts would improve my balance, agility and endurance.

Forever inspired by Bruce Lee, I knew the skill I wanted under my belt: Jeet Kune Do. It was convenient that Insane's dad, Jet Tanner, was an instructor, so this no-nonsense Vietnam veteran became my and Deja's sensei.

Antwon's garage became our battling practice ground *and* martial arts studio. As we grappled with the basics of Jeet Kune Do, Antwon practiced basketball, probably because he was wise enough to know about the blood and sweat that his dad was going to put us through! He had us punching this wooden board over and over with our bare knuckles.

"Harder! Punch it harder!" he shouted.

He was, he said, trying to build the calluses on our knuckles, but all I saw was grazes and blood. The big payoff was the knowledge that me and Deja would be smoking weed at the end of the pain.

The end result, after many weekends, was that I honed my technique in countless punch, kick and block moves, so I started incorporating this form into my dance moves, all ninja style.

I'll say with gratitude today that the moves you see from me on stage with the Black Eyed Peas, and the breathing techniques needed to endure a world tour, were shaped and rooted in a garage and backyard in San Bernardino with Jet Tanner.

He knew what he was doing all along.

He broke down each move, showing me how to build it into my dance set, stage by stage, move by move. It was like he was some crazy choreographer working through a ninja concept, and it was this martial arts form that became an integral part of my signature dance. That, in turn, inspired a ninja concept with my dress for battling. I started wearing crazy ninja boots, head wraps and ninja-style gloves.

All the pieces were in place: martial arts, breaking and hip-hop all meshed together, shaping me into a potential performer.

I can frame all those teachings within the benefit of hindsight now. At the time, I was just doing anything and everything that I felt would give me the edge. It's not as if I scribbled a strategy on paper. But I now thread all these events and influences together and see the biggest reason in an accidental sequence: Latino boy moves to hip-hop community. Hip-hop community inspires him to dance.

Dance inspires him to battle. Battle inspires him to win. Winning inspires him to learn martial arts. Martial arts makes him a better dancer.

Not that martial arts made me a mean fighter.

After about a year of training, Deja asked about our progress as fighters. "Hey, Jet," he said, "are we pretty good now? Do we know enough to defend ourselves?"

Jet looked us up and down and just said, "You know just enough now to get your ass kicked."

We had started hanging with Polo Molina more and more, and he was just happy that I was chipping away at my craft. He was the cool dude because he had the wheels: a Jeep, a Volvo and a Mustang. When all you've ever seen is an RTD bus route and Mom's battered Sentra, his collection represented one mean fleet of cars.

He took me and Phoenix around different all-age clubs to do battle and, one night, his act and nephew Little E stepped up to the plate. En route, Polo had talked up the kid as an MC of the future. So we walked in, expecting big things to happen.

And big things did happen . . . because Little E came face-to-face with William Adams—WilloneX—in an open-mic battle.

The crowd went wild as Little E—this little white boy—stepped up first. He was a midget with talent. He served Will.

Will stepped up, and, for a couple of rounds, let the kid have his shot. But, in the end, Little E was just a twelve-year-old kid rapping in a big man's world, taking on a dragon. We thought the crowd would sway toward the kid, the underdog. But no one in an urban club could care less about the white boy punching above his weight against the black champion. After humoring him for a bit, Will turned it on and smoked him.

It was as if Will was thinking "If you've got the nerve to step into my world, you'll get served like an adult." Swim in the ocean, swim with sharks—and Polo didn't like that.

As soon as Will finished up the inevitable victory, Polo was snarling in his face.

"Hey, you disrespecting my little nephew!"

That was the night that I learned how much Polo didn't like coming off as second best. It got a bit heated, and Polo shoved Will before Mooky stepped in as peacemaker. It was done; they squashed it and became friends.

It's all a bit hazy now, but it's enough to know that Polo agreed that night to ferry Will and Apl around town, as well as me and Eclipse.

Polo was part of the crew in those days, more linchpin than anything else, because Will already had a manager, Terry Heller. Terry was the man at that time, and he also had an uncle who owned a label called Ruthless Records. That said, Polo was still an ambitious cat who was playing the long game. He had four talented kids under his fledgling management wing, transporting us to battling arenas. Each week, he picked up his boys from Rosemead, then picked up his new boys from Los Feliz.

Will often took the wheel because Polo hated driving, and that one vehicle became an intense energy vessel all on its own, darting around Hollywood looking to make an impact on the same circuit. Those journeys were all about loud music, goofing around and free-styling; a traveling free-styling circus.

In terms of life, goals and creativity, we were on the same page, sharing the same dream. We were streetwise, we were hungry, and we thought no one was better than us.

There was something else we shared, something key: the desire to keep hip-hop on the up-and-up. We were in a West Coast era where the hip-hop scene was saturated by "gangsta rap," promoting themes of ghetto warfare, gun violence and women-for-sex. You think of gangsta rap and you think NWA—music which I listened to and had nothing against.

But me, Will, Apl, and Eclipse had been born into more underground hip-hop than mainstream hip-hop, so we didn't subscribe to lyrics about crack dens and AK-47s. We were more about promoting more feel-good, progressive hip-hop. We were about braggadocious hope, not braggadocious violence.

From the day we met, it was obvious that we had unity in spirit, intention and meaning. We just didn't know that this in-car union was the start of a beautiful alliance. It was that year—1992—when our shared intent sowed the first seed of the Black Eyed Peas.

MISFITS & MISHAPS

The first time I built with Will, he rolled me a joint. Not any old joint but probably the most expertly, perfectly rolled joint I'd seen—and he rolled that shit as quick as he rapped.

We had parked Polo's car outside a Hollywood club, the Graveyard Shift, for another round of battling, and he was walking-and-rolling and I was walking-and-watching, mesmerized. I couldn't take my eyes off his precision craftwork.

"You gonna smoke that?" I asked.

"Nah, I don't smoke . . . rolling it for you," he said.

And that was his icebreaker that said, yeah, we're cool, let the friendship and alliance begin.

I liked that he was a perfectionist, all about the pristine clothes, the focus to be number one, and keen on detail. Even his rolled joints were micromanaged. Not that he smoked weed. He'd once had a bad experience and never touched the stuff again. Whereas I had only ever had good experiences from the age of sixteen which explains why I was smoking three to four joints every weekend.

A few joints at the weekend couldn't harm me, right?

It was my stepfather Julio who, as an old hippie, unwittingly made me drug-curious. I uncovered his well-kept "secret" when I was home alone one day, having a good snoop around.

He had this brown wooden box—kind of like a big cigar box with a hinged lid—with the word BONK engraved on it, which, to this day, I still have no idea what that meant. But I wasn't interested in the wrapping, I was interested in the illicit contents: weed. I had previously observed him hiding this box, tucking it away at the back of the wooden bar in the den at the back of the house.

There was only one place I was headed next time he and Mom were out.

When I opened that lid for the first time, I smelled Dog Town all over again. I wasted no time diving into the virgin experience, taking his long wooden bong and packing it with weed. All I can remember is laughing. Watching TV and laughing.

Then I got the munchies.

And then I wanted to try some more.

Wow—I like this shit! I kept thinking.

The more I deeply inhaled and let the smoke fill my mouth, the higher I got. The higher I got, the better I felt. It was a guaranteed smoke of confidence and chill. I even convinced myself that I couldn't feel relaxed or be creative without weed. That was my flawed association: weed equals creativity.

From this moment on, I always had a smoke when hanging with my homies in the car, in Antwon's garage, or at Phoenix's house. It was the start of a beautiful friendship between me and weed.

That night at the Graveyard Shift, after rocking our respective battles, I listened to Will talk about the future—about his big dream and how he wanted to make records. He was here, there, and everywhere trying to make it happen. WilloneX was a mini-me version of the will.i.am you see today.

He exuded the kind of invincible aura that screamed: "I'm going to be somebody." Even today—with everything he's achieved and earned—he remains the same guy, still acting like the man who has nothing. He was all fire and hunger, from the way he dressed, the way he focused, the way he spoke.

Since boyhood, Will was fixated on the idea of making records. That is when he says he *knew* he was going to be a rapper and producer, staying in his room recording over tapes and making his own demos. When he wasn't making tapes, he was practicing dance moves and rapping. At nine, he was doing what he did as a Pea in the 2009 Pepsi commercial, rapping over Bob Dylan's "Forever Young."

Like me, he was raised in the projects of East L.A., and his childhood was almost a role reversal of mine: the African-American boy in a largely Latino community, raised in the Estrada Court projects in the Boyle Heights district.

He was born William Adams and was raised single-handedly by his mom, Debra. She, like Nanny with me, encouraged him to escape sameness and become unique. Will was the kid who set about learning music at age fourteen—a late starter by anyone's measure. He approached music like it was a new language. "If you want to move to Germany, you learn German. If you want to move into music, you learn music," he says.

It was when he was still in high school that he and Mooky started running

with a rapper called Eazy-E, aka Eric Wright, and he, together with NWA manager Jerry Heller, established a label called Ruthless Records.

That was a lot of street cred for Will, because here was the eleventh-grader hanging with the artist-of-the-moment, a little like someone in school today hanging with Jay-Z. Eager to impress, Will set out to conquer the MC battles at Ballistyx, performing as WilloneX.

His mom had ensured he attended a good school in Pacific Palisades—taking a daily hour-long bus ride across the metropolis—so as to better his life and prospects. Suddenly, the African-American in a Latino community became the African-American in a white-boy school. Like me, he had to switch it up and learn how to become a chameleon who straddled two separate communities.

Will is a natural-born storyteller, as fast, clever, and animated with his words in conversation as he is when rapping. He's shy—almost guarded—when you first meet him but it was also obvious that he was possessed by the spirits of ambition and talent.

His enthusiasm and charisma walk into a room and charge up the whole place. The man is a walking Energizer battery and true inspiration. Not just to the Peas but to anyone who works with him. Then and now.

Ask Bono. Ask Prince. Ask the Rolling Stones.

As the late Michael Jackson once said when he collaborated with Will: "He's wonderful, innovative, positive, and infectious."

Enough said.

He first met Allan Lindo, the boy we know today as apl.de.ap, during summer school at John Marshall High in Los Feliz.

Apl was born in Sapang Bato, Angeles City, in the Philippines, to a Filipino mom. His African-American dad deserted the family shortly after his birth, so his mom, Cristina, was forced to raise him and six younger siblings on her own. Apl was old before his years, chipping in when he could, working at local farms to bring in extra pocket money, picking corn and rice. But his life changed because of the Pearl Buck Foundation—when one of its commercials was broadcast on American television.

This foundation was set up to assist and better the lives of poorer children, and Apl was featured on the commercial that was seen by California businessman Joe Ben Hudgens. Mr. Hudgens picked up the phone, and, through a dollar-a-day sponsor program, adopted Apl and brought him to L.A. to start a new life. Apparently, there was a ton of red tape over the next three years, but the endgame was that Apl was formally adopted and moved to the West Coast at the age of fourteen.

That must have involved some heavy emotional shit with him leaving home and his mom, but he would grow into a man determined to make the American dream happen so that he could, in turn, financially assist his family back home.

It was Joe Ben Hudgens who I would know as Apl's father figure, and it was he who arranged for Will to take his adopted son under his wing, because Will's uncle happened to be Mr. Hudgens' former roommate. Consequently, Apl was invited to hang with Will and Mooky around Estrada Court to assist with his transition into American life. They have been inseparable ever since.

Apl is one of those rare beings: the most humble, genuine and strongest guy you could ever meet. For him to have arrived alone in America as a boy was a huge inspiration to me as a teenager. There I was, the kid living at home, whose horizons hadn't broadened further than East L.A. and Hollywood, and there he was, the same age, thrown into an alien land, detached from his family and crossing oceans to start over. Instead of shriveling into a ball, he got out there to maximize his new break in life, learning the English language as he went.

And he set about it with impaired eyesight.

He was born with astigmatism in each eye. When I first met him, he had what appeared to be some kind of nervous tic. He'd shake his head and blink repeatedly. Turns out he was shaking his head to establish focus. He sees outlines, not detail, more shapes than vivid color, but then you see how he dances, how he writes and how he thinks and it is mind-blowing. It's like he's sharpened his other senses to compensate for his poor vision. In terms of courage, independence and tenacity, Apl is the ultimate.

What showed up in all our stories were two common threads: we each came from hardscrabble backgrounds, and each grew up without having our real dads around. I'm convinced that within that hole in our lives, we found the determination to prove to these absent men—and ourselves—that we had value; that we would become better men than they ever were; that we wanted to do something with our lives and not settle as dropouts. In that common purpose, we each found a common love in dancing, music, and fashion. In that discovery, I guess we felt we owed ourselves something. As three different strands, we came together and formed the same knot.

We were all misfits, too: me the Latino adopted into the hip-hop community, Will the black guy in his Latino community, and Apl the Filipino adopted into an American family. Diverse enough but . . . the same. There was a definite serendipity to our coming together, even if it's more clear to us now than it was then.

It's because we were misfits that we appreciated everything unspoken about who we were as people. We would, in time, discover the real magic of this alliance, realizing that something "fit" as we merged and fused our energies, talents and beliefs. But first, we'd need to separately struggle some more and suffer some fresh kicks to the gut before we became one.

Nanny always said there was a God, and I trusted her when she said that. But I don't think I actually *really* believed it until the early hours of October 14, 1992.

I was fast asleep in bed, oblivious to the hour that was 6 a.m., when the

entire house started shaking, followed in an instant by the loudest, most humongous BOOM! When you live in Los Angeles, the first thought that flashes through your mind is *Earthquake!* And, in that half-sleep, half-awake blur, I was convinced the earth's core had just erupted and caused every tectonic plate to slip.

As I heard the commotion in the rest of the house—Celeste running screaming to Mom, Julio thinking the house was being robbed—I bolted to the window and saw what can only be described as the opening sequence to some kind of Armageddon movie.

Pockets of flames had broken out all across the road. Half of the concrete-slab sound wall—dividing us from the freeway—was obliterated, and one house down the street had lost a corner of its roof. Two parked cars were crumpled and, on the 10 freeway, all traffic had stopped because debris was strewn across the eastbound lanes. Motorists and neighbors were running around like headless chickens, and women were screaming. Just to add to the sense of surreality, an early morning fog drifted across the scene for further eerie, dramatic effect.

Within minutes, there were paramedics, cop cars and fire engines everywhere, lighting up the mist with flashing red, white and blue lights.

Turns out a private plane had fallen out of the sky and crashed into our street.

The single-engine Piper Cherokee had taken off from El Monte Airport, about two miles away, but it must have come down right away: it clipped the roof of a nearby house, cartwheeled into two parked cars and smashed into the freeway wall. The two people aboard, a couple from Las Vegas, didn't stand a chance.

All the neighbors rushed into the street, but Mom made sure me and Celeste stayed inside. We only realized it was a plane crash via the television news, because from the window you couldn't make out any plane parts in the wreckage. It was still pretty dark, and most of the plane must have disintegrated on impact.

I remember being excited by the fact that Rosemead—and our street—was leading the news coverage. The incident momentarily bumped aside the U.S. presidential election talk of whether Democratic nominee Bill Clinton had dodged his Vietnam draft call in 1969.

Everyone said it was a miracle that the house with the clipped roof had escaped major structural damage and the people inside were not injured. But, within all the what-ifs that normally follow near misses, all I could think about was our family's lucky escape as the plane dropped out of the sky, choosing where to fall with God's grace. Mimicking Nanny, I said a prayer that night—a big thank-you to God and Our Lady of Guadalupe.

Also making local headlines that day was news from Oxnard that nine juveniles had been held by police after what the media called "a graffiti spree." Some near misses were more apparent to me than to Mom that day!

There was another occasion, and another close shave, when I had good reason to thank God again—the time when I nearly burned down our garage.

I had managed to get hold of some M-80 firecrackers, mini-explosives loaded into a small red cardboard tube with a fuse stick. They were like mini-sticks of dynamite. I can't remember how I ended up with them and I can't say that I knew that they were illegal, either. All I knew was the instruction on the tube: *"Do Not Hold In Hand."*

Mom and Julio were out, so I shut the garage door—for privacy and better acoustics—and stuffed two or three inside a hole in the garage wall that Julio had never filled. When that shit went off, and with the echo off the walls, it sounded like one intense military gunfight cracking off. It was impressive but brief, and when the solo display was over, I wandered back inside the house.

Among the things that my ignorance didn't know was that when these M-80s go off, and the cracking and fizzing dies out, it leaves a small flame spark-ing in its stub. Somehow, some of these sparks leapt onto some old sheets lying on the garage floor. I only realized the enormity of my fuckup when I walked out back with a soda and saw smoke on the other side of the garage window. I ran to the front and it was much worse—I couldn't open the garage because flames were licking the underside of the metal door.

Where Julio's Mercedes was parked.

There's not a lot a teenage boy can do in those circumstances except panic. I ran into the street, screaming "FIRE! FIRE!" to alert the neighbors. Some-one phoned 911 and the fire engines arrived in tandem with the police, and, thank-fully, the fire was extinguished and confined to the garage.

I was standing in the driveway, staring at Julio's smoke-blackened Mercedes, when this fire marshal or detective came up to me, wanting to know what had happened. I lied like a stupid adolescent who thought that "I don't know" was a legitimate defense. But it's hard to lie when fear is dilating your pupils.

"You know you've got to tell the truth, son," said the fire chief, "because you know what happens to kids who start fires?"

Suddenly, being caught for graffiti didn't seem like such a big deal when measured against a possible arson charge.

I knew I was busted but couldn't help maintaining the denial.

Then, from behind, I heard a familiar wail: "HI-MEHHH! WHAT DID YOU DO?"

Mom and Julio had arrived back home, and my mother instinctively knew the truth. I think I pretty much gave away my guilt when I broke down in tears and ran into her arms.

That moment represented the lowest point and worst of times I'd ever experienced with Mom. She refused to talk to me for the entire month I was

grounded. The saving grace was that everyone accepted it was an accident, and there were no charges. The other saving grace, as Mom kept reminding me, was that the entire house—hadn't burned down.

As she often reminded me, half the time I didn't help myself. Which was true. But after near misses involving plane crashes, badass fireworks and run-ins with the law, don't tell me there's not a God. Because there is—and He's saved my ass more times than I can remember.

I view life as a chessboard. We're all moved around by God to different places, events and people until we're "checkmated" by destiny. Until that point, there are going to be times when you've just got to trust that things are heading in the right direction.

Even when it seems like everything is stagnant and pretty shitty.

That's easy to say in retrospect, I know. But it's something I now understand as I make sense of, and find reason in, all the twists and turns that conspired to create the formation of the Black Eyed Peas. Some of the chain of events involved me, some didn't. But, looking back on how the board ends up, it's hard not to see something predestined about each move that was made.

Foresight was not so easy in late 1991–early 1992. Personally, I think I was grasping at different vehicles, hoping one would transport me to the big dream.

Divine Tribal Brothers had become United Soul Children and then we had run into Will and Apl's Tribal Nation. With so much clicking between both tribes, we decided to merge and form a "super-crew" called Grassroots, allowing me, Eclipse, Will and Apl to double up our impact for battles.

But, under the umbrella of this super-crew, we maintained our separate units as ambitious artists. Will and Apl kept on with Tribal Nation which they renamed Atban Klann (the first word standing as an acronym for A Tribe Beyond A Nation), together with its other members, MC Mooky, DJ Motiv8 and a vocalist called Dante Santiago, who'd also been a mover and shaker on the scene at Ballistyx. At one point this super-crew was fifteen people strong as we attracted more like-minded creative types into the fold. Meanwhile, United Soul Children wasn't happening. Outside of school talent contests, its purpose felt redundant, so me and Eclipse decided to cut loose and form Rising Suns, leaving aside Deja, Phoenix, and Antwon.

It was a bit arbitrary, but we weren't in the mood to mess around. Deja, at that time, was going through a weird phase where he seemed to have the energy for nothing and Phoenix just lost interest. This coincided with a druggy phase he got mixed up in, which I'll get into a little later.

Antwon was all about acting. He homed in on that focus and, as things turned out, that was a smart choice, because he ultimately built a successful career, nailing roles in several movies and television series. Most notably, he landed parts in *NYPD Blue*, *Boston Public*, *CSI*, but his biggest run would be as "Skills Taylor" in more than a hundred episodes of *One Tree Hill*.

The great hope that was Rising Suns soon faded into nothing. In fact, during the scattered time we spent in Eclipse's mom's apartment in El Monte, we put together only two songs. There was no sense of momentum, probably because we didn't have a great rapper. I wasn't one, and neither was Eclipse. We were two dancers playing at the big game, and we became one of those stalled musical experiments in a long line of wannabe stars who formed a group or band because it sounded good in theory.

Meanwhile, Will and Apl were going places.

Will slayed everyone he came up against as Hollywood's MC champion. He didn't lose a single battle in an eighteen-month stretch, winning for about seventy consecutive weeks. He was untouchable. One particular night, he'd slayed the Chicago-based MC, Twista, and that was no mean feat because Twista once set a mark in the *Guiness Book of World Records* for the fastest rap. Hip-hop greats were bowing down to the boy from East L.A., and it so happened that Terry Heller from Ruthless Records was in the house that night.

Next thing we know, him and Apl rock up to announce that Atban Klann had landed a record deal, signed by Easy-E, together with another group called Blood of Abraham. Sixteen years old and still in high school, they'd been lined up to record a debut album, called *Grassroots*. Eazy-E's manager Jerry Heller had liked what he saw and wanted to launch them. First, they would get the chance to feature on Eazy-E's 1992 EP *5150: Home For tha Sick* on a track titled "Merry Muthafuckin' Xmas." But it was the prospect of their own album that was up there as the Holy Grail.

As far as hip-hop goes, the signing of Atban Klann couldn't have been more of a departure for Eazy-E. The theme of his lyrics was true gangsta rap: sex, guns, drugs, and cops. Will and Apl were all about peace-minded, universal love. Maybe Easy-E recognized the commercial potential in diversity? Not that it mattered.

They had struck gold, and the only way for them was up.

Senior year at Rosemead High saw a small miracle in our family, because I started to produce A grades and carve out a 3.8 grade point average, putting me on the path to graduate with honors, lighting up the road toward college.

Suddenly, that word that adults and teachers always dangled like a carrot became an option—"prospects" came into view. I interpreted "prospects" to mean something that enhanced my chances of "making it." That's probably the real reason the kid in me decided to knuckle down, study hard, and get good grades.

Plus, there was a part of me that wanted to prove to Mom that I wasn't a total loser. Whatever the reasons, I killed it in my senior year.

As I moved up at school, Phoenix lost himself. He went all-out with his drug experimentation, taking downers, acid, and mushrooms. He stopped studying. He stopped dancing. It was sad to see him become the burnout friend you didn't want to be around. He just freaked us out, and wasn't even funny anymore.

Drugs would never lead me astray like that. At least, that's what I told myself, because I wanted nothing and no one to get in the way of progress.

I should have remembered that mind-set when Karish came round to the house one afternoon when Mom and Julio were at work. The stormy nature of our adolescent relationship meant we were always breaking up and making up, and, this particular afternoon, we were making up. On the living room carpet.

I chose to have unprotected sex there and then.

I would soon learn that, sometimes, it's the most impulsive choices that end up having the most far-reaching impact on our lives.

On New Year's Eve 1992, I told myself that 1993 was going to be my year. Inspired by Will and Apl's journey, I'd find a way to rise up. But what's that thing that John Lennon said?

"Life is what happens to you while you're busy making other plans."

Cue one phone call from Karish.

"I'm pregnant," she said.

In nine months, my entire life would be tipped upside down.

The impact was a "get-real" check like no other, as if someone had dropped one big reality tablet into my heady cocktail of young love and lust, and then launched me into a parallel universe where I wasn't mentally ready or emotionally equipped. I was a seventeen-year-old expectant dad with the emotional age of a twelve-year-old.

Only two things were immediately clear: the thin blue line on the pregnancy test kit, and the fact that she was keeping the baby.

That blue line was starker and brighter than anything I'd seen, like a neon sign in Vegas that lit up with the words: "YEAH, YOU GAMBLED! YOU LOST!"

"I'm NOT having an abortion, Jaime!" said Karish.

"I don't want you to," I lied. "We're in this together."

With few words and little thought, that's how our decision was made. Mindlessly. We actually debated the merits of telling our parents more than we debated the wisdom of becoming parents at such a young age. In the end, we decided not to tell our parents. Not yet. There was too much other stuff to think about without including that shitstorm.

In those early days of her pregnancy, my mind lurched from the rational and irrational and back almost daily.

On one hand, I told myself that here was the woman I was going to marry, and a baby is what all married couples eventually have. It would seal our talk of "forever." I told myself that being a father mattered; that this is what adults did, and we had to be responsible. Which is odd when placed alongside the irresponsibility of the situation.

It was when fear set in—mostly at night—that the irrational thinking spun out of control, and triggered all sorts of escapist resolutions into my head:

Any second now, I'll wake up and none of this will be true.

Any morning soon, the dream catcher will catch this bad dream and throw it away.

Any day now, Karish will change her mind and have an abortion.

Or miscarry.

Or fall.

That's the kind of shit that goes through a kid's mind when caught in a pregnant girl's web. But, as the endless weeks passed, there was the growing realization that this was "daddy time," ready or not. Time to put away the toys and pick up the hard hat and tools.

I felt cornered by my own stupidity, but knew that I needed the dust to settle in my own head before kicking up a nuclear storm at home.

I dreaded telling Julio because it would just confirm that, yeah, I really was the fuckup he always thought I was; a kid having a kid, with no money, no job, nothing. That's why me and Karish figured that we'd have a good four months before she started showing; four months to get our ducks in a row; four months for me to step up and show everyone that I was prepared for the event, and *would be* responsible.

I lay awake most nights trying to figure it all out. That wasn't easy with the devil sitting on my shoulder, informing me that my future was well and truly over now. "No more clubs or parties . . . no more battling . . . no more good times," this inner voice told me. It was hard not to think that if the music shit wasn't popping off, then life was obviously giving me the message to give it up and get a real job.

And if life wasn't giving me that message, Karish certainly was: "You've got a baby to provide for now so that means taking responsibility."

"What do you want me to do, Karish?" I said, helplessly.

"Get a job . . . join the Army . . . but do something that will provide for your family!"

So I made the decision to follow in the footsteps of Uncle Louie and join the armed forces. It seemed the sensible thing to do, because a military life promised a steady salary, health insurance and a family home on base. It answered in one stroke all the questions that had kept me awake at night.

I even took the drastic step of cutting my long black hair, thinking that "smart" was a better look than "stylish"; thinking I've now got to make an impression, not a statement. I switched directions, walked out of hip-hop's back door and into freedom's front door. I was going to join the U.S. Air Force.

The Military Entrance Processing written test took place at a station in Alhambra, about ten minutes from Rosemead. Walking through that door is supposed to feel empowering, but I felt shoehorned by circumstances. My heart and soul surrendered to duty.

Everything about the military environment made my rebellious streak kick in.

I read the "Preparing for a MEP Test" pamphlet and realized I was stepping out of thrift-store clothing and into a straitjacket. It even had rules for sitting for the test: *"No earrings. Wording or pictures on clothing will not be tolerated. Wear neat, moderate clothing. Hats and headbands not permitted."* It also warned that the first thing they do is search for "illegal contraband," so that meant going a full day without weed.

The only aspect that sounded remotely rock 'n' roll was the promise that each processing station provided "personalized and professional attention." I looked at the cubicle where I would sit for the test—like one of those DMV driving test cubicles—and wondered about deliberately flunking the paper.

I don't even know why I am here, I said to myself.

I don't even want to be a dad, let alone a soldier, I added.

I was also honest with the male recruiter who greeted me that day. I told him my life was music, but this route was a necessity. I told him that many kids are comfortable with a regular, stable, and secure job . . . but not me. I was uncomfortable because this wasn't my dream, and, credit to him, he listened and understood. He reassured me that a lot of musicians had gone into the forces.

"Look at Elvis Presley," he said, "He became the king of rock 'n' roll!"

It was a nice try.

I was handed a pen and pencil and shown to the chair. I looked at the questions and wondered if anyone could fail *even if they tried.* I went through the motions, did my adult man's duty and walked out, like someone clocking on and clocking off. And that's what it would feel like every single mundane day, I told myself.

An orderly, disciplined, and conformist life stretched out before me like a prison sentence.

Back home, I pleaded with Mom that I couldn't do it. I couldn't take one more step inside a military building. Mom understood.

The difference with Mom's point of view was that she was still unaware of our secret. Within days, she laid out a bunch of college application forms on the table, agreeing that the military life wasn't the answer but reminding me "You can still go into the world of music, but you need college first."

I saw how much she was doing for me, and felt huge guilt because of the eagerness and hope that hadn't yet seen reality coming. Of the forms that I can remember, she was already imagining me walking into an academic life at Loyola Marymount University, near Marina-del-Rey.

In the meantime, we decided that I should go to school to learn another skill. I snatched at this idea to compensate for all that she did not yet know. So I found myself flicking through a pamphlet from Rosemead Adult School.

I looked down an endless list of tedious careers that made my soul flatline until I felt a faint beat of excitement: a career as an EMT—an emergency medical technician. That sounded like a cool option, with an element of living on the edge, and the pay was good at $12 an hour.

I enrolled for a six-week course, two hours every Tuesday and Thursday evening. I found myself studying hard, immersed in medical words and terminology, supposedly learning all about heart rates, blood pressure and anatomy. I say "supposedly" because the words went in one ear and out the other. The perceived excitement soon withered. It was only when it came to the final thesis that I found renewed interest, after being asked to write an essay about everything we'd learned and turn it into an oral presentation. Suddenly, here was a chance to get in front of the class of twenty wannabe EMTs *and perform*.

The tutor said he was looking for originality, so I started thinking about doing something spectacular, something no one had done before.

That's when the idea came to me: deliver my essay as melodic EMT rap. Not only did this conform to the requirements for "originality," it would also show the class that I was talented. There was also another method to my madness, because my brain was trained to store words in rhymes and associations, so this format became a surefire way to remember all those complex medical words. It was, I thought, an ingenious idea.

Over the following two weeks, I came alive with inspiration, dreaming up verses in my bedroom, treating this project with dedicated seriousness.

It was a school talent contest, it was a battle, it was a chance to shine. I'd found a way to incorporate my passion into the mundane. I even told myself that I'd be Los Angeles' first rapping EMT and would save lives with my in-ambulance performances.

On the big day, I brought my boom-box and mix tape to class. I drew the blinds, turned down the lights and burned a candle. Everyone looked at me, wondering what was going down, and the teacher—who took his task with the seriousness of a drill sergeant—eyed me suspiciously.

I had pictured every last detail in my head to set up the right ambience, even down to the incense stick that I lit before pressing "Play."

I cleared my throat as some scary underground beat came on.

And I started to rap:

> *"Ventricular septum . . .*
> *My rectum . . .*
> *Connected to his mouth . . .*
> *So kiss my ass . . .*
> *If you don't understand ass . . .*
> *The next man so I can just stand . . .*
> *Tell you what it means to be an EMT man . . ."*

I wasn't even in full stride when the music stopped and the lights went on. There was just silence. No applause.

"What is THIS?" asked the tutor, indignant.

"It's a rap, and it includes everything about—"

"It's a disgrace to the medical profession," he said, cutting in.

"But it's who I am!" I protested.

"It is NOT what an EMT is about!"

Anyway, he wrote "FAILED" across my work in big, fat red letters.

So that was the end of that.

Apl wasn't faring much better.

His adopted father, Joe Ben Hudgens, had started to wonder about his son's intentions in life. Apl would soon understand that "getting a real job" ran through America's work ethic.

"So, Allan," said Mr. Hudgens in his deep, serious voice, "what are your plans?"

"I want to do this music thing."

"Well, Allan, I don't think it's going to work out here if you pursue this music career!"

There was a lot more to that particular chat but the upshot was that Apl—the truly nomadic Pea—became the first to bolt for independence and move out of his home at age eighteen. He found a two-bedroom apartment in Hollywood with a roommate named Tommy. As our friendship solidified, we hung out in this dimly lit joint or the studio, shooting the shit. Apl was always chilling, thinking out loud about his ideas, writing down some creative shit, and Will was always pacing with his thoughts or dashing around in organizational mode.

I observed events from the periphery, fascinated by the process of watching friends go through the Atban Klann creative process. I didn't feel envy. I felt pride, and was happy enough to be hanging in their circle. It allowed me to vicariously enjoy their journey, making music. Some recording sessions took place in the L.A. downtown loft apartment of producer DJ Motiv8. It was more a makeshift studio than a professional setup: he had his workstation on one side of the room, and a microphone hanging down from the ceiling in a closet that acted as a vocal booth. But it was dope as far as I was concerned.

One day, I made the mistake of inviting Karish along. I don't know what possessed me to think that this would make her get it when she'd previously never shown an iota of interest in my musical career, but hope can be a desperate beast.

She was not interested in being there.

"Jaime, there's a baby that needs to be taken care of and this isn't how you're going to take care of your family!" she said.

She was up and out of that studio and I trailed after her.

Everyone from that time will accurately tell you that I was seriously pussy-whipped. I didn't have the nuts to be the alpha male, or have the wisdom to realize the necessity of having a life partner who supports your dream, especially when it doesn't seem to be taking off. I was too young to know that someone who *tolerates* your passion—or, worse still, resents it—is someone who'll never go the distance with you. Dreamers need someone who, when the chips are down and they think of quitting, is there to stop the pity party and lift your spirits. Like my wife, Jaymie. She is the first to kick my ass if I ever have a moment of feeling down; always there to remind me who I am because she understands the performer's spirit. But Karish never got me or my dream.

Mom still had no idea about the pregnancy. I kept going home and finding her at the table, surrounded by more college application forms. I didn't have the heart—or bravery—to tell her that she might as well forget it. I just stayed with her and went through the motions, feigning enthusiasm and continuing to live the lie.

"DO YOU KNOW WHAT YOUR SON HAS DONE TO MY DAUGHTER?" screamed Karish's mom in a red-hot phone call to my mom one unforgettable day in June 1993—one month before our high school graduation, and four months into the pregnancy.

That is how Mom eventually learned she was going to be a grandmother.

She didn't need to say anything. The devastation was written all over her haunted face. Then came the tears—the wails of "What have you done?" and "Why didn't you tell me?"—and then came the fury. It's like I'd let off another M-80 and burned down my entire future.

She wept and screamed for that future for days afterward, and couldn't look me in the face, let alone speak to me.

The only person who spoke to me inside the house was Julio, but that was only to say: "I cannot believe you, Jaime . . . you've messed up now . . . you've really fucked up now!" He kept saying it, repeating it like a bad chorus.

I couldn't deny what he said this time around. You could have slapped "LOSER" on my forehead and I wouldn't have complained too loudly.

When we held hands through our graduation walk in front of the whole school at Rosemead High one month later, it took the shine off the academic achievement I'd secured. Fatherhood at eighteen isn't the smartest career move in anyone's book. Watching your girlfriend sporting a cap, gown and baby bump as she accepts her honors is one sobering moment, let me tell you.

The next few months zoomed by, hurtling me toward another phone call from Karish's mom, this time screaming the news that her daughter had gone into labor. Hours later, on October 13, 1993, my son, Josh, was born at Whittier Presbyterian Hospital. My boys Deja, Antwon, and Eclipse all showed up, skipping studies to show moral support. The hospital waiting room resembled a scene from the movie *Knocked Up.*

There's not much I remember about Josh's arrival apart from how bloody it was. I was eighteen, and it was the most traumatic thing I'd ever seen in my life. It made my legs turn to jelly. But it was witnessing the afterbirth that finished me off.

I threw up. Then I came over dizzy.

Someone—I can't remember who—thought it would be a smart idea to let me hold my son for the first time, so I cradled Josh in my arms, looking down at him sleeping. His innocence came face-to-face with my ignorance, and all I could think was *"What the fuck am I going to do?"*

Like any child, Josh is a gift, and my love for him is beyond words. But, at the time, I must have looked like a deer caught in headlights because I felt so inundated with confused emotions. I was cognizant that this child was mine, but it also felt like I was pretending somehow.

I felt scared. It wasn't Josh that frightened me. It was the hugeness of the task at hand. Thankfully, there's not much time to dwell as a new father.

We decided that Karish and Josh should move in with us. So my bedroom became a studio apartment and nursery rolled into one. We couldn't afford a crib, so it was me, Karish and baby Josh sharing one queen-sized bed in a small-ass room.

Just think how nuts that was for Karish, transferring from a house where she lived only with her mom and then being crammed into a setup that involved me, Mom, Julio, Celeste and our newborn baby. Nothing went unnoticed. It was like our every move was watched, and Karish was soon looking to me, saying "What are you going to do? Are we going to live like this for the rest of our lives?"

On a daily basis, Karish was on me to get a real job. It became a collective echo in that house.

I wouldn't be much of a father in those early years. I was financially bare and emotionally immature. I was pretty lackadaisical about fatherly duties, too. I didn't want to change diapers. I felt weird holding him.

I'll never forget the time when I was home alone with Josh, trying to get him off to sleep, but he wouldn't stop crying. I was rocking him in my arms, mimicking Mom, but he kept crying louder and louder. I didn't realize that he was freaking out because I was freaked out and, before I knew it, he was wailing, turning red in the face. I lost it. "STOP! STOP!" I yelled.

And he screamed louder.

I was holding him in front of me with outstretched arms. I don't think I've ever felt so helpless and useless. I wept like a baby myself that night.

It wasn't that I was a *bad* father, I was just a *young* father completely out of my depth. Fatherly skills don't come easy when you're still a kid yourself, and I'm not sure they came easy to me for the next decade, truth be told. But within the new world in which I found myself, I knew one thing: I wanted to provide for Josh in a way my father never did for me.

FANTASYLAND

Right, Jaime," said Mom, "we're going to get you a job."

I left the house that morning knowing I had to do something because things were miserable. Me, Karish, and Josh were living off a shitty diet of pizza, chocolate-chip cookies and Sprite, eating food sitting on the bed and watching a small-screen television. Karish had insisted that we be self-sufficient, even if she often relied on Mom's occasional cooking and babysitting skills.

I wasn't the only one out of my depth.

I found myself at the First AME Church in South Central L.A. where there was a recruitment drive for summer seasonal work at Disneyland in Anaheim. Mom had heard about this "opportunity" because of her position working with the L.A. Unified School District, and I suspected that her "connections" meant this wasn't going to be a fruitless trip. I got in line with all kinds of kids looking to find a paying job and, sure enough, I got interviewed, scored high and had to choose from three Disney positions: custodial (clearing litter, cleaning tables, peeling gum off trash cans); beverages (serving drinks in the cafeterias with an endless smile); and parking attendant (welcoming and guiding in the millions). Each job paid $6.25 an hour and I would get paid every two weeks from the Bank of Disney. With Josh now eight months old, I was happy to be taking home whatever cash I could scrape. Even if Karish was the first to remind me that it was seasonal work and not a proper job.

But for me, Disney was a start, and I chose to be a custodian for one reason only: it placed me nearer the main action.

As mundane as I knew it was going to be—and as much as dragging my ass out of bed was going to be almost impossible—I knew that at the end of each day, there was the Disney parade. At least, that was the gloss I applied to a sense of obligation.

That summer of '94, I ditched the thrift-store clothes and jumped into my "costume"—an all-white janitor-style overall, with a circular name badge that announced "JAIME" beneath an all-ears logo of Mickey Mouse.

The dress code was worse than the military. No long hair, no piercings, no tattoos, and no facial hair. It didn't matter that I was a performer who wanted to let his balls hang. I had to be Disney squeaky-clean.

For once in my life, I had to conform.

As hideous as that straitjacket was, my attitude was simple enough: if I was going to work at the happiest place on earth, I was going to make the most of it. I got through the tedium of picking up trash and keeping the sidewalks clean by focusing on that nighttime parade, because my duties required me to walk in Cinderella's shadow.

In my mind, when that music started, I was one of the cast members; the happy janitor playing a supporting role to Mickey and Minnie Mouse.

I wore a vest that lit up and flashed like a Christmas tree, and walked in step behind Cinderella's glass slipper carriage . . . cleaning up great big steaming loads of horse shit that the humongous Clydesdale horses dropped en route down Main Street. That was part of my job description: to shovel hay-infested green shit left behind in Cinders' wake.

Walking in slow step—and praying that those horses wouldn't drop too many lumps of shit—I pushed around this yellow honey-bucket on wheels, with a medium-sized shovel clipped to my waist, and a small broom laid across the handlebars. Now those horses could shit, let me tell you, and when you're shoveling shit into a bucket with a smile on your face, it's a performance on its own: "Look at me kids! I'm picking up shit and *loving it*!"

Most of the time, I'd zone out reality and fall back on my imagination: picturing what it would be like to be one of those Disney characters, rocking out one of the carriages, impressing the crowds.

When in Fantasyland, escape to fantasyland.

I must have done something right, because I went from working two days a week to working four days a week to being called in on weekends.

Nanny was too ill by now to witness my minor contribution to Walt Disney, but we laughed one day when she reminded me, half joking, half serious, "Remember what Mickey says, Jim—'We're all allowed to dream!'—there are worse places to be!"

Nanny should have been hired by Disney when she was younger. She could have inspired dreams in more kids than Mickey Mouse himself.

• • •

As summer slipped into the shade of fall in 1994, I met a dude named Mr. Shah—one of the main men affiliated with Apl and Will. He was to them what Deja was to me: fellow school student and true confidant.

Mr. Shah was more of a cool writer than a great singer and he too had watched his two friends' ascent with Atban Klann, and decided that he wanted a similar slice of the action. But he wanted to try something different. He was all about the so-called "revolution of" *spoken hip-hop.*

Across America, this spoken-word poetry set to music was hyped as the cutting-edge sector of mainstream hip-hop, and open-mic battles broke out across the country. Basically, the tempo was slowed down and the emphasis was on the words, not the beats. I thought it was a bit corny but Mr. Shah was like Will—when he put his energy behind something, it tended to happen, for good or for ill.

"We should slow it down, and speak the hip-hop," he said one brain-storming day.

"Nah," I said, "I'm not into that spoken-word shit."

But Eclipse sniffed opportunity. "C'mon Tab, we should try this. What we got to lose?"

So me, Mr. Shah, and Eclipse formed a group named Pablo, and that decision consigned to history the faltering experiment of Rising Suns.

To assist us, DJ Motiv8 said he'd produce our tracks in his downtown studio, and so, from nowhere, a momentum built. Eclipse and Mr. Shah were all energized, and I went with the flow.

For the first time, there was real potential behind an outfit we were attached to, and the enthusiasm was contagious, even if I couldn't see how dancing could be incorporated. Hip-hop should be about rocking a place and going crazy, whereas this path seemed more pedestrian. The very concept seemed lackluster and didn't fire me up. None of it resonated, but it was typical of me at that time not to speak up and just fall in.

When Will and Apl moved on up to record their album at Paramount Studios with Ruthless Records, we rocked up at DJ Motiv8's studio as Pablo, and started creating music and lyrics. It was a hike, because without Deja it meant getting the bus from Rosemead to downtown, and the more we rehearsed the less money I had. That, in turn, meant there were days when I couldn't afford to show up—something that proved costly in terms of preparation.

The formation of Pablo was the first acid test of my professional capabilities; the baby steps out of the dream and into reality. I felt that pressure. We had allotted studio time, a willing producer and a serious intent that challenged all my pretensions. It was like someone had thrown a dinner jacket and tie on some casual proceeding and everything became strict, formal, and serious.

And spoken.

In the back of my mind, I knew Will and Apl were steaming ahead with Ruthless Records, so there was an expectation within Pablo to deliver. Mr. Shah and DJ Motiv8's great expectations turned the screw even tighter.

If there was one person I wanted to turn to at this time, it was Nanny, but she'd started getting really sick, in and out of the hospital. She suffered with diabetes and had had a heart attack, which really put her into a bad state. I remember when they brought her home and she was sat up in bed, looking like a pale shadow of her former self. Her cane was propped against the wall, and her characteristic zest had been drained out of her. No one had monitored my development more than she had, noting my improved skills each summer and Christmas.

"I'm proud of you, Jim," she said, "I always knew you had it in you."

If only she had known how incapable I really was.

When the day arrived for my first recording session, I knew immediately that I was out of my depth. I'd never been an MC, and had received no proper training. The studio environment felt alien, and it was clear to everyone that I was flailing. I had been thrown into the ocean without knowing how to swim, but I couldn't scream for help because that would have meant admitting failure.

Instead, I pretended I was having an off day because I didn't want to leave the party. The more dishonest I was about my talents, the more the faces of the boys registered disappointment (even if Eclipse always knew my weak spot).

DJ Motiv8's patience was wafer-thin: "Tab, get it together, man! You're not getting it and you're messing up the flow!"

Damn, I don't sound good . . . I'm not good enough, I thought.

"It's okay, man. I got it," I said out loud.

My big problem was that I was shy on the mic. Like, really shy—and it came across as intimidation in my voice. We were recording two tracks—"Open Your Soul Like A Window" and "The Green Opium Den"—for a demo tape, but when it was my turn to drop a verse, I was the only amateur in the room. I hated being the weak link, but I honestly felt that if I did it enough times, I could get it. But DJ Motiv8 didn't have time for rookies. He expected professionals in his studio to do a professional job.

During the second session and after about fifty failed takes, he lost it. "Tab, if you don't knock out your vocals, you need to get out of here."

Eclipse and Mr. Shah looked at me as if to say, "Hey, get it together. We've given you this chance and you're messing up. C'mon!"

We tried again. The music started. I counted down in my head. I gave it my best shot. "No . . . no . . . NO!" shouted DJ Motiv8. "You're fucking up, man!"

I was miles off what he wanted. When I tried to ramp it up, I ended up shouting. When I tried to do what they wanted, I was a tongue-tied mess. It was like the shy guy from school had returned to haunt me. I tried smoking weed and

even that didn't work. And when weed doesn't do the trick, you really are in deep shit.

I knew something was going down when I started receiving fewer phone calls to work in the studio. Then, eight weeks in, the phone rang at home. Both Eclipse and Mr. Shah were on the other end of the line, in a three-way direct from the studio.

"So whassup," I said, "when are we in next?"

Mr. Shah spoke first: "Hey, Tab. . . . we've been thinking. What do you think about being the hype man?!"

He said it with a glee that suggested I should be excited about being the warm-up guy for spoken poetry.

"I don't want to be the hype man. I want to be part of the group," I said, sharply. My heart raced like it does when you know something bad is about to go down. I could almost see Eclipse screwing up his eyes, not wanting to be there.

"Well," Mr. Shah said, "we feel you're not coming with it in the studio and the pressure's on, Tab. So we've no option but to roll without you."

"You're kicking me out of the group?"

"Man, I'm sorry . . . but we've got to roll without you . . . I'm sorry."

I was too cut up to say anything else. As much as I knew that spoken-word hip-hop wasn't my thing and that I'd struggled from day one, it didn't make it easier. It was like everyone was moving ahead but me, and someone I respected was telling me: "You're not good enough."

There is always that common question in life which asks how old were you when you first had your heart broken, and what was the girl's name? My answer is nineteen, and the girl's name was Pablo.

The Pablo experiment ultimately crashed, so it wouldn't have become anything, anyway. But that changes nothing of the crushing experience. Mr. Shah stayed working in the background with Will, and Eclipse wandered into another group called Dark Leaf. As for me, at the age of nineteen, it looked certain that I'd have to rest my dreams and place them in a box. Nothing was popping off. But I consoled myself that I still had my family.

It's like Nanny always said, family is the most important thing in life. The rest will take care of itself.

"I can't see you changing," Karish said one day, "It's not going anywhere. I'm done."

A few weeks into my time as a Disney employee, she was gone with Josh and returned to her mom's. Everything crumbled.

It was the first time that I understood that you could feel pain without anyone physically touching you.

In a short space of time, I'd gotten kicked out of Pablo for not being good enough, and lost my girlfriend.

I tried not to dwell on it but that's hard when you've nothing going on, so I smoked a ton of weed, and often dropped by DJ Motiv8's downtown studio to hang with Will and Apl as they worked on their album. It seemed the best I could do.

Will knew life wasn't too pretty for me. A blind man could have seen that I was glum, and he and Apl sensed that I was hanging around the studio to fill my time.

It was during one break that I wandered outside with Will into a parking lot one sunset evening, and we leaned with our backs against two cars, shooting the shit. One of them was his first car: a two-seated yellow Fiero. He was the first out of all of us to buy some wheels, which, in our eyes, was equal in achievement to landing a record deal, because it spelled freedom.

Will always was wise beyond his years. He was someone I'd learned to take advice from, professionally, and that remains the case to this day. I have huge respect for this man because of where he has come from, and where he has taken the Peas—to a stratosphere beyond any dream we could imagine. But on that afternoon in late 1994—a time when the idea of conquering Los Angeles seemed as likely as going to the moon—his sole mission seemed focused on lifting me.

I wasn't one to dampen anyone's spirits, but I had started talking, and the self-doubt started leaking out of the Pablo experience.

"I don't know what to do, man," I said. "I'm hurting here because I don't know if I'm good enough for this music thing."

When Will's eyes fix on you, they hook you and plug you into the great William Adams self-belief system; the one that says you can be anyone and anything.

"Tab," he said, "you know what you got that the other dudes ain't got?"

He let me think about it for a few seconds.

Then continued: "You got personality, dude . . . and presence. You can't pay for that, man. All you gotta do is let it out and let it shine."

There was a lot more blah-blah-blah and do-do-do, and we stood there speaking about the merits of being a "showman" and a "performer," and he made me see that presence and personality rocked a crowd. Not spoken-word hip-hop.

"I'm wack at rapping, Will, that's my problem," I said.

"It's not about being the greatest lyricist or rapper—it's about your *performance*," he said. "Don't let nobody tell you that you can't do something or you're not good at anything."

He was more fired up than I was, but that's Will for you—a man with the

empathy and compassion to want something for *you* as much as he wants it for himself.

He stopped talking and took a pencil from his pocket.

This stick of lead, he said, would train me to become a better rapper.

He placed it horizontally in his mouth, between his teeth and behind his tongue. He then started rolling his tongue against it, making the kind of sound effect that was a hybrid between lawn mower and machine gun.

He stopped, grabbed the pencil from his mouth and said: "And that's what you need to do, every single day."

Back then, rapping was tongue-trippingly fast with words and phrases merging into one long stream of rap, so it was all about loosening the tongue and the mouth. It was all about the speed, in line with artists such as the Fu-Schnickens and Poor Righteous Teachers.

It seemed a shit-ass crazy thing to do but I listened and obeyed, and the pencil-in-mouth regime became a daily discipline, applied with the same focus I'd needed to master the art of dance.

For days and weeks—each morning after getting up and each night before brushing my teeth—I stood in front of the bathroom mirror with this pencil under my tongue sounding like a kid killing the machine-gun sound effects.

I looked at my reflection and thought *Why am I doing this? What good is this doing?* But I stuck with it, repeating one phrase over and over: "Thinking about the things . . . when I was coming around" so that, with practice and speed, it accelerated in its delivery to a stage where I was streaming it as one merged sentence "Thinkingaboutthethingswhenlwascomingaround." It proved to be the vocal difference between firing single bullets and letting off a battery of ammunition through the gun.

And no shit, this technique worked. "Thinkingaboutthethingswhenlwascomingaround" turned into my own thoughts and rhymes, and I was soon standing in front of the mirror, stabbing at my own open-mic free-styling. I stopped writing verses and rhymes and started spitting from the top of my head.

With that small training device and a huge injection of his belief in me, Will rebuilt my hopes and erased my self-perceived inadequacies. He had trained my mind as well as loosened my tongue, and surgically removed the I'm-not-good-enough doubt that had crippled me after Pablo.

In early 1995, Atban Klann suffered a setback when Mooky was jailed for some assault incident. I don't know what he got caught up in, but it was something messy and domestic, and the upshot was him being sent to jail for six weeks.

I felt for Mook because he was a good guy and a Latino brother, but he was walking down the wrong path at that time, and it's fair to say that his girl

Jessie was a significant reason for his waywardness. She was not just a bad influence, she was trouble. We all wondered how jail would affect Mook, and, when he walked out six weeks later, we had the answer. He was a changed man.

Will and Apl had little time for Jessie, and Mook had not been out long when she kicked off a row with some of our DJ friends. Everything got ugly and heated and Mook started defending his girl which didn't go down too well. Then, in the heat of the moment, he quit.

We didn't hear from him for the next fourteen months. He, like Phoenix, had made his choice and bowed out, and his departure left a hole within Atban Klann, and maybe that was a bad omen.

The *Grass Roots* album had been shelved and gathering dust since 1993. Everything had been in place to distribute it through Relativity Records, but it never happened. For whatever reason, Eazy-E chose to use Atban Klann's commercial slot to release an album from another group called *Bone Thugs-N-Harmony*. I don't know the politics or the reasons, but I know Will and Apl were pissed. Not that all was lost, because their songs still had life in them, even if the album had flatlined.

As winter turned to spring in 1995, Will was buzzed because Eazy-E had phoned him, saying that MTV was excited about the song "Puddles of H_2O" and wanted to air it. This was due to be their breakthrough moment, launching them across America. You can imagine how excited Will and Apl felt after all they had been building for three years.

Then, one week later, Eazy-E was admitted to the hospital with suspected pneumonia. When doctors ran tests, they actually discovered it was AIDS. Within another ten days, on March 26, he was dead, at thirty-one, passing away at the Cedars-Sinai Medical Center. The speed of his passing stunned everybody.

With that tragedy, the MTV chance melted away. And without Eazy-E, Atbann Klann was going nowhere. Within the space of a week, Will and Apl went from potential heroes to a group without an album, without a label, and without Mooky. Suddenly, they were back to square one.

After all the sweat, toil and time that had gone into its creation, that was a sucker punch for both of them, but Will is not the kind of person to hold a pity party. He wanted to bounce back and maintain the momentum, and he told Apl that it was time to start a whole new thing.

A couple of days later, the phone rang at home. It was Will, inviting me to the mall.

We hung out and that's when he told me: him and Apl were performing under a new name—the Black Eyed Peas. That had been the name of Will and DJ Motiv8's production company in the first place, so out went Atban Klann and in came the Black Eyed Peas.

Everyone asks how they landed on this name. As the story goes, they'd been throwing all sorts of random names around that involved colors—like Blue

Unit and Turquoise Vines. As they continued exploring options, inspiration landed on "Black Eyed Peas," a subspecies of the cowpea bean which is popular in America's Deep South and the West Indies. The bean derives its name from its all-white appearance with a black dot in the middle, and it has long been regarded in the South as "food for the soul." It's a New Year's thing: eat it in January of a new year and it will bring prosperity. So it makes sense that a group intending to make money and music for the soul should be called the Black Eyed Peas.

Will then told me they had a first performance booked at the Glam Slam, a Hollywood club owned by Prince, who, in 1988, released a single of the same name. Apparently, Will and Apl had been discussing bringing me in a few days prior.

"So, you wanna come perform with us?" is how Will made the invitation.

Like I say, life is a chessboard and someone is always moving things around and removing pieces from play. One man's prison sentence and one man's death had changed the entire board, and would change the trajectory of my life.

I didn't hesitate one second when Will invited me aboard. Wherever he was going, I wanted to be on the same front line.

"I'm in—let's do this!" I said.

PIZZA & PEPSI

Within a matter of days, I was standing in a dark, back corridor, counting down to the debut gig of the Black Eyed Peas on a stage cloaked with a fog of weed smoke inside Prince's Glam Slam. The fact that I could breathe in such a sweet aroma *and* perform on the turf of the artist who always found his way onto my mix tapes was a bonus.

We were one of a few groups who performed as part of a Ruthless Records showcase. Will and Apl had maintained ties with the label even though they had been let go, and these showcase gigs—regular events on the music scene—allowed us to build our name. We rocked up dressed and ready, arriving together in Will's upgraded car—a red VW Golf—and we'd practiced as we drove into downtown. I can't remember the songs because we didn't keep them, but I remember the anticipation of stepping out in front of a crowd we knew would be 150-strong.

I wasn't "scurred." Will told me to "just do your thing" and I treated it like a battle. For him and Apl, it was just another performance under a different name, because, throughout their time with Ruthless, they had kept performing on the club scene, so it was a case of maintaining that momentum and me moving into the slipstream as part of the transition from Atban Klann to Black Eyed Peas.

Privately, I knew it represented a massive leap forward for me and there was no room for fucking up this time. I'm sure the Glam Slam performance was to test how much we gelled as a trio, because, as much as we were friends, we had never performed together. In many ways, that night was all about reinvention.

The moment I stepped into that Prince-owned territory, I was ready for the big time. Will and Apl's attitude was so relaxed that it made me feel there was nothing to prove.

Not that "patience" was the first word that sprang to mind when we checked out the audience: a mean-mugging bunch of thug-like cats with Jheri-curls, raider hats, and expressionless faces. It was more your gangsta-rap crowd, whereas we were more lyrical-miracle-braggadocious, rapping about skills and positivity.

Think about what people's first impression must have been: two black cats with thick, long Bob Marley dreds, wearing beatnik-style, old-man vintage clothing, accompanied by one theatrical, scary-looking Latino dressed all ninja-style.

There was none of the rap head's staples: no Tommy Hilfiger, Versace, or FUBU. Will always said that the clothes you wear don't make you hip-hop. That was a statement he would ultimately build into our first album, *Behind The Front*, making the point in the song "Fallin' Up": *"I see you try to diss our function by stating we can't rap/Is it because we don't wear Tommy Hilfiger and baseball caps . . ."*

We wanted to smash stereotypes—the dancing, the boundaries, and the clichés. We told ourselves that we were bringing the James Brown attitude to hip-hop—singing, dancing and doing it all.

We were about crazy dancing and fluid movement at a time when hip-hop was full of dudes "fronting"—acting hard while holding the mics and grabbing their crotch, bouncing but not dancing. It was like people were afraid to dance, but we wanted to be about high-octane energy and partying, incorporating anything from b-boying to free-styling and then, from me, kung-fu inspired moves. "It's time to ditch the hip-hop ego and run with the soul," Will had said.

As we launched on stage at Glam Slam, the looks on these gangsta's faces said the same thing: "Who are these little mothafuckas?"

We always thrived on a challenge.

We relied on a DAT tape for the beats as Will and Apl threw down the lyrics and I followed their lead, ad-libbing on the back of them. Club settings like Glam Slam were always intimate, highly charged affairs. Anything was liable to happen—as the first gig proved.

The moment Will started rapping, someone hurled an ice cube and it hit him dead in the eye. You could see the smirks break out on the audience's faces, but it didn't make Will pause. It energized him and he ran with it, free-styling with his anger about that very incident: *"Yo, fuck this shit . . . this MC just got hit . . . in the eye . . . but y'all can't stop my shine . . ."*

Or something like that.

Anyone who saw last year's E.N.D. tour witnessed Will fly with that same spontaneity when he free-styled using the BlackBerry Messenger messages that audience members pinged in; thinking in the split-second and turning it into a rap. That's what he's been doing since day one—he could change it up from any situation. If the lights went out, he'd rap about it. If a fight broke out in the crowd, he'd make a song about it. If the mic went out, we'd break into free-style dance. Fall down, we'd make a joke about it. Whatever we faced, we took in stride.

At Glam Slam, Will must have held his eye for half that show, but the crowd gave it up after seeing us free-style. We turned that audience around. Men standing around with all the rhythm of mean-looking statues were suddenly bobbing their heads and giving us props. It was like we had wandered into a lion's den of thugs and tamed them with nothing but performance, and that was some empowering shit.

I felt like a wall of energy that night, standing alongside Will and Apl.

This is it—this is family, I thought.

It wasn't the immature pretensions of United Soul Children or the fad that was Rising Suns. It wasn't the ill-fitting shoe of Pablo. It wasn't being forced down a road I didn't want to go down, like the Air Force or Rosemead Adult College. Everything we had known as friends was harnessed as one tight unit where there was instant chemistry. Everything gelled, effortlessly, and I knew our journey had begun.

If you ask me, 1995 was the year that represented the sign of things to come. Microsoft launched Windows 95, the DVD format was announced, and eBay was founded. Musically, the general public was embracing hits such as Michael Jackson's "You Are Not Alone," Alanis Morissette's "Hand In My Pocket" and Oasis's "Wonderwall." And Sade brought out a song called "The Sweetest Taboo."

When we three Peas came together, we instantly had our eyes on the main prize: visualizing taking hip-hop to a new level and touring the world. Our individual dreams were magnified as one, and we collectively imagined our future. We drove around in Will's VW Golf, going to a club or a rehearsal, and envisioned that one day the car would be a tour bus.

"Can you imagine touring around America?" we'd say.

"Forget that shit, can you imagine touring Europe?"

"Forget that shit, can you imagine touring the world?"

We always had the world in mind, not just America. So we visualized it. If there's a truth to the universe listening and then manifesting visions, it must have tapped into our brainstorming conversations inside Will's car.

Our musical direction was shaped by a bunch of influences: from A Tribe

Called Quest to De La Soul, from bossa nova to calypso, from Barry White to Stevie Wonder. We slammed it all into the same mixing bowl and came up with our own sound: hip-hop at its core but laced with Latin, jazz, and soul. We didn't want to be just another hip-hop trio. We wanted to change it up but keep it fresh, innovating and progressive.

We also knew we wanted to build in a four-piece band, because live instrumentation was just as important as rhyming. "Damn, if all we're going to do is go off the DAT, we might as well put the lyrics on that bitch, too!" said Will.

We agreed what we were driving at: we wanted to be a live hip-hop act, not just a rap group. We wanted to be about showmanship and visual imagery—create feel-good music, and a band was an essential ingredient of that aim. Without a band, we would have been a car without wheels.

Will—always the businessman and ambassador of the group—went out there and put together the band: Terry Graves as drummer, Mike Fratantuno on bass, and Carlos Galvan on keyboard. Several guitar players would come and go but first up was a man we called JC.

Will's philosophy was clear from the beginning: by introducing the element of a live band, we would be one step ahead of what the majority of the industry was doing or thinking.

Critics later compared us to the Roots, and Arrested Development, but as one reviewer once put it, the Peas "always had a sunnier disposition." That's because our lyrics focused on the positive. Our message was not only about vague peace and love. We had a theme we believed in: one nation, one race called humanity, and one diversity known as unity. We weren't about the West Coast versus East Coast hip-hop feud that was happening at the time.

Call us hip-hop. Or hip-pop.

Just so long as we were rocking our shit.

We rehearsed with the band about three times a month, experimenting with songs and coming up with set lists, mixing in some cool little free-styles. We usually practiced in the double garage at Apl's new place in Pasadena. Before moving there, he jumped from place to place. He must have lived in six different places between 1993 and 1996.

Apl and I used nothing more than a tape recorder to make the songs we dreamed up. Free-style "mumbles" turned into lyrics that turned into songs that turned into cassette tapes with song titles scrawled out in pen.

There was nothing intense about our rehearsal process. All I can remember is lots of fun, laughter, and weed. It must have been hard at first for the band to fit in, because we, as a trio, had a history and had already gelled, both professionally and personally. But that's the reality of collaborations—you throw shit together and hope for synergy. The two main pillars of the band were drummer Terry—a half-American, half-Japanese black guy with a great crop of curly hair—

and bass player Mike—a six-foot-tall, fresh-ass white boy from Milwaukee who wore glasses.

Terry worked at Virgin record label as an A&R man, but he wasn't at the top of the food chain so he couldn't do much for us as a band, connection-wise, but he brought a sense of organization to the group, always on top of rehearsal times and chasing the set lists. He had these big bulging eyes, like a bullfrog, that always told you when he was concentrating, and he was a super-nice guy and a capable pair of hands.

Milwaukee Mike looked nothing like your cool musician dude, at least not on first impression, but when he got on the bass, he killed it. He was a zany, wild Jim Carrey type who was always goofing around by making funny faces or silly-ass moves, and he was the perfect counter-balance to Terry's more serious vibe.

Despite other comings and goings within the band, these two would stick around until the year 2000, contributing their strong work ethic and their own musical stamp. None of us were the overzealous artists hell-bent on making music that *really mattered*. We were more go-with-the-flow types hooked on creating the party. At that time, of the three of us, Will and Apl were the most focused, and I was the functioning reefer head. But I could rehearse on the cloud nine of weed smoke and still get the job done.

After a few rehearsals in Apl's garage, we booked our first gig as an ensemble at an outdoor event at L.A.'s Peace & Justice Center, a venue known for celebrating up-and-coming groups in the city.

But no sooner were we into our set than we instantly knew that whatever had sounded fresh inside the garage didn't translate onstage. It was messy and disjointed and everyone knew it. We were like amateurs on "Showtime at the Apollo."

The first change we made was to get rid of the guitarist, JC. He'd brought along some woman, saying she was a cool singer so we tried her out on one song and she was horrible. The fact that we even allowed her to walk on stage is indication enough of how everything was too loose.

There was a lot of fine-tuning required, and we needed to work on our on-stage interaction, and agree who was going to talk first because, as MCs, our early eagerness had led to moments when we talked all at once, and it was a mess.

That said, it was the first time we had performed with our live band. We knew we liked the sound and knew we wanted to stick with the format, but practice would make perfect.

We also wanted to achieve "firsts," like Michael Jackson.

That man was a trailblazer: the *first* dude to have a video on MTV that impacted pop culture; the *first* dude who killed it with his dancing; the *first* one to connect his music with commercial brands; the *first* one to bring movie-production values to a video and tell a story, as with "Thriller."

Like Prince, his music always found its way onto my mix tapes, and—from hip-hop to pop—there are countless artists who today stand as by-products of Michael Jackson in terms of the bar he set in what he achieved, what he sold and the size of the entertainment monster he created. In respect to breaking molds and staying ahead of the game musically, he was a unique inspiration.

Like him, we as a group wanted our music to be multicultural and mirror our own life experiences: Will as the black dude, accepted within a Latino community; me, the Mexican accepted in a black community; Apl, the Filipino embraced by America. Crossing divides. Building bridges. Finding acceptance amid other races. That is what the Black Eyed Peas were about, as was mirrored in the lyrics to one of our first songs, "Joints & Jams":

"We're about mass appeal, no segregation/Got black to Asian and Caucasian . . ."

The concept was all built on one joint sucking in one people.

As one early reviewer would say about our music, "It didn't ask anyone to choose between class, race or national identities, it just embraced the concept of 'both or and,' encouraging flexible attitudes between all people."

I'm not sure even Will could have put it better.

My learning curve was steep in those first two years.

I hadn't started rapping until 1993, whereas Will and Apl had been running and rapping together since 1989, and Will had been an MC since '84. They were the experts, and I was still learning to crawl, at a time when we were creating songs for demo tapes.

I was still trying to find my voice and learn from two friends who were skilled architects—and partners—when it came to structuring song, format, beats and rhythm. Will and Apl seemed to be able to read each other's minds at times, and I was looking to find my place within that creative synergy. They had been writing together since age fourteen. I was eager to get in on that process.

Rule number one, as far as Will was concerned, was "Write from personal experience."

Rule number two was "Rhythm comes first, words later."

I absorbed it all from the edges as Will created the beat from some far-flung inspiration in his mind. He'd then play the beat, find the rhythm within that beat, and then find the lyrics. We'd sit around for hours on end, free-styling until we hit on something special, bouncing ideas around, creating just the right melody and cadence. For me, it was a master class under Will's musical and lyrical tutorship. Time after time, he showed me how we could make something out of nothing; how rhythm-became-mumbles-became-words became-lyrics-became-song.

Me and Apl would scribble thoughts on pads, envelopes, or backs of receipts, but Will never needed to write anything down. He always had it in his head, and this unconscious download of thoughts, lyrics, and ideas would just stream out of him.

The pen is too slow to capture his thoughts.

I'd only ever toyed with poetry and the odd lyric as a kid, trying to get deep with all that talk of my moons and horizons and suns that weren't rising. I fell into a trap that was common in the underground scene—full of artists trying to be over-elaborate and too deep, using words they had no idea about but sounded cool, spitting out grand words like "OSMOSIS! CHROMOSOMES! PROTONS! ELECTRONS FIRE THE NEURONS!" and all that kind of bullshit mumbo jumbo in the hope of sounding profound or clever. There was a train of thought among many in hip-hop that the more intricate it was, the better it sounded, even if it *meant* nothing.

Will's philosophy was hooked on simplicity—strip away all the big words, and work from personal experiences to create simple, catchy messages. Build on *themes* of style, skill, good times and braggadociousness.

Say what we mean to say.

Motivation wasn't always easy, especially when you're playing to crowds as small as fifty people. One time, at a club called Florentine Gardens in Hollywood, only twenty-five tickets were sold. But nothing topped the experience at some Black Expo event at L.A.'s Convention Center.

We knew it was going to be a vast expo, and that we'd have a humongous-ass stage to work with. But it was one of those times when grand expectations didn't meet with reality.

The setup was like a businessman's music festival with different stages, booths and events all taking place under one roof. The expo itself was packed, but the interest in our specific stage was empty. We walked out to see everyone chilling in the distance, and about seven stragglers watching us: three security guards and two moms with children. We looked lost on the massive stage, and the "audience" looked lost in the uninterested emptiness that surrounded them.

Will, Apl, and me looked at each other and thought: *Damn, this is embarrassing!* But we convinced ourselves that within that pocket of people remained the potential for word-of-mouth.

We got out there and performed our asses off, ignoring the bored and bemused faces that the kids threw back at us. That's what it was about back then: grinding out performances and maximizing any and all opportunities, big or small.

Those early months were all hit-and-miss because a few weeks later we performed at a bar called St. George's in Venice Beach. It was not far from the beach boardwalk, and was normally a venue that attracted poetry readings or live

acoustic performances by female singer-songwriters. But this one night, we got booked through one of Will's connections.

It was one of those small, intimate venues, but the upside was that it was a largely female crowd, and the actress and model Gabrielle Union—who we then knew as a twenty-three-year-old called Nikki—brought a whole contingent of female followers who were immediately converted that night into "Pea-bodies."

We were an underground hip-hop group from L.A. performing in the bohemian, surfer-dude spot of Venice Beach and we won over the female crowd, enticed by the elements of a live band and live free-style dance. As one woman told us that night: "You guys are giving hip-hop sex appeal!"

That's the time and place where we say the Black Eyed Peas attracted its first female fans. And as any man knows—once you get the woman's vote, the only way is up.

In those embryonic months, we had to be grateful for every opportunity, and, sometimes, that gratitude had to extend to accepting an appearance "fee" that was nothing more than food and drink. We still joke today that we literally performed for pizza and Pepsi.

When you're at the starting line and people don't know—or care—who the fuck you are, it's up to you to prove your worth, not up to them to pay you.

Yon Styles, an African-American from New York City, was our manager at the time. His management company was called Black Coffee Management, and his team was comprised of Eddie Bowles and another dude named Johnny Johnson, who was some financial whiz.

Will had met Yon outside a club called the Roxbury after beating one of his MCs in a battle. When Will told him that he was forming the Black Eyed Peas, Yon immediately offered to manage us, so he sealed the deal. He had enthusiasm and believed in us 100%, but he was always going to be the kind of manager who gave us a leg up, as opposed to the manager who would take us into a dream orbit.

After each performance, Yon and Polo Molina—who served more as our unofficial promoter back then—worked through the audience, asking if they were interested in seeing us again. Nineteen ninety-five and early 1996 were all about harnessing grassroots support from around Los Angeles. Our mantra was: "Pizza and Pepsi this time, but maybe $250/$500 next time."

If we could prove to a venue that we had a fan base with demand—and a strong mailing list—we could start charging on the door, and that is what ultimately happened. It was all about mailing lists, hitting the phones, and sticking up flyers.

As underdogs, we saw the size of the mountain in front of us, and only thought about the view from the summit, not the struggle of the climb. Along the way, we connected as friends before each gig, and at the end of each gig—always reminding ourselves not to take life too seriously. That's one thing I can say about life in the Black Eyed Peas: our friendship has always been a constant, bigger than anything we could achieve on stage.

We believed in each other. We willed each other on. And I drew inspiration from the two brothers climbing the mountain with me.

HELLOS, GOOD-BYES

I don't deal with good-byes too well.

Like the time when my half-brother Eddie wandered off into the sunset. Or when Mom upped and left with a suitcase to Mexico. Or when Karish walked out. Every good-bye I had known was hurried, and left me flattened in the aftermath.

The problem with saying good-bye to Nanny in 1996 was that I knew it was coming. I had time to prepare for the one thing everyone says you are always unprepared for: death. It was like seeing this humongous collision coming and yet knowing there was nothing I could do to step out of the way. Just stand there and work out afterward how I'd pick up the pieces.

She was seventy-four years old. The onset of diabetes had already weakened her system. When she suffered yet another heart attack, she had to be hospitalized, and she remained there—immobile and virtually unable to speak.

I visited her steadily over the next couple of weeks, but it was hard seeing this once vibrant lady reduced to a fragile shell whose skin resembled oversized clothes. On a couple of occasions, I had to walk out because I couldn't bear to see her so changed. I remember begging—not praying—for her to live: "Don't let her leave yet . . . don't let her leave yet."

I wasn't close to realizing the dreams that I wanted her to witness. It was because of her—and only her—that I was chasing them in the first place. But Mom and Julio had given me the heads-up: it was only a matter of time before she died. I remember the panic I felt as the tortured countdown started in my head. I thought of all the times when she encouraged me to escape my unhappy reality and fall back on my imagination. I wanted to sit again in that old Chevy truck in her backyard, with Lady between us, and drive and drive and drive . . . putting a million miles between Nanny and death.

When the inevitable time came, I took the bus to join the family at the White Memorial Hospital, on the streets sandwiched between the 5 freeway and the 101, and not far from El Mercado.

At her bedside, I was seated on a chair that was so low that it made me look up at her. She was so out of it that I needed to announce who I was. "This is Jim, Nanny." I took hold of her hand and talked. She wasn't really responsive, but I told myself she could hear me as I went on and on about all our times together and how much she meant to me in the memories that fill the start of this book.

She lay there seemingly lifeless, her hair wispy white and an I.V. in her arm. The only sound that came out of her mouth were these rasping breaths, which, whenever she tried to express something, came out as a groan.

I leaned toward her ear and whispered: "I want to dance with you again, Nanny." She breathed in—a groan.

That one sound killed me because it was her spirit trying to get up but her body failed her. This woman whose vibrant energy couldn't be stopped had to finally surrender.

We must have stayed with Nanny, as a family, for more than two hours that day, and she was still hanging on by the time I left. I told her I would see her tomorrow but I knew it was good-bye. I also knew I couldn't bear being around when she took that final breath. I placed her hand next to her side, and kissed her on the forehead.

I turned and hurried out of there as fast as I could.

Nanny died the next day while I was out trying to keep busy, running errands.

I arrived home and Mom was sitting down, crying. "She's gone, Jaime . . . she's gone" is all she kept saying.

In the following days, nothing made sense, as if gravity itself increased and my whole world imploded. Continuing without Nanny seemed impossible.

But then something saved me. I say "something" but I know exactly what it was—the God and the faith that Nanny had given me, together with her great spirit in the sky that was now watching over me.

Ever since that day, I have known—more than I have ever known anything—that she is always looking down on me in every situation and every decision I have made, good or bad, wise or foolish. I have always viewed her fire and spirit as the angel pulling me through whatever I face.

. . .

The memory of her funeral in East L.A. remains a blur.

I remember attending her service in a chapel and seeing her open casket on a stand with two large candles burning on either side. An organ played somber funerary music. I read a poem. I hadn't chosen it and don't even recall what it was. What mattered was what I said from the heart when my turn came to approach the coffin. Those words I remember vividly.

I whispered them like it was one of our shared secrets again.

I placed my hand on the backs of her hands, folded across her chest, leaned down and told her: "I cannot believe you have left me, Nanny. We had so many great times. I have lost a part of myself with you gone. You take it with you, and, in your spirit and through your guidance, I will become somebody in life. I won't let you down."

After that, the remainder of that day is a sketchy montage.

I remember one terrible detail: the lowering of her oak coffin into the ground.

I remember one obscure detail: that I wore my hair in a ponytail.

I remember one haunting detail: crying "Why? Why? Why?" and being held by someone.

I remember that Mom could hardly lift her head, and Uncle Louie stared into space.

And I remember the music.

In honor of both a Mexican tradition and Nanny's days at El Mercado, three mariachis stood behind the mourners, in a corner in the background, near a tree. As the coffin touched the earth at the bottom of the grave, they started to play.

As good-byes go, I guess it was fitting.

I moved in with Apl soon afterward. We had become best friends who rolled everywhere together, so it made sense to move out of Mom's and in with him. It was time to assert my own freedom and be my own man.

There has always been an easy synergy between Apl and me. We operate on the same frequency. Anyhow, life at home had become cramped and I was tired of feeling diminished by Julio's negative energy.

"You're not musicians . . . all you do is sit around and get high," he said, and that was pretty much the final nudge to find a place of my own.

Julio was the reason I place stock in the saying "Those who abandon their dreams will discourage the dreams of others," because he had been part of a band once, too, when he was younger. It was a Mexican band, and he played per-cussion, but his big plans never worked out. That probably explains why he was so insistent that there is no future in music. It was, maybe, self-protective on his part.

I just kept listening to Nanny.

Me and Apl didn't have too much money coming in so we couldn't afford a palace, but he had mentioned a studio in a small apartment block called Edgemont Manor in Hollywood. It was a second-floor, corner unit going for $600 a month—$300 each. That was expensive for us, but as cheap as we could find, and we figured that if we lived basic, we could scrape by without pleading poverty.

The day we went to view the place, I didn't know what I'd gotten myself into.

Walking up to its white-painted facade, the first thing that struck me was the graffiti on the outside walls. Real wack graffiti, not SKA art.

We walked up the stairs and tiptoed around a couple of spaced-out crackheads and empty liquor bottles. Once inside the grubby, unfurnished studio with no view, we discovered how paper-thin the walls were when we heard a couple beneath us engaged in a raging domestic. Some other dude was cranking out his heavy metal tunes not far away.

"Cool—we'll take it," said Apl.

I figured he had probably lived in worse places.

Once we had moved in and shut our door on the mess outside, we didn't care too much, because, we told ourselves, we were brothers living the dream in Hollywood, smoking as much weed as we liked, doing our own thing and writing songs. Base camp for our musical adventure.

We hustled so that we could get by.

We couldn't afford proper beds, so we slung two old mattresses on the floor, used the wall as a headboard, and used sheets as covers. We couldn't afford chairs, either, so the mattresses doubled as daybeds where we lounged around, thinking up raps and lyrics. There was a little kitchenette with a fridge and stove. Apl was the chef, and I was his assistant. We survived on a diet of weed, rice, beans and beef.

The main problem in that place was that we had cockroaches as fellow residents. We often opened the fridge and dozens of roaches scurried out, and that is why we were not too keen on keeping fresh stuff in there. It is also why we nicknamed the complex "Roach Motel." It was a desperate way of living, but we had no alternative, and the same can be said as justification for a new habit that we developed—stealing.

What you have got to understand before I go into detail is that we stole not to have stuff but to eat and survive.

By 1996, we had started getting paid for gigs but we are only talking $500–$800 a gig, and that had to be split between management, the band, and the three of us. When you are paying $300 each a month in rent, plus bills, that was not an income that stretched far. When a new season kicked in at Disney, I scraped the minimum wage but I still largely depended on help from Mom and Julio.

So when it came to getting food in, desperate times called for desperate

measures. There was a mini-mart around the corner and we devised a scheme where we walked in with a dollar, grabbed a two-liter bottle of soda costing ninety-nine cents, and took it to the counter. This was our "cover" for the meat and rice that we had already tucked down our pants. My job was always to pack in the meat, and Apl packed in the rice.

Beef, rice and soda was a step up from pizza and Pepsi.

At the counter, we paid our money with an honest smile and walked away with enough food and drink to last a few days. We became masters in the weekly execution of this sleight of hand. We were not exactly proud of ourselves, but if it meant avoiding starvation we could live with our guilt.

The problem with such a ruse is that once you become effective, complacency sets in, and if there is one thing that is guaranteed about life, it is this: whatever you're up to, whatever you think you're getting away with, and whatever your vices may be, life never, ever lets you get away with it in the long run.

In between the writing, rehearsing, and performing, Will networked his ass off around Hollywood, taking a ton of meetings in search of not just a record label but one that would "get it" and share our vision. As the captain of our ship, he was always out there hooking up meetings, and, when we were together, he strategized about things we should be doing or trying.

One day, we were discussing ways of amping up the entertainment, and he felt we were missing a crucial element. We were happy with our performance, dance segments, and the live band, but what else was needed? And that was when he announced the next dimension to our sound—female vocals.

Enter, from stage left, soul singer Kim Hill.

She had been at a BMI showcase where we performed in 1995 when she was introduced to Will. Around the same time, she'd started dating our tour/gig manager Eddie and she also knew our manager Yon, so she was virtually part of the extended family.

I had first seen Kim perform solo at Mogul, a club in Hollywood, and was impressed. She was sitting on a stool, with her tumbledown curly black hair, playing her guitar and singing true soul. Her voice wasn't extraordinary, but she had a soulful sound that was both edgy and ethereal. Unique.

Kim was an African-American who had lived in L.A. since 1993, having moved from Philadelphia, where she had studied violin and piano. She was about ten years older than the rest of us, so she had something of a big-sister vibe going on. She referred to us as her "shnoo-nahs." I have no idea what this apparent term of endearment meant, but she said things like "Hey baby shnoo-nah, how ya doing?"

Or, to me: "Tab! My little shnoo-nah . . ."

I have always remembered her for that, as well as for her ridiculously smooth complexion, piercing eyes, and endless collection of shoes. That girl loved her shoes and she had a fresh range and style!

I saw Will's logic in introducing her to our act because De La Soul, A Tribe Called Quest, and the Fugees had all incorporated female vocals; something to appeal to the female tastemakers. Kim was no Lauryn Hill but she was the next best thing and brought a new texture to our music. Prior to her introduction, we were the yellers: "YELL THAT—HAH! YELL THAT—HAH!"

With Kim on board, we could counterbalance the hardness of rap with her softness. It is the same today with Fergie. That is the beauty of how we have always written. One minute you hear the daba-daba-daba-daba-daba-daba-DAH! and then you heard Kim—or, today, hear Fergie—stroke it with a melody or a ballad. That was the ultimate mix we were looking for at the beginning, as we continued to experiment.

Kim was never fully installed as a member of the Peas, even though there has been much coverage in the past that she was the fourth member. It is more accurate to say that she *featured* with us, because she was still a singer-songwriter in her own right and still performed solo. She was also one of the first female acts that Will signed to his fledgling record company, I Am Music. The trade-off was simple enough: she helped us, Will helped her. She was not a constant feature at every gig we played, but she was regarded as part of the family from 1996 to 2000.

It was a natural fit for all four of us because we were at the same stage of hawking demo tapes around town. We had been prolific in writing material. We wrote and free-styled nearly every day, coming up with about fifty songs, or parts of songs, in our first eighteen months.

If there was one observation we all made about Kim, it was that she could talk . . . and talk. During gigs, there was a part where she sang and was then meant to say a few words. Just as with Fergie at today's concerts, Kim's interludes of audience interaction were intended to be *brief*.

Short, sharp, quick interludes.

The thing with Kim—and we made fun of her for this—is that she liked to spend time "connecting" with the audience, and her quick bursts of chat could often run into overly long monologues, like one of those inane, small-talk conversations between friends.

"You know," she would start, "today has not been a good day and let me tell you why . . ."

Or "Do you have that feeling when . . ."

Then she was off and running and we never knew how long she would be talking. Waiting in the wings, we would be foot-tapping and thinking "Just sing already!" We always dropped heavy hints afterward: "Yo Kim . . . uh . . . are you going to talk that much on the next show?"

"Well, you know," she said, "I've got to have my moment with the audience."

We "little shnoo-nahs" did not make a big a deal of it because when she did sing—on stage or in the studio—she always nailed it, and we thought she would soon get bored of her "connecting with the audience" moments.

As an MC, it was my time to slay ghosts and nail it in the studio.

We moved away from the tape recorder and Apl's garage and into our boy Ben Mor's studio to start laying down some songs. By this time, we were working on two or three songs a week. Ben—who would ultimately direct our 2009 anthem "I Gotta Feeling"—lived in the valleys somewhere out Tarzana way, and his "studio" was basically a bedroom stacked with all the professional equipment, but it did the job for the demo tapes we wanted to shop.

Outside of my Disney day job, we worked at his place in the afternoons and then me and Apl retired to Roach Motel in the evenings. The apartment merely became a place for us to rest our heads.

The moment I walked into Ben's studio, my insecurities went into a mental Pablo flashback: *I'm out of my depth . . . I'm hesitant in my delivery . . . am I good enough?* But the difference this time around was that Ben, Will, and Apl guided me and didn't saddle me with their impatience. The whole experience was the difference between gently coaxing a horse and whipping the shit out of it, and that allowed me to get out of my head and into the moment.

I don't remember the song I was doing—another one that never made it on an album—but I remember kicking my verse and then allowing myself to be educated by the masters around me.

"Hey, Tab, why don't you try it like this . . ." suggested Apl.

Then Will: "Just kick it the same way every time you kick it."

Apl is an incredible writer and Will knew song formulas. With those stabilizing forces around me, I couldn't go wrong. So I psyched myself up and tried kicking it a different way.

I launched in: "Let's demonstrate the real coordination . . ."

"Hold on Tab . . . slow it down, slowwwww it down," said Will.

I tried it again. Bang off tune.

"Nah, nah . . . you had it right the first time . . . just slow it down."

Okay. *Breathe. Sing.*

"Let's demon-strate . . . the real co-ordination/The way we impro-vise . . . gives you a timeless sensation . . ."

"Dope, Tab! Now with more ENERGY!"

I kicked it and nailed it.

"Okay, stop!" said Will, pulling on the reins. "Now let's do the next half of the verse . . ."

That's how I learned, by breaking down each verse piece by piece, as opposed to having to nail the whole thing in two or three takes. It was accepted that I needed to crawl before I could walk, and walk before I could run. The end result was that I approached each recording session with renewed confidence, not trepidation.

The first songs I laid vocals down for were "Change It Up," "Wise It Up," and then "ID4"; three songs that made it no further than being a demo tape, and yet, for me, these three songs represented a milestone in my journey with the Black Eyed Peas.

Once I was flying, there was no stopping me. I also wrote my first song called "Same Old Thing." It was a solo about not settling for the same old things in life, and it was the first time I had written a hook under my own steam. It was written by me, and produced by Will, and, even though nothing came of it, it told me that when the day came for us to step inside a real studio, I was ready for the big time.

We learned fast that the smog above Los Angeles was caused by the fumes from the amount of bullshit that gets spoken in Hollywood.

Booking gigs wasn't a problem and our mailing list was growing, but we wanted to be making albums and getting on the road. Yet every avenue we explored hit a roadblock built by a lack of interest, a lack of vision or a lack of imagination on the part of record labels.

Their diffidence stemmed from our being both underground and "different" from the usual hard-core hip-hop brigade. As misfits, we were searching for that one brave executive with a pair of nuts to go with a forward-thinking musical vision, but all we met were industry sheep.

Meeting after meeting came to nothing, and soon enough, Will's excited announcements of "Yo, we've got a meeting!" soon withered into "Whatever with meetings."

Hollywood was alien to me. Just because I was born in nearby East L.A. and raised in Rosemead didn't make me any better prepared for the dream factory of Tinseltown. But it didn't take long to understand that Hollywood is a place paralyzed in a no-man's-land between someone saying "yes" and someone saying "no" to the great dreams you have nurtured. A&R guys took meetings to check us out and cover their backs in their own empire-building strategy, but few were prepared to stick their neck out. Certainly, that was the case in the pre-digital age when CD sales still mattered.

Will had initially shopped demo tapes of "To The Beat Y'all" and "That's Right"—two very braggadocious songs that we felt best represented our sound. But perhaps they didn't have that crossover potential. We learned that much when Will returned all downcast from a meeting at one label where one executive

dished out another rejection with the review: "Great musicians but just not tangible."

Will adopted his diplomatic front, nodded and shook hands—then returned home to find out what the fuck "tangible" meant:

tangible: adjective—definite and clearly intelligible; something that can be held or touchable; not elusive

So we were left thinking "Shit, they don't get it—so let's make our music *tangible.*" We deduced that the label guy wasn't saying we were wack, he was just indifferent to our selections for the demo tape.

If our music was going to be "tangible," then what was it about?

It has to be East Coast, West Coast, and overseas, and have appeal in London, Will said, before disappearing into the bathroom. Our boy Poli Pol then played some crazy beat.

Seconds later, echoing from inside the bathroom, we heard Will shout: "That's the joint! That's dope—that's the jam. Turn that shit up!"

It was from the simplicity of that spontaneity that the lyrics became set in stone: *"That's the joint, that's the jam/Turn that shit up, play it again/We're going worldwide across the nation . . . we're on some northbound shit, some southbound shit, some East Coast, West Coast, London shit . . . "*

And that's how "Joints & Jams" was birthed—and it would become our first major single.

Countless Black Eyed Peas songs have depended on flashes of inspiration as opposed to sweating blood and spending hours carving out perfect lyrics. The writing process is an organic one that feeds and bounces off each member of the group. Once we have tapped into an agreed thought-stream, we can nail a song in an hour.

Anyhow, we thought "Joints & Jams" was more "tangible."

But again, when Will took it back to the label and started shopping it around town, no one was feeling it. I'm convinced that no one knew what to make of us or where to place us in the market.

You could almost hear the industry thinking aloud: *"They say they're hip-hop but one of them is Filipino and one of them is Latino. And the Latino looks Asian. Huh?"*

Financially, we had no time for those mental cogs to turn. We were effectively going broke, making just enough money to pay the rent and scrape by. We knew we had *something* but making it happen wasn't . . . happening.

That was the moment we flipped our strategy on its head and decided to run *without* industry support, and remove our begging bowl from under the labels' hands.

Fuck demos, we said, we will become masters of our own destiny. Cut our own album and take the music to the fans. If we created the buzz and built the momentum, the record labels would come knocking on *our* door.

The strategy was uncomplicated: hit the colleges and target the students because one day, those students will become interns and the chances were, in Hollywood, that they will become interns or A&R people at a record label. If we attacked the root instead of the top of the tree, we could climb and grow with our core audience. It was a deliberate word-of-mouth strategy in the days before viral campaigns, Facebook, or Twitter.

We traveled across Southern California playing colleges like Cal State Long Beach, Cal State Northridge, Loyola Marymount University and countless others. It was an endless tour of campus after campus, with performances in the afternoons or early evenings.

Alongside those bookings, we also maintained the underground scene with regular gigs at Dragonfly, Whisky, Mogul, Florentine Gardens, the Key Club, the Viper Room, and Club Fais Do-Do—an underground club once frequented by the likes of Sam Cooke, Billy Preston, and John Coltrane. It was a club that was in synch with our thinking with its racially mixed crowd and musically diverse bill. That's why it became one of the clubs that we *always* performed at. Our schedule was relentless but it had to be because we couldn't afford to stop, and the odd $250–$500 trickled in.

We popped up in the craziest places. Because of the four-piece band, few hip-hop venues could accommodate us, so we played rock and blues venues which made us more visible than we otherwise would have been.

Inspired by the sheer volume of our shows, we began working around the clock, writing, rehearsing, performing, and marketing. We designed our own flyers with the assistance of the creative flair of our friend Paul Chan. I guess he was the first to brand us—devising the first Peas' logo that said "BEP" as a simple tag with a fine-line typeface. I remember many nights going to some of L.A.'s undesirable clubs with pockets stuffed with postcard-sized flyers and then leaving early to stand outside the doors to catch the female audience as they were leaving. The flyer, back then, was a cornerstone of self-promotion, but Will, Apl, me, and Paul had to be slick about it because no club appreciated anyone promoting other gigs on their doorstep. But we were a determined bunch on our 2 a.m. promotional pushes.

We promoted ourselves like crazy, week in, week out. We'd all pile into Paul's black Chevy truck to head out on these pushes. The problem was that there was only enough room in the front for three, so sometimes I had to lie flat on the cold metal bed of the truck, head down and out of sight because carrying passengers in the back was illegal. For a long time, all I saw on the journey from the San Gabriel Valley to Hollywood was stars in the night sky.

Our marketing drive paid off because our crowds grew bigger. By the fall of 1996, fifty-strong crowds had swelled into 350–500. The sea of bobbing heads in front of us grew wider and farther and something told us that we were on the right track. That gave us enough faith to keep plugging away when the phones stayed quiet.

One face among those growing crowds was our old Atban Klann friend Mooky. I decided to invite him to a gig one night and he showed up, and the cool thing about Mook is that he held no resentment or jealousy. He came up to all three of us afterward and told us how "impressive" we were. I admired him for that because it couldn't have been easy for him to see me up there performing along-side Will and Apl. He had wandered down a weird path for a bit, but now he was back in the family, offering his full support. It was great to say hello to him again, and welcome him back into the fold.

Me and Mickey Mouse weren't destined for a long-term relationship.

Working shifts by day, performing at night and partying until the wee hours was an impossible lifestyle to sustain, so something had to give, and it was always going to be Disney. I say that as if it was a considered decision, when the truth is that I got fired. But I still like to think that I engineered it.

I slept in one morning and turned up so late that it earned me a reprimand and a verbal warning. If it ever happened again, "Don't waste your time coming back in," I was told by some Mickey Mouse–pleasing supervisor.

Sure enough, another morning soon came around when I didn't feel like getting out of bed and shoveling horse shit. I pressed the snooze button, giving myself an extra fifteen minutes to weigh my options.

By night, I was beginning to hear audience feedback: "Hey man, I love your music." By day, I was beginning to tire of the orders to "Pick up that gum" or "Shovel that shit." With that in mind, I made an executive decision to roll over and go back to sleep.

That meant having to get another job, but one that was less taxing on my time. I fell back on Mom's connections at the LAUSD and ended up working in the school kitchens as a lunchtime server, pulling in pretty much the same wage for fewer hours and less humiliation.

I went from putting horse shit in honey-buckets to placing lunch cartons, milk, puddings, and donuts on trays to hungry kids at three different schools: Griffith Elementary, Wilson Elementary, and Fairfax High. It was more mundane work, but, again, the thought of performing pulled me through.

I started wearing bandanas as head-wraps, knotted at the back. I refused to wear one of those wack hairnets so I improvised with a look that respected the rules and respected fashion at the same time. I wore all sorts of colors—green, black, brown, red, orange, and beige—and the schoolkids nicknamed me "Rambo."

That was when I decided to incorporate that look into our performances at clubs, and so the head-scarf, or bandana, became my signature look. A thrift-store jacket with some military-looking wrap was all people saw me wearing from 1996 to 2000. And the shoes and socks always had to match the headgear. I still remained fresh to death from head to toe.

One night at the apartment, Apl was cooking up our staple dinner of beef and rice when he decided he needed some soy sauce. So I returned to the scene of our mini-crimes at the mini-mart on the corner of Hollywood Boulevard and Edgemont.

With a nonchalance that came with practice, I tucked a bottle of soy sauce into my pants, grabbed the ninety-nine-cent soda and went to the counter with my dollar bill. It was when I was standing there, second in line, that I committed the cardinal sin of cockiness . . . and got greedy.

Out of the corner of my eye, I spotted a Kit Kat in a mini box stand and, as the Armenian owner served the guy in front, my hand did the surreptitious spider crawl, fingered one bar and slipped it into my pocket.

I slid the soda bottle to the man and handed over the one-dollar bill.

"And you're going to pay for the Kit Kat?"

"What Kit Kat?"

"I saw you, man. I saw you steal the Kit Kat. It's in your pocket!" he said.

I never was good at hiding guilt so I 'fessed up and, understandably, the dude was pissed. Especially when he discovered that the one-dollar bill was the sum total of the cash I had on me.

"You come in here every day and you DISRESPECT me like that!" he yelled.

To make a long story short, he threatened to call the police, but I begged him not to, convincing him that I had been caught short after leaving my money at home. He demanded Apl's phone number, rang him up and yelled: "IF YOU DON'T COME DOWN HERE RIGHT NOW AND PAY ME MONEY, YOUR FRIEND GOES TO JAIL!"

Apl guessed what it was about, turned up, and bailed me out with a $20 fine that had been demanded as compensation.

On the way home, he wanted to know what had gone wrong in the execution.

"I stole a Kit Kat."

"Damn!" he said, "I had to pay twenty bucks for a fucking Kit Kat?"

It is at this point that I would like to say that we learned our lesson. But that would be a lie. Two weeks later, we needed a new lightbulb to prevent us from sitting in darkness, and Apl offered to walk to the nearby Ralph's supermarket.

A new venue would cast less suspicion on him, he thought.

He breezed in, found a 75-watt lightbulb, tucked it in his pants, and was heading for the door when a member of security stopped him. A call to the cops looked certain. But, thankfully, he was blessed with yet another lenient manager who found a smarter way to teach him a lesson. He got out a camera and made Apl stand against the wall holding the lightbulb above his head. The dude then pinned the mug-shot on a mocked-up poster under the headline: *"SHOPLIFTING: Not A Bright Idea."*

After that episode, we never fingered another item in our lives. We figured that once you've been caught red-handed on two separate occasions, you know it's time to stop before the $20 fines and wanted posters make way for a call to the cops.

I think we knew then and there that we were living a charmed life.

GETTING SIGNED

In the latter half of '96 and early part of '97, some dark moods started knocking on my door, in what was probably a delayed reaction to many things: Nanny's death, the frustration of not getting signed and my guilt over Josh—a guilt that found traction in the echoes of my own fatherless childhood.

It was a time in my life when I seemed to be rushing around trying to get somewhere, but it felt like I was running in place, going nowhere. Within that void, I was a father by name and not by deed, repeating a history I didn't want to be repeated.

Josh seemed to spend more time with my mom and Karish's Aunty Gladys than with anyone else. I was so tied up gigging on Friday nights and the weekend, and Rosemead seemed an age away from Hollywood. These were the kind of feeble excuses that masked my surrender of responsibility as a father, and that was something that would eat away at me more and more.

On top of all that, I was sleeping in a roach-infested studio on a dirty-ass mattress with a career that wasn't popping off. As much as we felt we were gaining momentum, true success still seemed a long way off. I'd like to say that my confidence never wavered, but the truth is that I found myself assessing the difference between dreams and delusion.

This is all backstory to explain how I kept depression at bay: by trying out acid and magic mushrooms. As would become typical, I hit the experimentation hard—evidence of my incapability to do anything in moderation.

Looking back, this "promotion" in my drug-taking—from weed to hallucinogenics—was a threshold I should never have crossed. It opened the door into a wider curiosity further down the line, but depression and boredom are the worst kind of enablers. The logical side of my brain conveniently forgot about Phoenix's earlier downward spiral which I had vowed never to follow. My reckless senses just charged on through.

One evening, me and Apl took our one-eighth bag of mushrooms, kicked back and ate the caps, then waited for the trip to transport us to hell knows where. At first, the ride was fun, like some out-of-body experience; a state of lucid dreaming where everything seemed abstract but wonderfully alive. Time—and the hiatus between the dream and making it in the music industry—didn't exist.

But later we discovered the downside: the bad trips and the ensuing, even darker moods. Objects started morphing into other objects, inanimate ornaments and utensils came to life, and an out-of-body experience turned into a going-out-of-my-mind fuckup.

I had pinned photos of Josh on the wall opposite the mattress where I crashed, and I will never forget the time when I was standing, staring at his face—like I often did—and suddenly he started crying out, mouth agape, eyes pleading.

"Help me, Dad! Help me!"—his hands reaching toward me.

I was standing there, rooted to the spot, moaning and crying, screaming back at him that I had not forgotten, that I had not abandoned him. That whole episode haunted me for days, and you would have thought that would have been enough to keep me away from the wacky stuff.

But I also experimented with acid, and this time, I hooked up with Mooky and his then-girlfriend. We had headed west to Santa Monica beach, and thought it would be cool to watch the sunset after dropping some acid, but this was no enjoyable sunset. Mooky and Jessie started freaking out, saying I was turning into a skeleton in front of them. Then, I found myself wrapped within a trail of lights (I think the Santa Monica Pier came alive) and I could not see solid ground beneath me. I collapsed to the sand so I could feel the earth on all fours, but the sand started to fall like it was giving way under my weight. Then all three of us started freaking out.

To make matters worse, we thought we had lost the car keys in this falling sand and so we feverishly started digging on our knees, like three cartoon dogs searching for a buried bone.

To everyone else on the beach, we must have looked like three crazy beach bums who had just been let out of the asylum.

The final straw came back at the apartment when Apl started cooking rice after eating some more mushrooms. We were standing over the stove, trying to rap as he stirred. Suddenly, the rice turned into a thousand worms, mutating and squirming out of the pan.

"Fuck! FUCK!" we screamed. We backed away and didn't dare go near that pan for about an hour afterward, and we didn't eat that night. Instead, we tried calming ourselves with a free-style session but we couldn't string together one coherent sentence or lyric, like MC amateurs all over again—and that frightened the shit out of us.

"What's happening to us?" said Apl. "What happens if this shit fucks with us forever and we can never write again?"

It doesn't matter how irrational the thought process was, hearing Apl say that out loud was enough of a wake-up call.

"We are stopping this shit right now!" I said.

We threw the rest of the mushrooms in the trash outside.

Our time at Roach Motel was a trip in itself, and we learned two sobering lessons along the way: always pay for items at the counter no matter how desperate you are, and never risk your creativity for the sake of a trip.

It was weed and weed only from this point on.

I made that promise to myself.

I just didn't hear my demons laughing in the background.

I have this abiding memory of Will, as the producer, sitting in a chair in front of his drum machine with his collection of collaborators, and placing sounds under his microscope, manipulating samples from old songs or dissecting beats of his own making; taking a web of invisible threads and weaving them into a rhythmic masterpiece to which we then added lyrics.

By now, Will was a musician in his own right, not just an MC. Since 1995, he had been attending piano classes in Santa Monica to learn more about music. He wanted more than just the basic understanding he'd acquired as a teenager. He wanted to master it; to look under the hood and understand the mechanics of music—breaking down the structure of a song and the elements and chords and notes. That's the measure of the obsessive dedication he brought to the table.

By early 1997, we were making songs for an album which had no name and no distributor. It was a demo album with hope attached. We wanted to create a self-contained package with a professional gloss to deliver to a label and say "Here's who we are, here's our vision and here's our album."

In creating and recording our music, we used samples with live instruments. Every musical sample that people hear was once played live, so we wanted to re-create that raw form and incorporate it into our songs; minimal samples woven in with live instrumentation.

Sampling—the act of taking a portion of an old song, manipulating it and reusing it—was a device used in music since the 1960s, but it didn't become

widespread until the early 1980s, thanks to hip-hop, as producers built in sampled breaks. This device, in other words, meant the music would be the identifiable underlay but with different lyrics on top.

The first popular sampling was featured in Sugar Hill Gang's "Rapper's Delight" single in 1979 when they took a sample from "Good Times" by Chic, but instead of using a sampled break it used its own live band to make an instrumental copy so they could rap over it. And that's how we worked it, so that the overall vibe was not of a sample but of live music.

There is a big distinction between sampling and doing a cover. Music aficionados will already know that some of the most sampled artists are legends like James Brown, Quincy Jones and Michael Jackson. Beats and breaks from their hits provide underlays to hundreds of songs out there within hip-hop sampled jazz or hip-hop sampled rock 'n' roll.

Most hip-hop groups in the mid-90s were sample-heavy—using a sample the whole way through a song and rapping over it for three to four minutes. In some minds, that wasn't far removed from hip-hop karaoke.

Will wanted to change it up, falling back on his musical training to give samples his own twist. He wanted to use one brief portion before our own beat and chorus kicked in; taking a strand of DNA from one song and weaving it into our own to create a whole new beast. He wasn't reinventing the wheel, but he was providing the Peas with its own musical edge.

For "Joints & Jam," we took a piece from "Grease" by Frankie Valli, interpolating the melody and giving it our own interpretation so that the lyrics "Grease is the word, is the word that you heard/It's got groove, it's got meaning . . ." became "Jam is the jam, is the jam that you heard/It's got groove, it's got meaning . . ."

You hear that song today with a female vocal beneath the Peas' verses and it still sounds dope. This is what we did—creating a host of songs with our own signature across it.

We had moved from Ben Mor's bedroom studio into a professional studio at Loyola Marymount University (LMU) between Marina del Rey and Inglewood, just down the road from LAX airport. One night, after rocking a great gig for a bunch of students, we ran into student teacher Brian Lapin and engineering student Dave Haines. Brian was a keyboardist, and, because Carlos Galvan had left us, our chance meeting was serendipitous, filling the vacant spot. Dave—who remains our soundman genius today—set us up at the LMU sound studio. We had access to a full-on studio for the first time. I remember walking in and seeing the decks and the vocal booth and thinking it looked like something out of the movies.

For the next two months, we recorded songs with our live band and Kim Hill.

Sadly, there are no wild college campus stories to report because we were always there after hours. It was always dusk as we arrived, and beyond midnight when we finished.

The upside was that I wasn't working the school lunches anymore. I had quit when we decided to cut the album, because we were hitting the shows so hard that bookings had started coming in for afternoons as well as evenings. As things turned out, the income was now equal to what I would have earned in the kitchens.

In the studio, we must have put down vocals on a collection of about twenty songs and, aside from "Joints & Jam," it is the story behind "Fallin' Up" that sticks most in my mind. This song was written by Apl on the back of a bus as we traveled from Hollywood to 3rd Street in East L.A. We were sitting on the backseat of one of those orange and white buses, heading to meet up with some guy called Ray who supplied the weed, when Apl's inspiration struck.

"We be fallin' up . . . we be fallin' up," he kept mumbling, staring out the window—a man on a mission.

"Yeah, that's right, Ap—we be fallin' up," I said.

Around this time, there was all this East Coast versus West Coast shit in hip-hop, and we had this thing about wanting to become the modern-day pioneers of the genre, taking it in a new direction. It was that germ of a thought that turned into Apl's top-of-the-head free-styling.

"We be fallin' up, never fallin' down . . . keep it on a higher level, elevated ground," he rapped.

"Shit! That's it!" I said, and suddenly it was on.

Apl kept free-styling and it just kept on coming . . .

"Whether in your area, city or your town, Black Eyed Peas are known for getting down . . ." he rapped.

By the time we reached the stop for Ray's house, we were high on inspiration and didn't need no weed (but we bought a stash for later consumption!).

We took the lyrics and concept back to Will in the studio, and he was like "Yo, that shit is dope . . . we've got to record it!" He found an old-school CD from Brazilian artist Jorge Ben—a man renowned for spawning percussive Brazilian pop with his band Trio Mocotó—and we just listened as he went to work with his production magic.

"Yo, that riff right there!" said Will. "Let's take that guitar riff and redo it," he said, and he meshed bossa nova with rap and "Fallin' Up" was born.

When we weren't working, we didn't go our separate ways—we hung out as friends, playing miniature golf, going ten-pin bowling, or shooting pool. We remained as tight off duty as we were on stage.

We also kept performing, and, at one gig at Florentine Gardens, Deja spotted Fat Lip from the hip-hop group Pharcyde, who were on fire at the time with two big-hitting albums. His presence at one of our gigs was an endorsement on

its own, and it provided real hope for the first time that we were making an impact; that something big was about to blow.

Not long afterward, word reached us that DJ Mormile, the nephew of Jimmy Iovine, co-founder and CEO of Interscope Records, had given his uncle our demo tape, vindicating our target-the-college-fan-base strategy.

We knew that Jimmy was a big hitter, because he'd previously produced albums for U2, Stevie Nicks, Simple Minds, Dire Straits, and Patti Smith before launching Interscope in 1990. What was also significant was that it was a label with an ear for hip-hop and urban music. Interscope signed and launched Tupac Shakur, Snoop Dogg and Dr. Dre. A little more poking around in its history further encouraged me, because the label's first release in 1991 was Latino rapper Gerardo, who scored a top-5 hit with "Rico Suave." (As it turned out, Gerardo would eventually end up at Interscope as an executive, and he was said to be the man who brought Enrique Iglesias to the label in 1999.)

At the same time, we had been banging the publicity drum as best we could, doing local radio and television media, and featuring in some underground publications. A drip-drip-drip effect of publicity was building into an audible buzz that was getting us noticed.

That's when word came through that Black Coffee Management, responding to interest that was filtering through, arranged a Peas showcase event at the Dragonfly club on Santa Monica Boulevard. The club scene was beginning to rock again in L.A., and this venue had become a draw for record label executives to spot up-and-coming groups. There was more contract ink being spilled on its floors than beer, so this booking was our "this is it" moment. I smelled opportunity stronger than I smelled weed in the Roach Motel.

Everything we had worked for since we were kids—but especially over the previous twenty-four months—would ride on one night and one set, playing to the anonymous faces of the record labels we knew would be there: Interscope, Warner Bros., and Sony 550. This one event in 1997 was what we had engineered by design; the labels were coming to us, not us to them, after we had built our fan-base brick by brick.

We knew we deserved it—and that's why we didn't even think about failure.

It was time to be supermen and fly when that Friday night arrived. The place was packed with about five hundred people.

I wore some fresh outfit to summon the warrior spirit, and I hadn't felt so amped for a long time. Each of us was "on" that night, and I knew we were ready. There was not one iota of self-doubt among us. We thrived when we sensed the edge, and the night seemed loaded with expectancy. I checked in with Will's wild-eyed intensity, and saw Apl bouncing with energy. All three of us were humming generators backstage, waiting to release what even then we called "The Black Eyed Peas experience."

We launched into our set and won over everyone with "Joints & Jam," "Fallin' Up," and—for the crescendo—"Head Bobs," our most recognizable song at the time. It was our end-of-show rock song and was always guaranteed to ignite any venue. It was a song to lose your mind to, building and building into the head-bobbing chorus before getting real mellow; full of angsty guitar, drums and then soul, it contained all the dynamics to drive a gig wild.

When "Head Bobs" started up, I stage-dived into the crowd, as was my usual routine; being held aloft and passed around by a sea of hands, crowd-surfing. I thrived on being the orchestral conductor within that energy; diving in there, jumping around, pogo-dancing. Or, as the lyrics in "¿Que Dices?" better explain, in one of the raps I wrote: *My job is to mainly hypnotize/I'm a take over their thoughts and maneuver through their eyes/Visually on stage, the Peas we multiply/ We equal the sum of only one tribe . . ."*

With me squashed into the front of a heaving crowd, it was on; getting the crowd to bob their heads, singing the chorus out loud.

"YOU CAN BOB YOUR HEAD LIKE THIS—HA!"

Allowing the song to build and climb . . .

"WHEN WE'RE DROPPING BOMBS LIKE THIS—HA!"

I bounced around, left hand on mic, right hand in the air.

Gig after gig, I viewed the crowd as this pool which I wanted to jump into and splash around until everyone was splashing around with me. If I saw any dude standing with his arms crossed, being the reluctant, shuffling dancer, I'd be after him, getting him to jump around, looking to elevate the energy. With me on the mic in the crowd, and Will and Apl bossing it from the stage, it always felt like the whole venue was plugged into the same voltage that connected us as a group.

There was something about that showcase at the Dragonfly that made everything feel even more insanely crazy than before. At the gig's end, when we saw every hand in the air clapping and every face sweating and beaming within a multiracial crowd, we knew we'd rocked it. We sensed what Yon Styles was already waiting to tell us later that evening: that come Monday morning, there would be a series of meetings with each label. All three were interested in having talks.

That following week felt like speed-dating, music-industry style.

We shuttled between the L.A. offices of Interscope, Sony 550, and Warner Bros. as the subject of a bidding war. I felt like a passenger on some crazy magic carpet ride, being courted by labels talking up big promises and big money. This was when we fell back on Will's business-savvy direction. What he valued more than anything was the *right* opportunity, not just *any* opportunity.

We had all agreed on one thing: after having the patience to wait for this

breakthrough, we weren't going to lose our heads just because we'd been invited inside these music empires.

We all packed into Will's VW Golf—me, Apl, and manager Yon Styles—and dressed to impress. We presented ourselves as a package, in terms of both our image and our music. Armed with CD demo tracks—"Joints & Jam," "Fallin' Up" and "Head Bobs"—we put on our game faces.

Throughout all the meetings, I adopted the serious man-of-few-words persona. Not because it was a strategy but because I was as high as a kite, having packed in a ton of weed that morning. I couldn't say shit because my tongue was asleep. People in the meetings probably thought I was some chill dude, unfazed by the lure of show business, but image always has been deceiving in Hollywood.

My intake of weed was now as habitual and necessary as eating. Weed was as much a part of me as my blood and muscle. In the same way some people cannot start the day without coffee, I couldn't start it without weed. And, like someone attached to their BlackBerry or iPhone today, I always had to have it in my pocket, on my person.

What you've got to understand is that, by now, I wasn't doing it to relax myself, calm my nerves or whatever other bullshit justified why I was smoking it. I was doing it because I had reached the point that when I woke up, the first thing that I *needed* was to "wake and bake."

Warner Bros. was the first meeting and their guy was full of the big talk, seemingly speaking off some industry script and telling us how "we'll put you on every talk show, blow you up and make you big." We nodded our heads earnestly, but each one of us was thinking, *Nah, this guy doesn't know what we're about*.

Next up was Sony 550, then a division of Epic Records, whose most notable artists at the time seemed to be Celine Dion and Des'ree. Also, you couldn't walk through its doors without thinking "Michael Jackson."

The meeting was taken by a lady named Polly Anthony, whose own story spoke to our kind of perseverance. This was a woman who started out as a secretary before climbing her way to the top of the pile, so we had massive respect for her and everything she said. I'll never forget the moment she said: "And we'll get you on Oprah . . ."

Suddenly our stoic, professional masks fell and we're all thinking: *OPRAH! Oh, shit!* We were all fans of Oprah, and that was an enthusiasm that was hard to hide.

Polly was one intelligent woman who made all the right noises and said all the right things, and she offered big, cool bucks within a package that made us think, even as we were walking into the next meeting at Interscope to meet Jimmy Iovine.

We arrived at this humongous building in Santa Monica, and the first thing I noticed after stepping out of the elevator was the wall-to-wall framed pictures, plaques and commemorative records in honor of a range of artists: No Doubt, Dr. Dre, Marilyn Manson, Limp Bizkit, and Nine Inch Nails, to name a few.

We knew ahead of time that Jimmy was the kind of record-maker always looking for "something original, something different, and something with spirit," as he himself had said.

We carried out the same routine as we'd done at the previous two meetings, and played our demo tape of "Joints & Jam" and "Fallin' Up," followed by the somewhat grainy VHS-tape music video we had made for "Head Bobs."

There was no bullshit with Jimmy, and when he said he "loved it!" you believed him. Then he nailed it with an impressive pitch which I might not do 100 percent justice to, but my memory has remembered as something along these lines:

"Sure, I can give you as much money as you like because money is no object, but I don't want to just throw money at you and hope something sticks. I want to create a movement for you guys, and create something bigger than you've ever imagined. I want to work with you and for you, and blow you up into a monster group with as much support as we can offer. No matter how many records you sell, we'll build you up because I believe in you."

If I'd have been sitting at the negotiating table alone, I'd have bitten his hand off, but it wasn't enough for Will.

He remained impassive. Jimmy waited.

Will, turning to Yon and then turning to us, waited with that unmoved stare of his, and we all pretended to ponder.

At that impasse, I checked out the posh furnishings, the music awards, and platinum plaques. I saw a framed photo of Jimmy with John Lennon, and then one with Stevie Nicks. I then imagined a new frame with him and the Black Eyed Peas.

One day.

Jimmy started shifting in his big leather chair. He leaned forward and started stirring sugar into a cup of tea.

"*What* is it going to take to sign you guys?" he asked, almost exasperated.

"What about tour support?" Will shot back. "Touring is very important to us."

That is all we had ever visualized: going on the road and touring.

We looked at Jimmy who, distracted by the negotiation, had kept dropping sugar into his tea and stirring. "LOOK! You got me all nervous and now my cup's overflowed!" he said, "Okay . . . okay, I'll throw in tour support as well."

That was the deal clincher and we shook hands.

The agreed advance was roughly $500,000, which had to cover management commission, payments to the band, touring, and other expenses, leaving our individual slices at about $75,000 each.

I made an excuse to go to the restroom. Once I'd kicked open all the

cubicle doors to check that I was alone, I flipped open the cell phone and called Mom. I counted each tone as the phone rang. I was by the sinks, looking back at myself in the mirror, thinking *"This is it . . . this is it!"*

She picked up.

"Mom! We just got a record deal!!" I said, in one of those shouted whispers.

"What?"

I said it again, for both our sakes.

"We just landed a record deal with Interscope!"

"Congratulations, Jaime!" she said, not quite understanding the news but knowing enough to reward my enthusiasm with an uncertain "congratulations." Even though her comprehension was vague about what "a record deal" meant in real terms, I wanted her to be the first person I shared the news with—for all the sacrifices she had made; for all the shit I had caused; for all the doubts she'd ever had.

I walked back into the room and Jimmy hooked us up with a bunch of his label's latest CD releases. That evening, after the three of us had reminded each other to keep our feet on the floor and chill, me and Apl took our CDs to a shop called Penny Lane which exchanged CDs for money. We might have secured $500,000 on paper, but we were still technically broke and needed money to eat. That night, we used our exchange cash to buy a full-on dinner: chicken, rice and vegetables—and an ounce of weed.

We hoped that such a banquet was the sign of things to come.

One week later, the deal was signed, sealed, and delivered, and the check came through.

We were all together inside Yon Style's apartment when we read the words on the check together: *"Payable to Black Eyed Peas Music—$500,000."*

We must have looked at that check a thousand times, just to believe it was true. It was more money than our brains could absorb.

We had to wait for our own individual checks, so I asked for the group check to be Xeroxed. I wanted to take home something *real* to make Mom believe.

That check in my hand was the beans held in Jack's palm in the fairy tale *Jack and the Beanstalk;* a seed that would grow a tree-like beanstalk that would climb to a magic castle.

I took those "beans" home to show Mom, and found her standing in the kitchen.

I said nothing, and just put the copy of the check in her hands and let her read what it said.

She looked up at me, speechless.

There was delight on her face, put there by something I had achieved.

As she screamed and squealed, I actually became someone and achieved something—and it was something that broke the mold. No one in either the Gomez or Sifuentes families had previously achieved anything close to this.

Even Julio had to acknowledge it. He shook my hand and congratulated me, man to man.

Respect, at last.

It was also *touché*—my sweet vindication. Proof that music could be "a real job." Proof that I had been doing something more than just sitting around and getting high. Proof that Nanny's belief in me was well invested.

Consequently, that moment didn't only represent a turning point in my fortunes, it also marked a new beginning in my relationship with Julio, and, therefore, with Mom. We unlocked horns and relations improved ten thousandfold. That check allowed me to put money where my mouth was, so they finally cut me some slack.

Don't get me wrong, I wasn't taking anything for granted, because I knew this was still just my dream's opening sequence. The $75,000 was more money than I'd ever known but it wasn't steering me toward anything showy—no mansion or fancy cars.

That wasn't my style.

Worth more to me than all the zeroes on my share of that check was the satisfaction of making good on my big dream in Nanny's eyes, in her memory. Now, the rest of my family could respect those dreams, too.

We all laughed and celebrated that night. Then I told Mom exactly what I was going to buy when my slice of the money was received, because there was only one thing in the world that mattered.

EXPOSURE

It cost me around $25,000 to secure custody of Josh.

I know people say that having money isn't guaranteed to make you happy, but it sure can stop *un*happiness, and that's why my first chunk of cash went to rectifying one unhappy situation.

The moment Interscope bettered my life—the very moment I felt that check in my hand—I wanted to better my son's life, too, and after all the excitement had died down, the first thing I did was pick up the phone and call an attorney.

This was no rash, impulsive decision. It was something I had long thought about; the record deal just allowed me to accelerate what, for me, had always been an inevitable outcome. It helped that Karish agreed that Josh would be better off at our house. His weekend visits with his grandma were his happiest times, so making that arrangement permanent would bring stability. I always had an eye on the future that I was starting to build with the Peas, and Josh—now four—was always in that vision, too.

This isn't me holding myself aloft as some Dad of the Year because that was far from the truth and even when we were reunited, I would hardly prove to be any kind of role model. If I'm honest, I can't say that I really felt like his dad either—more like his twenty-two-year-old brother. Money didn't make me emotionally grow up overnight. It just made one decision possible.

That one decision—in terms of moving my son into a healthier environment—was the wisest one, regardless of my capabilities and limitations as a father. It was never about what I could offer as a dad. It was about returning him to a better *home* where there was constant love and support; the very home where his life had started.

I didn't think beyond that point, really.

That's why decision number one dovetailed with decision number two: to move out of Roach Motel and back in with Mom. It wasn't a very rock 'n' roll move—and neither was the brand-new green Honda Civic I bought—because me moving back home meant that I had to sleep on the brown couch in the front room. My old room had been turned into Josh's room, and Mom slept with him because she and Julio were one of those couples who, for whatever reason, slept in different rooms.

It sounds crazy looking back, but the imminent launch of the Peas would be taking me away from home and providing me with an erratic schedule, so I wasn't going to be home much, and it seemed a waste of money to throw rent at an apartment I would never live in. Mom didn't charge me rent for the sofa, and that allowed me to save money.

I treated my slice of the advance like treasure I didn't want to touch. When you have never had money and a sizeable chunk suddenly drops into your bank account, you hoard it like a squirrel hoards nuts, especially having spent the first $25,000. I didn't know how long the remaining $50,000 would have to last.

So there I was, the newly signed artist with Interscope, deciding to crash like a bum on a couch, and this would be my setup for the next three years. But that imperfect situation was tolerable because of the importance of having a family unit around Josh. Having Mom as the forever-present, doting grandmother was a godsend for a work-away single dad.

As for Karish, I think it tells its own story that she allowed me custody.

I think her mother's soul wanted to fight, but, at that time in her life, she had nothing to fight with, and so she stood aside with Josh's best interests in mind.

She agreed to me having full custody, leaving her with weekend visitations. I received a letter from the office of the District Attorney, Gil Garcetti, initially opposing my application unless I paid back the welfare payments Karish had been drawing after our split. I had to pay back that debt to the City of Los Angeles, but I was prepared to pay whatever it took to get Josh back.

I never understood the legal mumbo jumbo that followed, and I never needed to appear in court. I just took the phone calls and signed whatever documents I needed to sign. Once I had reimbursed the city and paid attorney fees, the final cost was $25,000.

Once that happened, the District Attorney's objections fell away and the

rest was a formality. The whole process took about ten days and, within three weeks of banking the record deal, Josh was back under our roof in Rosemead.

I banked the rest of the advance as savings.

I still couldn't believe the turnaround in our fortunes. For the first time, I now had money in the bank and a new car in the driveway and everything seemed as unbelievable as a lottery win. But that was the thing about good fortune on such a scale—it *was* unbelievable, to a degree that my brain couldn't compute.

Everyone tells you how to chase the dream, be positive, keep believing and never give up, because everyone can associate with the struggle or the pursuit or the hope. But few know how to handle the genie coming out of the lamp. There are no guidelines, manuals or prepared notes. Not even from the industry that has accepted you into its magic empire. It is just something you have to go through. But *no one* warns you that dreams coming true can be the hardest part. Especially if, like me, you're mentally, emotionally, and unconsciously ill-equipped for what you wished for.

Nothing really outwardly changed after being signed to Interscope.

It wasn't as if there was any artist development needed: we already had our look, the fashion, the vision, and the plan. In the eyes of the label and group, the great ship was already built and just needed to be pushed into the water.

Jimmy Iovine and an A&R man named Scott Igoe left the visual aspects in our hands, and our new life became a Pea's utopia: recording in the studio by day and performing around L.A. at night, with summer tours around America being eyed for the following year.

On the road—that was where we wanted to take our music. The cities of America were like the colleges and universities of Los Angeles—untapped places of potential fans. But first, we had to keep building momentum on home territory.

One night sticks out at Florentine Gardens on Hollywood Boulevard—a club once renowned as the favorite supper club of Humphrey Bogart, Audrey Hepburn, and Marilyn Monroe.

We walked in ahead of our allotted performance time to taste some of the opening acts. It was sometime around late 1997, and it was an event that our boy Polo Molina had thrown.

No sooner were we inside than we heard boos and heckles. I looked toward the stage and the opening act was just starting up—this little chubby white kid was trying hard to be the next Vanilla Ice in front of a mean underground crowd.

I felt for this dude, facing that wall of "Who the fuck is this?"

Then someone shouted, "Who's the white rapper?"

The kid on stage was from Detroit, and I felt sorry for him because he appeared to be drowning. It was one thing being a Latino rapper but it was *a whole other story* being a white rapper on the L.A. underground scene. Puerto Ricans had long been in the hip-hop vanguard but a white boy from Detroit? You could feel the whole club bristle when he swaggered on stage, but I gave him credit for one thing—he was fearless.

As he launched into his song, I worried for him. There was something about his voice and lyrics that grated, and a hook that seemed to start with a screech.

"HI! . . . my name is . . . /HI! . . . my name is . . ."

But that was half his problem. No one knew his name.

He was wearing a trenchcoat with glasses that flipped up, and he looked nothing like a hip-hop star. It seemed too gimmicky. Then, just as my reaction was nearing the line of "What the fuck is he doing?" he started to free-style.

And blew the place away. As an MC, he was incredible.

It was an onstage transformation and I scolded myself for having hasty first impressions. Afterward, I had to find this kid and give him props.

"Yo, you rocked it out there, son!" I said.

"Thanks, man," he said, head down, all coy and modest.

"Whassyername?" I asked.

"Eminem," he said.

"Good meeting you, Eminem, and congratulations, brother . . . that was fresh."

One year later, Dr. Dre signed Eminem after he won second place at some rap competition, and his first commercial release was the song he introduced that night at Florentine Gardens, "My Name Is."

The rest, as they say, is history.

"Fallin' Up" was released as our first single set in 1997, with "¿Que Dices?" as its B-side; it was a teaser for the album due the following year, and the video shoot broadened our horizons because it took us out of L.A. for the first time as a group—to Telluride, Colorado.

It wasn't memorable just because of the stunning setting—with the San Juan Mountains used as our location—but because the shoot marked the coming of age of a song written on the back of a bus, taking us from one mundane trip in East L.A. to the real deal of a video shoot.

We had previously shot an unreleased video on our own, for "Head Bobs," with a young director named Brian Beletic—who we had met at LMU—using an 8mm camera for his school project, in different locations around L.A., like Melrose and La Brea. That is why we rehired Brian to shoot "Fallin' Up"—and this time we could pay him. He still used some old grainy video camera, and the feel of the video was still guerrilla style. Ultimately, the video—shot in the mountains to

depict the "elevated ground" of where we wanted to take hip-hop—was aired on BET's Rap City, and I was home alone watching it on television, sitting in front of the same box where I had watched Boogaloo Shrimp, Michael Jackson, and Bruce Lee. And there I was, watching myself—and not sharing the moment with anyone. It almost felt like another one of those dreams that I was keeping to myself.

That video was our first real exposure to an all American audience. It also signaled that we had started our inch-by-inch climb out of the underground scene and into the mainstream—like ninjas pushing up street drain covers and rising up into the big, wide world.

Will led us to some gig at Luna Park, off Santa Monica and Robertson, because he said there was a female singer we *must* see. Will always had this thing about wanting to spot female artists *before* they blew up. Forever the producer-in-waiting.

I went along, standing at the back of the club as this hip African-American woman, originally from Ohio but living in L.A., ambled on stage. She was an Amazonian beauty with a big, wide Afro.

Then she started to sing. She had a unique sound—something rasping, scratchy, almost squawking and yet it still managed to sound soft; a cross between Eartha Kitt and Minnie Ripperton.

"Who is this woman, Will?" I asked him.

You could tell that the three hundred people were asking the same question as she took ownership of that little-ass stage.

"Macy Gray. Dope isn't she!" he said. "We should work with her."

That night, Will got her number and invited her to our studio sessions. The unmistakable sound of Macy Gray, this fellow dreamer who would become our sister, was going to be featured on *Behind the Front*. We had no idea what Kim Hill thought about it. All we knew was that this woman's voice was special and we wanted to use her.

We pretty much lived in the studio because—as remains the case today—that was the one place we preferred to hang. If I ever need plugging into life or if I am ever having a shitty day, just throw me into a studio. Then, as now, we holed ourselves away within soundproofed walls from 5 p.m. to 3 a.m. We are night owls. We do our best work at night. We had arrived with about thirty songs and then kept on writing and recording until we had built that number to a collection totaling fifty.

The studio is also our over-productive songwriting factory, pumping out material until we feel creatively spent. There is a true collaborative spirit that we each vibe off. We spend hours writing, messing around, and tossing up ideas as Will sits there and weaves it all together. And the one sound that always comes out of the studio is laughter. Somebody is always cracking a joke or acting the fool, and it is usually Will goofing around, being outlandish, saying something silly, making a silly face, or doing a silly dance.

The chief reason that the Peas have been able to stay together for so long is the constant laughter we share. We find it impossible to take ourselves too seriously. The spirit—in the studio, on the tour bus, on stage—is frequently upbeat and alive, and it is a combined positive energy—from group to band to producers—that is the key ingredient to our longevity.

I have learned to trust the studio as the one place in the world where, within the company of brothers—and sister—I feel open and safe enough to express myself. The studio has been a home, a training ground, and a refuge for sixteen years with the Peas, and I have never tired of its magic.

By late 1997, we had transferred our recording sessions to Paramount Studios, where Will and Apl had also cut their never-to-be-released *Grass Roots* album. As it happened, a handful of demo songs from that album were reincarnated to live again with the Peas on our debut album, *Behind the Front.*

We chose that title because of the certain "front" that many on the hip-hop scene were putting on—the posturing, the afraid-to-dance, the crotch-grabbing. So we were like "If you're the front, we stay behind the front."

A personal favorite song was "¿Que Dices?" because it was the track where I was first featured on the pre-hook—the confirmation that my baptism of fire as an MC was complete. The moment was made even sweeter because I got to use my native tongue in Spanish—the first time I could indulge my passion and give it up to my own people.

Then we recorded "Love Won't Wait" with Macy Gray for her first song on an album. Watching Macy at work in the studio was like watching a kindred spirit: she was hungry to work, intense, dedicated, and passionate. And her voice was infectious. "Hey Mace, that's one voice you've got there!" I said.

She laughed, as if she was almost embarrassed to own it—and there was a time when that was true, because, as a kid, she had been painfully self-conscious of that voice. So much so that she pushed all her efforts into the written word, studying screenwriting at the University of Southern California film school. But she kept writing songs for musician friends until she was given a break with some jazz band that encouraged her to go solo.

One other notable feature about Macy was her big feet. I was always noticing people's feet, and Macy's were bigger than my own size nines. Obviously, I didn't mention this to her because she would have fucked me up. She was one strong lady! But those feet always carried some fresh shoes, either something patterned and leather, or some colorful tennis shoe. From her voice to her feet, Macy was unique from head to toe!

It was always fun with Macy because of her contagious laugh. She was a great energy to be around, and it turned out that we were both single parents

chasing the dream. She was the mother of three young children from a former marriage, but they were living with her mother in her hometown of Canton, Ohio. It was a situation that almost mirrored mine: an artist relying on her mom as she built a long-term future. Hearing Macy's dedication and purpose made me feel better about my own sacrifices. Hearing her voice on the album made me realize what a powerful contribution she had made. *Behind the Front* was our seventy-three-minute debut, and would be one of five studio albums within the next twelve years.

It was pretty much the same album we presented to Jimmy before getting signed, save for a couple of fillers, "Say Goodbye" and "Positivity."

We don't say we made that music between 1996 and 1998. We say the music came from the time we started dreaming and working as kids because it was a collection of inspirations and influences from childhood and adolescence. Music that effectively said: "This is our life . . . this is our inspiration . . . this is the first album that reflects it all."

It is said that everyone must treasure the "firsts" in whatever we do or witness because the very nature of a "first" means it will not come around again: the sensation of that first gig, first record deal, first album; the first time your son speaks, says "Daddy," or walks.

Firsts are fleeting and need to be captured.

As a Pea, many firsts came thick and fast over the coming years, but, for me, they would gradually become devalued because of a substance dependency that threw down its seeds around this time. Over the next decade—between 1998 and 2007—I would get increasingly lost in the drink and drugs bullshit that escalated year after year. I declare that now in order for you to picture what follows and understand why some memories remain vague. Firsts that should be vivid and colorful memories were long ago rendered as pencil sketches in my mind, and it is only with the passage of time, and with the excavation of writing a book, that I have been able to fill in the blanks and provide some structure to the many scattered pictures. It has allowed me to better understand the unraveling that now began, slowly but surely.

It's hard to define what amounts to "critical acclaim" but *Behind the Front* made the critics sit up and take notice. We might not have rocketed up the charts, but we won across-the-board appreciation. My scrapbook has captured what my memory has forgotten, reminding me of those early reviews:

Elixir magazine—*"For a debut album, this is absolutely slammin'. Nobody has dropped bombs like these since the dawning of the Roots . . ."*

Request magazine college issue—*"The Peas deliver the most durably pleasurable debut thus far with . . . beguiling humor, incisive social commentary and easy-rollin' hip-hop grooves . . ."*

The bimonthly *Audiogliphix* in Philadelphia—*"Finally, a major label rap crew that breaks the intelligence barrier. BEP is to hip-hop today what War was to the rock/Latin/R&B nexus of the Seventies . . ."*

And *Interview* entertainment magazine in Hollywood gave us the biggest smile when it said that *"The only thing second-hand about the Black Eyed Peas is their thrift store threads . . ."*

At first, the buzz was mainly in underground publications or college magazines, but the more time passed, the more we received mentions within mainstream publications, from *Arena* ("looks great, sounds great") to *New Nation* ("an incredibly fine rhythmic debut") to *Music Week* ("a jazzy backing with funky songwriting") to *Melody Maker* ("an album that transcends all genres but sells out none").

I can't say I lost sleep over what the critics would or wouldn't say, but the commercial reality was that good reviews meant our music was getting noticed and that kept the label happy.

We never set out to be artists who were all worthy and profound. We were party people. We have never made music for approval. If we like it, we know millions of other people will like it, too. That's not arrogance, it is belief in our work.

Personally speaking, give me a bad review—and we've had our fair share over the years—and I hear familiar echoes: "You're not good enough . . . You can't do this . . . You're a failure." And that just makes me rise taller and say "Fuck you . . . just watch us turn this around!"

That's how I've rolled since high school—not really listening to what anyone else says—so the critic has always been as empowering as anyone who ever doubted me.

Interscope threw us an album release party at the Art Deco El Rey Theater in L.A. It was an intimate event for about five hundred people with a guest list that read like a Who's Who of the music industry, with movers and shakers whose names were lost on me.

They laid on the style that night, and the dressing room was like something straight from a luxury hotel, with plush furnishings and first-class catering. Gone were the pizza and Pepsi days, and makeshift dressing rooms created by wheeled-in curtain racks. It felt like we had won a competition to be VIPs for a day and some sponsor was laying on the big-ass treatment.

Our mini bar was stacked with free alcohol—as much as we wanted, as much as we could drink. There was free alcohol in the club (as there was in every club we attended as signed artists) and stubs of drink tickets became our new currency. From this day on, free alcohol was part of the rider at every gig and event. And there was always someone who had weed backstage.

Previously, I had only ever owned ten dollars and a dream, but now I found myself ingratiated with a world of sudden decadence and unrestricted indulgence. I was Charlie running around the adult chocolate factory.

Every temptation within me couldn't help but notice that hard work in the music industry came attached with serious partying.

That night, we performed a great set and I first rocked my somewhat theatrical, signature look in those days: one of those wide Chinese bamboo hats, the Kabuki mask, and the martial arts umbrella to add to my martial arts wardrobe. That was my warrior-like statement that stayed with me for the first two years, before being replaced by head-scarfs and vintage hats.

After the set, I got out of costume and let my hair down, hitting the drink hard and celebrating in style. I remember some Interscope dude shaking my hand and telling me to enjoy it because the real hard work was just around the corner. I had no idea what he was talking about. I was too busy enjoying myself.

I got smashed, like a teenager who had just discovered alcohol. I downed glass after glass of a cocktail called Adios Motherfucker—that head-numbing mix of vodka, rum, gin, Blue Curaçao, and orange liqueur. I can't remember much else. I know I felt elated. I know I was stumbling and giving high fives to people. I know I ended the night in my own bed back in Rosemead. For an album launch party, I was shamefully well-behaved.

That is the bit that I like to remember: being a happy drunk.

I was also, apparently, a bit of a social butterfly, circling the room and mixing with anyone and everyone, which, back then, was completely out of character. But drink coaxed me out of my shell and made me feel like the man of the moment with my two other brothers. Will gave some heartfelt speech that I cannot remember. He was the trio's mouthpiece—articulate, music-savvy, and intelligent. He was always going to be the Black Eyed Peas' ambassador.

As he spoke and everyone cheered, there was one anonymous face in the crowd that decided not to step forward and say hello. She was a California girl invited by the label, and we would later learn that she was impressed by what she saw, had wanted to introduce herself but the right moment had never presented itself.

But it wasn't a missed opportunity. Two years later, destiny would ensure that our paths crossed again with Stacy Ferguson, a singer/performer otherwise known as Fergie.

THE LONG ROAD

had signed a contract for an apprenticeship without having any real clue about
what the job entailed. I saw a three-album contract and the money, but I hadn't
thought too hard about the obligations and demands that would follow.

My child-like idea of the industry script went something like this: find
record label, get signed, release records, become huge. In my mind, there was a
giant expectation the size of a Sunset Strip billboard.

I had believed that when an album went on sale nationwide, the record
label machine automatically kicked in. I had become misinformed by overnight
success stories; the boy who still believed in the rags-to-riches fairy tale. Such
thinking was always going to lead to a rude awakening.

Sure enough, someone from Interscope mentioned promotional touring
and I was like "Yo, say what?"

I didn't know what this meant until it was explained that we would be
spending the first year banging the drum and getting our music out there. I was
soon to understand that we had not just entered the arena of performing but the
world of commerce. We were a brand as much as we were performers.

I hadn't realized that the first year as a signed artist would be pretty much
spent on a basic income with little extra money trickling in, save for the $75,000
advance which I had already banked, minus the $25,000 spent on Josh's custody.
We saw the odd trickle-down of some funds, but no big bucks. Essentially, the
advance was intended to incorporate expenses and touring costs, too. That made

me prudent in learning how to make $50,000 stretch over a twelve to eighteen month period.

I was soon educated into accepting that the Black Eyed Peas would have to mine, chisel, and carve our presence into the industry coalface before we started earning real dough. We had made the record labels come to us. Now we had to make the fans do the same. It was as if we had climbed and conquered the dream, stood on that summit and then looked to our left to find there was an even higher mountain to climb. Everest.

There are two tests that challenge the artist's passion. The first is how badly you want the dream. The second is how hard you are prepared to work when the dream presents itself.

I also understood something else: I had always shirked a true work ethic because I was the uninspired lazy ass who dragged himself around Disney and the school kitchens under the obligation of getting "a real job." But now I was being asked to do hard work in the pursuit of a passion and I couldn't wait to get out of bed in the morning.

I got to perform. I got to record. I got to travel.

I got to smoke more weed than my heart could desire.

It was, I told myself, the best job in the world—and it was time to get real and start trucking.

The promotional touring started almost immediately after the release of *Behind the Front,* and we were lucky enough to get invited onto the Smokin' Grooves tour, a hip-hop experience that began in 1996. It was like Coachella or Glastonbury, but on wheels. The festival circuit is where up-and-comers need to be, and this transported us out of L.A., to a more visible platform across the States. Smokin' Grooves was one of those much sought-after bills, so it was a big deal for our first time out. I felt that our stature grew almost overnight. When you have spent so long knocking on the door, it feels good to be invited inside to join the party. I guess it's a bit like being a virtually unknown presidential candidate: you hit the road to canvass support, raise your profile, and hope the people like you.

I remember Mom asking how long this first tour would last.

"Eight weeks," I said.

When the biggest gig you've done has only taken you away for a matter of hours and only as far as Hollywood, that kind of stint away from home takes some adjusting to, but I was lucky having Mom's support behind me.

"Josh and me will be fine," she assured me.

I might not have been the father whose hand rocked the cradle but I knew this mission—if successful—would provide Josh with a better life. I only had to think about the horse shit bucket at Disney to know I was doing the right thing by him.

Cypress Hill were on the 1998 Smokin' Grooves bill together with Wyclef Jean, Busta Rhymes, Gang Starr, and the headliners, Public Enemy. The Black Eyed Peas were billed as the "newcomers," and, as one reviewer would say, "the bohemian rappers." We liked being the unknowns; the underdogs. There are odds to defy and people to surprise.

Everyone on the tour had wild energy, everyone was a character, and everyone but us had hits, but no one could offer a live band and the break-it-down dance sections like us. We knew from day one that our appeal was found in not being a typical hip-hop group on the hip-hop bandwagon.

That is what the House of Blues–sponsored tour was all about: celebrating diversity within the genre, so it was the ideal platform to give everyone a first taste of the Peas experience, from Milwaukee to Minneapolis, from Chula Vista, California, to Camden, New Jersey. We always played at amphitheaters or outdoor arenas and traveled north, south, east, and west, and even dropped into Canada en route.

The first cool "trapping" our virgin eyes locked onto was the tour bus, wrapped with our album cover—the giant words of "*Behind The Front*" and "*Black Eyed Peas*" emblazoned across the side, back, and roof. We freaked out when we saw that one roll up. Imagine the feeling of seeing a six-foot version of your mug on the side of an Eagle bus; a traveling billboard. The most advertising we had previously seen was an ad in *L.A. Weekly* or a flyer posted on a notice board outside a club or pinned to a streetlight.

I am pretty sure that the people we passed in the streets had the same puzzled looks as the people who first arrived at the venues. As the first act on stage, the grass fields and sun-scorched knolls were always only half full as we began our set. The challenge was to turn the "Who the fuck are these guys?" into "Wow—these guys are fresh!" Just like we had that first night at Glam Slam.

What further encouraged us was the love we received from the other groups on Smokin' Grooves. It was surreal being on the same bill as some hip-hop heavyweights, and even more surreal to hear Wyclef Jean tell us "Yo, you guys have got something!"

Wyclef was Haitian-American and liked our multiethnicity.

"Black Eyed Peas!" he announced in that drawl of his. "You have something different. You got the Latino, the Filipino, the African-American. I like that . . . yeah, I like that!"

As rookies, that kind of love was a real shot in the arm that kept us buzzing for days. It was the first time that I understood what feeling "happily numb" meant without resorting to weed.

I was a single, twenty-one-year-old kid getting the opportunity to run rampant, rock stages, get faded *and* hang out with some of the most recognizable names in hip-hop. There was nothing to complain about.

We took to touring like ducks to water, not bothered by the constant trucking and the close proximity of the living quarters. We established "rules on the road" and they were simple enough: no stank-ass nasties allowed on the bus; no jerkin' off allowed, however lonely; and *definitely* no taking a shit on the bus. Leave all that crap for the hotels during stop overs.

I think the rules were out of respect to Kim Hill, because she had to survive on a testosterone-filled bus with eleven dudes. It's also fair to say that she was pretty high-maintenance, which was probably her prerogative as the only woman aboard. I am not saying she was a diva because there were no fits, tantrums, or anything like that, but I think she regarded herself as queen bee of the hive . . . and her dog, Chompa, as the freaking king.

It was one of those immaculately groomed Tibetan Lhasa Apso dogs, with clipped ears and an ugly snout. The thing to understand about these dogs is that they were bred to guard Buddhist monasteries, not Black Eyed Peas tour buses.

We men boarded the bus, ready for another trek across state borders, to find this furry little thing laying on the couch at the front end.

"Yo, any chance of us sitting down?" one of us always said, speaking to the dog like it was human while making the point to Kim.

"Can you not go sit in the back?" she said. "My little shnoo-nah is sleeping."

She called it her "little shnoo-nah." We called it a fucking nuisance. Her dog was sleeping, but we were the ones schlepping across most of America, needing some R & R. But there was always this assertiveness with Kim that eleven men didn't wish to take on. She had a confidence that was unafraid to state its preferences and so, whenever that damn dog wanted to stretch out, me, Will, and Apl took over the back lounge to avoid drama.

What we never told Kim was that Will had no time for her constant companion and she was probably lucky that it didn't go missing somewhere between L.A. and Kansas.

Whenever she wasn't around, Will shoved it off the couch with his foot and terrorized the poor little fucker with a menacing growl of his own. By the time we reached the end of the tour, the dog became surprisingly obedient—waking up and scampering off the couch whenever Will showed up.

After that experience, we introduced a new tour bus rule: no dogs allowed.

Our nickname on Smokin' Grooves was "The Good Samaritans" because we were the new boys and the nice guys; the well behaved freshmen at the hip-hop school. As newcomers, we were a bit timid at first, and soon understood our place in the pecking order—especially when it came to hooking up with girls.

Traveling music festivals always attract groupies who like nothing more than to be associated with the performers. These are usually the devotees of any kind of music that happens to be drifting through a sleepy corner of America. The groupies' collective mission is usually about securing backstage access and hanging with the main acts, and the trade-off normally ends in the party . . . the after party . . . and then the after-after party!

Sure enough, post-performance, we received our fair share of female attention, and, like dogs desperate to get their nuts off, we invited our favorite "fans" backstage, thinking it was on and popping.

Instead, once these girls had secured their all-access bracelets, they had more ambitious ideas. When there was star power like Busta Rhymes, Flavor Flav, and Cypress Hill sniffing around, there was no chance of us keeping any kind of sexy ass on our arm. In town after town, we three "Samaritans" were swooped on by the vultures looking for meat. So we lost the girls early on in order to earn our stripes. We just rolled with it and were like "Okay, whatever . . . this is your 'hood."

All groups and bands mingled and networked but me and Apl often preferred our own space, drew the curtains on the bus, and got faded. We had Public Enemy's Flavor Flav to thank for keeping us in the habit to which we had become accustomed.

He was a flamboyant, crazy-ass dude who was a real pogo stick of energy, always wanting to feel alive as soon as it was daybreak. He never allowed us to sleep in, and became our walking morning wake-up call—typical of the homie who always wore that giant clock around his neck on stage.

He marched on our bus and yelled "YO, Black Eyed Peas! It's time to wake your punk-asses up and smoke some WEEEEEEED!"

Invariably, our buses had pulled into the next hotel in the next new town having traveled through the night, and he was bouncing like a dude who had just walked off stage; hyper-loud and often shirtless. Always wearing that massive, toothy grin on his face.

I was no morning person. "Yo, Flav, give us another fifteen minutes!"

"No, TAB-OOOOO, get your ass out of bed you lazy mothafucka!"

He would clap his hands, turn on the beats, and shake us out of our beds.

I hated him for about five minutes, but always ended up laughing because here was one of the most iconic hype men in hip-hop dragging me out of my top bunk to share some weed for breakfast. It was almost a morning ritual.

One time, Will—probably the spiritually deepest of the Peas—tried engaging him in some mystic conversation about star signs. Will has always had

that depth to him, open to the alternative and the profound. He would talk about anything from cybernetics to astrology, and has always been keen to learn about anything involving self-growth, self-awareness and the bigger picture.

Whereas Flav never struck me as the kind of guy who was into all that shit.

But that didn't stop Will from seeing how deep the waters ran. Sitting opposite him on the bus one morning, an earnest Will suddenly asked: "So, what sign are you, Flav?"

"Huh?" said Flav, sitting and leaning back in a dense cloud of weed smoke that had just circled out of his mouth.

"What astrological star sign are you?"

Flav didn't flinch and his eyes widened. "I am . . . a TARANTULA!"

Will didn't know how to respond: "Oh . . . well . . . I'm a Pisces."

"Man! What the fuck! I don't know a damn thing about astrology!" screamed Flav.

Apl and me were creased up laughing on the couch because we were equally as dismissive. Will once told me I was a Cancer and explained what that said about me—hard shell, soft center, with a vulnerable side or something—and I was like "Whatever."

I'm more the person who wants to feel it, not think about it; to dive into life and not spend too much time trying to work shit out. Life's trials and tribulations have shaped me, not the one-size-fits-all characteristics of a symbolic crab. It's great. It's cool. It's Kumbaya. But it's not for me.

I found my spiritual place through weed, and there were copious amounts of weed on that tour, but that is all it was—weed. There was none of that shit Flav had struggled with in previous years—not that I saw—and none of the debaucherous rock 'n' roll stuff.

Not yet anyway.

I probably smoked about nine blunts a day. That tour was one giant mist rolling across America, leaving me in a perpetual state of easygoing slow motion until performance time. My clothes didn't smell of cologne and my hair didn't smell of shampoo. I was the weed equivalent of Charlie Brown's friend Pig Pen.

After our twenty-minute set, Apl and me loved nothing more than chilling post-performance with the rest of the audience. Being from L.A., we were constantly intrigued by what the vibe of each city was, what wardrobes people were wearing, and what people were saying about the music. We knew the temperature of the West Coast, but wanted to get a feel of the rest of America.

Meanwhile, Will networked, collecting numbers for one scouting mission that was already taking seed in the back of his mind: album number two. He scouted the talent, and we scouted the people. Sitting in the fields with the masses was informative. We called it "research"—using our anonymity to eavesdrop on the audience. The great thing about chilling in the crowd was that we rarely got recognized and we were able to sit back and enjoy the headliners.

Personally, no one had a bigger impact on me than the abstract, frenetic, "mighty infamous" Busta Rhymes. I had been fascinated by this dude ever since he first stepped out with the Long Island hip-hop crew Leaders of the New School in 1989, when he was sixteen, and he made me love L.O.N.S. with songs like "Case of the P.T.A.," "Sobb Story," and "International Zone Coaster." But his ascent really began when he was featured in A Tribe Called Quest's 1992 anthem "Scenario." Even to this day, play that song *anywhere* and it still gets people high. By 1996, Busta had gone solo and blown up on both sides of the Atlantic with two monster hit albums, *The Coming* and then *E.L.E. (Extinction Level Event): The Final World Front.* So it was an honor being on the same bill as him.

As a live performer, he was out on his own. He had always been exciting to watch. His ferocious presence and onstage intensity held the audience, the sun, and the sky in the palm of his hand, commanding attention.

When he came on stage, I went into a trance. Watching him. Studying him. I kicked back on the grass and learned: how he moved, how he carried the fans, how he kept it visually stimulating, how colorfully he dressed, and how his expressive character and facial expressions told a story. He was an all-round entertainer who was an explosion of energy, living up to his label as the "Tasmanian Devil on acid."

I like to think that watching Busta made me a better performer. He showed me by example how to embrace character, turn it on and keep it going. His stamina, rhyme schemes, and energy were incredible.

A couple of times I heard him come off stage and say "Son, I was hurting out there." But you couldn't tell. Whenever I felt sick, tired, lazy, Busta's example made me push through that wall, dig deep, give 1,000 percent and go BOOM! He taught me to take the show from hype to super-ultra-fresh.

Backstage, when Busta slipped the mask off and became Trevor Smith— his real name—he was a big hearted, humble guy whose muscular frame chilled on the sofa, all mellow and almost subdued, as if the very art of his performance had sucked all life and energy from him.

Leave the crowd wanting. Leave yourself spent.

In those days, I always wondered what Busta thought about the Peas, and it would take another twelve years before I found out. We were on the red carpet together for the 2010 BET Awards. Will took the mic on behalf of an interview for Access Hollywood and Busta admitted "There was a time when I didn't get it (the Peas) right away." Then he added: "But you guys kept it busy on stage when people were still coming in and you set the tone from the beginning of the tour, from the first date to the last date, from the first act to the last act, and that pace kind of made us get out there and catch a cardiac arrest!"

• • •

By the time Smokin' Grooves reached the West Coast, I like to think that the Peas had been positively influenced by the experience and artists that surrounded us. We had been on the same field as the champions of the game and part of an all-star team, and that whole ride made us hungrier. It made us want to work harder to get where Wyclef, Cypress Hill, Public Enemy, Gang Starr, and Busta Rhymes all were. Something inspirational rubbed off in the proximity to living examples who became brothers for two months.

"We'll get there. We've got the focus and dedication," we said to one another.

By the time the tour arrived in Los Angeles, we were ready for home.

For me, the L.A. gig was the sweetest of the twenty dates, and not just because it represented a homecoming but because the venue was the Universal Amphitheater, where me and Phoenix had once been booked for the aborted Ron Johnson show. As I saw it, this return was my graduation moment from the dreamer to the maker; life's full circle. Mom, Julio, Celeste, and Josh were all backstage, and it was their first real glimpse of my new world. I couldn't get over how excited Mom was.

I'll never forget providing the backstage tour, and everyone, from security to catering to the sound engineers to the other artists, saying "Hi," and, for me, it was that feeling that I presume bright students get when they show their parents around the university on graduation day and all the teachers and professors acknowledge them.

Acknowledgment. Yeah, that's what it was about.

I also wanted to share this first finish line with Josh.

All our families and friends were there, so, for the last song, I led him onstage before a packed arena. I led him out by the hand and he spontaneously started dancing. The crowd, Busta, and Wyclef started cheering and clapping. *Where the hell did he learn to move like that?* I thought.

Mom told me that when I had been away on tour, Josh had been transfixed in front of the television, watching the Michael Jackson video *Moonwalker,* day in, day out. Then, he got up and mimicked the moves and the moonwalk . . . and they were the moves he rocked on stage at the Amphitheater.

If ever there was a moment where the reality of being a father hit home, it was then. This kid watched and learned in the same way I watched and learned from someone like Busta. Josh's Michael Jackson was my Boogaloo Shrimp. My Mom was his Nanny. And I was the father that I never had in my life.

I looked at Mom at the end of the gig and noted her pride. I saw Julio smiling, too, and I thought about how long it had taken to earn this moment. Because that's what we are all chasing in the end, right? The pride of our parents. At whatever age we earn it.

At home, years of tension moved out and a new-earned respect moved in. Julio started confiding in me man-to-man, and happily helped with advice about future planning. It's like I had grown into the shoes that they had always laid out for me.

Josh's attitude improved, too. He opened up more, he became a happier kid, and he stopped being aggressive. I realized that within all these shifts that had taken place, Josh was now looking up at me, seeking *my* love, seeking *my* approval. And at first, it scared the crap out of me.

The boy in me who had barely grown up started to worry if I could ever measure up. I never, ever wanted to fall short or be a disappointment in my son's eyes. I didn't know what a father was, so how could I become one? I had no fatherly examples to pull from, only Mom and Nanny. And let's face it, I had been a shadow father up until this point.

"What do you want to be when you get older?" Mom had asked Josh one day.

"I want to be like Daddy," he said, without even thinking about it.

This kid who I had spent time with—play-wrestling, watching "Blue's Clues," going to Disneyland and Legoland—had me on the father's pedestal at a time when I didn't know who I was and didn't appreciate what being a father was about. Yet his future and dreams depended on the example I would be.

As Macy Gray once said about how she learned to cope with motherhood: "Having kids, and having to make money, and getting into all the details of a real life, you either grow up and get confident . . . or you jump off a cliff."

I didn't immediately feel the extra weight of that responsibility.

I didn't instantly feel an unknown piece of me wanting to run and hide.

All I felt, as he danced on stage and mimicked my martial arts poses, was pride.

"That's my son!" I shouted into the mic.

At some point during *Smokin' Grooves,* we went to the movie theater to see what we sounded like on the big screen. Warren Beatty had approved "Joints & Jam" for the soundtrack of a movie he had co-produced and directed, *Bulworth*—my first taste of the movie industry.

The movie was about a Democratic senator called Bulworth who delivered his message to the people of California by becoming an MCing politician, and then fell in love with a black woman (Halle Berry) who lived in South Central L.A. It was probably the cheesiest movie we had ever seen, but Interscope compiled the soundtrack and decided to place one of our songs. When you are young and just starting out in the industry, it doesn't matter how wack the movie is. Hearing "Joints & Jam" like that—and knowing it was being played in Regal Cinemas all across America—was sick. I wanted to toss the popcorn, turn up the lights, turn

around, and tell the rest of the audience, "Yo, that's my song!" But all three of us—me, Will, and Apl—remained seated, grinning quietly from ear to ear.

I don't think the movie made back its $30 million budget at the box office, but the soundtrack was cool and went platinum, selling a million copies and bringing us a little extra spending money.

I know that it certainly flicked a switch within us, getting us thinking about more ways we could license our songs with movies, television commercials, and radio jingles. We could have taught Warren Beatty a thing or two about rapping, but he taught us something valuable about the commercial world.

And my favorite line in the whole movie? When Mimi (played by Laurie Metcalf) watched Bulworth lose it on TV and said, "Would we be eligible for an Emmy or a Peabody?" I like to think it was one of those unintended double entendres that was a good omen.

It takes only one seemingly small choice to change the trajectory of the rest of your life. Just like the choice I made at my first rave in late 1998.

The rave was, ironically, at Glam Slam where our journey had begun three years earlier. I had never been interested in this scene before, but, out of part boredom and part intrigue, I decided to tag along with Apl and a few friends because of how sick they had said it was.

Raves were the new underground scene. L.A. was buzzing with talk of secret locations in the desert or warehouses downtown, and the street talk had changed from "You go to that club last night?" to "Shit man, did you go to that rave last night?" The buzz about different rave parties seem to spread by word of mouth, and it all sounded partly inaccessible and illicit—which meant that it had my interest.

At Glam Slam, I walked into that familiar foggy dimness and felt like a human who had landed on Mars. The club was thumping BOOM-BOOM-BOOM to hard trance-techno music. I don't think one person *wasn't* dancing—it was crazy. I didn't immediately realize that I was witnessing the next generation of music seething below the surface. Just as hip-hop was first confined to the streets and clubs, so was the rave scene. Its hypnotic sounds were not even being played on the radio, but it was a natural extension of everything that had gone before it.

If hip-hop was the faster version of disco—rapping over disco beats—then house music was a more uptempo brother of hip-hop, and then Chicago house became Detroit techno became universal trance. It was all dance music by a different name, but I had never seen people flipping out on this frenzied scale before, and especially with no singer-performer as the focal point. There was no stage. No performer. Just one DJ and audience tripping out.

One tribe.

The world was being led into the era of DJs as artists; into the arms and minds of people like Moby who would sell 2.7 million copies of his 1999 album *Play* with the kind of music that sent everyone delirious in Glam Slam.

People with beaming faces danced in a blackness which was pierced by darting webs of green and blue laser lights, and all you could see, against these pulses of rapid light, was some wild horizon of silhouetted hands. People were blowing whistles, waving glow sticks, and wearing crazy hair colors and clown-like makeup. On the floor, others were writhing about caressing themselves, and others cavorted with speakers or the edge of the stage. And the whole place was as hot as a sauna.

That is when I noticed everyone downing water, not alcohol. I couldn't marry the two: the uninhibited craziness with the fact that everyone was on H_2O.

I listened and sucked up the atmosphere. DJ Jean's "Launch" was playing, an iconic rave tune that summed up the hard techno beat; music on amphetamine—deeper, faster, monotonous and more dramatical, with countless buildups. I hovered on the edges near a booth that overlooked the tranced-out orgy and thought it was like a Woodstock of our time.

"YO, DUDE," shouted some guy standing to my left. "I'M ROLLIN'!"

"WHAT THE FUCK DOES THAT MEAN?" I yelled back.

"I'M ON . . . EX!"

"WHAT'S EX?"

"YOU GOTTA TRY IT, BRO—WAIT . . ." and he darted off.

Minutes later, this dude was back with a pill. Weed must have led me into a sheltered knowledge because I had no idea that half of Los Angeles was partying on this drug. There was no way I was saying no. So I got a hit—and swallowed my first Ecstasy tablet.

I washed it down with water.

"FIFTEEN MINUTES . . . THEN YOU WILL SEE!" screamed this random clubber.

But there was no instant high.

This shit is wack, I thought.

I retreated to a leather-padded booth in a dark corner and felt nothing but a sense of anticlimax. I observed the scene around me with a sense of detachment.

Next thing I knew, three girls sidled up next to where I was seated and were all over me, like Dracula's bitches.

"Hey mannnn, it's all lurrrrve," said one.

"You're bee-ewwww-tiful," said another, stroking my hair, caressing my hands.

"Look at your HAIR! Wowwwww!" said the third.

Just then, at the moment when everyone's behavior was starting to freak

me out, this intense wave of joy swept over me; a sensation that rushed through every vein, cell, and fiber.

"Oh fuuuuuck, I AM beautiful . . . look at how beautiful my hands are!" I said.

Suddenly, I was dancing like a crazy person, lost in the same transcendent state as everyone else and soaring above consciousness. I couldn't wipe the smile from my face. I felt on top of the world. It was a confidence I had never known before; the buzz of performing . . . without performing.

I wanted to feel it again—and that was the small choice I made. To start taking Ex. I found myself too preoccupied with the sensation it provided to hear the drumbeat of the distant nightmare I had just set in motion.

Polo Molina had always been one of the family, and I still regard him as the guy who gave me my first chance with the Ron Johnson audition. So when he came to us with an opportunity, we were intrigued. He had previously worked as a waiter at the Red Lobster before taking a job as a delivery driver for Frito-Lay chips but, like all of us, his vision and hunger eyed bigger dreams.

"I've been thinking," he said one day. "You should let me come tour with you guys."

"But you can't! What about your job?" we said.

"I'll quit and I'll make money—and make you guys money at the same time," he said, with the confidence of a hustler. If Will has always been our musical visionary, then Polo has always been the entrepreneurial wizard. And back then, Polo had spotted a new venture: to become the Black Eyed Peas merchandise man.

The next thing we knew, he reached out to one of his contacts and turned up with a box of five thousand white tees and black sweatshirts with the BEP circle logo emblazoned on the front, and sponsored by DaDa Footwear. It was our first-ever line of merchandise created under the company he simultaneously established: Grassroots Productions.

"What can you do with all that?" Will asked, bewildered by the scale of the first order.

"Set up a merch booth and sell it on tour," he said.

I didn't have as much confidence as Polo. Why would anyone want to spend money buying merchandise of a group who had not yet scored a hit single? I thought we needed to be more worried about making a hit record than selling product, but I admired him for putting it down because no one else—including Black Coffee Management—had thought about such a forward-thinking initiative. Not only that but Polo sucked up all the risk, invested his own money, and said he would pay his own ticket on the tour. All we had to do was provide him with the platform. So we agreed that he should quit Frito-Lay and join the Black Eyed Peas on some touring spot dates around Europe.

"Trust me," said Polo, "I'm not wrong—people are going to buy this shit."

We fell in love with London the moment those jet wheels touched down at Heathrow Airport. It had always been our mission to go overseas, and each of us had dreamed about one day playing England's capital city. You only have to look back to "Joints & Jam" to understand our long-term plan from the get-go: *". . . we want some north-bound shit, some south-bound shit, overseas, out of town, London shit . . ."*

We flew coach, but it felt like business class, because it was our debut transatlantic flight and we didn't know the difference. That coach seat with British Airways was the height of luxury as far as I was concerned.

We spent the eleven-hour flight conjuring endless possibilities now that the American borders had been breached. In the skies above the Atlantic, we planned it all: Apl is from the Philippines, we can perform there. If we go there, we can go to Mexico. If we can do Europe, we can do Africa.

We always were the types who wanted to run before we could walk.

But it was also the reason we had wanted Interscope to back us with tour support in the first place, because, in our minds, we were always an international group, not solely an American one.

We were excited about London because we felt that Europe "got" our music, even more than people did at home. It was much more forward-thinking in terms of music and fashion. London set trends. America caught on and followed. That's not my opinion. It comes from the mouth of history.

History is what kept us in a continual state of awe in London. We spent two days saying nothing but "Wow!" as we took in Big Ben, the Houses of Parliament, Buckingham Palace, and the Natural History Museum. We saw our first red telephone box, our first bobby-on-the-beat, our first black cab, and our first London bus. We hardly saw the inside of our hotel in Kensington because we spent all our time sightseeing.

It was weird landing as an American in England for the first time because I had only seen this place via television, and everyone I had seen was a lord of the manor, a royal, or damn rich. I associated the English accent with wealth. So when the young hotel receptionist welcomed us and wished us a "pleasant and memorable stay," I gawped at every precise word that came out of her beautiful mouth.

I looked at this sharp-suited lady and thought, *Wow—she must be rich!*

The weather was cold, damp, and gloomy, and the sky seemed suspended lower than it is in California, but we loved it because there was a sense of seasons. We walked in Regent's Park, where the leaves on the trees were already starting to fall golden and brown. If there is something perpetually showbiz about

L.A., there is something dreamy about being in London, especially for a Southern Californian.

We were also excited about our reception because we had arrived on the back of some serious airplay, and not only on the hip-hop stations. That is the smart thing about U.K. radio. It doesn't compartmentalize its music with pop-only, heavy metal-only, country-only, hip-hop-only stations. It has Radio 1—its biggest, non-commercial, mainstream music station. Its output is one diverse stream of music that reflects the city's tastes and musical heritage.

In 1998, it would play Nelly or Black Eyed Peas and then mix it up with some Gwen Stefani, Celine Dion, Kylie Minogue, or Deacon Blue.

Consequently, our airplay reached a far greater, more varied audience than it had been reaching via the niche markets of America. Maybe that's what explained the amazing reception that awaited us on two chilly September nights at one of London's premier music venues, the Jazz Cafe in Camden Town, a vibrant borough north of Regent's Park.

All roads led to Camden Town if you were a new band in Europe, and, prior to the Jazz Cafe's opening in 1990, the town's rough-and-ready pubs helped launch the likes of the Who, the Kinks, and the Rolling Stones. We were also happy to know that De La Soul—with the backing of one piano—had warmed up the hip-hop stage for us the previous year. But we knew London hadn't seen anything like us before—this insane-looking fusion of hip-hop-jazz backed up with a live band, non-hip-hop clothes, non-old-school, with three MCs who could kill the dance floor.

We were on the bill as part of a monthlong run-up to the MOBO Awards (Music of Black Origin) at Royal Albert Hall in October, and the Cafe was show-casing selected artists. The cool thing about the Jazz Cafe as a venue is that it suited both our lounge-oriented melodies and our jump-around energy. It can be intimate. It can be intense.

It was a sellout on both nights. We filled the main floor and the first-floor balcony with a capacity crowd of four hundred. There had been some buzz in the newspaper pop columns about *"the Black Eyed Peas making their UK debut,"* and it felt like the first real spotlight and sense of momentum had found us in London— five thousand miles away from the hometown where we had spent years trying to build our name.

It felt like instant recognition as opposed to the slow grind of L.A. I think this had a lot to do with Europe not being as cautious or as finicky. Back then, Hol-lywood clubs were full of people trying too hard to be cool and sticking with the tried and true. European clubs were packed with people who couldn't care less about what people thought and let go of themselves, with less rigid musical tastes.

As we rocked our gig, and the Jazz Cafe responded with equal energy, I don't think I had ever enjoyed myself so much on stage. The little-ass stage was a problem because it was the smallest we had ever performed on and we had to squeeze in there with the live band. It got comical at times because it was like we were using skipping ropes. How we didn't get entangled and fall flat on our faces I'll never know. But the atmosphere and our reception were incredible.

We were so close to the audience that we could reach out with our arms and touch the shoulders of the dudes bouncing in the front row. It was sweaty but sick, and we brought that place alive.

"This is where we need to be!" we said when we came offstage.

Apl, whose wide-eyed disbelief said it all, said, "Did you see how they were receiving us? I felt like one of the fucking Beatles out there!"

Outside in the lobby, we went looking for Polo to see how he was faring with slanging the merchandise. He had set up a table inside a farmer's market-style white tent in the lobby, and he was using a megaphone, just as he would at other venues and music festivals where we performed over the next year.

He looked like one of those newspaper sellers you used to see outside London's tube stations, shouting out the headlines. On the floor, he had a ghetto blaster playing our music.

Polo is a natural-born promoter, and he was effective with the merch because he thought outside the box to find ways of creating a spectacle that attracted customers. At future events, he started holding competitions, like spontaneous wet tee-shirt contests or games like "Who Can Bring the Best Weed to the Black Eyed Peas Tent?"—with me and Apl as the judges! Or "Who Can Dance Better than a Pea?" dance contests. Or he got us out there to have photographs taken with fans and to sign shirts.

As the weeks went by, and we finished our spot dates around Europe—including Paris and Amsterdam—Polo handed Will $55,000 in cash.

"What?" said Will. "You made more money than us!"

As a brand, we were up and running, as was Polo. We used the cash to pay for and then reinvest in new merchandise, only bigger and better: hats, hoodies, banners, and more tees. Not that Polo was satisfied with merely being our merch man.

The more he hung with us, the more he witnessed and the more he learned, and you could almost hear his mind ticking. "You know what," he said. "I could manage this . . . I could be your tour manager and blow this up big time."

When Polo said something like that, you knew it was going to happen.

He was the kind of always-thinking whirlwind we ultimately needed. He saw the bigger picture for the brand in the same way we saw it for our music. And, to be honest, the natural organizer in him was pretty much acting out the role of day-to-day manager as it was.

Europe was a great success, and we felt instantly connected to its people. We especially felt at home. "Man, we've got to come back here and record an album. London is where it's at!" we said.

After each gig in England's capital city, we went VIP to a nightclub called Chinawhite and I got shit-faced both nights. When the party finished at that club at 3 a.m., we then stampeded to another club called Paparazzi which partied on till 6 a.m. We had never experienced such endless nightlife in L.A. because most of the clubs closed at 2 a.m., and there was something special about weaving through the streets eating a kebab at those hours. I don't remember much about those two nights apart from the fact that there were, apparently, a lot of well-known British acts in the VIP lounges. I remember meeting some pretty boy band called Blue, but that's about it.

Will and Apl always partied hard, but, unlike me, they knew where the brakes were. I just downed Adios Motherfuckers, Long Islands, and kamikaze shots until I crashed. Being in London also provided the sense that I was on vacation, so I let myself go even more than normal.

I crashed out in a corner one of those two nights and introduced myself to the Australian singer-songwriter Natalie Imbruglia, who was also the star of her home country's soap opera *Neighbors*. I was smashed but not smashed enough not to see how beautiful she was.

"Hey, I'm Taboo from the Black Eyed Peas," I slurred.

She knew, she said. She heard we had played the Jazz Cafe and politely congratulated me.

I leaned across the arm of the couch.

"Do you know how beautiful you are . . . look at your eyes!" I slurred again.

She gave me that startled look that most sophisticated girls give the drunken idiot, but still managed to thank me politely. I was coming off as one of those belligerent old men, and she must have thought I was a real dick. Not surprisingly, that was pretty much the full extent of our conversation, so, after an awkward silence, I got up, said good-bye, and then fell over the arm of the couch.

Back in those days, first impressions in clubs were not my strong point.

On the positive side, the good news was that London is where we left our first faint fingerprint on the musical charts, breaking into the Top 75 for the first time as "Joints & Jam" reached #53. It was nothing to get excited about, but it represented progress. Sadly, the same could not be said for our path in America.

A review of the Jazz Cafe gigs landed in some London culture magazine and summed up our challenge. I didn't keep the publication's name, but I pasted the words into my scrapbook: *"This Californian crew mount an exercise in entertainment rivaling the Royal Variety Performance . . . mesmerizing onlookers as they perform dance routines of arena proportions. The Black Eyed Peas excel at their craft. What remains to be seen now is if the record company can translate such talent into real sales?"*

It was the last thing Will needed to read at the time because things were not looking good.

Behind the Front ultimately charted low on the *Billboard* 200 in the U.S., peaking at #129 and selling 300,000 copies. It was an average start, but we didn't do "average," and it certainly fell short of expectations. When a record label hands you a $500,000 advance, you better shift 500,000 copies.

By early 1999, we had also released three singles—"Joints & Jam," "Fallin' Up" and "Karma"—and not one of them had made an impact. We had not even registered as a faint blip on America's radar.

"We haven't even gone gold—this is not a good look!" said Will, and he kept scratching his head, trying to understand the low record sales. He is a man who likes to feel in control, and, with those sales, the vehicle was spluttering and going wayward. As he reexamined our strategy and direction, the highbrow *Independent* newspaper in London thought it knew the answer:

"The LA-based Black Eyed Peas eschew the gun-toting braggadocio of gangsta-peers, opting for a more socially and politically conscious brand of rap. It is probably this laid-back attitude that has prevented them from breaking into the mainstream . . ."

It also said I was "hip-hop's answer to Happy Mondays' Bez" and poked fun at my "Lawrence of Arabia-style headscarf with shades on top." I read that and thought, *What do these punks know anyway?*

Jimmy Iovine kept reminding us that we needed patience. "I believe in you guys and this is early days, so just keep doing your thing and knock out another album," he said.

But Will was stressed out.

He has always shouldered a lot of the direction and creative responsibility. It frustrated him that we had a critically acclaimed album yet had only sold 300,000 copies.

Jimmy could have carved his faith into his own forearm and drawn blood and it wouldn't have been enough for Will. He paced. He thought. He worried. He strategized. He talked to Black Coffee. He talked endlessly to Interscope. I think he had a Batphone or something with Jimmy, and was constantly staying on top of things even when we were on the road. It was hard for us all because we had never wanted our music to be measured by sales, but the commercial reality was biting.

To understand Will's frustration, you first need to understand something that has been part of him since his dream began: he never walked on the playing field to be a participant, he walked on with a desire to be the greatest. Number one. Unrivaled. That was the pressure he exerted on himself. Always.

I didn't see the need to panic but I've never wanted to be the Muhammad Ali of hip-hop. I had wanted the dream I was living and was hungry for success,

and, in my mind, we had a three-album contract so the only answer was to return to the studio and knock out another album.

The harsh truth is that I also didn't care as much as he did. At that time, my attitude was about having a good time and knowing that I had Mom's crib to retreat to. Looking back now, I had zero knowledge of the commercial pressures Will was shouldering. I relied on him to carry the weight and worry about real life in the same way that I fell back on Mom.

I was the kid who wanted to continually ride the roller coaster and leave the real shit of life to others. That is how emotionally stunted I was.

I guess I didn't want the party to end.

It is amazing how accustomed I became to the breakneck momentum and chaos of touring, so when the treadmill temporarily stopped and dumped us back in L.A., I was at a loose end and a little bored.

I managed to spend quality time with Josh and Mom, and continue our homage to Disneyland, but my energy got restless, and the problem with restlessness is that it starts searching for fresh senses of satisfaction to fill the void. Which might explain why this period represents the starting line for pursuing wanton pleasure: getting high, getting drunk, getting girls.

Week in, week out.

I had a bunch of girls on speed dial even though I had been seeing one particular girl—whose name is not relevant—for a long time. We had met at a college gig in 1998, but I acted like a sicko—the guy in a relationship acting like the single guy, living a double life and cheating left, right, and center. That relationship's importance to me is reflected by my actions. Enough said. What mattered was the chase and the conquest that my swollen ego couldn't resist.

It had not taken long for that ego to notice how being a signed artist attracted attention that I had never before experienced. The shy kid from Rosemead could now have his pick of the litter. It became a pissing contest for me to see how many girls I could get in one week, despite the "relationship" I maintained with lies and deceit.

When friends didn't believe that I was pimping, I was that guy who scrolled through the address book on his cell, hit up different girls and put their voice on speaker just to prove a point.

It was like I was telling the world "See! See what I'm about now!"

Girls were bitches—and, yes, that is how I viewed them. They were playthings that fed my need to feel good about myself.

I, like you, am horrified at reading this now, but that was me back then. That was who I was: mimicking what I perceived to be the cool rock 'n' roll lifestyle.

Ironic when you think about it. As a group, we did everything to put distance between us and the stereotypes of hip-hop. As a person, all I thought about was living up to the stereotype of the rock 'n' roll wild boy. I was a pathetic slave to the false notoriety of Hollywood.

I tried working out the "Why?" long before writing this book—with a therapist, during counseling—and the nearest explanation I arrived at was that, somehow, substance abuse filled the void that was left once a sense of achievement had been satiated. It has also been suggested to me that something in me didn't feel worthy of being a signed artist. I don't know about that. Sometimes, the reality is so twisted that I'm not sure there's much truth to understand. What's fucked up is fucked up. End of story.

All I know is that the addictive element of my personality chased a new obsession, and the more I indulged, the more I wanted it.

The more I wanted it, the more I needed it.

I was now smoking weed on a daily basis and popping an Ecstasy pill every other night. I had gone from smoking an eighth to a quarter-pound of weed, and then from a quarter-pound to half a pound and so on. Ecstasy tablets became easy to get, too. I had met this guy named Bubba in an L.A. club and had asked him for some pills after my Glam Slam experience.

"I've got as much as you can take," he said with a smile.

"You serious?"

"I'm serious—if you've got the dough?"

"I've got the dough," I told him, interpreting his question as doubt.

I bought twenty on the spot.

I had randomly found myself a supplier. Suddenly, it was open season and easy access to satisfy an illicit itch that would soon become habitual and excessive. I didn't care what people thought. I only cared about pushing life to the extreme; the thrill of finding the edge and teetering on it.

If we were on the road, I took my vices onto the bus.

If we were in Los Angeles, I wanted to be out almost every night.

Monday, I went to Joseph's; Wednesdays was Las Palmas; Thursdays was the Latin Lounge, and Saturday was AD. I drank Adios Motherfuckers like someone who had heard that the state of California was about to announce Prohibition the next day, and then I moved on to Champagne and Chambord, Long Island Iced Teas and, when eating in Japanese restaurants, I downed sake after sake.

In between times, I drank and got high with Deja at his place, or we'd drive around the freeways of Los Angeles, drunk, smoking weed, and rapping to beats playing on the stereo. I can't remember the times we drove out of our minds. We never stopped to think about the consequences because, within all that hyperactivity, I was having "fun" and being Mr. Popular, and Deja was hanging onto the same magic carpet ride.

I didn't realize that I was losing myself in the process. I was more inter-

ested in celebrating the false persona of Taboo from the Black Eyed Peas than in honoring Jaime Luis Gomez.

Outside of the studio and away from the stage, this period was the most fun I'd ever had, and I was deaf to the echoes of Dad's early life—the genes of a drinker now dripping into mine; that invisible and unconscious poisoned chalice being the one thing he had ever given me in life.

Maybe that's why Mom noticed the slippery slope long before anyone else—because she had seen it all before.

She was asleep in bed one night when she heard me stumbling about, so she got up.

I had been on another drinking and drugging binge and had woken in the wee hours to go for a pee. I was standing there, eyes closed, still swaying, releasing this giant arch of pee when the light turned on, and Mom screamed.

It turned out that I was peeing in the kitchen cupboard where the trash can was kept.

I remember the next morning for not remembering anything and for Mom's reaction. I walked into breakfast like nothing had happened. "Morning, Mom!"

She ignored me and left the room.

It took Celeste to remind me what had happened in the early hours. "She's worried about you, Jaime," she said.

I was embarrassed, and apologized, but I didn't see it as a big deal. I excused it as one of those sleepwalking accidents that happens to countless people. That's what happens when you're in denial. You ignore the small, embarrassing incidents without realizing that they are only building into one big, destructive event.

By mid-1999, I was ignoring all the small incidents. I didn't see the harm in having one more drink or swallowing more illegal chemicals. The dream I had chased all my life now became almost secondary to the warped experience of getting fucked up. I had boarded the runaway train stashed with bitches, drugs, and drink, and those trains shuttle you so fast across the Rubicon and into the longest tunnel that, before you know it, there is no turning back. There is only a guaranteed derailment at some unknown point in time.

For me, that point lay another nine years down the tracks and so, year after year, my intake of God-knows-what would continue increasing. I was putty in the hands of my own masochism.

Then life decided to play a sick joke. It would introduce me to the love of my life at a time when I wasn't ready for her. But that's what life does—it tests you at your weakest. At the crossroads where you decide to turn either right or left. It was as if God and Nanny were looking down at my behavior and asking, "Really, Jimmy? You *really* want to live like this?"

GETTING WARPED

It's fair to say that the deep and meaningful stuff of life hadn't yet crossed my mind. So I didn't give much thought to life's timing when Jaymie Dizon, a young fashion student, walked out of Dublin's, a club off Sunset Boulevard, and we crossed paths on the sidewalk. We locked eyes, and she was another possibility as far as I was concerned; another mistress behind the back of the "serious" girlfriend who I was still stringing along. I was not aware enough to view her as the angel-in-disguise.

The Peas had performed at the club earlier that evening before the late-night crowd arrived, and I happened to be leaving at the same time Jaymie decided to head home. I was twenty-four years old and she was twenty.

She was a beautiful Filipina with reddish hair, and when she smiled, I saw she had braces on her teeth. When a girl can still manage to look sexy wearing braces, it's something special.

As the hunter, I approached her with some lame line straight out of Joey's mouth from *Friends:* "Hey, how you doing?"

I didn't have much else to say because we were outside, so there were no dance moves to pull and no drinks to buy, and I didn't have a great game to spit anyway. The Black Eyed Peas hadn't taken off and I was still the dude living at home, crashing on his mom's couch. But we got to talking and I liked what I saw.

Jaymie is from the Philippines and had lived in Eagle Rock for a bit before moving to San Diego with her mom. Her parents wanted to ensure she received a solid education and didn't want her growing up in a bad area.

When we met, she had recently moved to Riverside and was in transition from being a nursing student to becoming a fashion student at FIDM—the Fashion Institute of Design & Merchandising, where she was about to start studying a merchandise marketing degree.

I don't know what my blah-blah-blah was, but, if you ask Jaymie today, she'll say that her first impression was that I came on strong. That is probably because I was expecting this spontaneous chat to immediately lead to her bedroom. That was my usual M.O. at the time: I was intoxicated, the girl was intoxicated, so let's go back and do whatever it is adults do.

There was a strip club called Strip Vale next door to Dublin's, and we parked our asses on a cement block outside with its shrubbery behind us and its pink-and-blue neon sign above. It seemed an appropriate backdrop for the life I had been living.

We did the usual small talk and she even said she had heard of the Black Eyed Peas, so I thought this particular conquest was a certainty.

"Right, then," she said, standing up. "We should get going."

I was convinced we were going back to her place.

"So here's my number . . . give me a call next week," she said, and she left with a friend.

She played hard to get, and I liked the challenge. It stretched out the chase.

Jaymie lived in Riverside and I lived in Rosemead, so that "long distance" facilitated my weird trip to keep a girlfriend in tow and one or two others on my arm. I had options in a town where people—professionally and personally—like to keep their options open. I guess that was the moment when life gave me a choice: to get smart or keep on playing dumb.

I decided to play dumb.

I decided that I wanted to have my cake and eat it.

As a child, Josh's abiding memory of me as a father is hard to hear.

This is what he says: "All I remember is you leaving. Having a black bag packed and walking out the door. You always kneeled in front of me before going and said, 'Dad's going to be gone for a while, but remember that I am doing all this for you.' All I wanted to do was watch television. But then, when your back was turned, I watched you leave."

I think it's the stuff that we *don't* communicate as kids that our parents need to know. The stuff I didn't tell my mom. The stuff Josh never told me. The stuff we're not aware of when it matters the most. Back then, reality was easy to leave behind the closed door of home, and push outside the rolling bubble of touring.

Between 1998 and 1999, Los Angeles was my intermittent stopover location because the touring juggernaut kept us focused on the endless promotion, forever sounding its horn in a new city and state. I lived out of the bag that Josh always saw in my hand. As much as I felt pangs of guilt, touring got me out of the box of Rosemead and opened my eyes.

By now, we had been on the road with Smokin' Grooves, the SnoCore rock tour, selected dates on the Lyricist Lounge, and a stint supporting OutKast. Then, in the late summer of 1999, we jumped back on the tour bus to join the punk movement.

Kind of.

We were booked for another traveling festival across America: the Vans Warped Tour—a heavy punk-fest going into its fourth year. In 1999, it had decided to diversify by incorporating other genres which is how we, Ice-T, and Eminem were invited to bring hip-hop to the roster in an odd juxtaposition alongside the likes of Suicidal Tendencies, Agnostic Front, Sevendust, Pennywise, and Blink-182.

I remember this outdoor tour as the first time we landed sponsors.

SilverTab—owned by Levi's—apparently liked our nonviolent stance that didn't cause controversy or riots. Which was weird when lined up alongside a motley cast of characters whose punk-rock music was riotous and whose followers seemed hell-bent on trashing everything in sight.

One hour into the first date and we knew it was an alien planet, far removed from anything we had witnessed in hip-hop. Everyone was pogoing, colliding in the mosh pit, crowd-surfing; savage faces contorted and screamed with unadulterated punk abandon to hard guitar and fast drums. From backstage, all I saw was a throbbing mass of rainbow-colored hair, skinheads, and tattoos with pierced noses, ears, and lips glinting in the sun, bodies drenched in sweat.

All artists were primed that missiles could be thrown at a second's notice, be it a projectile of phlegm or a half-filled beer bottle. In Denver, Vandals singer Dave Quackenbush was mid-set when some idiot hurled a bottle. It flew. He caught it. Then he said, "A free bottle—thanks, kids! You're not just a bunch of jerks after all."

The place went berserk.

And I loved it.

The combustible energy of that tour was sick. At the height of summer, it was always sweltering, and the heaving crowds were often hosed, water cannon style.

Within that chaos, I wondered how we would be received, and at first, we got the kind of looks that said, "You don't belong here." No one knew what to

make of my masked martial arts vibe, and Will and Apl's old-man vintage clothing. A review in the *Orlando Sentinel* summed it up when it noted *"the Black Eyed Peas received more gawking than mass dancing."* But we regarded it as just another opportunity to win people over.

That said, we were not encouraged by Ice-T's experience. He had gone on before Pennywise and the crowd thought he was wack. "RAP SUCKS! RAP SUCKS!" they chanted. "PENNYWISE! PENNYWISE! PENNYWISE!" they demanded.

Hip-hop's union with punk did not seem to have "forever" written all over it.

It was hard not to feel a little apprehensive about taking the Peas' progressive hip-hop into this Sid Vicious den for the opening date in San Antonio, Texas.

Before going on, the three of us huddled into a circle with the band and psyched ourselves. "Let's rock these mothafuckas!" we yelled. "Let's show 'em what we can do!"

We unleashed all that we had.

Even if our lyrics were not antagonistic and railing against society, we were hip-hop exhibitionists. I actually preferred the energy of Warped because it carried that "fuck you, I don't care" vibe. No guidelines. No rules. Anything goes.

It seemed fitting that when the Warped buses rolled into Florida and the city of Pompano Beach, police issued an edict to ban all onstage profanity. You can imagine how that went down and wasn't respected. It certainly wasn't applicable in Salt Lake City, where we had some serious racial shit to deal with.

Six tattooed, snarling skinheads greeted our arrival on stage with the bigotry we half-expected: "Fuck you niggers! Get the fuck back to Africa."

One Californian, one Filipino, and one Latino played through the abuse. We just played harder and faster as the crowds that filled both flanks stood defiantly with both hands in the air, flipping us the finger. We faced a thousand raised fingers before we ever saw candles or lighters being held aloft. We faced some difficult audiences initially, but soon enough, more and more Warped followers got into our sound, and the bigots were silenced.

The *Boston Herald* said we "were not a side-dish and punk had found its groove." What always sealed the deal was "Head Bobs." It was the jump-around anthem that punk rockers loved, and I just lost it—jumping on the speakers, running back and forth the length of the stage, surfing the crowd.

Apl climbed the amplifier stack and got the biggest cheer as he stood King Kong style atop the stack, and then leaped into a sea of outstretched arms. Four mad minutes of "Head Bobs" allowed us to rock it with the frenzy of punk stars, and leave stage with roars ringing in our ears.

In our books, that was some turnaround.

■ ■ ■

If there was one special quality about Warped, it was the backstage camaraderie. Anyone was allowed to play the warm-up or main stage, depending on what performance order prevailed on that particular day. The headliners, Blink-182, didn't care. The attitude really was that loose.

We were no longer the "Good Samaritans," either. With more white boys on this tour, things got a little crazier than weed. I tried cocaine for the first time. It was hard to refuse when people boarded each other's buses and started cutting up lines on the kitchen tops.

That shit tasted weird, and it made me roll my jaw and grind my teeth, but I'd found another string to my drug-taking bow, and I had acquired the taste. I didn't care what I was putting in my body. I was the kid who might as well have shoved his fingers inside the electrical socket just to see what I could feel.

We no longer lost the girls to some other group, either. The chicks were more than happy to hang with the Peas on this tour, and there were always random chicks up for a party—more notches on the bedpost.

The major pastime was basketball. Zebrahead, Blink-182, and Sevendust were our main rivals on the portable basketball court that the band had decided would be a good way to kill time. So we set up in parking lots in every city, and the Peas had a pretty mean team thanks to the ringers from the band: Terry Graves, Mike Fratantuno, and our newest additions—keyboardist Printz Board and guitarist George Pajon.

Printz was probably the most competitive, and during one match in Boise, Idaho, he made sure Zebrahead remembered he was there. Their vocalist, Ali Tabatabaee, went for a layup, and Printz, who is a thickset guy with dreds, came underneath and swatted his shot, hard. Ali toppled backward, slipped on loose gravel, and hit the deck. We knew by the way he fell that it was nasty. As he lay there screaming, no one wanted to touch him until the on-site paramedics arrived.

Printz was upset when he saw Ali being loaded into the back of an ambulance. He felt even worse when word came back that it was a broken pelvis, forcing Zebrahead out of the tour in only week two. We didn't let Printz forget that he had wiped out a fellow artist on tour. Very punk-rock behavior! Thankfully, that was the only disastrous moment I can remember from all the tours across America.

Blink-182 became our main *compadres,* as fellow Californians from San Diego. Travis Barker, Tom DeLonge, and Mark Hoppus always hung on our bus, cracking us up with their sarcastic sense of humor.

Even on stage, that humor counted. Once, when they were met with a lackluster reaction from one hating audience, they ended their spot with the words "THANK YOU! Thank you for not clapping—we really appreciate that!"

Those guys were a lot of fun, and Travis Barker was one cool cat and an incredible drummer. I remember when he first took off his shirt and I saw his entire

torso covered in this tapestry of tattoos. Even though it wasn't gangster tattoos, I hadn't seen body art like that since my childhood in Dog Town.

Travis was a hip-hop head, and this is probably why we hit it off, because he, too, wanted to explore other genres of music outside the box of pop punk. He even confessed to listening to more hip-hop than he did his own music, which made me laugh. After the tour wrapped, he invited me to his house when it was featured on *MTV Cribs* and I was one of his friends that was also featured. "Yo, this is my boy Taboo from Black Eyed Peas!" he said, introducing me on camera.

It was an odd way to make my debut on MTV.

It was probably one of the most ego-free tours I have known. But a few dates into the tour, it was noticed that one particular artist was always conspicuous by his absence.

"So why's Eminem not hanging with us?" someone asked.

It had been sharply observed by a few that he only emerged from his bus to perform, and then walked offstage and headed straight back to his bus, his head down, draped in a white towel.

"Maybe he just thinks he's too cool for us?" someone else said. There was some definite ill feeling taking root.

By now, the chubby white kid from Detroit who had opened at Florentine Gardens was a trim superstar who had exploded overnight. His debut album, *The Slim Shady LP*, impacted at #2 on the *Billboard* 200 chart and had sold almost two million copies, including 283,000 copies in its opening week. His success would become so humongous that Interscope would, in 1999, grant him his own label, Shady Records, and his first signing was his own rap crew D12.

The other half of D12 was a talented MC called Proof—Eminem's homeboy and hype man, who was a really cool guy, always easy to talk to.

It was his smiling face that greeted me when I knocked on Eminem's bus to have a chat because me being the person I am, I didn't want any bad shit to fester. "Who is it, Doody?" I heard Eminem say to Proof.

"It's Taboo."

"Come on in, brother," said Proof, one of the select few allowed close to Eminem.

Proof could not have been more friendly, but it felt like he was playing the role of gatekeeper. I thought back to how Flavor Flav had burst onto our bus without knocking, and how everyone on Warped had treated the convoy of buses like a giant open house.

Eminem was sitting on the couch, wearing a white tee and Jordan shorts, with his feet up. He was writing down lyrics on paper.

It was the first time we had seen each other since Florentine Gardens, and I congratulated him on his success. He was humble and clearly didn't wish to make a big deal of it. "So whassup, Tab?" he asked.

"Well, you know, you've been a bit secluded, and there are some on the tour who are starting to think you're antisocial," I said.

He stopped, put down his pen, and immediately became awkward. "It's hard, dude," he said. "Everyone wants a piece of me right now and I dunno . . ."

He looked to Proof for guidance, shrugged his shoulders, and continued, ". . . I just want to be private, you know."

"I just don't think it's cool to cut yourself off. You need to hang with us more," I said.

He shifted around uncomfortably, speaking about the "need" for security and the "embarrassment" of how that looked.

"I just don't want everyone to think I'm playing the big shot," he said.

This wasn't a guy who was so arrogant that he was on his own dick. He had holed himself away because it was easier than dealing with the trappings of instant celebrity—a security detail that made someone naturally shy stand out as something special. He may have been an exhibitionist on stage, but not as a private person.

"Dude, we're all artists here," I said. "Everyone understands—no one's going to hound you and ask for photos. Just give it a chance, yeah?"

I admire Eminem for what he did next: he emerged from his bus-cave to apologize to the other members of the tour, and at the next city, he started hanging out and playing ball. He was never going to become the great extrovert, because that's not his style, but he made an effort, and, after his own performances, he stayed behind and watched everyone else perform.

I felt sorry for him, because it was clear that his rapid success and fame had become almost alienating. Plus, he was under immense pressure to produce a second multiplatinum album to follow up the first. There was a lot riding on his shoulders. I saw how fame had made him retreat and become overcautious.

If that's what fame is about, I don't want to be famous, I thought to myself.

Even to this day, my mission is not about chasing fame or being the best-known Black Eyed Pea, because that is not my calling. All I have ever wanted is to be successful—the most successful I can be in what I do—performing.

Today, I better understand Eminem's internal pressure cooker. When an album has launched you into another orbit, the fear of failure is the worst kind of stalker. It no longer becomes about meeting your own expectations but the expectations of *others:* the fans, the label, the management, the media.

Back then, we were facing pressure at the other end of the spectrum, and when you measured Eminem's first-week sale of 283,000 albums sold against our total sale of 300,000 for *Behind the Front,* that pressure was obvious. Our second album, *Bridging the Gap,* had to live up to its name.

When we returned to L.A., I *needed* to party.

I loved the eternal high of being on tour—both drug-induced and performance-enhanced—and I wanted to re-create that feeling upon reentry to an ordinary life in Rosemead. I found it hard to return to mundane days that ended with me still sleeping on Mom's couch.

I felt like the little boy returning home from an adventure.

The money that I had banked from the road—the $2,000 to $5,000 per tour—was my party money to return me to the high.

I still wasn't paying rent or bills at Mom's, so I was comfortable, because I hoarded money the way a squirrel hoards nuts. I saved out of fear of losing it all. With zero prudent experience, I did not know how long it would have to last, so if I *could* hustle, I *would* hustle, and it seemed easier to get shit for free than put a dent in my savings.

Brands and companies throw free shit at you all the time as a signed artist, and that perk had started to happen in 1999. I was given boxes and boxes of free snowboarding gear from brands like Foursquare and Circa—snowboards, beanies, goggles, shell jackets, shoes. As a Californian who never went to the mountains, it was useless to me, but the hustler in me knew it had a high exchange value.

I made a phone call to my Ecstasy dealer Bubba.

I then made a call to Deja, asking him to do me a favor, without telling him what was going down.

I didn't want my best friend thinking I was a fiend. Which I was. But I was expert at hiding the truth from even the closest people to me. As Deja says today, "Everyone knew you were starting to get crazy, but no one knew *just how crazy.*"

I dropped the snowboard boxes at his grandmother's house in Alhambra, because that was where he was staying, caring for her after her recent illness.

He couldn't believe the merchandise I was handing over. "What's it all for?" he asked.

"You just need to drop this off and pick some shit up for me," I said.

I was using my best friend as an unwitting conduit for my dirty pawning trade, and it didn't even trouble my conscience. Deja rang Bubba and met at some faraway gas station in San Dimas off the 210 freeway.

As Deja today explains: "I give this dude the boxes and he gives me one of those yellow Perspex prescription jars. That's when I realized there were about sixty blue Ecstasy pills, and I started shitting myself because now I've got an hour's drive ahead of me and if I get pulled over by the cops for anything, it's a classic 'possession with intent to distribute' even when I had no intention to distribute shit. I was the errand boy holding the gun. I couldn't believe you'd put me in that position. So when I got back to Rosemead, I took five pills out for myself and thought *Fuck you.*"

Deja pretty much said as much when he rang me on arrival. "Yo, man, don't you ever ask me to do that shit again."

I apologized, but I didn't much care, because I had what mattered: the pills to party. I picked them up from Deja's grandmother's and then drove straight to the Flamingo Inn Motel in Rosemead to book myself a room and start the party.

From the outside, it looked like one of those motels that Thelma and Louise would flee to: it had pink doors to match its flamingo motif and was situated off Garvey Avenue.

This was my "party motel," where I took girls and took drugs and had some crazy times. It seems perverse now that I wouldn't give Mom rent to pay bills at the house but I happily spent money on seedy motel rooms to ensure a good time.

In my reconstruction of the tour-bus experience, I went on weekend benders.

I would check in on Friday evening, drop an Ex, turn up the music, and party all night. I did this almost every weekend. I took the "girlfriend." I took friends. The company didn't matter—I just wanted to get crazy.

We hit it hard, always going through the night until 9 a.m., and then spending all of Saturday in bed, coming down, feeling horrible, and recovering. Then, on Saturday night, I dropped more pills and partied in the same loop.

I started going to raves with Mooky, and we wore those zany glasses and finger lights. We earned the nickname "the twin peaks," because when we reached the peak of our high, we just lost it and danced till dawn. I wanted to always be in that "purple haze" that Jimi Hendrix sang about. He found it via LSD. I found it via Ex.

This was what it felt like to be on top of the world.

It made me happy.

I told myself that it made me happy.

And when my senses became immune to the buzz of one Ex, I popped a second.

When I plateaued on two, I took three; always wanting to climb higher and higher.

The morning after was always ugly, so the only way out of that feeling was to rediscover the "wow" from the night before. It was like I had mislaid a precious item—a watch, a piece of jewelry, a cell phone—and I panicked over its loss, frantic to get it back. Then I'd find it and feel like a king again.

Welcome to the vicious circle.

This was addiction—unknown, unnamed, unacknowledged—beginning its invasion.

An army of demons on the march, unseen.

■   ■   ■

We hit the studio in September to record *Bridging the Gap,* and that kept us occupied for four months, even if it didn't stop us bouncing around America, because we recorded a gang of collaborations with other artists at studios in L.A., New York, and Detroit. The latter was where we worked with the late and great hip-hop producer J Dilla whose legend remains carved into albums by A Tribe Called Quest, De La Soul, Busta Rhymes, and Janet Jackson. It was an honor to work with him even if that track, which I've now forgotten, didn't make the final cut.

From the start, we felt this second album was blessed because of the star quality that agreed to be featured and because of the effortless way the inspiration and music came together. If *Behind the Front* had established the platform, then *Bridging the Gap* would demonstrate a musicality that crossed all divides—bridging the gap between bossa nova and Latin, rock and hip-hop, soul and calypso, jazz and pop.

We wanted to deliver an international flavor and take this album to the wider world, beyond America, beyond Europe. This album was designed to be the bridge that connected us with all continents, and we eyed Australia and New Zealand for the first time.

Will's existing friendships and his relentless networking on Smokin' Grooves pulled in a collaborative lineup that meant I couldn't wait to get started each day: Wyclef Jean (played guitar and produced "Rap Song"); DJ Premier (produced "BEP Empire"); De La Soul (featured on "Cali to New York"); (Les Nubians and Mos Def (featured on "On My Own"); Esthero (featured on "Weekends"); and the unmistakable Macy Gray (featured on "Request Line").

Some people gave us stick by saying we were trying to ride the coattails of established chart-makers, but that was a low blow in a year when De La Soul had also hooked up with Chaka Khan, Common collaborated with MC Lyte, and Mos Def conspired with Busta Rhymes. When the opportunity arose to work with artists of such high caliber, it would have been crazy to say no. That's what we signed up for—to work with some of the best in the industry. The fact that opportunities presented themselves on our second album was one of those unexpected bonuses.

We arrived at Paramount Studios with our usual collection of fifty tracks written on the road, and then whittled that number down to the best fifteen. The end result was a cleaner-sounding album, still hip-hop but less underground, and also more up-tempo and energetic to reflect our time on the road.

We reunited with our sister Macy Gray, and she walked back through the doors of Studio C a transformed woman. She had gone meteoric with her song "I Try" which had sold millions on its way to becoming one of the biggest smashes of 1999 in Europe, and would later chart in America and earn her a Grammy for Best Female Pop Vocal Performance. Some music critics suggested we were opportunists trying to cash in on Macy's success, but they forgot, or didn't know, that she had been our sister when she was an unknown.

The best thing about Macy was that she returned to the same studio exactly the same person, with those big feet of hers rooted to the floor. Not even she could believe her own success in the year since we had last collaborated.

"My life's been like DISNEYLAND!" she shrieked, and then cackled with laughter.

For the album, we had wanted to do a second collaboration that paid homage to the Beatles by using a sample from "Baby You're a Rich Man," where we wanted to use the line *"How does it feel to be one of the beautiful people/Now that you know who you are . . ."* But, for whatever reason, Paul McCartney did not clear it. That's why we eventually ran with *"Request Line"*—an ode to ringing a radio station and requesting a song from the resident DJ.

Macy was one of the family even though she was closest with Will, and she clearly wanted more of our company, because one day she arrived at the studio all buzzed and shouted out, "Yo, Black Eyed Peas! You want to come on tour with me?"

That was her way of repaying us for the platform we had first provided with *Behind the Front.* We were booked as her supporting act for November 2000.

But first we had to cut the album that we would be promoting on that tour, hoping that *Bridging the Gap* would blow up just as much as Macy's *On How Life Is,* which had sold two million copies.

The two collaborations that I enjoyed the most on the second album were with my biggest inspirations—De La Soul and hip-hop's true icon, DJ Premier. These were two pinch-me-I'm-dreaming moments, and remain highlights of my career.

It was quite something to be singing on a track with the same boys whose posters had once adorned my bedroom wall, and it seemed fitting that the song we did with De La Soul was called *"Cali to New York,"* because it was a long-distance collaborative effort.

They laid down the vocals in New York, sent over the files, and we mixed it together from our studio at Paramount in Hollywood. That is how 90 percent of collaborations work in this day and age, creating the magical impression that artists are in the studio together. When I heard their voices on our track, that took some absorbing. And I can't lie: I thought back to that moment with Mr. Shah when I was kicked out of Pablo. If you had told that crushed version of me that I would be standing in a vocal booth laying down my verses on a collaboration with De La Soul, I would have had you committed.

And so would Mr. Shah.

But when shit like that goes full circle and returns with its reward, they are the moments when you thank God that you listened to no one but yourself.

Then there are other moments when you wonder what you have done to earn the right to certain opportunities: like the time we walked into a hallowed den off 37th Street in New York—D & D Studios—to work with a producer, DJ Premier, who, in my eyes, is the Quincy Jones of hip-hop. And for this collaboration, our mutual schedules allowed us to come together in the same studio, and it was an unforgettable experience. D & D was the ultimate hip-hop studio, the mainstream equivalent of Abbey Road Studios in London or Sun Studio in Memphis. It was where some of the greatest hip-hop albums were made, with the likes of the Notorious B.I.G. and Jay-Z, and DJ Premier was the resident alchemist.

We instinctively wanted to raise our game the moment we walked in. It was like stepping into a moody hip-hop video—thick with underground grime, graffiti all over the walls, and dudes free-styling in the corner. This became our weed-fogged heaven for the next two days.

DJ Premier was a hulking figure who worked with a cap swiveled back to front on his head, and we were in awe as he scratched and mixed "BEP Empire," taking bits from "Joints & Jam" and mixing it all into a new song. His hands moved like lightning, and his instincts darted around that deck as he took ingredients from one beat and chopped up pieces from another and threw them all together. Standing beside him, interacting with him as he wove our music like that, gave me goose bumps.

When we wrapped it up and returned to L.A., everyone thought we had packaged one special album. We listened to it at Paramount Studios—the different names, the disparate musical elements, the hip-hop, the hip-pop—and we could not have been more excited.

Jimmy Iovine had always said that because we were not classical hip-hop types, our songs had to be so much stronger, and we felt we had produced something adventurous and innovative. We were convinced that we had delivered an album that exceeded our expectations for its February 2000 release. When we emerged into daylight after four months in the recording tunnel, we felt everything was perfect.

When it comes to relationships, I am not so sure about that romantic cliche that says, "You just know when you meet The One." That sounds very Hollywood to me. If there is a connection, a relationship has to be built like all empires—slowly, painstakingly, and with care. No one just goes from the starting point of meeting to the stage of "Whoa—and here's your empire."

We need to lay the foundation, build it up, work hard, and grow strong.

At least, that is what Nanny always said.

What she *didn't* say was lay the foundation, build . . . and then demolish it.

That would become my warped interpretation, and one I acted out with Jaymie.

In fact, it would become a recurring theme in my twenties.

Get close to me and I'll push you away.

Show me goodness and I'll choose the poison instead.

I'd enjoyed several dates with Jaymie, and she was serious about honoring a committed relationship. The problem was that I wasn't. Even if I told her otherwise. I was still on some stupid-ass trip thinking that what she didn't know wouldn't harm her, so I kept juggling the obligation of the old girlfriend and had two other girls at the same time. I was two-timing, three-timing, four-timing, and still managed to sleep at night. I thought I was being the classic player when, in actuality, I was the classic, top-of-the-line jerk playing with people's hearts and messing with minds.

Jaymie was so good to me that I took it for granted. The most telling sign of that imbalance was December, 1999, when she asked me what I wanted for Christmas.

I was all about these new Air Jordan sneakers that had just come out in blue and black. "But don't worry about it," I said. "They are too expensive. Get me what you think I'd like."

When I went to her place for Christmas, she pulled out not just one but two pairs of Jordans, in both colors. She had been doing some freelance PR work outside her studies and had worked her ass off to afford this surprise.

You know what I bought her? Some chopsticks in a box.

The false gratitude she gave me hid the disappointment on her face, and I felt awful because it told her everything that I didn't have the nuts to admit.

Inevitably, the wheels started to come off my game plan, because the closer you get to someone, the more demands they make on your time, and the double life becomes harder to juggle. Eventually, she had enough of my bullshit and moved on. She got on with her life, advancing from being an intern to having a position with a company called Michael Stars before going on to work in fashion PR. She got her shit together faster than I ever could.

She broke off all contact.

Speak to Jaymie today and she will tell you that she always saw the good in me. "I always knew what you were capable of," she says now. "But I don't think you did."

Come the end of 1999, I celebrated the turn of a new century by getting high on Ecstasy and shit-faced on Adios Motherfuckers. Which is why I still cannot remember where I was or who I celebrated the millenium with.

All I knew was that the year 2000 represented our big chance with our second album, and that is where everybody's focus remained.

CHANGE IT UP

Our songs have been leaked!"

For a millisecond, the truth was difficult to absorb as our boy Dante Santiago was on the other end of the phone, sounding sucker punched.

"Tab, our entire fucking album is all over the Internet!" he said, ramming it home.

That was how I discovered modern technology had sneaked up from behind and mugged us in broad daylight. Will, and others, found out around the same time, at some frat party when a student DJ started playing our songs—three months before the official September release of *Bridging the Gap.* But for me, Dante was the bearer of bad news, after he went shopping in downtown Los Angeles and heard "Weekends" playing in the background at some shoe store.

"I didn't understand what was going on at first," he explained, "so I went up to the salesmen, asked where they got the music from, and this dude says, 'Online from Napster.' And all our songs were up there."

This was still the era when most people bought that old-fashioned concept called the CD. The idea of shopping for music anywhere other than Tower Records, Sam Goody, the Warehouse, or Virgin was foreign, because downloading music was in its embryonic—and illegal—stages. But Sean Parker's Napster experiment was ahead of its time.

Not that I could wrap my head around it.

Listening to music online? What's that all about?

It seemed crazy to me that our closely guarded album was now sitting on an untold number of home computers.

Napster.com was a file-sharing service that soon became dirt among artists, and no one put it better than Metallica's drummer Lars Ulrich when he said, "Sharing is such a warm, cuddly and friendly word but this is not sharing—it is duplicating."

Metallica and Dr. Dre were in the same boat as we were, and so was Madonna with the title track from her new album *Music*. But knowing that we were not alone on the victims' log didn't make the crime any easier to swallow. Especially when it soon became clear that we were powerless the moment our songs became available to the masses who had already downloaded our albums for free. Our songs were "old news" before officially being born, and Napster had stolen our thunder as well as our music.

We had been excited about *Bridging the Gap's* prospects. Then some tech-savvy student sits in a bedroom somewhere, dreams up some file-sharing concept, and we get killed.

Aside from the sick-to-the-stomach feeling of being cheated, the main emotion was confusion. We felt violated that our one piece of art—months in the making—was stolen and now hanging in someone else's gallery before we had even had the chance to display it, showcase it, and sell it. And there we were, left standing on the sidewalk, noses pressed against that gallery's windows, wondering "How did we get here?"

The inevitable after-the-fact inquiry took place, and we all met at the new Black Eyed Pea headquarters that Will had leased and converted from an old dentist's office into a recording studio with an office. This HQ, located between Glendale and Los Feliz, was christened "Stewchia" (some weird wordplay on "studio") and is today both the Grassroots and Dipdive main offices, reflecting Will's vision that this would become a music empire.

Not that the word "empire" was on anyone's lips that summer of 2000.

Will, Apl, me, and Dante joined Yon Styles and Eddie Bowles at the office, with the label on the phone on a speaker in the middle of the table. Will was really bent out of shape because we were not in control of our own music, and he, more than any of us, hates being out of control.

I don't think I have ever known such a somber mood in the camp. But, as a group, we have always agreed that whatever obstacles we face, we put our best foot forward and figure out the way across it, under it, over it, or through it—and this was the biggest obstacle we had faced since being signed.

The first priority was setting up an online presence so that we could remain in the game. We knew nothing about all things IT—we didn't even have a website. So that was when, and how, www.blackeyedpeas.com was born.

Will became an IT nerd overnight. Just like in the days when he wanted

to master music, he now wanted to become the Stephen Hawking of the Internet, vowing that if our music was to be downloaded, then *we* would be the ones working out how to monetize this shit.

We had been given a sobering lesson in how fast music could get out there, and, like Will said, we would heed this lesson, adjust to the future and turn it to our advantage. If downloading was the direction the world was going, we needed to turn such outlets into our friend, not enemy.

The Recording Industry Association of America (RIAA) did what it could to reassert control after the horse had bolted, suing Napster in defense of artists across the country. A federal judge in San Francisco saw it our way in July of 2000, when he ruled that Napster had "created a monster," that it was liable for countless copyright violations, and that it be shut down immediately (it would later be reincarnated under the same name, but this time as a legitimate online service). But what staggered us were the figures that emerged from that court case. At its peak, Napster had some fifty million users and an estimated 14,000 songs had been downloaded every minute. We would later learn that *Bridging the Gap* was downloaded around four million times for free, compared to the 250,000 paid-for in-store albums we sold. That was the extent of our mugging.

We really do need to wake up and get on this shit, we all thought.

Metallica and Dr. Dre sued Napster for copyright infringement, but it all felt a bit futile, because no amount of lawsuits was going to stop the future from arriving.

What we couldn't know back then was that a system called SoundJam MP had already been developed and this Mac MP3 player—devised by two software engineers—was purchased by Apple. By 2001, Apple used it as the base to launch iTunes. By 2003, the iTunes Store was declared open. By 2009, six billion songs had been downloaded. By 2010, the Black Eyed Peas were breaking records for the highest number of downloaded songs.

Sweet justice.

But ever since that Napster breach, Will never again allowed anything to leave the studio, and he always took the master copy home. It is a policy that remains in force to this day.

The September release date went ahead with the anticipated anticlimax. At 250,000 copies sold, sales registered lower than *Behind the Front*, and even though we made inroads on the charts by breaking into the *Billboard* Hot 100 at #67, it wasn't good enough. Bottom line: we had failed to go gold a second time, and excuses didn't matter. If there is one brutal truth in the music industry, it is that chart positions never lie, and artists don't get the chance to plead mitigating circumstances when it comes to contract renewals.

It didn't help that U.S. radio continued to seem indifferent to our music. Unlike BBC Radio 1, our home-country radio producers didn't think we "fit" anywhere. Urban radio didn't think we were urban, pop didn't appreciate our hip-pop, and hip-hop didn't think we were hard-core enough. We were "eclectic," everyone said, and it seemed America didn't have a clue where to place "eclectic." Our singles "BEP Empire" and "Weekends" became club hits, which was all good, but that only served to strengthen our underground status. It did nothing for our wider appeal to the masses.

What exacerbated matters was that Interscope was entangled in, and distracted by, merger talks with Polydor Records and Seagrams. Consequently, the PR push for the album was as full steam ahead as it could have been.

As Interscope—which had already purchased the Geffen and A & M labels—swallowed up more U.S. operations to become even bigger, we were understandably not on the executives' list of priorities. Fact of life: when it is the corporate dollar versus the creative dollar, corporate will always win. If you are one of the moneymen, what is your biggest concern going to be? A corporate merger that is guaranteed to bring in millions and millions of dollars, or the under-performing Black Eyed Peas who may or may not make $500,000?

That said, we expected more noise than we received.

Will summed it up best in some magazine article when he said, "All this album needs is the attention it deserves from the record company. From a musical standpoint, this project accomplishes everything we set out to do. We put in a lot of work and now all it needs is a little bit of support."

It was annoying, because one great album had been torpedoed by Napster and then sunk in a merger.

Meanwhile, we were witnessing two artists blow up after being with us in the same starting blocks: Eminem and Macy Gray. Regardless of the arguments about how incomparable our music and styles were, it was hard not to feel like being lapped on the racetrack.

We didn't understand what the formula was to reach their level of success, and some self-inquiry began within the group. What more do we have to do? What're we lacking? What're they doing that we're not?

We put all our shit under the microscope, but all the questions we asked, we couldn't figure out the answers.

Ultimately, we agreed that we could do nothing but keep on the same track, doing what we had always been doing. Belief in what you are doing matters most when things aren't going as planned.

Interscope accepted it was partly to blame for the album's adequate performance, and Jimmy Iovine's faith in us was unfaltering. He told us to concentrate on the music, not on unfortunate timing, and on the future not the past. "Now go out there, do the same thing and produce another fine album," he said.

If you were a basketball team trailing by fifteen points going into the last quarter, you would want a coach like Jimmy.

But we all knew that Album Three was our final contractual obligation. Jimmy could offer as much support as he liked, but the reality was that an elephant was in the room, tapping its wristwatch. We knew that this could be potentially our last chance. It was time to stop thinking about it, put our heads together, grab our balls, and get back to the drawing board.

Mom had invited my dad to the *Bridging the Gap* album release party at the Grand Avenue Club in downtown L.A. I think she thought it was a good idea to offer me the opportunity to rebuild bridges, now that I was established as an artist.

I suppose I was curious about the guy who had pretty much walked out on me, and to meet him again on adult terms.

Mom reintroduced me to him like we had never met. "Jaime, this is your father, Jimmy."

He seemed awkward at first. "Hey *mijo* . . . how are you, *mijo*? he said.

The strange thing for me was that I felt no great sorrow for the time we had lost. If anything, I looked at him like he was a mirror and I was trying to find myself in the image. I was standing there thinking *Damn, you're kind of ugly-looking. Do I look like that?*

There I was, expecting some kind of knight in shining armor to walk in the door and what I got was Tattoo from *Fantasy Island*.

As I'm analyzing all this, Will bounded over. "Shit, you guys have the same nose!"

So that confirmed it then: I had the wide, big-ass Gomez nose.

I think back to this scene now and observe its superficiality. In the emptiness between father and son, I seemed to spend those opening few minutes trying to fill the void by defining our similarities. In the absence of any substance or meaning to our "relationship," I only had surface appearances to judge. And even then, I spent those snapshot moments seeking to disown the inheritance of his DNA.

I knew all about his character, I thought, as framed by Mom's opinion. So the more distance I could put between how we looked, the better the chances of a fresh start. In principle, it sounded good: two men meeting for the first time, wiping the slate clean.

I could only spend about thirty minutes with him prior to the release party, and so he stayed with Mom, sucking up the life I now had. After that night, we kept in touch, and I started seeing him every other weekend at his two-bedroom place in East L.A. when schedules allowed. I met his new wife, Terry. She embraced me and seemed excited to get to know me.

The one person not around was Eddie—my long-lost half-brother. But

Mom had already forewarned me about "tension" on that front, so the question of his whereabouts was awkwardly avoided. I wanted to get to know Dad first, and then choose my moment.

Polo, the "brother" keeping watch from the edges, spotted this growing union with concern. As he observed: "You started going to dinners and shows together, and always going to his place, but this was a guy you hardly knew."

It was like anything else in my life—I threw myself into its phase until I drank the experience dry. First thing I noticed was that Dad was nothing like the man I had grown up hearing about. He was no longer drinking. He was an upstanding, softly spoken, middle-class citizen, earning a wage, working at a hospital; a reformed character, and an example of how we can all change for the good.

But of course, the intention of wiping the slate clean is almost impossible, because within renewed relations, the emotional questions always surface. Over a few weeks, I moved from superficial observations into more profound, introspective questioning; the kind of questions a kid asks quietly but internally about an absent parent: *Did you ever think about me? Did you ever seriously try to look for me? Did you not miss your son?*

I never vocalized them, probably because I feared the answer, and probably because I didn't want to stain the renewal. I didn't want to live in the past or hold grudges, but it was like Polo said: "There was a reason why your mom took you away from this man. Remember that as he becomes your new best friend."

Sure enough, over time, the cracks appeared and my resentments stirred.

At one show, Dad started saying how he had been there for me when I was younger, like he was taking credit or something. Then, he started talking to Will, pulling the East L.A. treat-me-as-a-homie card. I heard people laugh with him, and all that laughter seemed fake to me. It was like he came in the door, without any understanding about what it had taken for us to reach this point, and he wanted to be accepted before he had accepted me as a son.

His true colors really started to show when I was at his house for dinner with Josh one night, and I decided I couldn't avoid the Eddie question any longer. I felt enough ice had been broken to allow me to ask a reasonable question.

"So where's Eddie at?" I asked, choosing my moment, halfway through the meal.

Everything that had felt false and forced about our small-talk conversations was punctured by this moment of truth. Dad slammed down his fist on the table, silencing the room.

"Do NOT talk to me about him! That man is dead to me!"

"But why? That's my brother. What's wrong? Where is he?"

"DON'T TALK TO ME ABOUT HIM!" he screamed. He completely lost it.

In turn, something ripped inside me. I couldn't have him denying Eddie.

I had last seen him walking away with this man, and I had a right to know. I went loco and snapped.

"WHAT? Don't you come at me like that! Don't you diss Eddie like that!" I yelled.

We were standing up, head-to-head in a matter of seconds. The whole vibe scared Josh, and there seemed nothing left to say anyway.

It seemed to me that Dad had walked away from Eddie just like he had walked away from me.

"He is still your son, even if I'm not!" was my parting shot that day, as I slammed the door behind me.

After that, it was never going to take much to sever our fragile association, and one night the Peas had a show at Temple Bar in L.A. Dad couldn't make it—he never did see me truly perform—but his wife Terry turned up, with two long-lost cousins.

The problem was that they turned up without I.D., so the doormen refused them entry. Which was when Terry started causing a stink, saying she was Taboo's mom, and demanded to see the manager.

First I knew of it was when one of the doormen put his head around the dressing room door and said: "Tab, can we have a word—your mom is here and she's going crazy."

"My mom? My mom's not here," I said.

I walked outside and saw Terry.

"Hey, *mijo*," she started to say, "I was . . ."

Her audacity to claim me as her son was too much, and it opened the valve on something. "Don't call me '*mijo*,'" I shouted, "and don't say you are my mom because you are not, just as much as Jimmy is not my Dad. You disrespect my workplace and you disrespected me . . . now get out of here!"

I called Dad and ripped into him, saying a whole bunch of hurtful things that I now cannot remember. All I know is that he never called me again and I never called him.

As cold as this sounds, I found it easy to walk away, curiosity now satisfied. In total, he was back in my life for a four-month period that was as wasteful and meaningless as the rest of his role in my life. I felt neither richer nor poorer for the experience, and maybe I had only explored that path for one reason in the first place: because Dad was the gateway to Eddie?

I never did find out more about Eddie's fate: where he was or what he had done. It was a secret no one shared with me. I would have to wait a bit longer for life to reveal what everyone else was hiding.

In the weeks prior to the Napster leak, we had gone to "council," and held a big discussion about the way ahead, reexamining our setup and questioning if

Black Coffee Management was capable of riding with us to the next level. Yon was the main man who had taken us to the level of being signed, and made the dream happen but we felt we had reached the ceiling of our alliance. We had reached a natural "growing apart" stage.

Our homie Polo Molina was assuming day-to-day manager responsibilities, and was doing a good job. The more Polo became proactive, the less point we could see in retaining Black Coffee. With more profile-building tours on the horizon in 2000, we knew that we had to step up and make staff changes.

We had already begun looking around, and the dude who really impressed us was David Sonenberg from DAS Communications. He'd previously managed Meat Loaf, Wyclef Jean, Lauryn Hill, and the Fugees, and it was a track record that was hard to ignore. Bottom line: he had proved himself in the big league, Black Coffee had not.

We immediately sensed a synergy between DAS Communications as the strategy-making, umbrella company and Polo Molina as the day-to-day chief on the ground.

But, within all this, we wanted to respect Yon because he had been with us from the start, and we felt he needed some inclusion; work out a role somehow. It was always going to be a difficult conversation because of the friendships that existed, but we could not allow bonds to become our emotional handcuffs.

We met inside Studio C at Paramount where we had cut *Bridging the Gap*, and there was some awkward small talk before I broke the ice. "Yon, something is not working out and we have had to review where we are at . . ." I began.

When someone bristles halfway through a sentence, you know the chat as imagined in your head isn't going to pan out as expected.

". . . we have gone through a lot together and we have arrived at a good point, but we really need to burst through to the next level and . . ." I continued.

Yon's face turned to stone.

Will chipped in: "Look, we want to include you still, but we would like to bring someone else on board . . . someone with the experience of managing a big band . . . and we wondered if you were opposed to sharing some responsibilities?"

Stupid idea, really, but we were trying to be fair and find him a role out of loyalty. Not surprisingly, he didn't see it that way. He shook his head and rose to his feet. "Nah, if I can't do this on my own, I'm walking!"

And that's what he did that afternoon.

That was probably one of the hardest decisions Will has ever had to make. He and Yon had been tight since the day they had met, and had spoken daily. Yon dreamed with Will. But like I told Will: "If he's a true friend, he'll see the bigger picture and one day understand."

It was a sad day, but the excitement we felt about linking up with DAS

Communications told us we had made the smart choice. Jimmy Iovine also backed our decision, because he was once managed by David Sonenberg in his days as a music producer. So there was some good luck in the outcome as well.

David, who had established his business in 1976, placed us in the hands of his man Seth Friedman, a sharp guy with unexpected long-ass dreds. Seth was charged with orchestrating our "big breakthrough." One of the many things I liked about Seth was that he looked and acted nothing like a stereotypical manager. He always wore these dope-ass Jordans, too. He was young, hungry, and he exuded intelligence and capability.

With Yon gone, Eddie Bowles went, too, so Polo Molina stepped up from merch man to tour manager as well as our official day-to-day manager. It was perfect for the Peas because we already trusted this guy with our life.

Another key component in the machine was our business manager Sean Larkin. He had been around from the start, and the joke in the early years was that he always called us because it gave him something to do. Guys like Polo and Sean believed in our future long before anyone saw any shoots of success, and every team needs people like them aboard from the get-go.

Then there was another notable departure—Kim Hill walked out the door.

We had known our time together was coming to an end both before and during *Bridging the Gap*. On tours, nothing had changed in relation to her verbose monologues. When we were doing thirty-minute sets that depended on whipping up a crowd's energy, we didn't have time for two or three minutes of Kim's storytelling. It didn't help that in Denver during the Warped tour, when the punk-rock girls whipped off their tops, Kim appealed to them to cover up.

"Come on now, don't disrespect yourselves like that, ladies . . . put your tops back on!" she told them, which is the last thing anyone at Warped wanted to hear. It was the kind of place where everyone spits in the air and catches it in their mouth, and does everything their parents don't want them to do. The last thing we needed was Kim being the bum-out. Both on and off stage, her dynamic wasn't meshing with ours. The end result was that Kim left to pursue her own career.

Her departure didn't leave a great hole that couldn't be filled. We figured that we could call on Macy or Esthero if we needed female vocals. We agreed that the plan was to keep the Peas as a core trio. Just the three of us—as it always was.

Ironically, what came out of Kim's exit was the emergence of Will's voice. With tour dates booked, someone had to step up to the mic during Kim's segments and so Will announced: "I can sing the parts. I'll take on the duties"—and the cat found his voice. Will is no church-choir singer boy, but he has this raspy, cool, melodic style which, to our surprise, was neither pitchy or off-key. He had never believed in himself as a singer, so when he pulled it off we were like "Damn, who needs female vocals?"

■ ■ ■

The Hollywood scene has always been a freeloader's paradise for the famous, offering perks that come with the job. If you are deemed to be "somebody," you have an access-to-all-areas club pass and a free drink-as-much-as-you-can coupon.

I may have remained a "nobody" in the rankings of fame, but as a signed artist with Interscope and a Black Eyed Pea in L.A., I received a lot of love. I got accustomed to walking up to the main door to greet promoters, and the lines of people must have wondered who the weird-looking dude with Indian hair was.

But these gatekeepers at the velvet ropes were well aware.

"Taboo!" said Sarah, or another favorite promoter called Jen. "Welcome back!"

The doors opened, the promoters acknowledged me, the bouncers shook my hand like buddies before I was escorted to the VIP area. It was the sort of Hollywood bullshit that mattered to fragile souls such as mine.

I might not have been selling records but I was "recognized" and it meant that I never had to dip into my own pocket. When that happens in Hollywood, it becomes the same old story, because once accepted into the VIP den, a strange momentum starts to build.

The more you are seen out and about, the more club promoters recognize you. The more you are recognized, the more the social leeches want to be seen with you. The bigger the crowd of social leeches, the more popular you *appear* to be. The more popular you appear within this vacuous reality, the more you start to believe your own legend in the making, without even realizing how brittle it is.

At this time, Apl had started to withdraw from the social scene. It was the start of a personal deterioration that involved his own period of darkness and partying, but that is his story to tell, not mine.

It left me and Will, together with Dante Santiago and another "brother" J.J. Anderson, hitting the clubs filled with industry heads.

I was always the first guy at the club and the last one to leave, stumbling out. My boys were quiet observers of my increasingly wayward behavior, and were mildly amused at how drunk I became, and they were always bagging on me.

As I swayed and slurred, a blurred-looking Will invented a cover version of Eddie Murphy's 1985 single "Party All the Time," and he would sing "*Taboooo . . . likes to party all the time, party all the time . . . Tabooooo, likes to party all the time, party all the time . . .* "

It became the joke anthem among the Peas and friends every time I got wasted. I'd put my hands in the air as if it was a closing song at a concert, thinking the anthem was a compliment when the reality was that he was calling me out. When I didn't get the hint, he became more direct: "You need to slow it down, brother . . . you're kinda looking sloppy, falling over tables . . . it's not cool."

Will was trying to be the elder, wiser brother without telling me how to run my life, but I just waved him away. "C'mon, Will! I know how to take care of myself. I've got it," I said.

Not really, as I would soon prove.

One night, I was kicking it in Joseph's before Will arrived, minding my own business when this twitchy, bald-headed white dude called Chris introduced himself to me.

"Hey, Taboo, do you party?" he asked. As he said this, he made a deliberate point of rubbing the end of his nose, brushing his nostrils.

"Yeah, I party," I said, taking up the challenge.

In the toilet cubicles, we chopped up two lines of cocaine on a compact mirror he'd removed from an inside jacket pocket. Then we went to Chris's apartment in a gated complex off Sunset and Doheny. I staggered in with this stranger into a room full of strangers, buzzing with beautiful girls.

"Hey, girls, this is my friend Taboo from the Black Eyed Peas!" he announced to the room. For him: kudos by association. For me: recognition and respect.

It was a party apartment: just one couch, some cool leather chairs, a television that always played sports, and ashtrays brimming with cigarette butts. And people draped everywhere, entwined within the false bonds of Hollywood "friendships."

We did more coke and I drank so much that I can't remember where I ended up. I just remember snorting a line and saying "Yo, this shit is good. Where can I get it?"

"I sell it," he said.

So that's how I met my cocaine dealer.

Chris was a social cancer with tentacles that ensnared the weak. He wanted to fuck me up as much as he was fucked up. He obviously needed someone else who was lonely and pretending to be popular and I must have fit the bill. There are bloodsuckers like him lurking around every club in L.A., and I fell for it, because whether it was Hollywood or his apartment, there was always drink, always drugs, and always girls—and that was just the kind of life that I thought I wanted.

If the music gods blessed us with anything, it was two things: an unending passion for locking ourselves away in the studio, and the taste for touring. Both the studio and tour bus provided an abnormal existence away from everyday life; two weird and wonderful capsules of artificial, creative, and—for me—often drug-enhanced reality. I thrived on it.

We were always on the label about when and where the next tour was going to be. Will continually pestered them by phone, asking, "What're we doing this summer?" or "It's spring break—where we headed?" or "The kids are back at college—let's do the colleges again!"

There was something free, loose, and spontaneous about our tours and spot dates back then. We just rolled up, did our shit, unplugged, rolled on, and kept building. The live show was probably 75 percent of who we were as we fought for recognition.

Removed from all the album pressure, our sole mission was to rock it so that no one could ever walk away and complain about not getting their money's worth. Touring was also our bread and butter, and the gigs we had lined up—opening for Macy Gray, No Doubt, and Wyclef Jean on the MTV College Campus Invasion tour—earned us each about $40,000. Not great money, but enough to survive.

One of the best touring experiences of that time was when we opened for fellow Interscope labelmates Gwen Stefani and No Doubt that summer, ahead of the official release of *Bridging the Gap,* as they promoted their album *Return of Saturn.*

After the Napster episode had burst our marketing bubble, we threw ourselves into this tour more ferociously because it was our megaphone, our drums, and our radio around America.

No Doubt had cracked the charts the year we formed, with their album *Tragic Kingdom*, but things had really blown up for them after the hit ballad "Don't Speak" in 1997.

Gwen was a live-wire of a tomboy, all wide-eyed smiles, finely toned muscles, and pink-hued hair. The moment we first walked into the dressing room she embraced us, smashing high fives all round. I don't think there are many more down-to-earth artists out there, and she was cool to kick it with. That woman has a beautiful soul.

We opened for the openers, a totally mad crowd of punk-rock dudes called Lit who always gambled and played football. With all our energies combined on that tour—the insanity of Lit, the party fun of No Doubt, and the funk of the Peas—it was a riot.

We always set up a "free-style room" wherever we went, and Gwen loved it because of the energy we whipped up. Standing in a circle, each person took turns spitting a verse as Apl played a loop on his drum machine. These sessions built and built until one time, it was the turn of No Doubt's bass player Tony Kanal—the man whose relationship with Gwen had inspired "Don't Speak."

"No, no, no," he said, backing away, not wanting to take his turn, "I don't rap!"

But after being goaded by Gwen, he stepped into the middle and began, hesitantly. "All right . . . check it! Check it . . ."

The room started to laugh as he fumbled and grasped at anything that

would rhyme. ". . . I appreciate . . . all my friends around . . . uh . . . white, black, and brown . . ."

Everyone collapsed laughing, and Tony, who couldn't rap for his life, died on his feet. From then on, each time we saw him backstage, we said, "Hey, Tony! I appreciate all my friends around . . . white, black, and brown!"

But here's the thing. We repeated that joke so much that we ended up liking its simplicity, and, through repetition, it was adopted as our preshow anthem. To this day, in honor of Tony Kanal and our one-tribe mentality, we stand in a huddle in the wings backstage—group, band, dancers, management—and link shoulders. Will tees it up by saying: "Okay, so we are in (wherever) today and it's the birthday of (whomever) and the after party is at (some club). Okay! Are we READY? Let's go out there and rock this shit. One, two, three . . ."

And after that countdown, we say as one: "I appreciate all my friends around, white, black, and brown"—and we high-five one another Gwen Stefani–style. I am not sure Tony knows the legacy he left us but that is how memorable that tour was.

On stage, Gwen was a fireball, jumping up and down in a frenzy and doing push-ups to the beat of "I'm Just a Girl." I can still see her beaming as she comes out of her dressing room, running in place, waiting. That girl was like a boxer, psyched.

Her energy was infectious, and I couldn't wait to get out there because her fans were known for loving some rabid stage-diving action, and so I was in my element.

When we reached the "Head Bobs" moment, I told the audience to hold its hands in the air and let me fly. I did a running jump . . . and flew. A mass of hands passed me around like an inflatable human, and I never stopped enjoying the craziness.

At one gig, the energy was so crazy that the Peas turned into leaping lemmings after me. Apl stage-dived. Then Will. Then the band decided to join in. Printz left the keyboard and dived. Terry Graves put down his sticks and leaped. It was down tools time and jump. George, our guitarist, was itching to do the same. The only problem was that he was a bit heftier than the rest of us, and you could see the faces of the crowd turn from giddy excitement to "Uh-oh" as he put down his guitar. George probably needed a longer runway than the rest of us and struggled to get airborne but he dived, the crowd caught him . . . and then buckled. The funniest thing was seeing this human sinkhole open up in that mass of bodies, but give them credit, they held up and heaved him back to the front. Not surprisingly, it was George's first and last stage dive.

At the end of each show, all the groups returned on stage for Gwen's explosive encore song "Spiderwebs." and we pogoed and leaped around like it was Warped all over again. The first time this happened, I jumped on the riser with Steve, their trumpet player, and ran up to Tony Kanal and started hyping him on his bass before jumping alongside bare-chested drummer Adrian Young who—with smeared lipstick all over his face, leopard print hair dye in his buzz cut—was thrashing around doing a fine impression of Animal from *The Muppet Show.*

That's when I looked down and was shocked as shit to find him hanging out butt-naked. He had walked on in his pajamas and ended it naked.

Adrian was one of those exhibitionist but fun guys. He would always do something wacky like turn up to the after-party in a thong or walk in, make a loud grand entrance, whip off his clothes, and declare: "OKAY! Let's get this party started!"

The No Doubt after-parties were legendary for a bunch of single men. There were always lavishly themed rooms, and we used to send George and Printz out into the crowd to scout for the hottest chicks, each armed with twenty-five free party invites. The end result was the sight of an advancing, glamorous army of fifty different "options" with a beaming George and Printz in the vanguard.

They always did a good job hunting, until one time Tony Kanal raised an objection and shouted out, "Yo, who brought all these girls backstage?"

George, no doubt thinking he was about to be praised, raised a hand.

"Dude!" shouted Tony. "When you go out there and do it again, can you just make sure the girls are not underage!"

After that technicality, George executed the same hunt but was extra careful: he carded every young lady he invited backstage.

We had so much fun that I wasn't ready for the tour to end, but as we returned to L.A., word came through that *Bridging the Gap* was making noises in Australia where it peaked at #37 on the charts, and then in New Zealand where it hit #18. It wasn't an earth-shattering development, but for the first time we were making inroads beyond Europe.

It was progress.

Baby steps. But progress.

We had reunited with Macy, accepting her offer to open for her U.S. and European tours. We were performing in Chicago when, midway through our set, the band started getting excited—something about the way they were gesturing to one another and focusing on a certain section of the crowd.

It was during a breather between songs that George Pajon let me know that he had spotted Prince in the audience.

Prince had, apparently, come to see Macy perform, but all I cared about was knowing that somewhere in the darkness was the man who featured so prominently on my mix tapes as a kid, and was responsible for my first record purchase.

I spent the rest of the performance thinking about the prospect of meeting him backstage.

But it must have reached a certain point post-performance when I thought it was not happening because I left for a club with Will and Apl, and got typically wasted. Another night came, went, and was forgotten in a drunken blur, and I didn't think too much about the missed calls on my cell until I saw George in the lobby the next morning.

"Where were you?" he said, "I kept calling and calling and you didn't want to know!"

George, with the franticness of a friend who knew I'd be upset, had tried to let me know that Prince had finally showed, and invited the band back to his hotel for a jammin' session.

"You picked up at one point, Tab," he reminded me. "And said, 'Whatever with that,' and I don't think you believed me. But man, you should have been there . . ."

In my drunken oblivion, I had missed out on a dream meeting as our own band jammed with Prince. It took me the rest of the Macy Gray tour to get over that one.

When we arrived in London with Macy, I walked onstage at an empty Wembley Arena—then the city's biggest indoor venue—and it was vast. I couldn't believe its size compared to the little-ass platform at the Jazz Cafe on our last visit to the English capital. This was a real stage in an arena with a capacity of 12,000.

Being inside Wembley Arena provided us with a taste of the action we dreamed about, but we dreamed even bigger than arenas and amphitheaters. We wanted the Holy Grail of touring—a stadium tour.

As an artist, that level of tour requires sales and a fan base that can guarantee sold-out audiences of 50,000 in city after city. Once again, our imaginations were running before we could walk, but while we rocked Wembley, I pretended in my own mind that we were at next door neighbor Wembley Stadium.

Any stadium.

After the show, George told the story of how he, too, walked out into the arena with Seth Friedman as the seats started to fill. George was also in awe of the whole setup, and he turned to Seth and said, "Look at this place! Do you think we will ever get to play venues like this?"

"Never going to happen," said Seth.

Giving Seth credit, he had yet to fully understand us, and he hadn't been immersed in the studio with Will and the band, where the collective vibe was that we were making music and were part of something that we wanted the rest of the world to hear. What we felt every time we made music, and especially on that stage at Wembley, was a calling, not some wistful hope.

So when I heard the doubt from Seth, I quietly told myself what I always said in my head when I heard someone say something would never happen. *"Oh, you don't think so? Well, you watch me! You watch us!"*

The MTV College Campus Invasion tour was a timely downsizing experience before I got too big for my boots, returning us to student-band stages and crazy college crowds—our core audience. It also teamed me up in person with De La Soul, who, like us, were opening for Wyclef Jean.

Having collaborated long-distance, I was now able to sit down alongside my idols and get to know them as people. Posdnuos, otherwise known as Plug One or his real name Kelvin, was a favorite of mine, a real cool cat who was into his shoes. Everything he wore on his feet was fresh, and it was to him that I first expressed another far-flung dream and said, "I want to have my own sneaker one day."

I had been looking at people's shoes and feet all my life. Some girl at Janson Elementary School can probably take credit for that, because one day she came up to me, pointed at my shoes, and said: "Jimmy Gomez! Urgghhh—look at your shoes!" Then she looked in horror at my fingernails.

"Urrrgghhh—your fingernails are dirty, too!"—and she ran off laughing to tell everyone.

After that, I scrubbed my shoes—and nails—harder than my Uncle Louie, living and dying by the maxim that you can tell a lot about a person by looking at their shoes. Even today, there are three self-pride rules I abide by: smell good, taste good, and look good.

And if you wear dope shoes like Posdnuos, it will be the first thing I notice. (Thinking back to the conversations we had about sneakers and brands, it came as no surprise in 2006 when De La collaborated with Nike to create the Nike Dunk.)

On this tour, it dawned on me that we—the group fighting for recognition—were on equal footing on the roster with De La Soul, the group that, in my eyes, was legendary. They had started out in 1987, and yet were still an opening act on a college campus tour. It seemed odd when set against the pedestal they had occupied in my life. There was this weird moment after one show when Maseo, another of the trio, said to me, "You guys are the new breed . . . the up and coming. We're still trying to pave the way and do our thing and . . ."

I lost the rest of what he said because all I heard over and over was this hero of mine saying, "Still trying to pave the way and do our thing . . ."

What the hell, you guys are amazing and should be headlining your own tour, I thought.

Soon followed by another thought: *Shit, we can't be here in twelve years "doing our thing."*

Life was good in the Dog Town projects, my home.

Childhood costume:
as a pirate in Dog Town.

Driving to an imagined
destination with our dog,
Lady.

Nanny, looking beautiful as
ever in the good ol' days.

Mom, Nanny, and me.

A rare moment of togetherness
with my stepfather, Julio.

An early twenty-dollar performance, stage-managed by Nanny.

With Mom, as a difficult teenager—and rocking the hair!

My hands were full
as a teenage father
to Josh.

1998: Performing at
Dublin's in L.A.
with Apl (left).

The pre-Fergie days: performing as a trio. Photograph courtesy of George Pajon.

2003: Outside the Elephunk tour bus. From left to right: me, Apl,
keyboardist Printz Board, road manager Bobby Grant, and guitarist George Pajon.

Photograph courtesy of George Pajon.

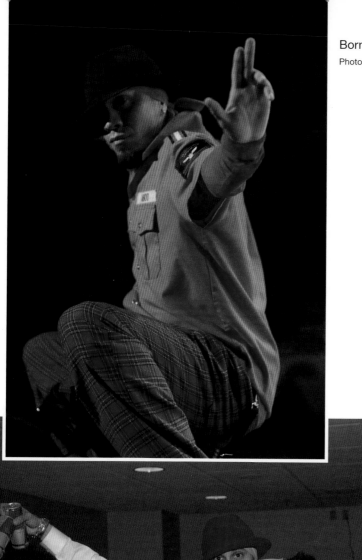

Born to perform.
Photograph courtesy of George Pajon.

2005: Me and Apl in the dressing room with Fergie, who had joined the group two years earlier . . .
Photograph courtesy of George Pajon.

The Peas and the band Bucky Jonson. From left to right: George Pajon, Printz Board, me, Fergie, Tim Izzo, Will, Apl, and Keith Harris.

The exhilarating exhaustion of touring:
finding rest at some airport.
Photograph courtesy of George Pajon.

Smoking a victory cigar with road manager and "camp counselor" Bobby Grant.

Photograph by Dina Douglass/Adrena Photography.

This was a sight that Bobby and the band were used to seeing. As our success increased, my personal decline began. Photograph courtesy of George Pajon.

Monkey Business tour: Sting and the band backstage. Photograph courtesy of George Pajon.

Sting's backyard, Stonehenge: Fergie, Apl, Polo Molina, me, and George Pajon.

Photograph courtesy of George Pajon.

Momentous day: in the recording studio in London with the one and only James Brown.

Photograph courtesy of George Pajon.

With the Black Eyed Peas management chief Polo Molina. Photograph courtesy of George Pajon.

My "brothers" Mookie and Deja.

The police mug shot, on the day that changed my life: March 27, 2007.

Without the love and support of Jaymie, I don't know how I would have survived.

2008: "Jaymie Dizon, do you take me, Jaime Gomez . . ."
Photograph by Ingrid Sanchez, I Studio Photography.

Time out at the Acropolis in Athens during our 2010 tour.

We've come so far from performing at Dublin's in L.A. Our biggest show yet: the E.N.D. tour. Photograph by Misha Sundukovskiy.

Solo segment: riding the *Tron*-like motorbike above the crowds during the E.N.D. tour.

Photograph by Misha Sundukovskiy.

The captain of our ship, Will, leads from the front during the E.N.D. tour.

Photograph by Naomi Pajon.

Show your love, Pea-ple,
and "put your hearts up . . .
put your hearts up!"

Photograph courtesy of George Pajon.

The happily-ever-after: with Jalen, Jaymie, and Josh.

Photograph by Crystal Ogilvie, About Face Imagery.

If their story told me anything after all our ponderings about the formula for success, it was that we needed to keep evolving, whatever happened. Our two albums had been a gumbo of different inspirations and musical elements, and, if we had pretensions to conquer the world, we had to keep mixing it up.

De La Soul, the inspiration, suddenly stood as a salutary lesson.

I think that the second half of 2000 demonstrated how we had stepped outside the hip-hop comfort zone, having shared the college campus hip-hop beat, or ska-pop with Gwen, or R & B/Soul with Macy. We actually felt more comfortable with audiences that were ethnically and culturally diverse.

The De La story must have played on my mind a bit, because my scrapbook from that tour has captured a review that clearly meant something. This one college publication said: *"While most students are familiar with De La Soul and Wyclef, they may not be acquainted with the Black Eyed Peas . . . they may not be heavy hitters now but they may be 'bridging the gap' to stardom and are poised to blow up."*

Another student review, from Berkeley, California, said we were *"creating a new subgenre within hip-hop . . . where the vocal aspect of songs takes a diminished role and the beats and background music stay in a supporting role."*

They were indicative of the reviews the album received, and signs that our audiences—as opposed to industry critics—were getting it. They may have only been student forecasts, but I pinned my optimism on them.

Just in time for Christmas 2000, we received an offer out of the blue. The soft-drink maker Dr Pepper asked us to provide music for its "Do What You Wanna Do" television commercial campaign, with a bounty of $100,000 each.

The DAS Communications linkup had not taken long to pay off.

The money was a saving grace. It allowed me to give Josh a special Christmas, and I bought myself a new car—a Honda SUV—and that was the extent of my wise investments. Admittedly, a large chunk of that change was also thrown away on drinks and drugs, because now I had some real dough to flash around Hollywood. It was dispensable income and I dispensed it on guilty pleasures.

When news broke about our collaboration with Dr. Pepper, some purists in the hip-hop community accused us of being sellouts, and we knew there would be accusations of "grasping," because we had discussed it all during our own soul-searching process about getting into bed with corporate. But after throwing it around, we agreed on one thing: the music *industry* was about getting visibility and getting our music into as many ears as possible—and the one hundred G's helped at a time when we needed money. It made no sense to turn it down.

It was like Will pointed out—do you think Run-D.M.C. weren't "selling" Adidas when that is all they wore on their videos, or other groups were not "selling" Tommy Hilfiger by being loud and proud with that brand? The difference is they were not getting paid because no one had woken up to the corporate wisdom for artists. By and large, the industry was still lying back in its hammock, thinking that it was all about CD sales and chart positions. But our Napster scars pre-warned us that we had to learn about other ways of making music work and finding fresh revenue streams.

Anyhow, Dr Pepper's message "Be You . . . Do What You Wanna Do" was a perfect fit with our take on life, so it was not as if we were selling out on our principles and attaching our name to any old product.

I didn't really care what anyone else's view was. Why would I? I was the kid who was accused by Latinos of being a sellout for hanging with a black hip-hop crowd and "dressing like a nigga." Being accused of selling out professionally was just another example of haters trapped in the time warp of an outdated mentality.

Today, in 2011, when brand sponsorship and corporate marriages are commonplace, the arguments we heard then seem as old-fashioned as the CD itself. It is the way of the world now, and you didn't need a crystal ball in 2000 to see it coming.

No one thought about looking into the future when we performed at a multi-act radio show, the Jingle Ball, in Minnesota, the week before Christmas, and found ourselves on the same roster as the three chicks from the group Wild Orchid.

We didn't give them a second thought until one of them, Stacy Ferguson, got her hustle on and stopped Will for a chat. We had been walking down a corridor with Nicole Scherzinger—a member of Eden's Crush who had also performed—when Stacy, walking alone, stopped us. She was this striking, blondish-haired beautiful woman who sparkled, and she wasted no time in telling Will how long she had wanted to work with him and how she had been thinking about going solo after almost a decade with her group. It was true Fergie: ballsy, flattering, charming, and direct—and that was when we learned she had been in the crowd at the El Rey Theater for our first album launch.

"I don't think this Wild Orchid thing is working out for me, and I need a producer," she said, confidently.

"All right, cool," said Will, "Give me a call and we'll make some tracks for you."

We wanted to build on our growing position Down Under, so we jumped aboard the Big Day Out (BDO) music festival in January of 2001 that hit Sydney, Perth, Adelaide, Melbourne, and the Gold Coast, before moving to New Zealand. If Europe felt like the conquering of a new frontier, then Australia felt like landing on the moon.

I had never felt so far away from home.

We didn't realize what a big deal the festival was until we got there, and if I left with one echo in my head it wasn't the music but a regular chant from the crowds. "AUSSIE, AUSSIE, AUSSIE . . . OY, OY, OY! AUSSIE, OY! AUSSIE, AUSSIE, AUSSIE, OY, OY, OY!" chanted 65,000 people.

We were part of a forty-strong, diverse lineup that included the Happy Mondays, Limp Bizkit, Roni Size, At the Drive In, Placebo, and some other new boys going by the name of Coldplay, promoting their album *Parachutes.*

I didn't pay too much attention to the lead vocalist Chris Martin, but the Peas' band said they "sucked" live. Chris was apparently deathly afraid about getting onstage in front of so many people, so much so that he didn't want the main spotlight on him, and this stage fright apparently took away from the performance.

When he performed "Yellow" and "Shiver," his stage presence was stiff, and when he sang, he either looked up to the skies, eyes closed, or looked down, eyes fixed on his guitar. He looked intimidated, performing in front of such a vast crowd. I think BDO 2001 was a time when Coldplay were yet to come into their own. In that respect, we were all still growing. It's just hard to believe how cripplingly shy Chris was when that image is juxtaposed with the presence of Coldplay today.

I fell in with a great group called Grinspoon, a rock band from New South Wales, and what I liked about these dudes was that they named their group after Dr. Lester Grinspoon, a professor of psychiatry who supported the medical use of marijuana. With a name rooted in weed, they were always going to be cool with me.

The scale of the BDO event was colossal.

As we performed, we saw all these straining faces of people pushed up against the barriers, and dozens of people were carried to the front, unable to cope in that heaving, swaying mass of bodies in such heat. The whole scene made the Warped tour look tame.

Tragically, that was the year a sixteen-year-old was crushed as the crowd surged to see Limp Bizkit in Sydney. We were in catering at the time, and knew nothing about it until reading the news in the newspapers the next morning. The girl had been critically injured. Six days later, she died, and Limp Bizkit pulled out of the tour.

That event punctured what had, up until that point, been a pretty blissful tour, and it made me extra cautious about how much I hyped the crowd with my own stage dives, seeing what it could lead to.

Aside from that incident, Australia and New Zealand could not have gone any better, and we felt that, overseas, we were hitting hard compared to our domestic performances. Just as we started to wonder when the same would happen in America, our February 2001 release of the Macy Gray collaboration—"Request

Line"—became our first entry onto the *Billboard* Hot 100 at #30. It made the Top 40 in most countries.

Then, the accompanying artsy-fartsy video caught fire, receiving endless airplay on MTV and VH1. We felt truly visible for the first time.

I won't forget making that video at a soundstage in Hollywood because I woke up with a cluster-fuck of acne all over my face, and one humongous, ugly pimple sitting like a volcano between my eyebrows.

"That's a nasty outbreak," said the makeup artist, plastering on her concealer.

"Yeah, can't understand it," I said, knowing full well it was the scars left behind by the various chemicals in my bloodstream.

The great surprise of that video was that a) you couldn't see this violent outbreak on my skin, and b) we received our first major nod from the industry with a 2001 MTV Music Video Award nomination for Best Hip-Hop Video.

I wish I could remember what happened at the ceremony, and how it felt to be there for the first time, but my memory is a blank, and we didn't win anyway. Maybe my memory was saving itself for another time further down the road in 2003, when the night would prove unforgettable for all the wrong reasons.

PEAS & LOVE

Fourteen years before I was born, Alfred Hitchcock went location-scouting in Sonoma County, Northern California, and came across Bodega Bay, and decided it was the perfect, moody setting for his 1963 horror movie *The Birds.* In 2001, will.i.am went location-scouting and came across the same sleepy harbor town, and felt it was the perfect, isolated setting to start work on our next album.

It was time to remove us from the "distractions of Los Angeles" and transport us to a place where, as a group and band, we could "focus" on the most important album of our lives; our third and final obligation under our first contract, our seventh game in an NBA final.

"We haven't proved anything yet," Will said, "and we need to get away from L.A. and nail this."

Previously, I had pushed his stressing to one side, but even my head had now found room for some worry: *What if this one bombs, too? What if I have to get another "real job"? What would I do?*

It wasn't just the isolated setting that focused the mind.

I had never seen a house as vast as the one in Bodega Bay. Not even in the movies. It was this brownstone, modern-architecture, big-ass crib on a hill with a backyard that was the Pacific Ocean. We had a massive kitchen with an island, a master chef's grill on the patio, a swimming pool out back, and a set of old wooden steps that zigzagged down to our own private beach. It was the kind of crib seen on the front of interior-design magazines, located in the type of town you see on postcards.

I also saw why Alfred Hitchcock chose the location: the sky was full of birds, but, at least according to the book on my bedside table, they were more black oystercatchers and long-billed curlews than killer blackbirds. That also explained why the most exciting activity going down in the area was the twitching of bird-watchers, who were everywhere with their binoculars. All anyone seemed to do in that town was "watch": whale-watching, sea lion–watching, bird-watching. One thing was certain: I could have scoured that open landscape for hours with a pair of binoculars and never found one dealer in sight. Will had chosen well.

Bodega Bay was effective in causing a temporary hiatus in my partying (even if I did bring a healthy supply of weed). I also started smoking Salems, a disgusting menthol brand, and they became my fifteen-a-day habit, which was a horrible substitute for the real pleasures in life.

This base camp was "home" for nine men—three Peas, George Pajon, Terry Graves, Mike Fratatuno, plus manager Polo and producers DJ Motiv8 and Dante Santiago—for three months, from the start of June until September 12 when we had to return to L.A. for a mini-tour. Keyboardist Printz was the only one missing, because of a temporary "misunderstanding" with Will over something, but "Leaver 2001"—as we nicknamed him after that—would be back within five months, rift healed.

We also took a woman along for the ride—Terry Dexter, a female singer-songwriter who Will was nurturing as a solo artist. He thought she could be featured on the odd song. But for me, she was Kim Hill without the sister vibe, and I personally couldn't understand why she was there. After some time had passed, I don't think she could either.

We worked every day, starting around 5 p.m. and going through until 4 a.m. and then waking at 1 p.m. the next day to start all over again.

I took my new Akai MPC-2000 drum machine to make beats because I wanted to use some alone time—about two hours a day—to learn another craft. I had watched Will and Apl with their producer hats on and realized it wasn't my strongest point, so I was keen to learn a new skill in my own time. I just closed my door and got to work on that 64-track sampler, approaching it like I had with b-boying and MCing: a skill to be crafted come what may (it would take a good two years of repetitive practice before I felt anywhere near capable).

Will also had a new piece of equipment: his first Pro Tools rig—a mixing board and recording software that provided us with a mobile studio and allowed him to move away from his laptop for the first time. And so we got to work, creating about thirty songs in those three months.

It was often Terry and Mike in one room, Will and George in another, and me and Apl in another, as Motiv8 and Dante floated from room to room. I felt for

Terry Dexter, locked away in a house with all these men. She seemed lost, hanging around waiting to be called without really fitting into the way we worked. I think she spent more time on the phone than she did recording. She was a sweetheart, but I don't think she could wait for those three months to end.

Being honest, I wasn't digging the energy in that house, either. Great location, but the vibe was off. It wasn't Paramount or Stewchia, and I felt displaced. Even as we were making different songs, I was thinking, *This doesn't feel right,* and that didn't help a creeping anxiety about the album's fate.

It didn't help the flow that we had to leave the house for seven days to shoot the Dr Pepper commercial which didn't go down too well with the band. Mike Fratantuno was especially unhappy about how much time that jingle took up. "I thought we came here to get away from distractions? I thought we were here to make an album, not commercials!" he said.

When you've got ten people in one house, living on top of one another 24-7, there's always going to be tension and frustration, especially when the pressure is on to deliver.

One morning summed up that uncharacteristic cloudiness more than any other when George came up from his basement room to make breakfast, only to find Apl—who prided himself on his cooking just as much as Will did—already using the pan. This scene only makes sense when you understand that both of them were drunk after going hard through the night.

George watched Apl doing nothing but staring at the pan, trying to process what he wanted to cook.

"Ap!" said George, his patience running out. "Look at you—you can't even see!"

Which Apl misinterpreted as a slight against his poor eyesight.

"HEY!" he shot back, "YOU GIVE ME LOW BLOW, I GIVE YOU LOW BLOW!" And he retaliated with "Look at YOU! You don't need to be eating no more!"—a clear dig at George's weight.

It was like watching a married couple bickering, and I thought, *This isn't what we are about . . . we are normally fun and laughter.* As good as Will's intentions were to remove us from L.A., it was proving to be a dumb-ass move the more time dragged on. Thankfully, Apl and George kissed, made up, and cooked breakfast for everyone, but I don't think any of us believed the album was coming together up there, even though we had about ten songs "selected."

We decompressed by escaping solitude and heading into San Francisco every Thursday and Friday night to party at two hip-hop haunts that reminded us of the L.A. underground scene: the Justice League and the Maritime Hall. It was the equivalent distance of living in Malibu and heading to West Hollywood.

The Justice League was the kind of cavern that had attracted acts like De La Soul and the Jungle Brothers, so we naturally gravitated there, and Polo arranged for us to hold our "Pea-Pod" charity event, which we had been doing in L.A. every Christmas since 1999: a platform for new musicians, dancers, MCs and poets to come perform and bring a toy in support of the Five Acres Children's Home in Pasadena. We couldn't do toy drives at the San Francisco Pea-Pod because it was summer, so, instead, we held live jam sessions.

These sessions became jam-packed, and one time, this white lady walked in carrying a big-ass tuba. It was so big, she might as well have been carrying a piano on her back. I had seen pictures of this instrument with British brass bands and orchestras, but had never seen one stomping into an underground nightclub before.

But this woman stepped up and belted out this big, funky sound.

Elephant, we thought.

Heavy. Fat. Thump. Thump. Thump.

"Elephunk!" we said—and that's how we found the name of the album which, ultimately, would become all about trombones, fat bass lines, fat grooves, and thick horn arrangements.

It was also the trip that introduced us to Polo's lifelong friend Bobby Grant, this wild-haired student with a Don King 'fro who was local, and had done a spot of club promoting. It was he who'd fixed us up at Justice League. We also held Pea-Pods at a jazz spot named Storyville.

Essentially, these nights became an excuse for us to test the beats we had been working on at the house. We got a sense of what was working and what was not, and we always had a blast in the process. As a result, we also hired Bobby, and he remains an integral member of the family today, as our indispensable road manager. The name of the album and Bobby Grant were the two good things to come out of our time at Bodega Bay. As I packed my bags on the penultimate day, I don't think I had ever yearned for Hollywood so badly.

I was fast asleep when Will burst into my bedroom, freaking out on a hysterical level. "Scoot over! SCOOT OVER!" and he jumped on the bed like a frightened kid.

"What the fuck Will?"

"Shit, man, this is scary . . . WE'RE BEING ATTACKED!"

I looked at the terror in his eyes and thought the house was being robbed. I glanced the bedside alarm clock: 6:30 a.m., on the morning of September 11.

"America is being attacked. It's the end of the fucking world, brother!" he then said. I was still coming around and none of what he was saying was making sense, but nothing would make much sense that day.

Will had been watching TV downstairs and had already seen the two planes hit the World Trade Center towers. "Turn on the TV! Turn on the TV!" he screamed, refusing to get out of bed. I flicked the remote, and it took my eyes

a few seconds to adjust to what I was seeing—two smoking silver stacks in Manhattan.

"I saw the second one hit . . . right into the building . . . BOOM! . . . I tell you, dude . . . this is it! We're being fucked . . . WE'RE FUCKED!" said Will.

Even though we were three thousand miles away in a sleepy outpost of Northern California, the distance did nothing to dilute that electrifying fear we felt as Americans. Planet Earth—civilization as we knew it—felt like it was spinning out of control.

Across the bottom of the television screen, reports started breaking of other planes flying loose and wild in the skies—silver birds hijacked as bombs and heading for the Pentagon, the White House, and God knew where else.

We both bolted downstairs where the rest of the group—minus Apl— stood gawping, hands held to mouths, watching the news. When we watched those towers implode, the house fell into emotional chaos. Will couldn't contain his fear. Terry was wailing. And there was a general sense of caged panic. Apl wandered sleepily down the stairs, wondering what was going on. He looked at the television, looked at us, and thought we were watching some movie until everything was explained.

One by one, we made frantic calls to our families.

"We've got to go home . . . we've got to go home!" Will kept saying. "We've got to book a flight now." But we soon realized there were no flights going anywhere. So we booked three SUVs and one U-Haul for the band's gear, and headed on the six-hour journey south. No one said a word as we headed home, locked into unfolding events on the radio.

Back home in L.A. and back with Josh, we held a family prayer, and, in that moment, I didn't want to leave the borders of Rosemead ever again. The dream we had was eclipsed by a living nightmare, and the business of the Black Eyed Peas seemed irrelevant and trivial. Yet we were supposed to start another American tour two days later, on the thirteenth. None of us were in the mood and we discussed pulling the plug, because what citizen wanted to party and jump around with all that shit going down?

Will went to visit his grandma, a wise woman who was to him what Nanny had been to me. When he phoned us, one by one, to share her rational perspective, it made us think again, because they were wise words from someone who had lived through segregation, war, and suffering. Her words went something like this:

"If God didn't intend for you to help people with your music, you wouldn't be going on tour. Now, you need to provide therapy for people in this time of crisis. Your music matters, and you are one of God's angels. If everything stops because of this, the terrorists win. You should do the tour."

That clarion call returned us to the road, but Will was adamant about one thing. All the work we had done in Bodega Bay was finished. "The world has changed," he said, "and those songs don't mean anything no more. We're throwing it away and starting again."

IYDKYDG was the acronym for the If You Don't Know You Don't Go tour. Basically, us, Black Starr, and Bismarck toured America on dates tied to a Coca-Cola promotion, which meant none of the acts could promote the tour or sell tickets. Only Coca-Cola.

The size of our audiences was dependent on how many people were "lucky" enough to buy a can—and find tickets attached. Willy Wonka style. If you didn't get a winning can, you didn't know about the concert: If you didn't know, you didn't go. Get it?

It seemed a pretty dumb premise to me, because what happened if you got a ticket but were a fan of Celine Dion or Britney Spears? As a result, the promotion was sporadic. In some cities, there was strong promotion. In others it was weak. But we weren't complaining because we were being paid $7,500 each, a week, to play along.

The funniest outcome happened in New Jersey, when we turned up and realized either people didn't drink enough Coke in that state or they didn't listen to enough hip-hop. Only thirteen people showed up in this big-ass hall. Thirteen people scattered alongside one metal barrier on the front row with a big yawning space behind them.

If I had been Coca-Cola's marketing team, I would have been embarrassed as shit.

We couldn't stop laughing as we walked on stage, but Will made the most of a bad job by shouting out, "YO, WHASSUP NEW JERSEY! HOW Y'ALL DOIN'?" treating it like we were playing to a full house at Madison Square Garden.

We decided to use spontaneous initiative and turn this night into a personal show for each audience member. We grabbed a fruit basket from backstage and handed out apples, oranges, bananas, and grapes to each person, asking for their name and where they were from. Will then started free-styling about their bios, their shoes, and their clothes, and, in the end, we made the best of a bad job.

Thankfully, a lot more people drank Coke in Manhattan. We did a gig at Sounds of Brazil (SOB's) in Soho, around four hundred people showed, and it turned into an amazing night.

It was only a few weeks after 9/11, and as weird as "entertainment" still felt, we took the words of Will's grandma with us, and reminded the crowd that terrorism won't stop the world turning and won't stop music being played. The cheer in that moment gave me goose bumps, and validated our decision to remain with the tour. At the end of our penultimate song, we held a minute of silence for all the lives lost, and then everyone held their lighters aloft for our closer, "Positivity."

That was an emotional time when everyone felt the nation's back was

against the wall. But in that hour onstage, we felt hope, and that is the power of music: it heals, it galvanizes, it empowers.

Outside the walls of SOB's, we detected a worrying undercurrent as people started hating on Middle Eastern people. We heard it in conversations in the street, in cabs, and in restaurants, and we sensed suspicion at JFK airport.

We saw anyone who was remotely dressed as a Muslim being searched more vigorously than we had noticed before, and, in Manhattan's din, we watched as one man drove by in his car, passed a young Muslim man, and shouted from his car window: "Fuck you, towel head!"

We kept saying the same thing over and over to each other: "Have you noticed how racist New York has become?" The city had lost its love in collective grief and fear.

As a Mexican-American, I felt sorry for Muslim-Americans. We were all Americans—in a country that preaches to the world about democracy and the way things should be—and yet we had regressed, pointing fingers with eyes and minds that could not discern one rabid bunch of terrorists from one wider group of citizens. What would have happened if black people had been in the cockpit of those planes? Or Mexicans? Would every black person or Latino be accountable for that, too? Was every Basque region resident a terrorist in Spain? Was every resident of Dublin, Ireland, a member of the IRA? It seemed like some irrational madness had taken over New York, and fear had dragged us back to the Dark Ages.

The whole vibe made us speculate that one terrible injustice perpetrated against America was spawning an even bigger injustice against humanity at large; that the West now judged anyone of Eastern origin with suspicion, without applying context or compassion.

It is all we spoke about on the plane back to L.A.

In the weeks before Christmas and the New Year's festivities of 2001—when all I wanted to do was party—I noticed one thing about taking Ecstasy: I had begun to feel immune to it. When I wanted to be rolling, I felt little or no buzz. It fizzed when it should have exploded.

So there was only one thing to do: take more.

And more. Until I felt the euphoria I expected to feel.

I wanted to recapture how it felt the first time back at Glam Slam, but Ecstasy overkill had desensitized me. Pushing the extremes—oblivious to the dangers—was my only escape from the plateaus I couldn't tolerate. Chasing that elusive virgin experience is the very trap that hooks thrill seekers like me. I don't want to think about how much MDMA my brain and nervous system had to deal with back then, because, instead of taking one or two pills, I dropped five or six at a time. That was the type of person I always was: the obsessive gorger.

I did the same with espressos. I did the same with cigarettes. Until I drank so much caffeine and inhaled so much nicotine that I was physically sick—and never touched the stuff again.

Ecstasy never made me sick. It might have made me feel horrible the next morning, but not sick enough to be turned off. I just kept hitting it harder and kept drinking myself into oblivion. That was the fucked-up thing—I was taking Ecstasy to make me feel something, and then drinking myself to the point where I couldn't feel anything.

All I know is that I couldn't go without those pick-me-up doses for the nights in Joseph's, because I needed to feel on-point within VIP lounges. It gave me that confident, arrogant edge. Like the night when I saw Rick James in Joseph's.

I was alone, getting drunk, when I saw him and started singing "Super Freak" in my head, staring at him like some starstruck kid. For me, he was someone I respected because of his music, but he was also known for his wild living and I liked that. The notoriety. The legend.

Fucked-up and still a legend.

He caught me staring, wandered over and introduced himself. "You like a smoke? You got papers?" he asked.

"Nah, but I've got a blunt."

"A blunt? Never smoked a blunt before . . ."

Rick James has never smoked a blunt before?

We went outside and shared this big-ass cigar of weed, and that night I smoked him out. In my book, it didn't get more notorious than that. There were countless other nights where I felt some self-important attachment to celebrity when I had no clue what "celebrity" meant. The bigger the name that accepted me, the more I felt included. The equation was as shallow as that.

Club A.D., off Highland, was another of my loyal haunts. I loved that place for its hip-hop and house music and multiple dance floors. It was my VIP version of Ballistyx, and I would get in there, dance, and a circle would form, throwing light on me in the center.

I was doing my thing one night when I spotted Justin Timberlake watching from the edges, and I pointed at him, calling him out as if to say, "You gonna bust, Justin?"

He was with *NSYNC at the time and they were at their peak after the album *No Strings Attached* had sold almost ten million copies in 2000, so when I pointed at him, the place went crazy. His grin told everyone that he was happy to pick up the gauntlet.

I went first, letting him know that I was all about killing the circle. I stepped out and he stepped in, a Hollywood repeat of me versus Z-Crew but this time Black Eyed Peas versus *NSYNC.

As we danced, this crazy energy that we had started began to spread from the epicenter to the rest of the dance floor, and the whole place was bounc-

ing. We were like, "Yo, look what we did!" and that's how we hit it off and swapped information.

"We should do this more often, Jay!" I said.

"Sure thing, hit me up sometime," he said.

At Stewchia, Will had been kicking it with Printz in the week before Christmas, dropping some ideas for a ringtone people could download for cell phones.

Will came up with a beat, and Printz disappeared into another room to create a guitar part. By the new year, when work started for real on *Elephunk* at Glenwood Studios in Burbank, me and Apl heard the loop, and the three of us started thinking about lyrics, extending it from ringtone to song.

With our experiences in New York fresh in our minds, we started thinking more about President George Bush, his declared "War on Terror," and how "it will not end until every terrorist group of global reach has been found." An era of war and hatred, not peace and love.

There was one famous scene from 9/11 that I kept replaying in my head: Bush at some elementary school in Florida reading a book with some kids when one of his guys leaned in and told him that America was being attacked. Instead of citing emergency business and getting the fuck out of there, he remained seated and carried on reading. I suppose that was meant to be "presidential" but I couldn't help but think of another word: "nonchalant."

Nonchalant—seconds after being told a second plane had hit the World Trade Center.

What was that all about?

I started reading more, and learned that the CIA's George Tenet was apparently told about the attack when the first plane hit, and before the president had arrived at the school. The whole thing seemed like madness, as if something was being swept under the rug, and we were left to guess at the reasons and the truth.

This was the kind of shit I was bouncing around as we hung in the studio, playing with lyrics. The creative process is always the same with us: Will at his mixing board, where he *always* sits, Apl lounging on the couch, and me pacing by a far wall or corner. I would write something down, ask Apl to check it out, and then kick it for feedback.

To this day, me and Apl write our lines on paper but Will "writes" in his head and goes directly to recording, scooting back and forth in his chair between his mixing board on one side and his mic on the other. He free-styles his verses, and edits as he goes along. Me and Apl need to scratch and build the verse in longhand first.

I wrote random notes as I imagined God looking down on the madness and speaking to the world: "Not the same . . . these days are strange . . . is the world insane? Peace and love . . . suffering . . . the youth are dying young."

Will approached it differently, as the kid going to his mom for answers. "What's wrong with the world, Mama?" And Apl went dark—viewing the war as a burden with "I feel the weight of the world on my shoulder . . . as I'm getting older, people get colder . . ."

After about an hour or so, and after exchanging some thoughts, we had our different verses and felt that we had what we were looking to say.

Time went by and we had this song for a while with a simple hook that ended "Where is the love . . . the love, the love," and we were sitting around thinking who could feature as male vocals to give it the big message it needed. Names I cannot remember came and went without resonating.

One afternoon, I dropped into the label for some business and met with Ron Fair, executive A&R on the album and president of A&M Records under the Interscope umbrella. We discussed the names that had been thrown around when I had a burst of inspiration: Justin Timberlake.

Justin was red-hot as an artist and was going to break off to launch a solo career once the latest *NSYNC tour was over so, taking off from that night at A.D., I hit him up on the drive home, and told him my sister would love tickets to their L.A. date at the Pond in Anaheim. I became the coolest brother in the world when Celeste got to hang backstage with Jay, Joey, Lance, J.C., and Chris. As we left the concert, I told Justin that I had this song I wanted him to listen to.

Later that week, I played it over the phone from the studio. He loved it.

"Dude, this is a smash . . . it just needs a bigger hook," he said.

"I know! We're looking for some Marvin Gaye-style emotional hook . . . just something, you know?"

"All right, I get it . . . let me get writing," he said.

One hour later, he called me back. "Tab, I got it!"

Over the phone, he started to sing, a perfect falsetto.

"People killin', people dyin'/Children hurt and hear them cryin'/Can you practice what you preach/And would you turn the other cheek . . . Father, Father, Father, help us/Send us some guidance from above/Coz people got me, got me, questionin' the love . . ."

"What do you think?" he said, deadpan.

"THAT is the shit we wanted!" I yelled.

I couldn't wait to phone Will. Which I did about thirty seconds later, more excited than I had ever been over a song.

"Will, Will . . . you've got to hear what Justin Timberlake has come up with!"

"Justin Timberlake? The dude from Backstreet Boys?"

"*NSYNC."

"What the fuck, Tab!"

"I'm telling you, Will . . . I'M TELLING YOU . . . this is big!"

I'm not sure what excited me more: the actual song, or the fact that I was spotting something *before* Will for a change.

As iffy as he was, he heard my passion and his boy-band cynicism gave way to give it a chance.

I felt zero pressure because I had no doubt in my mind about what I had just heard. I felt how right Justin's hook was in my gut, in my heart, in my soul, and with him about to do some solo shit, it was perfect timing all round.

Ten days later, in March of 2002, Justin walked into Glenwood Studios.

Looking like shit.

Heartbroken.

He had just broken up with Britney Spears, and, for the first two hours, he just occupied a chair and talked about nothing else, unburdening himself. It is not relevant to know what he said, but everyone, the Peas and the band, let him pour it out.

It didn't seem to matter that he had known us for the equivalent of five minutes. It was clear that he needed someone—anyone—to listen. His evident agitation required that comfort. I think his openness endeared him to Will. Justin was a young cat then, and we all saw his hurt and pain, and that was some real shit he was going through. I'm not sure we were the wisest relationship counselors in the world, but we were there, and we were patient until he was ready to record his bit.

I actually think his suffering made him better that day, because he went into the vocal booth and poured all his heartbreak into that hook. He shit on that song, and the studio was blown away by his harmonies, the way he hit his falsettos, and the whole way he was trained.

In a matter of minutes, he had given "Where Is the Love?" the golden touch.

I started jumping up and down. "I told you! I fucking told you!"

Will was at his mixing board, and I was standing up, leaning across it. He looked up at me as his trademark grin spread across his face. "Dope," he said, nodding his head.

I remembered what Justin had done once when *NSYNC won one of their first MTV Awards—an astronaut on the moon trophy—and, in a goofy acceptance speech, he delivered a spontaneous ditty: "We got a moon man! We got a moon man!"

The moment he walked back into the sound studio, I went up to him and said: "This song? We're gonna get a moon man! We're gonna get a moon man!"

He didn't laugh. Not in his heartbroken state. He just smiled bravely.

I felt like a jerk.

Until he said, "This song is bigger than a moon man, Tab."

I suspect his label, Jive Records, also thought the same, because not everything ran smoothly in the months afterward. Many stress-head executive-to-executive meetings took place with our boys at Interscope because Jive worried that it would "compete" with the hoopla around Justin's solo debut album, *Justi-fied*. Negotiations took place to ensure we would release it as the first single from the album in June of 2003, and Justin would release his album that August, to avoid a clash and yet provide some element of cross-promotion.

Justin's credit also became an issue. At first, we had permission to use his name on the single but Jive worried this could dilute his own album's marketing.

For us, "Where Is the Love?" was a majestic song, but it was the first of many, so, once we had added Justin's hook, we put it to one side and kept writing, recording, and collaborating, working with our old homie from the Warped tour, Travis Barker, and then Papa Roach.

Being back in L.A., working between Glenwood and Stewchia, felt good. I never felt like turning out the lights and leaving the studio in darkness to go home to Mom's couch. I wanted to stay up through the night and watch us, as a team, give birth to more beats and music, and dovetail this work with the guilty pleasures within Hollywood's clubs.

I think I worked best within that creative, fucked-up axis.

I think I worked best with distractions around me.

I was at the L.A. Lakers Parade of 2002 after they stormed the NBA Championships with a 4–0 series win over Allen Iverson's 76ers, and I took my place outside the Staples Center to cheer my friend Kobe Bryant home. I was mingling in the crowds, stacked with people from East L.A., and I got a tap on the shoulder. "Hey, are you Taboo from the Black Eyed Peas?"

I thought the guy was stopping me to ask for an autograph or something but then he said, "I know your brother Eddie—he's always talking about you, dude."

Eddie. The kid I had last seen walking away from Dog Town, leaving me his toy robot; the brother Dad had refused to acknowledge.

"How is he? *Where* is he?" I asked.

But this dude evaded all that, and instead gave me a number I should call "and then you can ask all the questions you like." The number I called belonged to Rosie, Eddie's then-girlfriend.

When she picked up and I told her who I was, her reaction was as if *she* was the long-lost relative. "Jimmy? Oh my God! Eddie's going to be so happy!"

"Can I speak with him?"

"He's in jail, Jimmy," she said, matter-of-fact, "but he'll be out soon!"

Time went by and he called me on his first day out of prison. Two days later, I arrived at this first-floor apartment in East L.A., wondering what he looked like and without even thinking what we were going to say. Rosie opened the door,

with his two-year-old daughter hiding behind her legs. She was the female child version of Eddie: dark-skinned, jet-black hair, and a little chubby.

Eddie was waiting for me in the living room. I was one of his first visitors from the outside world.

Gray hair. That was the first thing that struck me as I walked in and saw him.

Gang tattoos covering his arms and neck. That was the second thing as we hugged and embraced. "It's been a long time, brother," he said in this high drone of a voice that he had developed.

Then three tattooed teardrops running from his left eye. That was the third thing as I checked out his face, trying to recognize the young kid behind the old man's face on this thirtysomething guy.

I knew instantly that he'd done some dirt and gone down the path Mom had warned me about. I followed Mom and became a Black Eyed Pea. He followed the gang and became a member of Primera Flatz. My heart sank for him. I felt disappointed.

"So, homie," he said, "I missed you, man . . . it's been years . . ." and we talked about how "Pops" and him had went their separate ways. Eddie didn't have much else to say other than he had been locked up, and all he wanted to talk about was me.

"I'm proud of you, little bro," he said. "You've made a life. Look at me . . . I can't go nowhere," and all this sadness and fear poured out of him because it became clear that he was a marked man on the outside. Imprisoned by the gang life that sought reprisals.

"If I go outside that door, I fear for my life," he said, and then he started showing me all his tattoos, "You see all this right here . . . that's scarring. Everything . . . it tells my story right here, homes."

I didn't know the life he was talking about. I didn't know what he had done or what he had faced and I didn't ask and he didn't go into details, but I wasn't going to sit there and judge him based on the markings I saw.

"Look at you," he continued. "Look how good you look. I'm proud of you—you did it for the Gomezes!"

I did it for me, I thought, but didn't correct him.

I was with Eddie for about two hours that day, and I sincerely tried to reignite the embers of our childhood. I invited him to a party for my son Josh, and he showed up, but he sat in a chair in a corner all night because he didn't know how to socially engage with people on the outside. This world—and certainly my world—was alien to him. I was trying to build bridges between different planets.

Fast-forward a few weeks, after we had seen one another a handful of times, and his girlfriend Rosie called me. "Hey, Jimmy, me and Eddie would like to ask you for a favor . . . uh . . . do you think you could loan us some money?"

And with that question, that was the end. I knew it was too good to be true that our reunion was about love, about being brothers, about actually enjoying one another without involving what I did or who I was. It was the briefest of reunions.

Eddie is my brother. I love him for that. I love him for the kid he was and I have compassion for the man he became. It's just that I don't have a relationship with him because we come from different worlds now and for that—for rescuing me from the gang life that may or may not have enticed me—I will be eternally grateful to Mom. Thank God for a mother's foresight.

Living life as a pinball, it was understandable that my erratic ways were hard to tolerate and one night, the old girlfriend got suspicious about whether I was telling the truth or not about being at Stewchia until 3 a.m. I couldn't blame her, based on my track record. On any other random night with some random chick, her suspicions might have been well founded. But not on this night, because me and Will were locked into some groove.

She rang me on the cell as Will was editing at the mixing board, and the next thing he heard was my defensive stance in a heated phone conversation.

"Why don't you believe me? I AM in the studio," I said.

"Bullshit," she said.

I held out the phone, away from me, to get proof. "Will, let her know I am here, that it is you . . . just say something!"

"HE'S IN THE STUDIO!" Will shouted.

"That IS Will's voice!" I yelled.

"Bullshit," she said.

"Ah, just shut up," I said, done already.

"*You* shut the fuck up," she said.

"No, *you* shut the fuck up!"

We went at it back and forth like a game of tennis until I cut the call. Will kept his eyes on the board, head down, and said, "There's a song in that, you know."

"Huh?"

"Shut up . . . Shut up. It's a song," he said, as calm as you like.

Most times, that is how organic and spontaneous it is. One flash of reality or a seed from one personal experience. Will then started talking about his experiences—having a romance but then having to go on tour and how shit got out of hand—and he started to free-style: *"Girl, me and you were just fine (you know) /We wine and dine/Did them things that couples do when in love (you know) /Walks on the beach and stuff (you know) /Things that lovers say and do I love you boo, I love you too . . ."*

And we kept kicking it and, within an hour, we had the song "Shut Up"

(so at least one good thing came out of my relationship which soon ended). The lyrics were dope but the problem was that Will was singing the girl parts—and that sounded wack. This was no song where he could slip into Kim Hill–style shoes, because for it to work it *needed* to be an argument between male-female warring protagonists.

Dante insisted that it had to be a powerful female voice, and we tossed some ideas around such as Terry Dexter, a girl named Debi Nova, and Eden Crush's Nicole Scherzinger.

"Why don't we put Stacy in there?" said Dante.

Will had already made it clear that he never saw us adding another Kim Hill to the mix, and would only add guest female vocals again if the material really warranted it. Even though that material had arrived, he seemed hesitant.

In the same way that Will had been reluctant about featuring the voice of bubblegum pop with Justin, he was equally wary about introducing someone with an 80s-style b-pop pedigree, but Dante persuaded him to give the Wild Orchid girl a chance.

They called her up then and there and she came in the following week. Fergie said she was "nervous as hell" that day, but it didn't show. I arrived to find her dancing in front of a glass door with her back to me, practicing some moves as she waited. I didn't recognize her immediately as the girl from that Jingle Ball radio gig and I thought, *Who's the sexy chick dancing?*

She saw me in the mirror, watching her dance, spun round, and was like "Hey, whassup, I'm Stacy!" and she struck me as real talkative and outgoing. As she spoke, she kept moving on the spot to a subtle beat, like she couldn't stop or something.

I took one look at this white girl and thought there was something special about her; she exuded star-quality aura from day one.

She was still reinventing herself at this time, midway through the transformation to becoming Fergie, the hip-hop chick with the rock 'n' roll vibe; still at the half-caterpillar, half-butterfly stage.

She walked into the vocal booth that day with about five men on the other side of the glass sitting in imminent judgment. She was only there to record vocals for one song. She knew it. We knew it. She would go on to to pursue a "solo package" with Will, but as far as the Peas were concerned, this was a tryout for a one-off song.

But that understanding started to warp like plastic under heat the moment she started singing her vocals to "Shut Up." Within thirty minutes and two takes she destroyed it in there.

Like a seasoned pro, she knew about thirds, and layering, and stacking, and she brought that song to life. But it wasn't just the voice that impressed, it was the *performance* she gave. The majority of people walk into a booth to lay down vocals and concentrate on the delivery, keeping the mouth close to the mic, not wanting movement to affect the projection of the voice. But Stacy started rocking out like she was on stage, in her zone—and kept her vocals pitch perfect. It was incredible to watch. She was a fireball.

For me, that was the moment that "Stacy Ferguson of Wild Orchid" was kicked to the side, and Fergie was born.

Or "Fergie-Ferg," as we would grow to know her.

We knew we had found the perfect fit for "Shut Up," but Will also knew the power of that one song was in danger of eclipsing the rest of the album, especially since Ron Fair was such a fan of Stacy's, having worked with her and Wild Orchid at RCA Records. "They were the greatest white-chick harmony band of all time, but they got caught up with bad luck and bad hair," is how he put it.

So when Will went in to play *Elephunk* in late 2002 for Ron Fairs, he walked in with a few selected tracks but kept "Shut Up," tucked up his sleeve. He wanted the hard work of the Black Eyed Peas to shine first and foremost, to let our strongest tracks like "Where Is the Love?" speak a power on their own and demonstrate that we had an album that was original, powerful, and ready to take on all that flossy, glossy shit that was around at the time. Instead of delivering an album with one or two good songs, we felt we had created a whole record from start to finish.

So we were surprised when Ron didn't like it, and he especially didn't rave about "Where Is the Love?" which we considered the strongest track. "It's not very good," said Ron, and we were like "Whaaaaat?"

Together with Will, the song was reworked, adding new strings, and lines from the verses were switched around. "Buffed up," said Ron. We also added "Hey Mama" and "Hands Up" to the album, and Will produced "Shut Up" as the white rabbit out of the hat, and it was given the green light.

When we went to Record Plant Studios to mix the album and add some finishing touches, we prepared ourselves to walk tall into 2003 with a new album as three Peas. We were satisfied that *Elephunk* was our best work. Three brothers. Three musketeers.

During those long days at Record Plant, Pharrell Williams was also recording next door, and he walked in when we were sitting around, playing our songs, and he kicked back to listen. At that moment, Jimmy Iovine also walked in and we were surprised to hear that he had not yet heard the album so he pulled up a chair.

"Shut Up" came on.

When Jimmy heard it, he couldn't hide his excitement. "Who's the girl on that track?"

"Stacy Ferguson," we said.

"You *need* to put that girl in the group!"

I think all of us shifted uncomfortably in our seats when we first heard that, and we went away to discuss the suggestion that seemed loaded with label expectation. It was not a decision that was going to be rushed, because we had reservations. Not only because we ideally wanted to remain as an all-male trio, but because Stacy had made it clear that she was a solo artist who didn't wish to be part of a group. So would her heart be in it?

We also knew that one great recording session did not mean she was going to "fit," even if we agreed she was telegenic. Bringing in an outsider was a hard concept, especially at a time when we felt freer after ditching Kim.

But with open minds, we invited Stacy to join us on our trip to the four-day Falls Festival in Australia in Lorne, where we shared a bill with Jack Johnson. It was one of those casual "come-along-for-the-ride" invitations, but we all knew that it was the do-or-die experiment.

Thrown into the deep end without a rehearsal; a live audition, if you like.

She had never before performed with a live band or with in-ear pieces, and we were no Wild Orchid. In terms of initiation ceremonies, it was potentially brutal. But if there was one thing I would discover about Fergie, it is that she is unfraid of taking chances.

Before going on, we had given her the chill-out pep talk. "Don't worry about fitting in, just do your thing . . . We've got your back, we'll fill in any gaps . . . Just let it come to you."

"Okay, got it," she said, without a flicker of intimidation.

We were probably two songs in when I thought, *Okay, she works.*

She didn't know her spots, and not everything was slick, but it was her presence: she strutted on stage like a veteran rock 'n' roll chick and . . . BOOM . . . impact made. She transferred what we had seen in the vocal booth to the stage, multiplied by ten. What she unleashed that day was some inner wild animal that Macy, Esthero, and Kim never had, and that crazy energy matched our own. She may have been untrained Pea-style and rough around the edges, but so were we at first.

I think any other female debutante in that scenario would have withered or drowned, but Fergie seized it, stepped up, and carved out a slot that we now could not survive without. What further impressed us was that she was eager to learn, and—like us—she was clearly a perfectionist. We could have scoured the earth and placed job applications in every city in the world looking for the attributes she brought, and found no one. And she had dropped into our lap with a serendipity that had been trying to make itself known since our first album launch at the El Rey Theater in 1997.

She fit in with the same amount of ease socially, too, and the two of us hit it off immediately. She was then what she remains today: a regular, humble girl who could not be more down to earth if she tried. Somebody very real but blessed with star appeal.

She started coming to Club AD with us, and we'd all pile into her white Mustang drop-top and head out there, together with her friend Eileen, and I found a dancing kindred-spirit in Fergie.

We fed off each other's energy. I would do a move. She would do a move. And you'll still find us breaking out, mirroring each other on stage to this day.

As founding Peas, me, Apl, and Will had been tight since way back, and in walked this stranger from Hacienda Heights who fit in like some long-lost relative, and she was sexy without being catty, confident without being arrogant, strong without being over-domineering, and tomboyish without losing her femininity.

With Fergie's very positive vibe added to the camp, we found ourselves sparking even more creatively. We even added another song, "Fly Away," to the album; a song that was initially intended for her "solo package."

Elephunk was ready for release and the Peas were now a quartet.

We wouldn't know it straightaway but in Fergie, we had found our missing ingredient to the magic formula we had long been searching for.

STRATOSPHERES

If I had experienced a premonition of the whirlwind that was about to suck us up and drop us in another stratosphere, I would have probably put it down to a delayed hallucination from the 'shrooms and acid I once did. As the summer of 2003 arrived, we released our first single "Where Is the Love?" from the album *Elephunk*, and it exploded with such force that it turned self-belief into disbelief.

What happened over the next year or so was life-changing, somehow made sweeter by every struggle, frustration, and setback we had faced because it was a dream that arrived not pristine and artificially new but vintage-looking and worn, made in a different age and stained with the deposits of sweat, blood, and tears that it had collected in the eight years it spent in the making.

Half my problem was believing that something good was actually happening. Being in a good place used to mess with my head. I carried around that "too good to be true" doubt that made me feel like some impostor in my own dream; that someone would one day say I wasn't good enough and then ask me to leave the stage.

When I started thinking that way, all kinds of destructive shit started to happen. That's why, on a personal level, hell was about to kick in during the fall of 2003, because I was about to meet myself—and my dream—head-on at the crossroads. On a professional level, the sudden change for the Black Eyed Peas was about to make its velocity known.

That change began inside the West Arena in Phoenix, where Justin Timberlake and Christina Aguilera's co-headlining tour, Justified & Stripped, kicked off with us as the supporting act. We opened on June 4, 2003—twenty days before the official release of *Elephunk.*

All we had planned for was the tour's end, in St. Paul, Minnesota, on August 24. It was, as far as we were concerned, a rare platform that provided us with another crowd—the pop crowd—to win over. Our final taste, as it turned out, of being chameleons and underdogs.

It was Justin who first suggested the idea that we join him on his forty-five-date tour with Christina. The lateness in booking the tour meant that tickets had already been printed, so we were an invisible supporting act until the actual night, and that omission tapped into our old music-festival mentality of taking people by surprise and making them sit up and take note.

We only had a twenty-minute set, so we concentrated on the fast, intense, high-energy songs, and then ended with "Where Is the Love?" with Fergie singing Justin's hook. It was never going to be protocol for the headliner to join the supporting act on stage, and we were cool with that. If anything, Fergie's voice added a new, special quality that was not there before.

The single was released twelve days into the tour, and, suddenly, we found favor with the U.S. radio stations. A door that our music had been banging on suddenly opened into a nation's consciousness, and it was being played *everywhere.* Friends phoned us from different cities, from inside shopping malls and taxi cabs. I saw radio towers in my head, sending out sound waves of Black Eyed Peas music across the world.

It was then that something amazing started to happen.

With the arenas 95 percent full of 20,000–25,000 crowds as we closed with "Where Is the Love?" we noticed that the first two rows started joining in, singing the chorus. A few days later, it spread four and five rows back . . . then ten rows back . . . then fifteen.

"That's dope!" we said, seeing for the first time the power of radio play.

I watched it build as we sang, spreading like some freak wave from city to city.

"Did you see that?" the band said to us after each performance, and we all started to view the arena's seating like a graph where the colored blocks just kept on growing, charting our popularity.

One week later, it reached rows halfway back, to the point where we heard our own words returned to us in unison. By week four—at the tour's midway point—the whole arena was consumed by a mass rendition of "Where Is the Love?" and it was an incredible feeling to see the entire crowd standing, arms waving, singing it out loud; down the sides and stretching out in front of us. I couldn't wipe the smile from my face when I saw that ripple happen every night.

We were suddenly Pea-approved by a massive mainstream audience, and Justin's people took note. From once being worried about the song diluting his solo work, they asked that "Where Is the Love?" be included in *his* set, not closing ours. We, the supporting act, were promoted to accompany Justin, the headliner, and so, having started and finished our segment by 8 p.m., we walked back on stage around 10 p.m., introduced by Justin to his sold-out venues, "Yo, these are my boys . . ." he said, "GIVE IT UP AGAIN FOR THE BLACK EYED PEAS!"

And the place roared.

Seth Friedman's doubts on the Macy Gray tour fell away when he said, "The moment I saw these arenas singing 'Where Is the Love?' I knew something big was happening."

Ironically, the ripple effect spread faster across the Atlantic Ocean than it did across America. London—the city where we always felt our music was embraced quicker by radio and by people—went #1 that fall, and we stayed there for six weeks. "Where Is the Love?" became the U.K.'s twenty-fifth-best-selling single of the millennium, and it was also the best-selling single of 2003. It's not hard to see why London is set in stone in our minds as the place where we first blew up on the charts.

We didn't make the same impact on the American charts where we reached #8 on the U.S. *Billboard* Hot 100. A few months later, as the song gathered momentum around the world, we shot to #1 on the *Billboard* 100 Top 40 Mainstream chart, which is based not on sales but on radio play—a sweet irony after being untouchable and unplayable since 1998.

Elsewhere around the world, constant phone calls brought nothing but good news as we hit #1 across the rest of Europe, Australia, and New Zealand, and blew up in Asia and Latin America. Our international market was much stronger than domestic sales, and we kept saying how much overseas was kicking America's ass. Our "Joints & Jam" philosophy was becoming more than a lyric or a hope. Our single was a monster across the world.

We kept saying it out loud—"Number one around the world . . . Number one around the world"—as if repetition would make it easier to accept, and I thought about Jimmy Iovine, the man who had spent millions backing us even when the odds did not look good. It is often believers that will carry your talent across the finish line in the end, not luck.

We also recognized that years of touring festivals and college campuses had given us a solid foundation to build on; eight years of bricklaying. Had we been a group who arrived overnight with just one hit, we would never have been in such a strong position to push on, but now, with festival recognition behind us, we had the world to go at. And that mattered as we set about capitalizing on the global interest we had harnessed. We knew that if we kept our foot on the gas, our international reputation could only keep growing, so Ron immediately got to work with Seth and Polo to organize a nine-month run of spot dates around the world to start the moment Justified & Stripped wrapped.

That kind of follow-through after the breakthrough is probably one of the most important periods in an artist's career, because it is a relentless and demanding schedule, hitting the tour bus and spot dates with the intensity of a presidential campaign. The industry is full of hard-luck stories about one-hit wonders, and we were adamant that that not be our fate. It was going to be the hardest we had ever worked, but the more we broke our backs, the bigger the payoff would be.

Years on the road had prepared us in a small way, but the *Elephunk* experience was a new beast, because the breakneck conveyor belt we jumped on dragged our asses out of bed at 5 a.m. and didn't dump us back to our hotels until 1 a.m. We did three shows a day: television breakfast shows like *Good Morning America* and *Good Day LA* at 6 a.m., the tour at 7 p.m.; and our own late-night club dates at 11:30 p.m. that had been booked at the outset.

Inside the arenas, everyone was there for Justin and Christina. Inside the clubs, we still needed to jack off to our own shit within our own hour for our own fans. It was the balancing act between reaching out to new fans and honoring the small but loyal fan base we had built up since 1995.

As the song's success kept snowballing, we had this running joke with Seth Friedman and Polo about whether having a sudden hit meant we would get instantly rich—which, of course, we didn't. Not immediately. Not on the strength of one song. But it didn't stop me from asking "Yo, are we rich yet?"

I asked it so much that it was decided to attach it to *anything* that happened afterward:

"Congratulations! You've just sold your first million!"—"Yo, Seth . . . are we rich yet?"

"Hey, guys—you've been invited to the VMAs!"—"Yo, Seth . . . are we rich yet?"

"You've just gone double platinum in the UK!"—"Yo, Seth . . . are we rich yet?"

"Does anybody need anything?"—"Yo, Seth . . . are we rich yet?"

There was always an underlying reason behind the joke for me, because money was my only measure of success. The day when I had a million in the bank, could buy my own house, and move from Mom's couch was my tidemark for declaring "success." It was about success, not fame; something enduring, not fleeting, and our first hit single had made me hungrier.

Every day felt like a celebration, but with every celebration came an excuse to drink. I guess the only way to explain it is to ask you to remember the last major celebration or achievement you had, and you probably wanted to go out, get drunk, and celebrate with that "I've earned this" mentality.

That was my thinking every day for the first year of breaking through.

I became used to living life at 100 miles per hour, so I drank to keep the fun going, to unwind, and to celebrate; three reasons in one. I was no longer partying on Ecstasy and cocaine. All I was doing was harmless stuff: starting the day with a daily helping of weed, and then ending each day by raiding the minibar and downing the vodka miniatures and half-bottles of wine before sinking into five hours of sleep. Drinking not only became the climax to a routinely thrilling day, it helped knock me out. Vodka and wine became my rock 'n' roll version of hot chocolate before bed. I didn't have time to think about what I was doing because we were too consumed with keeping busy, being tired, and keeping the show on the road.

I could blame MTV.

Because it teased me with the words: "If twenty years is not a reason to party, we really don't know what is"—which is the last thing you need to tease a party animal with.

We had been invited to our first VMAs at Radio City Music Hall in New York, where we gave a preshow performance of "Where Is the Love?" on an outdoor stage before the ceremony began, marking the twentieth anniversary of MTV. The problem with a preshow slot was that it gave me plenty of drinking time at the main bar before we took our seats. I got pissy drunk. The star power, the prestige, the ongoing disbelief, and the alcohol all went to my head, even though I had listened to Polo when he said it was "important to be professional tonight, Tab."

I wore a fresh outfit—red glasses with a red leather hat and black leather pants, matching the color scheme for the music video—and happily accepted the free half-bottles of wine, drinking it like water. I never sipped wine. I only gulped it.

First one, then two, then three.

In the space of an hour.

Polo gave one of those "Don't you think you need to slow it down!" nudges, a serious hint delivered through gritted teeth and nervous smile, and his frustration got worse the sloppier I became. I started trying to accost other artists, walking up to the likes of Jay-Z and 50 Cent only to find Polo's arm hooking my neck and dragging me back into line. Polo always said that when I drank, I turned into someone else—the belligerent, tedious drunk who was loud and embarrassing. He was one of the few people who could get away with saying that, because he was like an older brother who always checked me. Not that it did any good back then.

My problem was that once I started drinking, I couldn't stop, and I had the alcohol tolerance of a teenager and the appetite of a hardened veteran. So this big night was not looking good even before the ceremony began. What made it worse was that we had been booked for a special performance of our single at a private after-party for Justin Timberlake. It was a big night for us, Polo had constantly reminded me, dropping anchor-sized hints on my toes.

I had not been in my seat long when I started getting antsy, and the wine started taking hold. I acted like one of those drunken idiots in the street, hollering wildly when Madonna and Britney shared their French kiss moment and laughing like a hyena at host Chris Rock's jokes. He was funny, but not *that* funny.

Apparently, Will and the band were embarrassed by my exaggerated reactions, and by the fact that I was swaying even in my bucket seat, with a lolling head, and it soon became clear to everyone that there was no way I was making the Justin gig.

"We'll do it with the three of us," said Will. "Just get him out of here before it gets any worse."

Polo was furious. At the next break, he guided me from my seat and I stumbled up the aisle, out the door, and into the street. As soon as the outside air hit me, I was gone, so Polo slung one of my arms around his neck and walked me home; the silently fuming father leading his drunken teenage son home.

Luckily, our hotel was only two blocks away, and he dumped me in my room, dropping me on the bed, leaving me sprawled out, facedown.

"I'm sorry, Polo, I let you down, huh," I slurred.

"You are a disgrace, brother," he said, "and you've disappointed me and let down the group, the band, but most of all, yourself. You've worked so hard to get to this level and you're treating it like one big party. What is wrong with you?!"

He ranted a bit more and then came his parting shot: "I do not understand, why you want to fuck it all up before it has even started?" And then he walked out, leaving me to sleep it off.

What is wrong with you?

Echoes of what Julio always said.

Why do you want to fuck it all up?

Echoes of how my father lived in his youth.

I woke the next morning, still in my clothes, half-remembering the lecture, and I grabbed the newspaper hanging from the outside door handle to see if we had made any photographs on the red carpet. No. The only MTV item making headlines was the media's excitement over that Madonna kiss with Britney; a moment of VMAs notoriety that, thankfully, eclipsed my own.

That morning, I made my apologies to the group for my behavior, and vowed never to let them down again. I told Polo I would never be a disappointment in his eyes again. I would step up from this moment on.

What I said was so impassioned that even I believed what I was saying.

■　■　■

We were reunited with Justin Timberlake on the European leg of Justified & Stripped. I forget where we were, but one night we had come to the end of another performance of "Where Is the Love?" and were doing our onstage good-bye routine when Fergie gave him a hug, Apl shook his hand, and Will got all cool and shook his hand and then dropped into the splits, which the crowd loved. So I tried to follow suit, but, as I dropped, my leg went one way and my knee the other, and the shot of searing pain told me straightaway that it wasn't good.

It turned out that I had torn my meniscus and the doctors insisted I rest, otherwise it would get fucked up even more. So that took me off the *Elephunk* train for about six weeks.

Physically, I appreciated the breather; but, mentally, I never was any good at just sitting around. It got frustrating hobbling on crutches, feeling like a grounded astronaut. The worst frustration was when we learned that "Where Is the Love?" was up for the Mainstream Top 40 Track of the Year award at the 14th annual Billboard Awards: our first-ever nomination.

I was reduced to sitting at home watching the ceremony on the television, eating chips with Mom and Celeste as Will, Apl, and Fergie lived it up at the MGM Grand in Vegas. I sat there, leg propped up and crutches to one side, feeling sorry for myself, never thinking for a single second that we would nail it, but then it was announced we had won and I leaped up and started bouncing around on my good leg. The cameras panned around to capture my partners' faces, and I couldn't stop yelling for them. Then Will got to the rostrum, made a great speech and gave me a shout-out: ". . . and we want to thank Taboo, he couldn't be here tonight because he's injured his leg but this is also for you, brother . . ."

I raised one crutch in salute and told Mom that I couldn't stay in. This was a moment that deserved a celebration, so I went into Hollywood with our old friend Paul Chan. It seemed appropriate that the man who first designed our logo that appeared on flyers around L.A. now shared the fact that our name was carved into the gold plaque of our first trophy.

I hobbled into my usual haunts, Joseph's and then A.D., and told everyone we were Billboard winners, and the drinks came thick and fast. As the three other Peas celebrated and did media in Vegas, I got shit-faced again in Hollywood.

There was a special intensity about 2003–04, and the schedule reflected it, as the *Elephunk* ride became a whirlwind that took us around the world at a mad speed for nine months. We were here, there, and everywhere promoting the shit out of ourselves: the support act for the Dave Matthews Band; holding our first headliner dates in Sydney and Melbourne; performing a series of spot dates around the world.

The album reached #14 in the *Billboard* Hot 200, #3 in the U.K., and sold eight and a half million copies worldwide. Its official release date may have been June 2003, but the life of the album lasted until the end of 2004. Apart from my six-week layoff, our feet didn't touch Los Angeles soil for about a year, as we added some exotic stamps to our passports with performances in places like Singapore, China, Vietnam, Malaysia, Japan, Taiwan, India, and Israel, as well as the usual stops of every major capital city in Europe. We also did Australia and New Zealand, where the album went #1.

It was a ride we never expected, and it catapulted us into a different stratosphere. They were long-ass days that were punishing, and I was often dead on my feet. We did our own makeup and grabbed catnaps on green-room sofas, studio floors, or the tour bus.

Until you have lived the onslaught of three shows a day, it is hard to explain the exhaustion and sleep deprivation, but we knew that the brutal schedule was our one shot, and, if anything, it tested our mettle and discipline, and made sure that we were serious about what we had wished for.

We were booked by every television network, every chat show, and every radio station, often dividing up the welter of interviews between the four of us. That shit went so fast that we hardly had time to catch our breaths and gather our thoughts. It became like a runaway train, getting faster and faster, and that became the pace of life. We laughed and screamed like crazy cats on a crazy ride, smoking weed to keep grounded. Once you have been through an experience like that together—living, eating, sleeping, breathing, and surviving the craziness—it cements the unity, and because we were adjusting to a new life as a quartet with Fergie aboard, that kind of baptism by fire could not have been better timed. We were just thrown into the deep end, and the more we swam, the more we gelled, and the more our performance synergy improved.

In total, we would do four hundred sixty-five performances or appearances over the next year; and in the first six months, "Where Is the Love?" stood tall as one of the biggest-selling singles of 2003, selling around two million copies worldwide. Not bad for a song that started out as a ringtone.

When that weird animal called fame attaches itself to your success, the most bizarre things can happen, and the following story proves that fame doesn't change the person, it changes the people around the person. Which is why I take you to the Canadian border for one of the oddest stories of our travels.

Management had forewarned us that if we had any weed by the time we reached the U.S.-Canada border, to make sure we had smoked it because the border patrol cops like nothing more than searching tour buses for all sorts of substances. But, being the dumb-ass, I forgot that I had stashed some weed under the mattress of my bunk. I didn't realize this error until the men in uniform had walked their air of authority onto the bus with a thoroughness that made me

feel like a Mexican druglord. Then, the shit went down. "Whose is the last bunk to the left on the top?" asked the officer. I 'fessed up, and they said they were placing me under arrest, and I was taken off the bus to the patrol's office. I saw the rest of the group and band's faces thinking it even if they weren't saying it: "There's Tab . . . and another dumb-ass episode."

I had been busted for less than a gram. That was sloppy.

I sat in this holding area and the officer, all stern and serious, told me that we could "play this the easy way or the hard way, seeing that you have less than a gram."

I listened, desperate to discover the easy way.

"The hard way is that you pay the fine, which is five hundred dollars, or you can—" And this smile broke out across his face and his colleagues started to smirk. "—you can sign an autograph, take a picture with us, and make our kids very happy."

At first, I wasn't sure if he was serious, but he wasn't joking. The dude wanted an autograph.

So I signed the picture, and we burned rubber getting out of there, and I screamed with relief all the way across the border and into Canada.

One of the most poignant trips was to Apl's home country, the Philippines, where he was treated like a king when we arrived. When I saw the mass media and crowds that greeted us at the airport, it made me think of the kind of reception the Beatles used to enjoy. Fans screamed his name and offered us fruit, bread, and flowers. Forget the red carpet. This was royal treatment, Apl style. I was just happy that the brother I had shared an apartment with received such a deserving reception in such an unforgettable way.

He was a little overwhelmed. He is so humble and such a class act, and he knew that everything he had sacrificed had paid off; the Prodigal Son had returned home. When we met his mom, Christina, for the first time, we saw the love that existed and better understood the sacrifices he had made to improve his family's future. Forget about rising from the projects in East L.A. That was no comparison to the boy rising from an area in the foothills of the volcano Mount Pinatubo, an area that resembled a jungle, where locals live in grass huts with tin roofs and every "house" has a pig or two as a sign of wealth.

Seeing with our own eyes the background and the odds that he overcame—as opposed to seeing photographs—gave me a renewed admiration that remains immeasurable.

I also enjoyed my first visit to the Motherland, Mexico City, but I can't pretend the reception was the same. No one knew me and no one knew what to make of me. I swear that half of Mexico thought I was Asian! I was just happy to be on Mexican soil, reacquainting myself with my ancestors and getting to see the world. I felt no strong attachment, not having any family there, but what mattered was not so much the roots of being a Latino, but a Latino representing his people wherever I am.

Not many hip-hop groups would have the chance to take their music around the world like we did, and we soon moved on to attending the MTV Asia Awards in Singapore and the MTV Latin America Awards in Miami, where we were awarded Best International Hip-Hop/R&B Artists above the Beastie Boys, 50 Cent, OutKast, and Usher.

I was the group's spokesman that night because I was the only one capable of providing the acceptance speech in Spanish. I said how proud I was to be a Latino member of the Black Eyed Peas, and I think that was the moment my fellow Mexicans sat up and realized I was not Asian but one of them, standing on top of the world.

I like to think those nights demonstrate that I had short spurts of good behavior; when the soul occasionally forced the ego to tap out. *Elephunk* was a dream ride, but nothing was more surreal than the time when a childhood wish came true; a night that has gone down in Black Eyed Pea folklore as the time when Taboo finally had a one-on-one with his idol Prince—and still managed to fuck it up. When sober.

It was either the night of the Oscars or the Golden Globes. I can't remember. All I know is that there were a lot of actors at Prince's crib on the night we were invited to one of his after-parties.

Having missed meeting him in Chicago with Macy, life had awarded me a second chance. Only this was no backstage jammin' session. This was an invite to walk into the Kingdom of Heaven.

An all-purple furnished heaven in the Hollywood Hills.

All the way there, Apl kept making fun of me for fanning out before even meeting the guy, because it was all I could talk about.

As I walked inside, my feet crossed the famous "love symbol" of the Prince motif, set in black into the polished white floor. I scanned the room, ignored the Champagne and spotted some recognizable faces: Denzel Washington, Reese Witherspoon, Pamela Anderson, and Spike Lee, and then Penelope Cruz and Salma Hayek gossiping in the kitchen. I saw Cher. Then John Stamos. And then I saw and heard Prince as he started jammin' in the living room. It was the coolest thing I had ever seen—Prince, up close and personal.

I didn't think the night could get any better until Apl tossed me a mic. Me and Apl—the only two Peas there—followed-up Prince's showcase of genius, and Apl started free-styling, laying down some verses as we attempted to hype the A-list crowd. Prince—wearing a pristine purple shirt and white pants—stood

to one side of our guitarist George Pajon and our homie J.J. Anderson at the front.

Then it was my turn to be MC on the mic, and I wanted to use the opportunity to connect with Prince and win his respect with an impassioned rap. I started to bounce and hype the audience that was about a hundred and fifty strong.

"Say rock that shit!"

And the crowd gave it back to me. "ROCK THAT SHIT!"

"Say, That funky shit!"

"THAT FUNKY SHIT!"

And then I kicked it: "The roof! The roof! The roof is on fire . . . We don't need no water . . . let the mothafucka burn . . . burn mothafucka . . . burn . . ."

That was when I noticed Prince whispering in George's ear and George relaying something to Apl. Seconds later, just as I was getting into a rhythm, Apl stepped in, grabbed the mic and said, "Yo, Prince wants you to get off the mic, dude."

It was like someone had just removed the needle from the record and stopped the party. I spent the next hour stressing out about what I had done wrong, and it didn't bode well when Prince's assistant approached me and said, "Would you mind him speaking with you once the party is done?"

As guests drifted away, me and Apl were summoned to the downstairs music room, which was stacked with amplifiers and guitars. On the walls, there were framed album covers and platinum discs. We perched on the edge of two amplifiers, and then the main man—petite, serene, and chill—walked in, and my private audience with Prince began. Even though we were seated, we were still on his eye level. He is that small.

Then he started to talk, looking directly at me.

"My brother," he began, "I need you to understand that the only reason I took away your mic was because of the foul language you were using in the house of Jehovah."

He couldn't have been more serious. Not once did that pencil moustache twitch.

I tried to apologize. "I'm sorry, I didn't mean to disrespect . . ."

But he continued: "The slave master has you trained to always use foul language."

The slave master?

Prince, noting the frown, smiled like one of those teachers who pities the dumb kid.

"What you have to understand is that we all must grow and learn. I want the Black Eyed Peas to come on tour with me but I want you to first learn from this experience . . ."

"Cool," said Apl, chipping in.

". . . but I wouldn't want you using foul language again," said Prince.

I didn't really know how to respond. All I could think about in my confusion were the lyrics to his classics like "Sexy Motherfucker," "Erotic City," "Nasty Girl" and "Sex Shooter." I couldn't connect the dots between his constant cussing and his sermon to me now.

He said some more profound things about life and how he had learned, and then said: "You have to train to learn how to hype a crowd without using the kind of language you used in my house."

He spoke with the soft-spoken compassion of a priest, and I was kneeling at the altar of a megastar who was bestowing on me some life lessons. (I later found out that he underwent some kind of spiritual awakening in 2000.)

When he stopped speaking, we were suspended in this moment of reflection, and all I could hear was him breathing, in . . . and out, in . . . and out. And that is when my idol worship got the better of me.

"Taboo," said Prince, "I would love for you to do a prayer with me."

"You serious?" I said as more of a statement than a question.

"Would you like to pray with me, brother?"

I jumped up, fisted the palm of my hand, and blurted out: "Damn, Prince, you're the SHIT! Thank you, man . . . tha . . ."

And then realized what I had done. Apl looked at me like I was an idiot, and the look of disappointment on Prince's face will stay with me forever. We must have been in there for about forty-five minutes and it was ending perfectly—until I cussed again.

"You see, my brother," he said, "you will never learn. After all this training, you still use foul language." And he wished us well before leaving us in the hands of his assistant to let us out.

"FUUUCCK!" I said outside, hating myself.

"You see, that's the problem with you, Tab," said Apl, grinning, "You'll just never fucking learn."

The next time I saw Prince was backstage a few months later in L.A. at the 46th Grammy Awards, when a dream night saw us nominated for Record of the Year and performing "Where Is the Love?" on stage with a forty-piece orchestra and the band.

Prince opened the 2004 ceremony with Beyoncé, performing classics like "Purple Rain" and "Let's Go Crazy," and when he saw me, everything was cool. I just don't think he was ever going to invite me to free-style again. We had a few words and he wished me luck for the night.

We all took our families that night, and Mom was my guest. We sent a

limo to pick her up in Rosemead after it had first picked up Apl's adopted father, Mr. Joe Ben Hudgens. The parents of the two kids who battled at Ballistyx and slummed it at Edgemont Manor were now going to see them perform on the biggest stage in music.

As Mom said that night, it was one thing to see me get a record deal, and one thing to see me in concert. But this? "This is the Grammys, Jaime!"

I know, Mom. I was pinching myself, too.

That night was a bonding moment that made all the trials and tribulations seem irrelevant. But before the ceremony, and after rehearsals that afternoon, I took a moment to savor it alone—and share it with Nanny.

I sat in a chair near the front and counted the steps to the stage.

"One day, you will be climbing steps to perform in front of the world. Believe that, Jimmy. Believe it," I heard her say.

I did a full three-sixty and scanned row after row of the thousands of deserted seats behind me, climbing from the arena floor to the steep tiers that rose into glass-fronted suites, stacked three high. Above them, some one hundred fifty feet high—were the names of basketball legends, hung from the rafters as giant purple and gold jerseys: number 25, Goodrich; number 42, Worthy; and number 32, Johnson—legends almost as good as my own childhood hero Michael Jordan.

We had always watched the Grammys on television as kids, and they came back to us as a montage of memories that afternoon: the first time a hip-hop song won a Grammy with MCs DJ Jazzy Jeff & the Fresh Prince, aka Will Smith; the first time we saw MC Hammer perform and then Belle Biv Devoe do their thing; and the iconic moment when Michael Jackson won for *Thriller* and had Brooke Shields on his arm. And there we were, walking in those same shadows with a dressing room in the same corridors stained by the sweat of the L.A. Lakers.

"Way to go, Jim! Way to go, Jim!"

That night, the *Washington Post* said we gave *"the most impassioned performance of the night,"* and it was mind-blowing to think that we killed it in a broadcast to twenty-six million people around the world. It was a perfect evening which not even I could mess up.

The Black Eyed Peas have won six Grammys in total up to 2011, but we still haven't won one of the big ones, and we still haven't won on camera; we've won those awards that the telecasts deem not important enough to broadcast. But that elusive moment is something we are still shooting for. Life is all about finding new dreams.

As the Peas' momentum continued, it seemed to positively affect the whole album. As well as radio play, corporate America, political America, and world-famous brands wanted to surf the wave with us. It was as if we became hot overnight and everyone wanted a piece of us.

The NBA adopted "Let's Get Retarded" for the play-offs, which was huge for us as basketball fans. As part of the deal, we changed it up by tweaking the lyrics and renaming the track "Let's Get It Started" for a more sport-appropriate anthem (as incorporated on the album's second run). It meant that we were in constant NBA playback on ABC, and, as the song's popularity spread, it led to an invitation to perform at the Democratic National Convention in Boston.

By doing that, we were lending support to the presidential campaign of nominee John Kerry. None of us were politically rabid, and this was the first time we had ever gotten involved in political issues. But we were moved to support the Democrats because we just wanted George Bush out of the White House. In traveling the world, we had seen and heard how much he was being viewed and ridiculed; this war-mongering idiot representing America. As far as I was concerned, he was embarrassing to have as a leader. Lending "Let's Get It Started" to the Democratic campaign was part of the message for the nation to get a new chapter started.

It was probably the most unanimated crowd we had ever performed for, but there was good energy that day. And even though Bush won a second term that year, it felt dope to be a part of something on that scale, making our convention debut.

Also making his debut that day was a black senator giving his first keynote speech. I didn't get to meet Barack Obama (only Will met him a few days later, at some rock 'n' roll gala dinner) but, in my book, that memory has not gone down as "the day we played to the National Democratic Convention," but "the day we played to Obama"; the day when a leader was born and change got started.

Away from the political stage, Apple also wanted to adapt our music and use "Hey Mama" for the launch of its new television iPod campaign, and that collaboration was sweet justice for us after the Napster episode, because it meant our music was associated with the opening of the iTunes Store. Ironically, it was "Let's Get It Started" that was an instant download success, selling 500,000 downloads in the U.S. alone. We were in charge now. Not Napster.

Popularity for "Hey Mama" also grew, and it eventually ended up getting used in *Garfield: The Movie* when Garfield and Odie had a Ballistyx-style dance-off.

It didn't matter whether we were reaching Democratic followers or Garfield fans, these two singles were proof that brand association was thinking outside the box, and taking chart music with it. Even though both songs only performed okay on the charts, we were reaching millions through other mediums, and, in turn, our brand was growing alongside our music. The first step that we had taken with Dr Pepper had proven a wise one.

■ ■ ■

Every change in fortunes leads to someone, somewhere, spending time with a calculator working out the portions of the pie before the gold dust has even settled. So when drummer Terry Graves' hand was raised in the air asking for a pay increase, it was disappointing, because he became expectant at a time when things were in transition.

We had always recognized Terry's role and contribution, because he had been there from the start and was regarded as an essential part of the band, Beat Pharmacy. But he wasn't as indispensable as he seemed to think he was, as time would prove.

Terry was disgruntled, suggesting he was the "Musical Director" and therefore deserved an increase, but what irritated management was that he was making a fuss about this at a time when we needed to be focused, pushing forward.

Will and Polo both acknowledged Terry's previous value and input, and suggested that they would take a favorable look at his pay down the line, but asked if he could wait a bit longer. But that wasn't going to happen and, after a heated conversation with Polo, Terry left. When he left, Mike Fratatuno left, too, because they were best friends and he didn't appreciate the way the situation had been handled. I respected his loyalty, if not his argument, and Mike going was a big loss. It was sad to me that just as we made the big game, two key players who had got us there decided to bow out over the terms and conditions box at a time of dizzying transition. I couldn't really understand the hurry, but that wasn't my business to understand. What mattered was finding an equally good drummer as a replacement. What happened is that we found an even better one in Keith Harris.

Keith, the funky drummer from Chicago, is hands down one of the best musicians I have met in my life, and he demonstrated his professionalism on his first day when he came to his first show with music sheets of every Black Eyed Pea song, written out in his own hand.

This dude was on point from day one, and reassured everyone that he was the man for the job. He brings an intensity and a timing like no one else, and the way he plays is flashy, tossing those sticks like a juggler. He was so good that we started to test him—throwing a bottle of water at him mid-set, but he caught it, kept playing, drank it and kept playing, and never missed a beat.

The new setup meant a new name for the band: from Beat Pharmacy to Bucky Jonson, and these guys—Keith (drums), Printz Board (keyboard and trumpet), George Pajon (guitar), and Tim Izzo (sax, guitar, and flute)—are the backbone of the Black Eyed Peas, as well as producers and cowriters. Without their skills and camaraderie, we would never have survived or achieved what we have achieved. Every time I step out on stage, I ride their brilliance, and feel that rare connection and cohesion between group and band. Sometimes, I look at all the different components that make up the Black Eyed Peas—from the Peas to the band, from dancers to stage crew, from wardrobe to makeup, from management to catering—and it seems we have been blessed with the kind of like-minded people who make the experience feel like family and enrich the journey we would all share together.

Within the family, our new sister had fit in like she'd always been one of us. I had viewed Fergie as Joan Jett crossed with Madonna; the rock 'n' roll girl with a pop track record who liked listening to groups like Guns N' Roses and Led Zeppelin. That she made the transition into a Black Eyed Pea so effortlessly speaks to her versatility as an artist.

Our sound was different, and better, because of her. She was as powerful and hard as she was sensual and soulful, and her inclusion provided that cross-over into pop-rock that we never had before. As she carved out her role, she became the siren of what she refers to as "the four-headed dragon," and, throughout 2003–2004, she started to unveil, bit by bit, the marketable sex appeal that also brought the "wow" factor to the Peas.

At first, she let her voice speak for itself, often portraying this tomboyish white rapper-girl vibe, with the blue tracksuit tops she wore in honor of *Elephunk*'s cover color scheme. But then the cutoff tops came out and showed off some ripped abs, and the world flipped out. We may have previously had a cool vibe with something vintage, abstract, witty, and different in terms of our dance and live band, but Fergie added the sex appeal that made the spotlights brighter.

Since then, Fergie has personally evolved through various stages: from the tracksuit-wearing hip-hop girl to the sex-bomb babe with the hard-core body to the current style icon with her own solo fan base alongside the Peas.

Her whole package—the firebrand energy, the voice, the look— contributed such synergy that it was hard to see how we had ever functioned without her.

Not that her transition was all plain sailing.

She, like me, would have to get used to swimming in the deep end when it came to rapping, and I'll never forget the first time we took to the stage as the Peas with Fergie, when she was getting her feet wet prior to the Justified & Stripped tour. It was a spot date in San Diego at some place called the Belly-Up Tavern, and we jumped into a segment of free-styling, which came naturally for three MCs, but not the new female vocalist, and, because it was a spontaneous thing, she had no warning.

Like I said before, though, Fergie—all 5'4" of her—runs from nothing.

We were on stage before an audience of about a hundred and we all kicked our verses before we gave up the mic to her, hoping she had used the time

to think about the direction she was going in. The beat had been hard, and we had given it some intensity, so the tempo was raised and ready for her to ride and give it everything she had. She had the look, the energy, and the moves . . . but then she started channeling the Jackson 5.

"ABC, easy as 1-2-3/as simple as do-re-mi . . ."

All the guys just looked at each other. *Huh?*

"ABC, 1-2-3, baby you and meeee . . ."

It was funny as fuck—and a little awkward—but the audience must have thought it was all part of the schtick. We did have some gentle words to say afterward, and I think it was Will who said, "Yo, Ferg, you seemed to be stretching there a bit . . ."

"I didn't know what to say!" she said. "So I just ran with what I knew!"

It was agreed that free-styling was not going to be her strong point. And if she did have to spit from the dome again, we told her to feel free to scat and do some la-la-la's or da-da-da's.

Just no more ABCs and 123s.

We all like teasing one another as the Black Eyed Peas, and sometimes, the humor can be merciless, but no one is better at mimicry than Fergie, because "doing voices" has always been her thing.

One little-known fact is that she used to be the voice of Charlie Brown's curly-haired sister, Sally. If you watched *It's Flashbeagle, Charlie Brown* or *Snoopy's Getting Married, Charlie Brown* or *The Charlie Brown and Snoopy Show* in 1984 and 1985, that is when you will have first heard the voice of Fergie. She also does a dope version of Veruca Salt from *Charlie and the Chocolate Factory.*

She had also starred in the variety show *Kids Incorporated,* which had a similar format to *The Mickey Mouse Club.* She had her first agent at nine and then went from teenhood into Wild Orchid. As someone who had worked in the entertainment business all her life, she had never known too much "normal"; a social misfit, if you like. Another misfit.

She joked that she used to sing about anything she saw as a kid, making up songs about food on the table or people in the street, and tap-dancing to her made-up lyrics.

She was raised in the Hacienda Heights district of Los Angeles, and grew up vowing to be a performer. Which explains the hunger she arrived with as a new Pea.

Onstage, we have an awareness that each of us knows what the others are thinking and where the others are, like we have eyes in the back of our heads. It's like a sixth sense, and there is nothing better than having your family onstage, feeling good and seeing them smiling and joking as we perform.

U2 have always been an inspiration to us that way. They stuck together first and foremost because of their friendship, and have remained a tight-knit family through all trials, tribulations, and solo projects. If we could have the longevity of groups like U2 and the Rolling Stones, that would be a happy future, because the Black Eyed Peas is an army, a tribe, a coalition of nations and a family under one roof, and it has provided me with the biggest sense of belonging I have ever known—and gotten me through some of the worst scrapes imaginable.

HAZY DAYS

The Black Eyed Peas actually call it a "fam-er-ree," not "family."

One day, Apl made an impassioned declaration about the importance of our band of brothers and sisters sticking together, and, with his Filipino accent, he mispronounced "family" as "fam-er-ree," so it stuck. What wasn't lost in translation was the sincerity of his message, because life has been our teacher, struggle has been our patience, music has been our medicine. Especially on tour.

When you are thrown together as a group of people into the melting pot of a tour, it is like being strapped into the greatest, fastest, wildest ride ever, and we seem to have been strapped in for the majority of our time between 1995 and the current day.

When you wake up wondering what city you're in, what time zone you're in, and what day of the week it is, you know you're on tour. Within that exhausting exhilaration, it is the sense of "fam-er-ree" that provides the only compass points and handrails.

Of course, when a juggernaut keeps going long enough, there are always going to be the occasions when the wheels come off, and that is when the true bonding takes place—in the trenches of a crisis. I have had to fall back on the memories of others to piece together the events of our time on the Caribbean island of St. Maarten, but most of the "fam-er-ree" agree that in terms of wheels coming off, overall craziness, and my drunken oblivion, nothing pushed the extremes more than this one night during the seemingly endless promotion of *Elephunk* in 2004.

We had just done a stint in Europe where we had frozen our asses off and "not won a sausage"—as one newspaper put it—at our first U.K. award ceremony, the Brit Awards in London, where we were nominated for best pop group and best international act. Polo was proud of me that night because I stayed sober. I must have been too busy trying to stay warm in the Arctic weather that the English call "a cold snap."

I probably felt the cold more because it was around this time that I dropped the head wraps and let the Native American hair grow long—not that it did anything to clear up the general misunderstanding about my origin, because I now went from the "scary-looking Asian guy" to the "scary-looking Asian guy with the long hair."

With London's freezing temperatures behind us, and after the promoters behind St. Maarten's Heineken Regatta threw a decent amount of money our way to perform at the end-of-race celebration, we couldn't wait for some fun in the sun on Kim Sha beach.

It was one mad party for four days as both sides of the island—Dutch and French—came together for a lavish celebration, Caribbean style.

When we arrived, it seemed like my idea of heaven: booze and women *everywhere.* The first day, we had a ball. The second day, we had a ball. And the third day was our last true day to party, because we were performing on the fourth and final afternoon.

I knew on day one that serious fun was on the agenda when I found a local guy who sold coke. It never took me long to find an outlet when I was traveling. It was always the same routine: someone local attached to the promoter asks if we need anything—and that was my sign.

"Yeah, actually we do . . . you mean *anything*, anything?"

"Yeah," says any guy in every city, "like whatever you need."

"Like, you can hook me up with some shit?"

"Some white shit?" he asks.

"Yeah, cool," and so, whether it was Ecstasy or cocaine, it really was that easy because, as the VIP guests of a town, the street's concierges want to ensure you are looked after, and indulging my recklessness was the only way to look after me then.

As on the previous two nights, I was wasted by 9 p.m., and our last party night in town ended with me stumbling out of a strip club, draped between the shoulders of Polo and Will. Which is when Nick Lauher turned up outside, walking into this scene after some date with a girl. Nick was on his first run with the Peas as an assistant, learning the ropes about life on the road, so when Polo asked him to be my crutch and "look after Tab," he probably thought it was part of his duties.

Poor kid had no idea what he was wandering into. All Nick remembers is that I could "barely stand, let alone talk," and he just did as he was told.

As Polo and Will disappeared, I was left on the sidewalk hanging off Nick like he was a coatrack. Apl and our drummer Keith Harris were also there, wondering where we should go next, when this 250-pound, 6'3" black guy—a promoter we barely knew—pulled up in his jet-black BMW, music blaring. He said he knew another great strip club, so, with nothing better to do, we all jumped in and headed for another hour of free drinks.

I also knew that we had a healthy supply of weed, stuffed into my side pockets. In the car, I was in the backseat, squashed up next to Apl who was squashed up next to Nick, and Keith was in the front passenger seat. I was too faded to notice that our black promoter friend was tearing along the roads at some ridiculous speed, and I was too far gone to notice the blue flashing police lights that had been tailing us.

As we slowed and pulled over, the promoter dude told us, "Do not worry, guys . . . I own this island . . ." and he started talking all kinds of big-man shit. The problem with that was that he then started giving attitude to the cop, and that meant the cop asked us all to get out of the car. The problem with *that* was that my pockets were stuffed with weed. So as we clambered out, I started ditching these great big clumps of weed, palming them off to the new boy, Nick, who looked the most innocent out of all of us—fresh out of college, fresh-faced. But as Nick tripped out of the door—last one out—one bag of weed dropped from his pocket, and this cop's flashlight caught it—and us—red-handed.

Everyone was told to put their hands up. We were under arrest.

With me unsteady on my feet and Nick the college kid sweating it that his dropped ball had landed us in the shit, it did not look good for the headlining group of that weekend's regatta celebration, as we were handcuffed one by one and put into the back of the police Ford Explorer.

As we were driven away, the promoter dude was still ranting, trying to explain that we were the Black Eyed Peas doing the main show that weekend. His words hit a wall of indifference, and then, with ironic timing that somehow summed up our predicament, "Where Is the Love?" came on the radio.

"Turn it up! Turn it up!" I shouted, shuffling forward, thinking I could reach forward and turn the dial—while handcuffed. "That's our song! That's our song!" I kept shouting.

"I don't care who you are, I don't care what song is on the radio," said the officer. "Sit down and shut up!"

As much as the cop was giving us shit, we only thought he was taking us in to teach us a lesson. So when I got to the front desk, and they asked my name, I wasn't taking it serious because a) I was wasted, and b) experience had told me that being a Black Eyed Pea carried its own get-out-of-jail card.

After being told to empty my pockets on the table, I found twenty-two crumpled U.S. dollars, two tens, and two singles. "Here! Here!" I said, offering the desk sergeant all the money I had. "Take it . . . let me pay you off . . . let's get out of here . . . you want an autograph?"

"TAB! What the fuck are you doing?" Apl asked.

It soon became obvious that the St. Maarten's police were not as lenient as Canadian border cops.

My bribe didn't help the situation, and the desk cop now started barking, ordering us to line up, backs against the wall, and stand still and not say a word.

My pants, undone like a beach bum's, fell down to my ankles. I bent down, pulled them up. They fell down. I bent down, pulled them up.

"Stand still!" the officer shouted.

I stood upright—and my pants slipped down again.

We ended up being put into a dank, nasty-ass holding cell that smelled like piss. A somber-looking Keith stood there, both hands on the bars, looking out into the dark corridor. Apl sat down in a corner. I fell down, slouched on a bench. Nick, looking like a deer caught in headlights, paced the cell, and the local promoter dude could not stop yelling in his half-French, half-Dutch lingo.

The cop was unmoved, turned the key, locked the gate, and told us we would have to wait until the "prosecutor decides what to do with you on Monday morning." It was Friday night, and our highly paid gig was the next day.

Nick—no longer enjoying his first touring experience—started freaking out like a little white boy. "Oh shit! Oh shit! They're going to take away my license . . . I didn't come here for this . . . I can't be in here till Monday . . . I can't!"

"Nick, will you relax and stop freaking us all out!" said Apl, always cool in a crisis.

Keith still stood at the bars, as chill as can be. "Everything happens for a reason, man. This concert could be a wrap if we don't get outta here . . ."

As Nick continued muttering to himself, I was laid out, oblivious.

Oblivious, that is, until I suddenly bolted upright and started yelling "HEEEEELP! HEEELP!" at the top of my voice. I screamed out twice, apparently, and then fell back into my slumber. I've no idea why I did that. It's what the guys told me I did.

Meanwhile, Mr. Big Shot promoter was still shouting his mouth off. "Let us out now!" he screamed—this time in English—"This is an outrage! You will pay for this!"

The cop, who was at a desk around the corner, obviously had had enough. He appeared at the bars again, unlocked the door, and said: "All right, you guys want to fuck with me . . . EVERYONE OUT!"

We were led, single file, up some metal steps which led to a big-ass steel door which this cop heaved open. "Inside—all of you!" the cop said.

What opened up before us was this warehouse-sized, two-floored, main prison that adjoined the police station: a hellhole with small-ass cells crammed with mad-looking people who were banging their metal cups on the bars and pounding their fists into the cement walls. It is a vague scene in my head but the guys said the noise was frightening, like caged rabid wolves smelling fresh meat.

"Oh fuck!" said Nick, now wetting himself, "They're going to beat the shit out of us . . . they're going to beat the living shit out of us!"

In hindsight, he probably had good reason to panic: no one knew where we were and we seemed to be going nowhere fast inside this international hellhole. But I was so wasted that they could have told us we were going to spend a hundred years and then get beheaded and I wouldn't have given a fuck. I just shuffled along, mindless to the seriousness of the situation.

Which was probably for the best.

The cop had shown us what lay in store, and after the five minute sneak preview of our futures if we didn't shut the fuck up, he returned us to our holding cell, where, next door, we spotted some dude alone behind bars. He got to talking to the promoter in local lingo. The promoter then relayed the good news: they won't put us in the hellhole, he said.

How does he know? we asked.

Because he's been in here for six months, he said.

How a puddle didn't form at the feet of Nick at this point, no one knows.

Ask him what he's in here for, we said.

"For trying to cheat at a local casino," the dude told our promoter.

Then the imprisoned one asked what we were in for.

"Drugs," the promoter told him, and this other guy started getting all excitable, apparently.

"What did he say? What did he say?" asked Nick.

"He said we're fucked," said the promoter.

"Oh God! Oh God!" said Nick, now physically quivering and starting to cry.

Two of the guards laughed at his whimpering. One grabbed a loaf of bread and started picking off chunks and throwing it between the bars into the cell, like he was feeding birds. The other guard passed through one small glass of water for all of us.

"Drink?" he smirked. It was obvious they were fucking with us and getting a lot of pleasure from it.

It was sometime after midnight—after four hours in that shit-hole—when a senior officer showed up, said he had spoken with the regatta organizers, and he was letting us go as an exception to the rule. His parting shot was: "Drugs of any kind are not tolerated in St. Maarten, and we do not care who you are. We never want to see you in here again, do you understand?"

We nodded our heads like naughty schoolkids, gathered our possessions, and got out of there. Nick, today Will's right-hand man, ran out of there like the place was on fire, and he was the first on the street, hailing a taxi, and vowing: "I am *never* coming back to this shit-hole ever again! Fucking dictators!"

In the taxi on the way home, I started waking up and everyone was calling me a crazy-ass, drunken fool—or words to that effect—for making matters worse by trying to bribe an officer.

A lot of my impulses during this period didn't come from much intelligence.

It also helped that I was so hammered that I couldn't remember much and, when you can't remember much, it's hard to feel shame. But if any of us thought we could walk out of there and keep the incident as a secret between us, we were mistaken. You can't go for a shit on a small island without people talking, as we soon found out.

The very next morning, the hotel left a complimentary copy of the local newspaper at each guest's door, and the front page headline that day was loud and clear: "BLACK EYED PEAS IN JAIL AT HEINEKEN REGATTA."

That one took some explaining to Polo, but the main concern was that the headline didn't cross over to the mainland and spread across America, and, thankfully, it didn't. We were free (if a little notorious locally). We had survived. The "fam-er-ree" had come through and Nick eventually stopped shaking. We did the show. We rocked it. And afterward, there was only thing left for me to do—go out and get hammered again. I drank myself into oblivion again and had to be carried back to the hotel, propped up, feet trailing. Lesson of the previous night unlearned.

St. Maarten was not just the place where we got out of jail. It was the place where I realized I could not stop drinking. I was at the drink-anything, sleep-with-anything, take-anything stage of self-destruction, and not even a horrible night in a shit-infested hellhole was enough to stop me. It was on the flight back home from Europe when I realized it.

I had sobered up but felt hungover, sick, and disgusting. I knew how bad I felt, and I said to myself that I cannot keep doing this. Then, in the same breath and within a split-second of that same thought, I was already thinking about getting wasted back in L.A.; planning the very thing that I was pushing away in my head. Now *that* was fucked up.

I was the opposite of the health freak who goes to the gym in the morning, releases those endorphins, feels sore, and then, that same afternoon, feels like going back to the gym again. To feel good. To recapture that feeling. Only mine was the unhealthy version.

I was the drinker who went from binge to binge at clubs or in restaurants; the kind of drinker who never admitted to any problem because I had passed it off

as "social drinking" for so long without realizing its excesses. But it didn't matter what form of drinker I was. The bottom line was that I couldn't stop.

I have always said that *Behind the Front* marked the time for me when one arm changed into a monster. With *Bridging the Gap*, it was two arms, and by the time *Elephunk* came around, I had become a total, egotistical monster.

At this stage, I started looking into the mirror and not liking what I saw: the bad skin, the gaunt cheeks, the haunted eyes, the color of a ghost; the vacancy sign that hung from every aspect of me that I didn't recognize. I stared back and hated what I saw.

I told myself that I would, I will, I want to stop.

I told myself to get a grip.

But I lied to myself every time I saw myself staring back, because each time I saw the drink or the drug, I did it anyway. Fuck it.

There were small pockets of time when I cared about what I was doing to myself, but they were pushed to one side by the larger taste for the wild and the reckless.

The shrinks will tell you—as they would ultimately try to tell me—that this is how much love I *didn't* have for myself; how much pent-up resentment there was about a childhood with an absent father and present stepfather; how Karish had never made me feel like a man; and how much I didn't think myself worthy of the dream I had made happen. Within all that psychological stuff, the boy in me felt lonely and the man—the performer, the artist, the party animal—tried to discover an authority and respect that he felt he never had in life.

Deep shrink talk.

I haven't spent too much time exploring that one opinion, so I can't say whether I agree or not. But, as with most people who aren't prepared to help themselves when the red flags start appearing, it would take life's natural course to make me realize a thing or two on my own.

I've realized one thing on this journey: life never lets you escape taking responsibility in the end. It charts your course with a watchful eye, and the more you ignore the warning signs, the more punishing the backlash will be.

From 2004 to 2005, the scale of my guilty pleasures went something like this: I was spending about $600 a week on Kush, i.e., Hindu Kush: the *crème de la crème* of weed, and the most powerful shit on the market. I could now afford a higher grade because of the influx of money coming in from *Elephunk,* and Kush is the difference between having a gourmet meal and McDonald's; the smell, the taste, the high was something else.

Even the grade of weed I was buying was a sign of me moving up in the world. I had started with the dirtiest Mexican weed, made up of sticks and stems, then this guy called Bucky provided dubz of weed called "Acapulco Gold"—so-called because of its little gold flakes—and that was another step up. I then moved on to "Chronic"—a green form of weed with no seeds, and when you've reached the Chronic stage, there is no turning back. From Chronic, I moved up to the next level, to "Tone's weed"—yellowish and kind of fluffy, much softer in texture than the others, and then I ran into a guy called Mitch who said he could get his hands on some Kush. One of his terms and conditions was that he only met "big-weight" orders, and that's how I got to spending $600 a week on half-pound, half-ounce bags.

I was smoking six times a day: gutting a fat-ass cigar and re-stuffing the paper with Kush to create the finest blunt. I had that first thing in the morning, then mid-day, then mid-afternoon, then around 6 p.m., one around 9 p.m. and then another just before bed.

It's fair to say that I was living—and functioning—within a perpetual haze.

When I was drinking, getting faded just added to the fucked-up experience, and as the weed became stronger, the drinking got worse. From raiding the minibar post-performance, I was now enjoying all-night solo binges. Previously, I downed vodka and wine to unwind and help me sleep. Now, I was emptying the bottles—and ordering more—so that I could keep drinking through the night, alone, whenever the mood caught me.

No one, in the group or the band, knew the extent of my alcoholic appetite when that hotel door slammed shut and I hung the Do Not Disturb sign on the handle. It wasn't every night, but it was often enough.

As for my intake of Ecstasy—costing about $200 a month—I always kept a supply close at hand, but it really depended on how much clubbing we were doing. When we did, I would pop four, five, six pills. One time, I took ten—one after the other—because finding the buzz became harder and harder. And then there was cocaine, which I was using more and more, to stay awake, to stay high, to feel amazing. I had my supplier in Chris, and I was probably spending $100 a month keeping that supply line open.

That was my diet of indulgence: a happy cocktail of Kush, booze, Ecstacy, and cocaine. Alongside that, I started to believe in all the Hollywood bullshit, and I developed this warped sense of entitlement, expecting to receive the same star treatment that a life on the road had conditioned me to expect. The attention received on tour made me feel important, and I became attached to that importance, as if all the acclaim, album sales, perks, VIP treatment, prestige, and starry perception added extra value to me.

Whenever we had downtime in L.A., I developed one of those you-don't-know-who-I-am? mentalities, and if I walked into a restaurant and was told there would be a fifteen-minute wait, I told them: "I don't wait fifteen minutes. I need a table now."

I remember that and cringe now.

But when that didn't work, I managed to remind them that I was a Black Eyed Pea.

When that didn't work, I got even more pissed, thinking up a bullshit attitude.

What? You don't know the Black Eyed Peas?

You don't know Taboo?

Well, you better damn know.

It was the same at clubs. If some chick at a bar didn't know who I was, I told her so as to impress her. If some dude disrespected me, I dropped my status all over his nuts. I found myself becoming intolerant, irritable, and impatient with "normal" life. We had lived life at such breakneck speed that when it slowed to an everyday, pedestrian pace, I was a bundle of pent-up energy revving on the spot.

My whole mind, body, and nervous system had been amped up to live in a whirlwind, and were so accustomed to life at full throttle that they couldn't cope outside of a schedule that did not involve being here, there, and everywhere, on this TV show, on that TV show, in this city to that city, from that continent to the next.

The moment I stepped off the conveyor belt, I was lost.

A robot trying to feel human again.

Because that is what touring makes you feel like.

I struggled with having time on my hands. So, during the non-touring periods, I created a high-speed social life to compensate. I used drugs to replace the high of the performance. I surrounded myself with fellow partiers to replace the adulation of an audience. And I went out of my way to show people I was the star and the player-pimp, flashing his status and money around.

"Let's not do dinner for four, let's do fifteen—and I'll pay for everyone. No problem."

"Bring your friends, drinks on me, let's party!"

"Look, I've got the money. Stick with me. I'll show you a good time."

"You want that shit you see in the shop window—I'll get it."

"Let's keep the party going . . . let's keep rocking it till seven a.m. That's what we do on the road."

Business manager Sean Larkin became alarmed at the spending patterns he saw coming through on my bank statements. Why was I spending $250 a time on bottles of Champagne, sometimes twice a night? Why was I taking out $250 a day from the ATM? What was I doing spending money like it was going out of fashion?

I didn't think it was smart to tell my business manager that I was buying popularity and spending more money on drugs than the average family spends on their weekly food shopping at Vons. So I made up some bullshit about "entertaining" and "expenses." There is no way he believed me.

As for how I justified it to myself, this was Hollywood; this was rock 'n' roll and this is what people did: from Jim Morrison to Jimi Hendrix to Keith Richards to Slash. Why couldn't I, as a hip-hop artist, have the same lifestyle and be as notoriously wild?

Every month, when home, I held what I called "Celebrations": dinners that started out at places like T.G.I. Friday's and Dave & Buster's or Japanese restaurants, before we moved onto the clubs. Friends would bring friends and their friends would bring other friends. "Drink and be merry, bitches!" was my toast, my shout, my starting gun for the night.

"What are we celebrating this month, Tab?" someone always asked.

"Life—and how good life is!" I always said.

I wanted to be viewed as the always-happy, super-cool, party guy. Misery loves company, and I loved having as many people around me as I could, whether I knew them or not.

It didn't dawn on me for one second what a joke I was, because everything was too much of a blur for any kind of self-awareness to kick in.

Like father, like son.

The Hollywood bullshit version.

As a "fam-er-ree," it is the laughter that sustains us. I said it earlier and I will say it again, because it is the one sound—one beat—that has never changed throughout our evolving sound and music.

If I think of times on the tour bus and planes, and in the studio or backstage before a concert, I hear laughter. I see Will's eyes-alive grin as he listens to some beat that he gets a feeling for; Apl's bushy-tailed head nodding as he cackles out loud to some mad memory; and Fergie breezing onto the scene with her arriving catchphrase—"Whassup, bitches?"—before spreading her positive energy and launching into some funny anecdote or impression.

So it is genuinely hard for me to remember any really sad times as a group, but I think the toughest hit we took was when a fire broke out at the studio as we recorded *Elephunk* at Glendale Studios, and we lost about $500,000 worth of gear.

It was one of those nights when I was at home, having already done my session for *Elephunk,* and Will was working late into the night with Apl, Dante Santiago, and singer-songwriter Toni Braxton, producing a track that Will was working on with her. Because it was Toni, it was decided to create a more moody ambience by lighting some candles inside Studio A. Girls like candles in the bathroom. I guess Toni liked candles in the studio.

When she left, it was apparently around 2 a.m., and Will, Apl, and Dante

went to the catering room, grabbing something to eat. It was then that an assistant sound engineer burst into the room and started yelling "FIRE! FIRE!"

When everyone went into the corridor, Studio A was aglow.

Apparently, one of the candles had somehow set fire to one of the microphone shields. Two engineers fought it with extinguishers before the firefighters turned up, but the damage was done—the studio was a charred mess, and the band lost guitars, amps, a keyboard, and a drum machine, and Will lost a stack of his latest recording equipment. I don't think anyone could believe how quickly that shit had taken hold, and it was by the mercy of God that no one was injured.

The first I knew was when I turned on the television the next morning and saw local "breaking news" about the studio fire. Sadly, George Pajon found out the same way, but his discovery was more devastating—because some fire chief was holding up two of his prized but blackened guitars for the news cameras.

For weeks, he kept saying, "Irreplaceable, irreplaceable" when he spoke of those guitars, and only musicians will understand his loss, because of the sentimentality attached to these prized possessions. One of those guitars lost in the fire was the acoustic one George had in the hot tub at Bodega Bay, and as he kicked it, with feet dangling in the water, he played a guitar part which excited Will. "That line there—that's it! That's it!" he shouted, and, in those bubbles, with that guitar, "Smells Like Funk" was born. Like George kept saying—irreplaceable.

The Bucky Johnson side of the "fam-er-ree" took an emotional hit on that one—Printz lost one of his keyboards, too—and things were grim for a few days. But the main thing for me was that everyone was safe because it could have been a lot worse. The fire was caught just in time, allowing everyone to get out uninjured and none of the previously recorded *Elephunk* material was lost.

Will said it was a sign that "our music brought heat to Glenwood Studios," and that *Elephunk* was "on fire as an album."

We never did light candles in the studio again.

My friends said I exhibited classic Dr. Jekyll-Mr. Hyde behavior: one minute I was an easygoing, pleasant guy you can talk to, the next I was a belligerent drunk.

There was no starker example than the evening when I went to dinner in Pasadena during some downtime in L.A., and decided to treat Mom, Celeste, Josh, and Julio, who was part owner of this restaurant called El Cholo.

It was supposed to be a rare chance to catch up as a family, and I was okay at the start of the evening, telling stories from the tour, the places we had visited, the plans for a fourth album. But I started knocking back the tequila, one after the other, and I could feel it taking over me.

Suddenly, I was at the table and Julio said something—I don't remember the exact words—and it triggered the past and that was all it took to light the fuse and let him have it. Just when we all thought that years of childhood shit was consigned to the past, I vomited it onto the table.

"You told me I wasn't good enough . . . you treated me like shit . . . you were mean to me as a kid . . . I didn't feel love from you . . . you were a jerk to me . . . why did you make my life so difficult . . . you turned every day into a battle . . . you only wanted Mom, not me . . ."

I was drunk and ranting.

Mom tried reaching out to calm me down as my voice got louder, but I interpreted that as her defending him again, so I let her have it, too. "You always did take his side . . . you were always weak . . . you never stood up for me . . . you let him talk to me like shit . . . you were no mom to me!" I said, a final lie aimed at wounding.

And then I saw Celeste, staring at them both around the table, lost. She started to cry. Mom started to cry and Julio just looked shocked to shit and didn't retaliate. Everyone just stayed where they were, and the whole restaurant had fallen silent.

I have never spoken about that night again until writing this book. Like most awkward moments in our family, it was brushed under the carpet and avoided. We never spoke about it and never addressed the issues again. I think it was just understood as me getting shit off my chest, uncorked by drink.

I just wish I could say that's as bad as things got.

If I were to retell every last incident, bump, and scrape that I experienced during my descent to rock bottom, it would read like one boring—but colorful—misdemeanor rap sheet from 2001 to 2007. Anyway, my brain cannot piece together or make sense of all the foggy details from my hazy days. I think it has only retained an edited version of the main events to make me remember *just enough* of the episodes as a constant reminder of how bad things were. I recount them now as they are framed in my mind: a montage of flashbacks that serve to remind me of the person that I never want to be again.

Belfast, Northern Ireland—we performed a spot date and went to a club where, with all the Peas and band being single, we were a terror. Our Black Eyed Pea status had started attracting women to the VIP section like bees to honey. Girls would even ditch their boyfriends or dates to hang with us. Star association is a weakness of human nature that we played on. Inevitably, this upsets the guys.

"Why is it girls only? Why can't we come as well?" one Irish guy started saying from the other side of the roped-off area.

I started smirking. The guy grabbed the chain around my neck. Printz decided to punch the guy in the mouth. Next thing we know, there are five or six other Irish guys piling in, and the whole VIP is a wrestling mess until the bouncers

restore order. We get to stay. The Irish guys get thrown out of their own club in their own 'hood.

At the end of the night, the manager warned us that these guys would still be waiting outside, probably with backup. So he snuck us out a back door and we made it to our hotel. But, fueled by drink, all I could think about was how this one guy had disrespected me and grabbed my chain. That punk.

By sneaking out a back door, I felt weak.

So I decided to be a hero. I raced to my room, tore down the shower curtain and grabbed the silver pole, ran through the lobby and out into the street, waving the pole around like a ninja intent on killing someone. I was a madman flailing and screaming, "COME ON THEN YOU MOTHAFUCKAS—BRING IT."

"Yo, chill, Tab!" Printz screamed after me. "It's over, dude, let it go!"

There were two blessings that night: first, I didn't find those Irish guys when I returned to the streets near the club, and second, no policeman spotted me looking armed and dangerous. Printz and George eventually calmed me down. The next morning, they said they had never seen me lose it like that before.

"You've got some fucking anger issues there, Tab!" said Printz.

I laughed it off.

Los Angeles, California—I was in a club. Don't ask me which one. Just one of my regulars.

I was already pretty far gone. Printz introduced me to this Indian girl he knew. She was with her boyfriend who was not introduced to me. Apparently, this girl had wanted to meet me and explain how much she liked our music.

"So you like me?" I asked this fan, and she nodded, fanning out.

I grabbed her face between both my hands, brought her face to mine, and tried sticking my tongue down her throat. She struggled. She screamed. Her boyfriend tried to hit me. Printz couldn't believe it. Apparently, that lost me a fan that night, but I didn't give a fuck. "She said she liked me but if she didn't want to fuck me, then she can fuck off," I said.

Printz looked at me like someone he recognized but wished he didn't.

To that couple today, I am sorry. That wasn't me. Well, it was me . . . but you know what I mean.

Maui, Hawaii—after a two-night run, we went to a club and I drank about nine sakes and felt like I wanted to carry on performing. I was with Apl, Will, and Polo, and there were these performers onstage who were wack. I thought I could do better.

I jumped onstage, interrupted the show, grabbed the mic and started hyping the crowd: "SAY HOLA, HOLA, HOLA!"

The crowd fell quiet, probably thinking "Who's the drunken idiot on stage?"

224

"SAY HOLA! HOLA! HOLA!"

I faced a floor of statues, unmoved, just looking at me.

"C'MON! SAY HOLA! SAY HOLA! SAY . . ." and that's when Polo jumped up and grabbed me like he was a bouncer getting rid of a nuisance. Back in the VIP section, Will and Apl looked like they wanted to disown me.

"We're leaving before you cause any more embarrassment," said Polo, disappointed.

Again. On the walk home, I was unable to control my bowel movements and I shit on myself, and it poured down my leg and stained my pants. Anyone who passed me couldn't avoid seeing—and smelling—the mess. It was, said Polo, one of *his* most humiliating moments.

Beijing, China—our boy DJ Motiv8 was doing a spot in a club in Beijing. Inside, I bought some Ex, and downed eight pills over the following four hours.

I was dancing, drinking water, when I started feeling horrible. It felt like my head had been locked into a turning vice. My jaw was really tight, my heart was thumping, and it felt like my eyes were rolling out of the back of my head. I started cracking my teeth, I was grinding so hard. I started staggering, all disoriented, and Polo decided to get me out of there and take me back to my hotel room. I took a cold shower, desperate to sober up and feel better. I got out naked, left the bathroom and shut the door behind me. But I had turned left out of the hotel room, not right into the bedroom, and I was naked, dripping wet in the hotel corridor.

I was still rolling hard and shuffling more than walking, going in a deluded search for a phone at about 3 a.m. I got in the elevator, slumped against the glass, and waited for the doors to reopen. When they did, I found myself at the lobby level.

I walked out into the marble surroundings, naked and fucked up, and the guy at reception spotted me. He ran up to me and threw a coat on me like I was a fire to be put out. He placed me in a chair where I was hunched over, shivering.

The reception guy rang our road manager, Bobby Grant, and told him: "I'm sorry to bother you, sir, but we have found one of your principals in the lobby . . . naked."

First thing Bobby did when he came to retrieve me was ask for the closed-circuit cameras tapes. In playback, he watched me wander the entire length of my floor's corridor, bouncing off the walls, before circling the lobby. "You looked out of your mind, dude!" he said, the next morning at breakfast. "You out-did yourself last night!"

When everyone else was laughing, Polo leaned over and said, quiet and serious, "You're losing it, brother, and you're worrying me. You've got to start getting a grip."

. . .

Flight from Australia to L.A.—We were somewhere above the Pacific heading east, and I had downed about five glasses of wine in quick succession. I had been given some strong sleeping tablets and read the standard warning that mixing sleeping pills with alcohol can be dangerous.

Sounds edgy, I thought.

I wonder what happens when you do?

So I took four, and washed them down with more wine.

I don't remember blacking out. Because I thought I was sleeping. But what happened, as later recounted by Will, was that I started having convulsions, like I was having a seizure in my seat. The flight attendants were so alarmed that they spoke about diverting the plane and landing early. "No one knew what the fuck was wrong with you!" said Will.

Luckily, there was a doctor seated two rows back, and when he saw the sleeping pill pack next to the arm rest, he did some shit that stabilized me.

All I knew was that I woke up groggy, with a killer headache, and Will was there.

"Tab, you better say thank you to the doc behind you . . . the dude saved your ass."

I looked behind me and saw the doctor. Then I saw the magician David Blaine looking at me. I had no idea what I had done or how serious it had been, but the look in his eyes—the concern, the pity—made me feel about two feet tall.

Polo was furious, probably because he had felt out of control at 35,000 feet. "Damn, Tab, you could have overdosed. What kind of shit were you pulling this time?"

David Blaine interrupted us. "You gave everyone a scare there. You going to be okay?"

"I'm okay, just a bad reaction or something," I said.

Polo and me both knew I was lying. "One of these days you're going to fuck up big-time or you're going to kill yourself! Is this the guy you want to be? You want to be the fool from the Black Eyed Peas?"

In my eyes, Polo became the moaning parent I chose to ignore time and time again.

Each time he spoke like that, trying to drum it into me, I felt guilt for a few fleeting minutes, but the more I thought about his advice, the more I viewed him as a stepfather telling me what to do; telling me that while everyone else in the group or the band could drink and handle it, I could not. In my head, I vowed to prove him wrong. Not by staying sober but by keeping on drinking and building a stronger alcohol tolerance and asserting my control over the demons that I would not allow to have the final say. *Oh, you don't think so? Well, you watch me.*

. . .

Elephunk took us back to the Big Day Out festival in Australia and New Zealand, three years older and this time with Fergie. It was one of the sickest lineups we had ever shared: Metallica, the Dandy Warhols, the Flaming Lips, Basement Jaxx, Massive Attack, the Strokes, the Darkness, and two new breakthrough groups—the Kings of Leon and Muse. That was a big-time bill as far as we were concerned, and the best bit about it was that we played when the sun was still up and came off around dusk, giving us plenty of time to watch the headliners perform.

It was the festival which showed us how big "Shut Up" had become on the other side of the world: it was #1 on the national ARIAS chart while we were there, and that single was far better received in Australia than it ever was in America.

When we hit the main stage and they went crazy for "Shut Up" and then "Hands Up," it felt amazing because it cemented our confidence in our global position; seeing was believing.

Australia was the place where I got my first tattoo, as encouraged by our road manager Bobby Grant. Getting tatted-up was either during BDO or a tour we made to Oz later that year, in 2004. I can't remember which. But me and Bobby sat in the chair, side by side, and this was when I had "Spirit Warrior" stained into my forearm in Chinese and Japanese letters.

I was finished before Bobby—four hours before the tapestry on his upper arm was done—so I went with his girlfriend at the time, an Australian chick named Samantha, to grab some food at an Italian restaurant. She was a cool, designer-by-trade woman who I didn't know very well, but Bobby was our common bond, and as we left him in the tattoo parlor, he joked with her: "Just look after him!"

In normal circumstances, that would be an innocent thing to say, but, deep down, Bobby was probably worried that his girlfriend was a lamb being led to the slaughter.

Sure enough, two hours later, Bobby got the call that he dreaded.

"Uh, Bobby," Samantha apparently said, "I don't think Taboo is very well. I think we might have to get him to the hotel because he's vomited everywhere and has now passed out."

I had not shared with Samantha that I had gone to the toilet twice to smoke some weed on top of the copious amounts of wine I had been drinking. I didn't want to give a bad first impression. The poor girl had to nurse me until Bobby reached us about ninety minutes later, and this brother, who has put out countless fires for me, helped pour me back into the hotel.

The next morning, I felt an embarrassment that I rarely felt because I had made a fool of myself in front of Bobby's woman. That wasn't cool, and I apologized. I sat down with Bobby and had a chat that I had never had with anyone, not

Will, not Apl, not Polo. That's probably why Bobby is also called the "camp coun-selor." Behind his Don King hair, crazy-ass humor, and zany behavior, there is an intelligence and wisdom that many have fallen back on.

We sat across from each other in a corner of the hotel, learning forward because this was going to be a whispered moment of vulnerability as far as I was concerned.

"Yo, Bobby, you drink Scotch and keep it together. How do you do it?" I asked.

"I just know when to stop," he said.

"But I *can't* stop, Bobby. I want to stop and I can't stop," I said.

Bobby had his theory: I was someone who didn't go to college, so I had never "learned" how to drink, and I was binge-drinking in the same way college kids did. But my binge-drinking coincided with the Black Eyed Peas blowing up, so the "celebration" was magnified. He spoke about self-control. He mentioned the phrase "drinking in moderation." He told me, "You just need to slow it down. You can do it, brother."

He had so much faith in me that I just nodded my head and agreed with him.

No one realized how incapable I was, or understood how much I was out of control behind the partying front. Not even me. But during my sober windows, it started to frighten me. Having made it, I started to worry about losing it—the dream. But then the ego kicked in, rose up, and invited me to drink that fear away, swallow it down, or snort it up. And then I didn't care anymore.

I chose to escape fear, instead of facing it. I chose to be reckless, not responsible. I chose to carry on flailing, instead of asking for help.

I chose to be an idiot—then blamed everything and everyone else around me.

MONKEY BUSINESS

James Brown is coming into the studio," said Will.

Out of all the things that he has ever said, that announcement in the fall of 2005 was time-stopping. At first, I thought he was punking us, but when Will has that focused, edgy vibe going on, you know he's serious.

"When?" I asked with Apl and Fergie.

"In the next hour," he said.

Suddenly, we were rushing around, fanning out at the prospect and making ourselves look pristine, because musical royalty was about to walk through the door. This was going to be our historic day, when the Godfather of Soul graced our studio—and our album—with his presence, and permitted the Black Eyed Peas to be one of the very few acts he has ever collaborated with; one of those rare times that not even some of the greatest musicians of our time had been afforded, and yet there we were, in a studio in London W4, about to get funky with an icon whose artistry and songs had paved the way for our kind of music. James Brown constructed the bedrock of hip-hop and inspired a nation of people to stand up and be black and be proud, at a time when "black" was not accepted in society. It is too easy to talk about privileged moments and surreal experiences on the journey we have enjoyed, but this was one of those personal wonders that you want to trap in a snowglobe and keep on the shelf. And the best thing is that I remember it. Not faded. Not drunk. Not absent. Just alive and present and soaking it in.

We had decamped to London for three months to record our fourth album, *Monkey Business*. We wanted to zone out somewhere that inspired us. Where better than the first place where our music was first and foremost appreciated. London had always had a special place in our heart so we headed there from July to October to build on our success and prove that *Elephunk* was no fluke.

London's vibe has always inspired artists from the Beatles to the Rolling Stones, Jimi Hendrix to David Bowie, Led Zeppelin to Eric Clapton. We wanted to tap into the sounds, fashions, and energy as "research"—allowing us to feel what people in the clubs were rocking out to, and then fuse it with the international flavors we had collected from our travels with *Elephunk*.

Unlike Bodega Bay, the creative vibe clicked from the day we moved into our rented home in a cul-de-sac in Chiswick and the nearby Metropolis Studios, an impressive setup in an old Victorian building, the Power House, which was set back from a busy main road and backed onto a common. With a bus depot as a near neighbor and old-fashioned semidetached houses across a street lined with oak trees, it was classic suburban London, but close enough to feel the city's pulse.

I guess the locals have grown used to all sorts of Bentleys and limos turning into the main driveway marked out by a very English, ornate, wrought-iron arch. But not even the esteemed history of Metropolis Studios had previously seen the likes of James Brown walk through its doors.

Three days earlier, we had been at the MOBO Awards—when Public Enemy received a lifetime achievement award—when we scanned the room and Will spotted the legend himself. "Shiitttt," he said, "it's James Brown!"

All four of us were like groupies standing on the edges, wondering whether we should make an approach, and then Will pulled himself together, walked up, and told him how much we loved his music. "One day, we would love to work with you," he said.

"All rigghht," said Mr. Brown, in that coarse squawk of a voice of his. "We'll make that happen."

Within seventy-two hours, true to his word, he was making it happen.

He walked into the studio—the arrowhead of his entourage—looking immaculate, dressed in a sharp-ass violet suit and maroon shirt, with perfect jet-black hair all done up, and black shoes so shiny that a Marine would have been proud. There were ten people flocked around him: four female backup singers, three members of his band, and three assistants. He was glowing. Not walking but gliding. Oozing charisma. We were the kids, standing in awe, bowing down, thinking, "Here's the Jedi Master . . . and we're about to vibe out." It was like the court of James Brown in our own corner of England.

He sat down on the edge of the couch, with his foot tapping to a rhythm already in his head. He looked around, checked out the band, checked out the setup, and, with us hanging off his every word, he said, "You know! I don't really do collaborations. I'm James Brown. But some'ing told me that I needed to work with the Black Eyed Peas . . . and that is why I'm here! So let's work."

Will already had the foundation of a song, and he played him the beat, sitting there all nervous as we awaited the Godfather's approval. Mr. Brown listened, thought about it, nodded his head, and then grunted. These grunts, we soon learned, were sounds of his approval.

The reason I keep on calling him "Mr. Brown" is because when he came in, Will was like, "Yo, what up James, how you doing?" and that's when his right-hand man, Bobby, made a point of etiquette: "Well, one thing I should say is that we have a system here and we don't call anyone by their first name. We refer to each other as Mister or Miss or Mrs. So you is Mr. I Am, you is Mr. de Ap, you is Miss Ferg, and you is Mr. Boo," he said, referring to me, "and Mr. Brown is Mr. Brown. Okay?"

Mr. Brown took charge pretty much from the moment he arrived, getting all vocal and barking instructions with that staccato delivery of his. "Okay, I'm going to tell you . . . what we're going to do," he said, gesturing for his band members and ours to go into the studio, ". . . y'all go in there and I'm going to give you direction!"

Over the next two or three hours, we learned how he demanded nothing but perfection. There was no margin for error with Mr. Brown in the room. He expected nothing short of excellence every second. We created, honed, and polished the track "They Don't Want Music"—but not before we were handed a lesson in funk.

The band was in the main studio, his backup singers were in a side room, and Mr. Brown was with Will sitting at the mixing board when our saxophonist Timmy Izzo started playing, getting into it.

"Nah! Nah! Stop!" Mr. Brown yelled, rising from his seat. "You're not feeling the funk, boy! I'm not hearing no funk. Let me show you what FUNK is . . ." and he walked in there, took the sax off Tim, and started demonstrating funk, with sound effects from his own mouth. On the spot, in his groove, and using some kind of indecipherable grunting noises, Mr. Brown went: "heyda-heyda-hadahum . . . ahuh-henuheyda-heyda-HUM!"

Which was kind of hard for Tim to follow, but he tried again. Wasn't right.

Mr. Brown sent his guy into the studio to get on the sax—and then he didn't do it right either. "How am I . . . going to teach . . . this young man . . . if I bring you into the booth . . . and you can't even do it right? Let's do it again!"

He was standing there, like a conductor, directing the band from the

outside, telling the saxophonists how to play the sax, telling Printz how to play the keyboards, telling Keith how to play the drums.

"Boy!" he barked to Keith, "you can't play funk sitting down!"

Keith stood for the rest of the session.

All the time, Mr. Brown was telling his band how to kick it, but communicating his demands via a secret, grunting code that was known only to them. He went "HEH!" and his band stopped. "HUH-HUH!" and the horns played. "HUH-HA!" and the ladies started singing. I was in awe watching it all come together as he basically bossed the studio with nothing more than some "Gotta get a HUH!" and some "Gotta get a HA-HUH!"

The funniest shit was when Printz, one of our own perfectionists, felt that one of the backing singers was off-key. The whole ensemble was in full flow when Printz waved his hands and stopped the action. "Hold up! Something sounds a bit funny in the chorus."

Mr. Brown's people looked horrified.

Printz, thinking he was making a valid point, went on: "It's not right . . . maybe . . ."

"Son!" Mr. Brown interrupted. "Never . . . NEVER . . . stop the music!"

Printz, realizing the extent of his audacity, mumbled something but all I heard was Mr. Brown add: "Let me tell you some'ing. I've been doing this for fifty years. Fifty years. And it's *exactly* how it's supposed to be."

Printz retreated behind his keyboards, lesson learned (but he'll still maintain to this day that one girl was off-key and all he did was offend Mr. Brown's biased favoritism).

When it was time for a break and lunch, we all went to the catering room upstairs above the studio, and Mr. Brown was the last one to make his entrance. When he did, he approached the table and clapped his hands: the signal for an assistant to come up and brush his hair from behind before he sat down. He then sat down—aware that all eyes were on him—and before you knew it, someone had placed a napkin across his lap, and then, as soon as his plate arrived, another assistant was cutting up his meat.

It was servitude on a monstrous, iconic superstar level, and I was just sitting there, trying to keep my mouth from falling open. Okay, it was strange, but I wasn't going to judge him because that was James Brown sitting right there.

James fucking Brown. Even if he wants someone to sit there and have someone twiddle his toes and polish his nose, that was cool with me . . . because that was James fucking Brown! The President of the United States had his own flunkies. The Queen of England has her own servants. And James Brown has his servants, too.

Back downstairs, it didn't take long to wrap up "They Don't Want Music." He nailed the hook in two takes and we were out of there.

"I'm only going to do this twice!" he had pre-warned us.

Two takes was all it needed to capture his signature on our album. He could have done it in one imperfect take and it would have been enough. All he's ever had to do is go "HUH—I feeeeel good" and it's unique. The man is unrivaled in history and he gave us authentic funk on *Monkey Business*. I still look at that track's title on the album cover—"They Don't Want Music" (*featuring James Brown*)—and say a quiet "wow" to myself. It remains one of the greatest memories of my life.

If there was one period that summed up the extremes of both good and bad, it was 2005 to 2006, and the recording and touring of the *Monkey Business* album. In terms of the group and band's chemistry, everything gelled like never before and we were on top of our game, in the studio, on the road. We had always loved playing together, but this was a new kind of synergy, built on the back of the confidence our breakthrough success had given us. The momentum felt unstoppable.

In terms of my descent, everything felt equally unstoppable, but only because there were no brakes. London inspired us creatively but, as a 24/7 party city, its energy only served to further enable my drinking and partying, as will become clear.

Monkey Business represented the growth of our success, in the sense of we had already accomplished #1 hits, had pretty much traveled the world, got to perform on the big stages like the Grammys and had mixed it with the Who's Who of the entertainment industry. We were no longer viewed as a support act. In fact, 2005 was the time when we went from Black Eyed Peas to *the* Black Eyed Peas; three letters that denoted a big shift and elevated our emphasis, our status, and our brand. If *Elephunk* was our key into the established kingdom of music, *Monkey Business* was about strengthening that brand, following up quickly and cementing our position. I was about adopting the Michael Jordan spirit.

When Jordan first came up, he was a kid trying to make a name. He was known for one thing—his killer slam dunks—so he had notoriety. He didn't win a championship, but he had notoriety. Over the years, he became a team player, took his game to the next level, and became a leader—to the point where he won six championships. That was the spirit the Peas needed. We had come up with our basic skills with *Behind the Front* and *Bridging the Gap*, and we got noticed with *Elephunk*. But if we were to become true champions, we had to take our game to the next level—evolve—and we needed to pass the ball better around the world, as opposed to doing the one thing we were known for.

For our fourth album, we wanted the international feel to be stronger, and for the album to better reflect how we played live, to have more of a party feel,

from the beats we had to the types of instruments we used. We wanted it to make people move, have fun, jump around, and not take life too seriously. Serious messages get lost over time as events and society change, but fun music and party anthems live on, and we have always preferred a catchy song that stays in the head and impacts a wide audience. We've never been so self-important as to think that our music must really, really matter all of the time. But what it must do all of the time is entertain.

As we headed into the studio in London, we hadn't really had the time to draw breath because everything had moved so fast, but the *Elephunk* road trip had made us hungry to record another album and lay down the kind of music and sounds we had tuned into in our travels, from Europe to Japan to Brazil. That is why *Monkey Business* would draw on everything from big pop hooks to old-school funk to hip-hop to bossa nova.

Our time on the road also inspired the album's title, for a couple of reasons.

Firstly, we were overseas—I can't remember exactly where—and we were inside the back of an SUV, being taken away from a venue. I think it was this incident when all four of us began to understand the scale of our success. Because the van was stopped and hemmed in by an excited crowd that started banging on the sides and the windows. I remember looking at Fergie and seeing her face match my thoughts: *What the fuck is happening? Why is this happening?* It was the craziest thing we had been through. The whole vehicle started shaking and these faces and palms were pressed against the front, rear, and sides as we were completely mobbed, and that is when we all started laughing, and I said, "I feel like we are monkeys in a cage right now!"

"Feeling like monkeys" was a long-standing joke since *Elephunk,* because as our profile increased, the label and management guys sat in plush offices in L.A. and New York and just kept cracking the whip and filling the schedule, without understanding how grueling back-to-back dates and city-to-city traveling can be; without comprehending what it is like to leave a venue at midnight, travel to an airport, fly to the next city at 2 a.m., arrive at 4 a.m., check into the hotel at 5:30 a.m., and then try to catch some sleep before the next day starts again.

Each time a new date was squeezed in regardless of logistics, we shrugged our shoulders and said out loud: "Sing monkey, dance monkey, get on stage monkey." The Black Eyed Peas always did the impossible when it came to making insane schedules happen, and I can say without fear of being challenged that we were—and remain—the hardest-working, no-frills, no-bullshit group, band, and crew in the business.

"Monkey business" was also the constant theme of our time together on the road—always laughing, acting the fool, or punking one another, and this is reason number two behind the title.

We had drinking competitions on the tour bus, fruit-platter fights in dressing rooms, and pillow fights on the planes—using those mini-pillows as missiles—and whenever we came across the Canadian pop-punk band Simple Plan, we'd wait until they went on stage, and then remove every stitch of furniture—couches, chairs, tables, and fridges—from their dressing room. This habit began when our paths first crossed at BDO in 2001, and it just continued whenever we shared a bill, because they were both easy prey and good sports.

I always looked forward to them finishing their set and returning to a bare dressing room with not a bottle of water to drink, and then we'd hear them curse us: "Fucking Black Eyed Peas!"

Meanwhile, in-house drinking competitions allowed me to bury my habits in the old excuse of fun. I like to think my reputation as a drinker was notorious, if not quite unbeatable, and everyone tried to take us on, especially me and George Pajon. We were the anything-goes kind of drinkers who never refused a shot or a challenge, and I remember when two new dancers joined the crew—Dion and Marvelous—and they saw a pale-faced Mexican and chubby Cuban and figured they could win. "You don't want to take us on, guys," warned George. "We've been doing this for a while now."

They didn't listen and, needless to say, those poor guys had to be loaded onto luggage carts and poured into their dressing room, vowing never to drink with us again. As much as everyone criticized me about my alcohol tolerance, I still had this amazing ability to keep on drinking even when wasted. Which made me unbeatable as well as incoherent.

Our level of alcohol competitiveness probably went too far in January of 2003, when we were on the tour bus in Tampa after the Buccaneers had won the Super Bowl and we got involved in some serious post-game partying with the Buccaneer cheerleaders. As a result, I was asleep on the tour bus by 10 p.m.—an event which is viewed as a small crime in our camp.

Falling asleep early on the tour bus is a punishable offense—which I'll come to in a bit—but George didn't want to punish me, he wanted to challenge me. He snuck on the bus and shouted in my ear, "YOU ARE ASLEEP, TAB!" and started hassling me about not handling my liquor.

"Okay, let's battle!" I said, jumping up, still drunk.

George whipped out a bottle of Jack Daniels like it was a gun from a holster.

He took a swig. I took a swig. He took two swigs. I took two swigs.

And then the last thing George said that night was the boast that

declared: "C'mon, Tab, is that all you've got?" and he downed the whole bottle, about two-thirds full.

Within seconds, he collapsed in a heap and fell flat on his face.

I was standing over him, screaming "YOU SEE, GEORGIE! You can't even handle your liquor!"

Which didn't provoke a response.

"George! Look at YOU . . . finished the bottle but lost the battle!" I said, goading him more. He lay there, face crumpled into the carpet, not moving a muscle.

"George?"

It took a few minutes before we realized that George was out cold and had downed so much whisky that he had suffered instant alcohol poisoning. He didn't leave his bed for three days and didn't stop aching for a week. Which, in my book, left me as the winner by a knockout.

Instead of challenging me, George should have left me asleep and allowed me to suffer the punishment that befalls every other premature sleeper on the tour bus.

Normally, when someone falls asleep in the front lounge of the bus with their shoes on, it is customary for the rest of the group to write a whole verse of a Black Eyed Peas song on their face. As Apl found out, when, after an afternoon of drinking, he crashed out on the couch and woke with the lyrics of "Fallin' Up" written out—with a black Sharpie—all over his forehead, cheeks, and chin.

The title *Monkey Business* is not just an album title. It represents the spirit of the Peas, because we are always dropping bombs on each other. It requires a thick skin and a merciless humor to be on our tour bus, and no one is safe from the bagging, the sarcasm, and the punking. We should have remembered that when we were invited to some Playboy Mansion–type place in Los Angeles when some fun-in-the-sun failed to turn into a laughing matter.

We were told it was a meeting with *Hustler* magazine to discuss a possible interview and photo spread, and so we arrived by appointment, pulling up at this grand mansion in the Hollywood Hills. It was the kind of opulent home that screamed mega-millions, set in manicured gardens with neat little hedges and one giant pool out back.

I remember it was a baking-hot afternoon, where girls were wearing next-to-nothing bikinis with high heels, draping themselves over the lounge chairs and sitting around the pool. The moment we all walked in—me, Apl, Will, Polo, and our two friends, J.J. Anderson and Sebastian—we were thinking the same: "Party Paradise."

The first thing that ran through my mind was getting to the bathroom, dropping some Ex, and, with so many girls around, getting the *real* party going. I didn't pay too much attention at first to this black dude who was supposed to be the "pimp" for these girls. He acted a little awkward and suspicious, but I guess he was no more shady than any other pimp in that setup.

I sat down poolside and this chick started coming on strong. Apl rolled a blunt and we all started smoking. Then some other blonde said, "Who wants to go in the pool?" and Polo's arm went straight in the air. The problem was that this girl, wearing an ankle-length summery dress, didn't have a bathing suit.

But she said to Polo, "You go in naked, and I'll go in naked . . ."

Polo didn't need to be asked twice. He got out of his clothes and jumped in but she was still standing on the edges, reluctant . . . until he pulled her in, fully dressed. I was observing it all with mild humor, and starting to get faded, when . . . BOOM . . . this door broke open and about twenty police officers, guns drawn, burst in.

"NOBODY MOVE! HANDS IN THE AIR . . . GET AGAINST THE WALL!"

The whole place scattered with screaming girls, and it was mayhem. When someone asked what the fuck was going on, some cop said it was a prostitution ring and everyone was going to jail. The cops lined up girls on the right and men on the left.

In the melee, I was frozen to the spot, standing there, as high as a kite, with a blunt in my hand and pills in my pocket. I looked to my right, and Polo was standing alone in the middle of the pool, looking as bewildered as the rest of us, and, as the manager of the group, this was a probably a nightmare he didn't wish to handle naked.

We both looked across the deck, and the suspicious-looking black guy— now unmasked as the undercover cop—had grabbed Will and was dragging him, violently, by the side of the pool. That was enough to trigger Polo's protective instincts, as a brother as well as a manager.

"YO!" he shouted, scrambling out of the pool, "what the fuck do you think you're doing with my artist?," and he started pulling on Will's arm.

"Put your hands up!" the cop yelled.

I used the distraction to drop the blunt and toss my pills behind a small hedge.

"PUT YOUR HANDS UP!" the cop shouted again.

But Polo—who said he sensed something wasn't quite right with the setup—was defiant. "HE IS MY ARTIST AND YOU HAVEN'T EVEN READ HIM HIS RIGHTS!"

The next thing I knew, Polo smacked the cop in the face and they both fell backward into the water; one naked man and one man wearing the full-on S.W.A.T. gear. Polo's protective streak knows no bounds.

The cop came up spluttering for air and saying: *"Punk'd!* It's *Punk'd!"*

Polo, misinterpreting the protest, had the upper hand in the grapple and said: "I'm a punk, am I?" and he smacked him in the mouth one more time. Which is when the panic-stricken producers from Ashton Kutcher's MTV show *Punk'd* came rushing out from their hiding place with their full—if a little late—disclosure.

Apparently, I had been the main target of the prank until Polo stole the show.

Will had set up the whole thing with Ashton Kutcher, designed to give me a scare about my partying ways. I don't need to tell you that it was the one *Punk'd* episode that never aired, and I was spared the "monkey business" humiliation of being set-up—and faded—on national television.

We liked our life in London town for those three months of recording time in 2005. We actually rented three houses in Chiswick: one for the group, one for the band, and one for management. Our "home" was in a corner of a cul-de-sac, with a high brick wall that separated us from an over-ground section of London's Underground (subway). We had one of those tall, narrow London homes with rooms that were as small as fuck. London living is *not* for the claustrophobic.

As soon as we walked in the front door, the house started climbing up some narrow, spiral that went four flours high, and none of us will forget those horrible stairs as we hauled Fergie's eight suitcases to the top. But, suitcases aside, it was great having a woman aboard, living among us, and fitting in. I'm not sure what her views were about sharing a home with student-living men, but she never complained, and when it came to cooking, she was chief taster, I was chef's assistant and Apl was the head chef. I bonded more with Fergie on this trip as a sister and friend, because on days off she took me shopping to Oxford Street, Regent Street, and Bond Street. I think that is when she realized that my taste for shoes was almost as strong as hers!

I remember two things about Chiswick. It was very leafy with large trees on the common and trees on the street, with big-ass canopies of greenery shadowing bus stops and houses. When all you are used to is towering palm trees, seeing these dense, low-lying branches every block or so takes some getting used to. It also seemed to be a town filled with fertile women. I have never seen so many pregnant women and mothers with babies. I looked around and thought: *Is that all you do around here? Make babies?*

Our house was like base camp before we took the fifteen-minute drive to the studio, where we all bounced between different rooms and studios on a factory floor that processed our music on some kind of assembly line that took a song from pre-creativity (thoughts/inspiration) to creativity (writing/recording) to refining (polishing/mixing).

We came and went, back and forth, room to room in an almost choreographed collaboration, jumping from studio to studio, switching and swapping with equal input. It was starkly different to our disjointed, loose, and frustrating time in Northern Cali on *Elephunk*. In London, we had become a slick, well put-together, creative machine.

Fergie put it best when she described the creative energy of this time as "a creative waterfall which just fell down into this huge ocean that is *Monkey Business.*"

At 9 p.m. every night, the drinks always arrived and the studio got used to my shout: "Yo, it's WINE TIME!," which meant I could get loosened up and get my taste on for the night ahead, because when we were done at 11:30 p.m., we hit the clubs, taking the Tube into Victoria Station and then hailing a black cab to our regular clubs—Chinawhite until 3 a.m., and then the open-all-night Paparazzi.

We went there every night, and that allowed me to transfer my Hollywood lifestyle to London. But this was more excessive, because I was now allowed to party and drink every night for a solid three-month block. My body now attuned itself to binge-drinking on a daily basis, and each night always ended the same— everyone drifted away, I became annihilated and always wanted to stay, even when it was obvious that I'd had enough. That was me: first one to start drinking at the studio, last one to leave the clubs around dawn.

Most nights, I was with our homie J.J. Anderson. J.J. is this African-American bear of a man who has always been a motivational force, confidant, and spiritual advisor to the group. He is invisible to the fans and yet ever-present in our lives; always the life and soul of the party on the tour bus or charter planes; always bouncing around in the wings at concerts. His father worked as a security specialist for Muhammed Ali, Sugar Ray Leonard, and Mike Tyson, so he grew up on those blurred edges of the spotlight, and he has shared our journey, trials, and tribulations as much as anyone. And this cat can party with the best of them, so when everyone was leaving me slouched in a corner of Paparazzi, I would always collar J.J. to stay with me. What he rarely knew was that I had nearly always popped some Ecstasy, so I was always much more fucked up than he realized. I can still see us now, shuffling out of that club at 7 a.m., walking outside and reacting to daylight like Dracula, and J.J.—suffering and rubbing his shaved head with both hands—saying "What the fuck, Tab! Why you keep me out so late, bro?"

He vowed never to let me lead him astray again, but he always stuck with me. Without J.J., God knows which gutters in the London streets I would have ended up lying in.

We would get back to the house and sleep till 1 p.m., and then it would start all over again: work, work, work, party, party, party. I even wrote a song with Apl that summed up our London life, "Working Seven Days A Week." It didn't make

the final cut, but the lyrics pretty much summed up what we were about back then and went something like this: "*Wake up, We smoke, We eat, We smoke/We work, we eat, we smoke. Wake up/We drink, we drink, go out to clubs, and do it again . . . *"

The songs that did make the final cut didn't include a big-feeling song on the scale of "Where Is the Love?" because the content was lighter and more party oriented, but I felt we delivered a more solid album. For me, it set the standard of our future direction. "My Humps" turned into a monster hit, but not in a socially conscious way. "Don't Lie" was different than "Shut Up," but in the same vein "Don't Phunk With My Heart" was Bollywood inspired by the bhangra clubs in London, and "Pump It" was an anthem inspired by the European club scene. It was also used for the Best Buy television campaign in the U.S. in another corporate string we added to the branded collection.

Monkey Business wasn't just recorded in three months in London. We recorded on the road during spot dates and trips to Brazil, Japan, France, and Berlin, and that kind of system was a challenge for Fergie, by her own admission. She was used to blocks of centered studio time and then blocks of touring, but the growth of the Black Eyed Peas was all about a moving energy; about recording and writing and touring at the same time. Always was. Always will be. And the more she found that groove, the more she excelled, and "My Humps" was the song that first showcased Fergie's solo talents—the first song that featured mostly her voice and paved the way for her solo success.

Even today, if we're touring in Europe and have a day off, we find a studio to record. Touring inspires us and it's those inspirations we wish to capture in the studio, catching the moment. If we are in a club in, say, Athens or Barcelona, and we hear music or pick up on a certain vibe in a club, that is what we want to build on in a studio the very next day.

"Pump It" is a prime example of working and recording on the move— literally. We were on the bullet train in Japan heading from Tokyo to Yokohama, and we were drinking sake and getting drunk, except for Will who was tucked away at the back of the train, listening to some CD he had bought in Brazil entitled *Brazilian Tunes*—which is why he bought it—but it turned out to be some surfer-rock songs. He was pissed at first, but kept listening and there he was, deep into the music via his headphones when he suddenly heard the Dick Dale song "Miserlou" and he jump-started his portable recording tools on his computer . . . while we are doing about 150 miles per hour.

He was loving the guitar riff but we had no idea what he was listening to. All we heard was him shouting out "Louder! . . . LOUDER! . . . LOUDER!" which made him look like one of those crazy people who sit on trains alone and hear voices.

"Louder! Turn it up—LOUDER!" he kept shouting—a DJ without an audience.

By the time we reached the hotel, he was bouncing with energy in the lobby, and he told us all: "I've got one! It's going to go "Pump it—LOUDER! Pump it—LOUDER!"

On the flight back to Tokyo, he tightened the beat from his seat on the plane. He then recorded some vocals in a park in Tokyo. And that was how "Pump It" first came together, and that is how we like to work . . . by keeping the energy moving.

Over the years, we have been lucky enough to see the world and stay in some amazing places and enjoy some ridiculous five-star hotels. We have arrived by private jet, by boat, and by helicopter, and have lived a life that our ancestors would find mind-blowing. But *nothing* compares to the time when we got to stay in an Englishman's castle.

Sting's castle in Wiltshire.

Will had been working with Sting in 2004 when, with *Monkey Business* in mind, we decided to sample the melody from his 1988 hit "An Englishman in New York" and add our own lyrics for a song called "Union," which ultimately featured Sting's vocals.

Our version was not about feeling "alien" anywhere but about finding unity and harmony and equal opportunity in society, based on the Three Musketeers' mantra: "It's one for all and all for one" (about as serious as the album got).

It was one of the first ideas we had for the new album while still on the road with *Elephunk,* so when Sting found out we were booked for our first appearance at the U.K.'s Glastonbury Festival—a festival we nicknamed The Mudfest—he invited us to stay at his "house" for two nights.

I was expecting some large mansion, as we all got excited about visiting this musical great and seeing his studio. Then we rocked up on the day and couldn't believe our eyes. We had seen some big-ass cribs and Hollywood mansions before, but we pulled up outside of that mothafucka and were like, "Oh shit! Sting's 'house' is a castle!" A seventeenth-century Jacobean castle named Lake House.

This dude has forty rooms to rattle around in, a lake in his backyard, a meadow for a garden, and a three hundred fifty-year-old tree where he swings in a hammock between its branches. He grows his own dairy products, has his own cattle and chickens, and has a field of organic fruit. I was standing there, mouth falling open, as he greeted us and welcomed us to his home, telling us he always feels better when the place "comes alive with people." It turns out that

his hit "Fields of Gold" was inspired by the surrounding fields and meadows. No shit.

We each had our own room, which I wasn't too cool about because that place was as scary as fuck. It had all these old-ass pictures of lords and dukes from the shires and shit, with eyes that followed you through the dark hallways. I was in there about five minutes before I decided it was haunted. There was some old English medieval times shit going down, and me and Apl joked that it was the last place on earth you would want to do acid, because those dukes would come alive and have you jumping out of the windows.

Sting is one deep-centered spirit, and he was sitting there all chill and Zen while I was sitting there, feeling restless, legs bouncing. Thank God for his ten-year-old son Giacomo, because as Will, Fergie, Sting, and his wife Trudie discussed all things philosophical, deep, and Tantric, this kid—the biggest character in the house—kept me and Apl more than occupied. I don't think I have ever met such a confident, outspoken boy with such a strong personality, and he took us to the fields on the bikes, and on a tour of the castle—the highlight of which was playing the drums in the attic converted into a music room.

This kid was running the show, and calling us on all kinds of shit. When he saw us smoking a cigarette outside, he observed us for a bit, then said, "Oh, you smoke like Mexicans."

This kid was *tough,* and had a confidence that you had to admire—probably because he'd always had such a strong family unit around him. He was the kid I wished I could have been, and he had the security I wished for mine one day.

That was the observation I took away from those two days. The advice I took away was from Sting, and it spoke to the spirit of the Black Eyed Peas. He told us that friendship was sacrosanct within a group; having constant respect for each other and the band throughout all trials and tribulations. "You will have creative differences and petty shit will get in the way, but if I learned anything from my days with the Police, it is to stay grounded and protect the friendship that you have," he said.

The next day, he decided he wanted to show us some sights. "You want to go see Stonehenge?" he asked.

"Stonehenge? With the stones and shit?" we said.

"Yeah, it's right across from my house," said Sting.

So we visited his ancient near-neighbor, Stonehenge, to complete a surreal weekend.

I came away from those two nights thinking, *This is success, this is what it's about*—this was years of being on top of his game and making the right decisions and doing the right things as an artist, a philanthropist and an entrepreneur. I think life sometimes introduces you to living and breathing examples of the people we can become as human beings, and here was life offering me a better version of the life I was leading—someone who had known the industry, known success, and known the spotlight and come out of it intact. Such an example registered at some level, even if it wasn't acted on straightaway.

Years before Sting bought Lake House, the English came up with a saying: "A man's home is his castle." Among the Peas, we had our own variation of that theme, believing that a man's home was a sign of success. We had always said that the moment we bought our first homes—outright, with no mortgage—was the moment we could truly say we had achieved in life. For us, success was measured in bricks and mortar, not album sales or chart positions. So, at the age of twenty-nine—after banking my first million and before setting off to record *Monkey Business* in London—I moved off Mom's couch in Rosemead, bought my first property in Walnut, outside Los Angeles, and dived into the world of independent living. For the first time in my life, I could stretch my balls, put my feet up, and transfer into the home the kind of freedom I enjoyed on the road.

With business manager Sean Larkin's guidance, I had found this two-story, four-bedroom house, and I bought it outright for $500,000. It was nothing fancy. It was an ordinary suburban tract home, painted beige and tan with an average backyard. The most lavish item on the inside was the projector screen I bought to watch movies, and the most expensive item on the property was the brand-new red Hummer that General Motors had given each of the Peas, as part of a sponsorship deal. It seemed more rock 'n' roll than my Honda Civic, even if a Hummer wasn't my style, but it was free and it was a perk I wasn't going to refuse.

Even though it was my first house, I treated it more like a base. I wasn't into interior design or any of that shit, so I didn't hang any pictures, place pretty plants on stands, or have any frills and shit. It was a classic bachelor pad: stark and bare with one table, four chairs, one couch, a bed, a fridge, a microwave to substitute for the oven I never used. It was a soulless place.

Back then, I didn't need a "home." I just needed a place that me and Josh could call our own, and all that really mattered to me was having the privacy to smoke as much weed as I liked in my bedroom, as I played the role of being a single dad.

I had not moved in long before the Peas left to record *Monkey Business* in London, and Josh returned to stay with Mom for three months. "We'll be a proper father and son living at home when I get back," I told him.

It was one of those empty promises that regularly fell out of my mouth back then.

■　■　■

After returning from London, and with the *Monkey Business* album almost complete, I made my first break into acting. This was one of those accidental dreams that arose organically instead of by design.

Ever since 2003, an agent named Sarah Ramaker, from the Paradigm agency, had been saying I should explore an acting career because I had what she called "a distinct look." I think that was her way of saying that my scary-looking face was a hidden gift.

At first, I thought this was just another Hollywood agent blowing smoke up my ass. "Why is this lady asking me to act?" I said to Deja. "I'm not an actor. I want to do music." Even though I had been inspired by Bruce Lee as a kid, the big screen had never really appealed or seemed like a possibility, but the more Sarah floated the idea by me, the more "Why me?" turned into "Why not me?" But, as with b-boying and MCing, I didn't want to leap into the circle without first understanding the basics of the craft, and so I signed up for acting classes at the Gloria Gifford Conservatory School of Acting, where I went every Sunday morning from late 2004, whenever I wasn't recording or touring.

It was one of those decisions that, when taken, made me wonder why I had doubted it in the first place, because the moment I walked through those doors, the environment felt as natural to me as the stage. There had always been a sense of the "theatrical" about me in terms of my performance and costume, so acting felt like a natural extension in the end. I felt more and more liberated and comfortable in a class that involved around twenty-five other students. As my confidence grew, I was then introduced to a male acting coach, Cary Anderson, who then took me under his wing to develop my basic acting skills with one-on-one tuition.

Throughout this process, Sarah continually handed me scripts so I could practice my delivery, and she threw me into auditions so that I could get used to reading to a camera (and get used to the rejection!). After a year of tuition and practice, nothing seemed to be popping off, and I had almost relegated my prospects to the back burner to concentrate on *Monkey Business* when the phone rang while I was in London.

"Hey, Tab," said Sarah, "there's this movie called *Dirty* . . . there's a role that would be perfect for you . . . and the casting director wants to give you a shot."

I felt challenged by a new skill. I felt butterflies in my stomach for the first time in a long time, and I saw something that involved me as an individual that was not reliant on me being part of a quartet. I was sent the script for my return to L.A., and, after a successful audition, I landed the small part of Ramirez in *Dirty*. During two days of filming in some familiar streets of L.A., art suddenly imitated the life that Mom had never wanted me to know.

My role? A *cholo* from East L.A., hired to kill.

How did I prepare? I just thought of Eddie and tapped into that parallel universe. With that irony, I took my first tentative steps into Hollywood, and decided I liked acting and wanted to do more. Which was good, because when the beautiful Jaymie Dizon walked back into my life in 2005, I needed to be the best actor out there. I had to play the role of the guy who had changed and got his shit together.

ANGELS & DEMONS

Ever since Jaymie walked out of my life in late 1999, I had often thought about her. In all the comings and goings of female attention, and during all the time I was standing in the shallow hell of Hollywood, my mind always managed to trace its way back to the one connection that had felt the most alive, even if its value had been lost on me at the time.

It was during the sober windows that I wondered how she was doing and where she was, and, even though I had treated her badly, my arrogance was so solid back then that it never shied away from the idea of reaching out.

I finally acted on that idea backstage at NBC's studios in L.A. when we were booked to perform "*Where Is the Love?*" and "Hey Mama" on the *Tonight Show* with Jay Leno during the Elephunk run. I was excited about doing the show, and, out of all the people I knew, I wanted the person who I hadn't seen or spoken to for three years to see it and share it.

I texted her out of the blue: "*I know you probably don't care but tune into Jay Leno. We're on—check it out.*"

I can't say I was confident about getting a reply, but, after the show, my cell vibrated and illuminated green: "*Congratulations—a lot of thrusting and gyrating of the hips!*"

So began the usual game of text tennis. "*Maybe we can have lunch soon?*" I suggested.

"*I don't think so,*" she replied.

"Maybe lunch next year then?"

"I don't think so."

"Maybe in two years?"

I raised it to five, seven, and ten years, and she still said no, and after that night's brief burst of re-contact, another year and a bit drifted along until I was back in L.A. after recording *Monkey Business* and decided to fire in another random attempt.

"Maybe we can do lunch this year?" I texted.

"Okay—but you're picking me up."

We went to a Cuban restaurant in Torrance. It was one of those rare days in California when it was raining, and I picked her up in my red Hummer. I saw this different woman darting through the rain, under an umbrella. She had gone from a rock-style fashionista to bohemian chick: little to no makeup, one of those billowing, flowery skirts, cowboy boots, and aviator sunglasses.

At that first lunch, we kept it light and adult, catching up. I told her what the Peas had done. She had noticed, she said. She told me she had graduated from FIDM, and was now working in PR at the Michael Stars label.

And she had a boyfriend.

"Cool, I'm glad you're happy," I lied, "I'm glad we can be friends."

We carried on this platonic pretense, going for a few lunches over several weeks without anything ever happening, and we started dining at a Japanese place in Walnut when, one time, we loosened up over a few sakes and the pretense fell away.

She admitted she wasn't happy in her relationship. I admitted I wasn't happy being the single guy, bouncing from place to place.

"I don't suppose Josh is happy with that, either," she said.

We confronted the past for the first time, and, thanks to the sakes, gave each other a dose of honesty.

She was scared of me, she said. I had hurt her more than I knew.

"You left," I said. "You quit at the first sign of trouble."

"Do you still love me?" she asked.

"I've never stopped loving you," I said.

I told her I had messed up. I was sorry.

"How do I know you won't hurt me again?"

"That's not me anymore," I said. "I've changed."

When those words came out of my mouth, it wasn't exactly a lie because I had changed in this way: I was now successful and not "a broke-ass rapper." I now had my own bank account with money in it. I now had my own place and not just Mom's couch. I was now going places and could be the provider. So much of the landscape and the fortunes had changed around me that it appeared to be a transformation.

"If you gave me another chance, this time it will be different," I said, using that line that no girl should ever trust.

What I concealed from Jaymie that day was the downside of "change." In 1999, I was not an addict, just a jerk. Now, in 2005, I was unable to free myself from the weed, the drink, and the occasional burst of Ecstasy. I was useless in the face of an inner destructive force that had not yet fully revealed its worst to me, but I also knew that I wanted this woman in my life. She had come back to me for a reason. She knew me like no one had ever known me, and she was the smartest, most solid, beautiful, intelligent woman I had met. And, for some reason, she still loved me.

I wasn't going to lose her again. So it was safer to rely on the outward appearances of change than admit to being damaged goods.

"I can see it in you," she said, "I can see a big change."

Within a few weeks, she had ended her relationship and we had decided to give it another go. Building trust would take time, but we vowed to wipe the slate clean. I felt in a good place with that decision we had taken. Maybe I felt like Jaymie could be the answer—the missing piece—because I now had the house, I had the money, I had the girl and the dream career was getting bigger and growing stronger. I guess I was the guy who had it all.

Around the same 2005 period that Jaymie returned to my life, two other not-so-good influences moved in with me at the Walnut house. We'll call them "Heckle" and "Jeckle," as opposed to their real names, and I had known them both from childhood days in Rosemead. But what I learned is that a shared history in childhood doesn't guarantee you'll be brothers, especially when those friends viewed my life and its accompanying lifestyle as the one magic carpet ride they could hang onto and enjoy.

I had introduced this duo into my world because, as the success grew and I was advised to set up a corporation—Tab Magnetic—I needed help with day-to-day management, general organization, and looking after Josh. It didn't matter to me that these two Latino neighbors had zero experience in any of those departments. I just viewed them as two extra pairs of hands, and they were from the 'hood and, therefore, I could trust them.

Heckle had been a next-door neighbor since we were kids, and he was this small, chunky dude with a big-ass mop of curly hair whose obnoxiousness I mistook for the kind of attitude I could use in a guy. I paid him a salary to be my driver, assistant, and babysitter to Josh.

Jeckle was someone I had known since fifth grade. He was this short, bald-headed guy with pock-marked skin, and he could cook, so that's why I hired him as my chef. His 'fee' was being allowed to live rent-free at the house with all bills and food paid for. I told them both that if they stuck with me, I was going to change their lives for the better. It really was a case of the blind leading the blind.

My sister Celeste was also supposed to move in, but after a couple of visits when she witnessed the disorganized, sparse, student-living-style setup, she stayed with Mom. I don't blame her, and looking back, it was just as well, because this would turn into a pretty dark period, and the energy in that house had a bad vibe about it. Mom obviously had her concerns, too, for Josh, who was now somewhere between sixth and seventh grade at school. "Why are you taking Josh away from me to live with you and those two characters who know nothing about my grandson, and don't know anything about running a home?" she asked, with understandable bafflement.

"Because this is my son and I need to take care of him," I said, unaware of the absurdity of how this intention lined up against the circumstances.

What I was trying to show Mom and Jaymie and everyone else—feebly—was that I was growing up and "doing the right thing," and I was trying to show Josh that I could step up as a father and be there for him. The truth is that I was crashing around, acting on impulse, responding to all this inner pressure and guilt I felt to be a man at the age of thirty when, in actuality, I was this emotionally unaware kid whose only reality had been the rolling bubble of stages, tour buses, and hotels and the pleasures of getting as faded and as drunk as possible.

I wouldn't blame Josh if he looked back on this time and said "Yeah, you paid for this and that and provided the nice new house, but you were always touring, and even when you were home, you were never really there."

I loathe looking at myself now through his eyes back then, because God knows what he saw and didn't say or whether he was cognizant of the fact his dad was slipping away. If he felt the detachment, Josh never said anything. He was just this kid who quietly kept himself occupied, went about his own business, did his homework, watched television, played games consoles, and helped himself to snacks from the fridge. He was a resilient kid who never acted out or screamed or kicked. He soaked up the bleakness of that house like a sponge.

Meanwhile, I would lock myself away with Heckle and Jeckle in the master bedroom, sitting on the bed with the curtains drawn, passing the blunt around. There wasn't one hour of this period of my fatherhood when I was not faded in some chill cloud. And Heckle, the so-called babysitter, played along and lived my life vicariously. Jeckle followed Heckle's lead like a sheep, and no one inside the house attempted to bring me to my senses. Because for Heckle and Jeckle, this, too, was a life of decadence they had never tasted before, and they didn't want it to end. I invited them into a rarefied world under the cloak of employment, and it went to their heads as much as it went to mine.

Like classic enablers, all they wanted to do was enjoy this association and party.

"You want to party?" they asked, "Great! Let's go party!" and so we dropped Josh at Mom's and then hit the Hollywood clubs.

"Who's got the coke? Tab's got the coke!"

"Who's paying for the drinks? Tab's paying for the drinks!"

"Who's getting the burgers? Tab's getting the burgers!"

Within this circle of death, I was the cave-dwelling Grinch who stole Christmas, whose heart had shrunk so small that I was too busy selfishly indulging myself to show love to anyone, let alone be a father.

Thank God for a clear-headed mom and girlfriend who kept knocking on the door of my consciousness. And Jaymie kept asking, "Why do you have these guys in your life. What exactly do they do apart from live off you?"

Jaymie saw a lot more than Josh in terms of my lifestyle, and what my two assistants "assisted" me with, even if she didn't realize the extent of my drinking or cocaine use. Effective concealment is part of the addict's game, and I managed to hide from Jaymie the worst excesses of my behavior because we were dating and not living in each other's pockets. The real conflict between the person I was and the person *she thought I was* would come further down the line, the more inseparable we became.

Monkey Business was released on June 7, 2005 and set down our marker in the mainstream market that we were more than just a hip-hop group. But now everyone else started paying more attention to the smorgasbord of music we provided and that probably explains why it was widely described as our "crossover album," as we headed out on tour.

First, we toured Latin America in October–November of 2005 before launching into the main headline event—the sixth Annual Honda Civic Tour that took us on thirty-four dates between March and May 2006. What I loved about this tour was the fact it was our own shit; our first headlining experience. We now had our own support act—"the Pussycat Dolls"—and it felt as if a bigger world of opportunity had opened up for us. We were no longer riding someone else's wave, and the tickets sold were because of what we attracted, no one else. When you've spent almost a decade in somebody else's wake it is a good feeling when the stage opens up as your own.

Now, instead of Polo and management guarding every penny of a limited budget, we had corporate sponsorship paying for the whole thing via Honda and co-sponsor Verizon. We started flying first-class and being put up in five-star hotels, and the whole tour had a lavish feel about it. Honda even made ten limited edition Black Eyed Peas Monkey Business Honda Civics. It suddenly felt like money was no object in some Black Eyed Pea Magic Kingdom; like we had paid our dues, shoveled the shit at Disney and now here we were, leading the parade.

The scale of the tour felt even bigger when the second leg kicked in between July and December, because now the realization dawned of how much we had grown on *a global scale* in the time since *Elephunk.*

I looked at the tour itinerary, stretching from midsummer to the end of the year, and it was exhilarating just looking at the dry list of countries and cities: Moscow, Tokyo, Hong Kong, Shanghai, Mumbai, Tel Aviv, Honolulu, Bogota, Buenos Aires, Panama City, Mexico City, Manila, and Santiago as well as our usual stops across America, Canada, and spot dates in Europe. The album went on to sell ten million copies worldwide, four million of which were sold in America and one million in its birthplace, London.

We also saw our growth on a logistical level because our whole setup expanded to meet an increased operation. For our travels across America and Canada, the band got its own separate bus (by the end of *Monkey Business*, Fergie would get her own bus, too), and we started getting teams: a glam team, a grooming team, a wardrobe team, tour management, and a security detail.

Our road manager, Bobby Grant, now had a proper crew working with him. Previously, everything that had constituted a concert performance had fallen on him—that meant setting up nineteen instruments, placements and applications on stage to make a live show with three Peas, four musicians and sound equipment, working in tandem with our long-standing sound engineer Dave Haines. Now, Bobby—who had been road manager, stage manager, and production manager rolled into one—had a sixty-man crew/entourage to free up his leadership qualities. The Black Eyed Peas had grown from an eleven-strong unit into a monster touring machine, and yet we knew that this was just the start and that we had bigger and better still to come.

In my eyes, the scale of the Black Eyed Peas' reach had grown beyond the dream. It felt like one minute it was 1997 and we were running nonstop with our heads down, touring and recording and striving to make shit happen, and the next it was 2006 and we were selling out tickets in every corner of the world. It took time for me to absorb the hugeness of what we had built. In fact, I don't think I really believed it until I saw these heaving crowds across the world with my own eyes; different creeds and native tongues singing our songs, hands in the air, partying.

The craziest sight actually happened on New Year's Eve, 2006 at Ipanema Beach in Brazil, to the south of Rio de Janeiro. We were booked to headline a New Year's celebration and had been expecting the kind of crowd that turns up for summer-season gigs at Santa Monica Pier back home. But then we turned up and saw the reality. It looked more like the Hajj pilgrimage to Mecca in Saudia Arabia. I had never seen so many people.

People talk about "seas of people," but this was no sea, this was an ocean—a density of people packed onto the beach and streets, stretching back as far as the eye could see. Before going onstage, as we were standing in the wings

not believing our eyes, organizers told us that there was an estimated one million people out there.

Flashback to the days of performing to twenty-five people, and the disbelief is obvious. Those Brazilian people gave us a lot of love and they rocked that beach that night. It is indescribable what it is like facing a million people singing your songs; a million people holding lighters or cell phones in the air; a million people jumping and fist-pumping. It gave me chills as we closed out with Where Is the Love? and wished everyone a Happy New Year—and then the thrill turned into one scary-ass situation because this human ocean started rising and moving toward us. There were no barriers and no sense of crowd control and this swell started coming down the sides and around the back of the stage, and we felt swamped.

Only one word was going through our minds: stampede.

It turned from beautiful to frightening in a matter of moments.

To one side of us was the sea, and everywhere else was covered by people. There was no way out. Our bus had been drowned somewhere in the middle. We grabbed each other but felt paralyzed as a unit.

The next thing we knew, we were bundled into the back of an ambulance backstage and sitting on its stretchers in the windowless rear, and the driver turned on the sirens and lights and cut an emergency passage through the crowd and to the airport. We laughed with relief—and disbelief.

The *Monkey Business* touring didn't just represent an increase in our global profile and scale of operation, it marked an escalation in my drinking.

I was now drinking *during* performances, on stage.

Away from home, away from Jaymie, away from Josh, I hit it harder than ever before. I had gone from raiding hotel minibars to binge drinking through the night to now chugging one-liter plastic bottles of Arrowhead, emptying out the water and refilling it with white wine—a Chardonnay, a Pinot Grigio, a Chablis.

Sometimes I downed two bottles per performance, sometimes three.

Everyone thought I was taking water onstage to keep hydrated, and the more I drank and stumbled, the more it looked to the crowd that I was having a good time, because the spontaneity of our gigs was all about hanging loose, jumping around, and partying. I became expert at performing under the influence.

I got away with it until New Year's Eve 2005 in Las Vegas, during a show at the Hard Rock Cafe. We were halfway through our *Monkey Business* set and I had already downed three bottles when we launched into "Don't Phunk With My Heart."

I was drunk, so what follows is an indistinct version of events, but I was standing at the very front of the stage and there were a few celebrities in that night, sitting in the front row. I remember looking at Elizabeth Shannon, Brian Austin

Green and I want to say Alyssa Milano (or someone who looked like her), and it was those three faces that I was focused on and performing to, looking at them dead in the eyes.

I was kicking my verse—"*Baby girl you make me feel/You know you make me feel so real . . .* "—and I went for this quick-motion half-jump when I slipped and both feet went under me, and I dropped ass first onto one of the front-of-stage monitors. BOOM!

Numbed with alcohol, I jumped back up in a split-second but I saw the wincing faces in the front row looking back at me, and Elizabeth Shannon had cupped her hands to her mouth. Then the pain followed the visual: this searing pain that shot right up my back and into my neck.

Will, Fergie, and Apl were oblivious because they were on the other side of the stage doing their thing, but the band later told me that they "felt the pain just watching you fall."

I knew I was in trouble because I was stooped like an old man. Crooked.

I moved back to the center of the stage, looked left, and saw Polo. "What happened? You okay?" he mouthed. I pointed to my back but rolled my hand in a circle, indicating that I would go on, thinking that I could walk it off.

Somehow—and probably due to the anesthetic of alcohol—I played through the agony for the next three songs.

By the time I boarded the charter flight back to LAX that night, I was in the worst pain of my life; the kind of pain that brought waves of nausea. I was unable to sit down or lie on my back so I had to lie flat across three seats. "Polo, I think there is something wrong with me, brother."

In the back of my mind was the following day's performance that we were flying back for in downtown L.A. I've got to get straight for tomorrow, I kept telling myself.

Jaymie was waiting for me at the airport and she took me straight to the hospital in downtown L.A. Within an hour of being admitted into the ER, and after an X-ray, the diagnosis was through: I had broken my tailbone.

"But I've got a performance tomorrow night," I said to the doctor.

"You won't have a performance for the next three months," he said.

For the next three months, my enforced rehabilitation was sitting around on a special doughnut pad: a furnished version of an inflatable rubber ring.

Jaymie was my nurse and Heckle and Jeckle finally had some real assistant work to do, and, thankfully, everyone agreed that weed was a necessary medicine to keep my chill.

There were some small mercies within the suffering.

The injury was perfectly timed between tour dates, sandwiched between the October–November 2005 Latin America leg and the March–May 2006 America–Canada leg, so I didn't miss out on the real business end of touring, just

the odd spot date here and there. The only thing this injury really impacted was my role in the "*Pump It*" video–with its "drunk at a party" theme and scenes of street dance, road rage, and excessive partying.

The irony was not lost on me.

I was supposed to swing into the party scene on a harness, but that was floored by the injury. Instead, I had to settle for a quick walk-on cameo role.

The biggest setback in my rehabilitation, after three months of sitting on that doughnut, was the fact that the tailbone didn't heal properly; it had re-set into a fish hook. It was recommended that I start going to an acupuncturist, and this Chinese guy worked his magic and massaged the small of my back week after week, making me feel more and more comfortable.

I almost started to believe in this alternative Eastern medicine shit.

Then one day, he told me to brace myself because "I am going to break it back, otherwise you will have discomfort for the rest of your life."

No dancer or performer wants to hear that kind of prognosis.

So I lay there on my side, in one of those open-backed gowns they give you, and he said, "Okay, Jimmy . . . knees to your chest . . . prepare yourself . . ."

I was trying to look behind, over my shoulder. "Prepare for what? Is this going to hurt?"

"Just reeee-lax," he said.

With that warning, he shoved two fingers up my ass.

"WHAT THE FFF . . . !!!"

It's hard to leap up and hit the ceiling when some dude is treating you like a glove puppet, and he had these two fingers, hooked up, poking around my anus, trying to grab the tailbone, and I'm rolling around like baited fish, screaming and hollering "GET YOUR FUCKING FINGERS OUT OF MY ASS!!!"

I lost it. That was an alternative medicine violation.

He popped out his fingers, looked as stunned as I had looked ten seconds earlier, and I was up, dressed and out of there in about sixty seconds flat. Did he break it back? Nope. I was like "Yo, fuck it—let it grow back the way it's going to grow back" because no injury—no nothing—is worth some dude's fingers in my butthole for three to five minutes. I am pleased to say that in the year 2011, my tailbone is still fish-hooked, and it hasn't affected my walking, dancing, or rapping. Personally, I think the acupuncture trauma was God's way of teaching me a lesson never to drink on stage again.

It rarely happens that we leave a stage feeling deflated, but when we first performed in South Africa during the Elephunk run in 2004, we walked away feeling a bit low and disillusioned. Not because we had given a bad performance, but because every face in the crowd was white.

Performing in the land of Africans and not one black face to watch us, and there we were at the "Ten Years of Freedom in South Africa" concert, com-memorating the first decade since apartheid.

It was a shocking reality to our perceptions—naïve or otherwise—because this scene informed us that our music was not accessible to the people we ex-pected it to reach, and our concerts were not affordable to the people we wanted to entertain the most—the very African people to whom Nelson Mandela had given a voice. It left a kind of sour taste in the mouth as we headed back to L.A., and we vowed on the plane to return and give a free concert for the underprivileged people—black or white—as part of our mission statement for our Peapod Founda-tion, which now, for the first time, could set its sights outside of America.

We had driven through Johannesburg and toured the surrounding areas, and we had seen the affluent, pristine areas with grand houses, manicured lawns, and U.S. Open–style golf clubs—beautiful neighborhoods. And then, in a crude juxtaposition, we saw the ghettos and the poverty in the shantytowns on the dirt roads, and found resilience behind the rickety structures of plywood and tin-built homes. It was for that neighborhood that we wanted to come back.

On an evening in late May, 2006, in the weeks after the Honda Civic Tour had wrapped, we returned to keep our promise, and, this time, what we saw made us happy: forty thousand people from underprivileged backgrounds filling Johan-nesburg Stadium. The sight of those beaming faces, and hearing all that African chanting, was an experience that instantly relegated the one million of Ipanema Beach to the back of our minds.

On real human occasions like that, I didn't care what people said about us selling out. I didn't care about industry talk about "hip-pop" or "crossover" or "main-stream" or any of that shit. Because for the next two hours, our music was giving back to people who didn't have clean daily water to drink and had never before seen a live show in any kind of venue. This was music serving its higher purpose.

Prior to the concert, we traveled to Soweto to stage an artistic workshop with a local record label, Ghetto Ruff, and we visited children from the Belleh Pri-mary School and the Umbuyisa School of Art. As we drove in, our minibus became the Pied Piper as all these ecstatic kids ran alongside and behind, smiling and waving as they tried to keep up on the dusty roads. They raced up to surround us and greet us with high-fives.

"We cannot believe you are here," said one kid, "Not even Snoop both-ered to come visit us when he came to South Africa. Thank you. Thank you for coming."

That entire day was humbling. We thought we had known struggle in East L.A. but this was struggle on a different level, and yet that didn't lessen the mes-sage we arrived with: to tell these kids that dreams don't recognize class or back-ground, and that there is no such word as "No."

I'll never forget when Will held up this fourteen-year-old boy's arm and told everyone: "He is fourteen. When I was fourteen I started a group that became the Black Eyed Peas. I, too, came from a poor background. We all did. But I have made it—and so can you." And that small cheer was the biggest cheer we ever heard.

Then there was the boy named Bongeni Moragelo. He was nine, from Soweto. He had this chubby, round face and wore this fresh patterned sweater, and we could tell he was itching to perform as he shuffled forward, unable to hide his eagerness. Everything about him exuded "attention-grabber"—one of those kids who stood out and caught the eye.

We offered him the mic and he killed it. He was a rapper and dancer, but what struck me the most was his fearlessness, seizing this one moment when the spotlight had found his corner of obscurity in Soweto. I saw his hunger—his desperate need to perform—and recognized my own youthful passion. I saw Will at Ballistyx in the way he moved and rapped, furiously spitting into the mic. There is talent like Bongeni scattered all over the world, just as we misfits were scattered around L.A., just looking for an outlet. He was genuinely that impressive that we invited him to perform with us in Johannesburg, and his face lit up when we offered him that chance.

On the night, Will—who took this kid under his wing and eventually ended up sponsoring him—gave him the big build-up, and as this little kid stepped out onstage, the place roared for him. He free-styled and back-flipped like a young Apl, and the place went crazy.

Only when you have seen a young kid from Soweto own his fifteen minutes of fame on a stage inside a stadium inside a city he never gets to visit can you begin to understand the power and unity of music and art. This kid was no different than us. He was born to perform—you could tell that by his spirit—and he held a dream just like we all had. Making that dream come true in front of 40,000 people was a beautiful thing. That boy, his face, and that concert was the most vivid memory of the whole South Africa trip. Which is strange when you think we also met with Nelson Mandela the morning after the show.

In looking ahead to this momentous introduction, I could not have been more excited. "Whaaaat? We're going to meet Nelson Mandela! Shiiiit—that's crazy!!!" I said, when we found out. He was the Martin Luther King of South Africa; the freedom fighter who dared say "Si, se puede!" in his crusade against apartheid. When you talk of dreams, of achieving the impossible, of falling up—Mandela stands, defiant fist in the air, as the ultimate example. None of us could wait to meet him. Will even brought his grandmother, Sarah Cains, to share the once-in-a-lifetime trip and experience.

But that day, visiting him at his house at the Nelson Mandela Foundation, never did start well for me because after the Johannesburg concert, I got as drunk as fuck. I decided to celebrate the history of the occasion by drinking from 11 p.m. to 5 a.m. As ever, I didn't think about what I was ruining the next day. I never could think that far ahead.

I dropped into bed somewhere around 6:30 a.m., completely forgetting that our lobby call to visit Mr Mandela was 8 a.m. I came downstairs, feeling like death, and saw Will in a smart-ass white suit, with his grandmother looking the epitome of grace. I saw Fergie all pristine and made-up, and Apl looked fresh and ready. And I was standing there, still wearing the same clothes as the night before: a camouflage army jacket with black pants. This was my state of readiness and preparation to meet one great man.

The brutal truth is that I could have had an audience with God and it would not have mattered. I would have acted the same way. It embarrasses me now to think that I wasn't sober enough to savor the occasion. I cannot even recall the build-up, the location, or the grounds we traveled through, because I was asleep in the back of the minibus all the way there, trying to shut out the vocal excitement of Will, Polo, Fergie, and Apl. Everyone was head over heels with joy and I was the zombie trailing behind, as we were met and greeted on arrival by some dignitaries and an MTV film crew who were tagging along to film some behind-the-scenes footage.

I stepped inside this illustrious museum-like place and it felt ornate and stately. Stuffy. Official. It made me feel stifled and clammy. I stepped outside, on a back deck overlooking some gardens, to steal a moment and have a cigarette. I was pacing away from the building and just steadying myself when I heard them closing the glass double-doors I had walked out from.

"Way-way-wait! I'm part of the group!" I shouted, ditching the cigarette.

But the doors still closed, and this security guy was left looking at me through the glass, wondering who is the dude in the camouflage gear.

I knocked again. "I'm one of the Black Eyed Peas . . . I'm with them," I shouted, pointing inside to the "fam-er-ree" who hadn't yet realized I wasn't in the huddle of people at the reception.

I saw a circle forming and then activity, smiles and handshakes—and that is when I first saw the tight crop of silver hair belonging to Nelson Mandela, surrounded by one MTV camera, photographers, and aides, gradually making his way to meet the Peas. I knocked harder on the glass and, all the time, a second MTV camera was on me, flashlight beaming, catching me caught out like some idiotic scene from the movie *Trading Places*.

One of the thug-looking security guys finally got word to let me in, and he opened the double doors. "You need to be more prompt. When the group goes, you need to go," he said, and then he let me inside.

I had already made a spectacle before being the late guy, hurrying in to

stand alongside the rest of the group. "Heyyy, glad you could join us!" said Will, ironically.

Seconds later, I was reaching out my hand to greet Nelson Mandela.

He looked like the wisest of old men, and age had rendered him a lot weaker than the powerful man he once was, but his smiling presence was still immense. He spoke in a quiet voice, supported by two aides who flanked him, and everyone leaned in to listen to what he had to say. He said how happy he was that we were there even though he didn't really know much about our music. We all laughed on cue. He asked us about the concert. Will and Fergie did all the talking. He asked them to speak a little louder because his hearing was not what it used to be. We all laughed again on cue.

As he spoke, Fergie beamed, fluttered her eyelids, flicked her hair, going all girly-coquettish on him. I swear she was flirting with him! We kept bagging on her for that afterward, and, like she said, how can you not find such greatness attractive?

Outside, we had a photo call on the steps and it is that image, captured on the front page of the Johannesburg newspaper The Star, that hangs in a frame on my office wall today, making me feel both privileged and disappointed.

It shows Fergie and Will flanking Nelson Mandela, each holding a hand to steady him, each looking as happy and content as two kids sitting on Santa Claus's knee. Then me, standing behind the three of them, looking as pale as a ghost, forcing a half smile. It brings disappointment because I remember the lack of respect I showed for the occasion, and what was running through my mind:

How much longer is this going on for?

Damn, I can't wait to go lie down.

Damn, that pillow is going to feel good.

That is the sad truth behind that momentous day. I had switched overnight from an appreciation of one humbling moment with a nine-year-old performer to a state of disrespect for one of the greatest leaders of our time.

I have never been one of those people who gets overexcited by award ceremonies. I grew up watching the Grammys and the American Music Awards, but was more turned on by the idea of *performing* on such a stage than being handed a trophy on one. Even when my ego was at its most inflated, I recognized early on that award ceremonies were grandiose events that gave record labels an annual chance to jack off and showcase their talent, and then that talent had the chance to say to the world "Look at me . . . aren't I special!"

Recognition is all part of the game, but the Peas have always been about earning that recognition first and foremost as performing artists, and that true sense of recognition comes only during a tour, in a direct interaction with the fans, not via some grand ceremony in New York, L.A. or Las Vegas. Don't get me wrong.

An award holds a value somewhere in the pecking order of accomplishment but it doesn't—or shouldn't—provide an artist with any sense of validation just because they have a gold trophy in their hands. I have seen some gushing speeches, in both the music and acting industry, and I am always left thinking "Really? It means *that* much to you?!"

We won our first Grammy in 2005 with "Let's Get It Started," after performing an opening medley of that song with Gwen Stefani and Franz Ferdinand. I can't forget that occasion because I had the flu and was as sick as a dog. Moments before going onstage, I was laid out, curled into a ball, sweating and aching, but the "sing monkey, dance monkey" autopilot kicked in and I somehow struggled through. I can't say that winning the Grammy made me feel any better, either, because we won it off-camera, and that served to heighten my sense of anticlimax surrounding awards season.

We were kicking it backstage in the dressing room, pre-show, when a member of the Grammy staff knocked, popped her head around the door and said: "Just wanted to let you know, guys," she said. "Congratulations—you won the Grammy for Best Rap Performance by a Duo or Group!"

"Oh, so it's not going to be on camera, then?" we asked.

"Nah, unfortunately it's not one of the awards that is televised," she said.

And we just looked at each and burst out laughing. So that was our first HUGE Grammys moment, captured backstage and off-camera. We then discovered the actual Golden Gramophone was sent to us by mail; there was no grand hand-over on the day. Months later—months, not weeks—some UPS guy knocked on the door, not knowing he was delivering a Grammy to this random guy in Walnut, and said there was a package for me. I opened it and there it was—my trophy of delayed gratification.

Same thing happened in 2006 when we had four Grammy nominations and again won for Best Rap Performance by a Duo or Group with "Don't Phunk With My Heart." I know they are still victories, but it is not something I attach myself to with any great sentimentality. It is a memory, and takes its pride of place on my shelf in my office as an ornament of what we have shared together.

I guess our biggest awards moment came at the 2006 American Music Awards, when we picked up three AMAs, for favorite rap/hip-hop album with *Monkey Business*; favorite rap/hip-hop band, duo or group; and favorite soul/R&B band, duo or group. But, again, we had to laugh at our awards jinx, because, yes, these awards were televised but no, we weren't there to collect them, because we were on tour in Costa Rica. So our first visual acceptance was via satellite from some jungle location, meaning we had to do pre-recorded acceptance speeches from afar just in case . . . three times. It is perhaps no wonder that we don't feel attached to the award season's sense of occasion. It's like we said to ourselves that night, as we raised a glass of Champagne and I got wasted again: "What would

we rather miss out on? Earning $600,000 from a tour or jerking off in public for the sake of an award?"

I know what I would rather spend my time doing.

Just in case any of us were in danger of getting carried away with our growing profile in 2006, life threw us a grounding reminder of what *true success* was all about when we landed a dream gig and were booked to open for the Rolling Stones.

The Stones have historically tapped into a variety of acts as openers for their U.S. tours, so it was not as if we were being singled out as an exceptional talent. But we were still honored to have been chosen to kick off their On Stage tour for a couple of dates in Boston, before we handed over the baton to Maroon 5, Pearl Jam, and John Mayer.

All I could think about during the build-up was the fact I was going to meet the god of bad-ass rock 'n' roll: Keith Richards, whose notoriety I had been mimicking all along.

We arrived at the venue of Fenway Park, and suddenly our Monkey Business tour felt like it had been shrunk in the wash. It was like I had just wandered in from the streets of Rosemead and found myself overwhelmed by the skycrapers of Manhattan. The stage setup dwarfed even the vastness of Fenway Park.

From the back, there were four different floors that rose from the center of the field, and part of the stage elevated and extended about a hundred feet into and over the audience for the performance of "Satisfaction." Then, the extension retreated and a giant set of inflatable lips, covered in flowery prints, rose up like a hot air balloon, and loomed over the crowd in time for "Honky Tonk Woman." That is the most I remember of the two nights, except that we opened our forty-five minutes set with "Hey Mama" and closed with "Let's Get It Started."

The details of our performance are sketchy, though I have a vague memory of the crowd cheering when I pulled off my jacket and the audience—from the sixty-year-olds to the twenty-year-olds—applauded my Rolling Stones insignia T-shirt.

Backstage, we didn't get to hang with Mick Jagger or Keith Richards. It wasn't that kind of tour. They weren't that kind of group. There was no sense of inclusion from them, just a very distinct feeling of separateness. I think the most chat we exchanged was a "Hi, guys!"

At the time, I partly understood. *It's the Rolling Stones*, I thought, *they are hardly going to kick it with a hip-hop group from Los Angeles who, when measured against their run, were still wearing diapers.*

I thought that way until we toured with U2 in 2009. More on that later.

I observed the Stones long enough to see Keith Richards up close and personal—and what I saw shocked me. He probably didn't look any worse than he did thirty years earlier, but all that ran through my mind was *Wow—you look fucked.*

He was reptile-looking with all this sagging skin, clearly ravaged by years of partying. He may well have been a living musical legend but he was also a living and (still) breathing example of what years of drugs, drink, and partying do to someone physically. I think I was too caught up in how he looked to appreciate anything else going on. Because here was this guy who I had stupidly thought I was modeling myself on, in a party-animal sense, and here was the reflection of a possible version of my older self.

I went back to the hotel that night and examined every shadow, bag, and flaw under my eyes and across my skin, wondering if my comparable apprenticeship in drink and drugs had caused any noticeable damage yet.

"Fuck dude, you've got to stop," I said to myself in the mirror. I did this often now—staring at myself in the mirror, having a word with myself, urging myself to get sober.

The Rolling Stones gig told me three things: a) as much as I admire the talent of Keith Richards, I never, ever wanted to end up looking like him; b) I didn't want to be still performing with the Black Eyed Peas at the age of sixty; and c) but in the meantime, this is the kind of stage we need to be on one day.

We detached from the side of the Rolling Stones and then walked back into the spotlight as headliners—booking for our first million-dollar gig.

Polo announced that some guy in America was prepared to pay us a cool one million for a one-hour show. Just in case we couldn't work it out, he added extra perspective when he said: "That's just over $16,000 a MINUTE, you guys!!"

It was a fee to be split among the group, but we all raised a glass and remembered the time when we performed for Pepsi and pizza. All this shit was happening as if to remind us of how far we had come, and you would think it made me deliriously happy, but I can't say that was the emotion I felt. Yeah, it was crazy and we jumped around like excited kids for a bit, but I think my heart, mind, and soul were now so clouded that it rendered my spirit almost ambivalent to such good news.

I was like "Wow—that's crazy. Okay, cool"—and then I wanted to party as before, using such news as hooks and excuses to celebrate and drink.

I am not really sure I fully appreciated the significance of such moments. I see the significance now, in writing it all down, but ask me if I can remember that $1,000,000 gig, where it was and who it was for, and I draw a blank.

These were incredible moments that deserved to be everlasting in the memory, but, for me, they haven't been registered in the way they deserved to be. Our first $1,000,000 gig and the Rolling Stones concert today stand as vague milestones, not vivid memories. I lay them out now to illustrate the peaks we were riding as a group, and the blur I was drifting through as a person.

■ ■ ■

After the Monkey Business tour, I brought my drinking home and was downing wine and hitting the vodka or sake every other day. I would wake up, call out to Heckle and Jeckle, and call some other boys and get everyone to meet me at Benihana's Japanese restaurant at the Puente Hills shopping plaza off the 60 freeway. This became my regular haunt by day before going out at night.

I was sitting there drinking sake by noon so that I could get fucked up by 2 p.m., go home, smoke a blunt, pass out, and wake up at 6 p.m. so that I could get ready for the nighttime drinking shift at my clubs in Hollywood.

With this drinking, the ego was irritable and aggressive, which is sad because I used to be the happy drunk who was unthreatening. I now switched and became one of those embittered, mean-spirited guys who was disrespectful to those closest to me, and even to random strangers.

Take the time when I went for lunch with Jaymie at Benihana's.

I was being loud, the center-of-attention guy, and had been knocking back the sake when, for some reason, I decided I wanted to buy everyone around me some shots.

There was a plump-looking lady sitting nearby with her family and I noticed she wasn't drinking. When someone wasn't drinking, they weren't having fun.

"You need a drink!" I shouted out, looking at her. "Get that lady a shot!"

She smiled, embarrassed, desperate to ignore the belligerent drunk. "I'm pregnant," she said. "I'm not drinking."

"You're not pregnant! Have a fucking drink!" I said.

"No," she said, cutting me dead.

There was something about the way she declined that stung me.

"You don't need to be eating anyways! You're not pregnant—you're just fat. You're a fat woman! Fuck you!"

I embarrassed that lady in front of her family and the entire restaurant. They all got up and walked out, but, as she passed our table, she stopped, looked down at me, looked at Jaymie and said, "I feel sorry for you . . . you're too good for this loser."

Jaymie was mortified. I am mortified, reading that back. But I managed to deflect it as a one-off at first, blaming it on all sorts of bullshit like the pressures of the tour and then blaming it on the presence of Heckle and Jeckle living at home. Which led to a convenient conversation about positive change and Jaymie moving in. We had spoken about it before, and our relationship was moving quickly so it kind of made sense.

It was now me, Josh, Heckle, and Jeckle, and Jaymie living under one roof.

The problem with that increased proximity to one another was two-fold: there was no longer a hiding place for my addiction or short fuse, and, as far as

Heckle and Jeckle were concerned, there was now a woman in the house who made no secret of the fact that she didn't understand what their purpose was. In her eyes, they represented a threat to my well-being. You can imagine the all-round awkwardness and tension in that domestic set up, and it was never going to take long before that friction blew up.

Inevitably, it happened when I wasn't there, when I was away on some spot date in America, late in 2006. I heard about it via phone via Jaymie, and both sides had locked horns in the kitchen over something and Heckle started yelling at her.

Jaymie gave him a piece of her mind, told him to pack his bags and leave, and he did, quickly followed by his loyal shadow, Jeckle. That same week, she handed in her resignation at work and announced that she would now be taking care of Josh full-time. "We're going to be a family," she said. "Just you, me and Josh."

At home, I used the "going to the bathroom" excuse as cover for doing cocaine when I wanted a little bump and to feel the buzz. When Jaymie woke in the middle of the night and found me sitting up watching a movie on the television, I told her it was insomnia and I couldn't sleep.

"But it's 6 a.m.," she said.

"That's the effect of touring," I told her. "Messes with your body clock."

When you are a performer, you can forever hide behind excuses of tour schedules and adrenaline to cover up the shit that you are doing to yourself. I had spent so long kidding others and masking my excesses that denial became my daily performance, trying to fight off the ultimate exposure and being seen for the fraud that I feared I was.

The thing is, I wasn't in self-denial, because I had looked into the mirror so many times and acknowledged my addiction. But that admission didn't grow beyond a whisper behind locked doors, and as I would later discover, if you're not admitting it out loud, you're actually admitting nothing.

I like to think there is a point of clarity within everyone's vast denial, and for me, that moment came after Jaymie walked out on the back of some big-ass argument in which I disrespected her once too often. Even angels have their limits.

The next day, we were supposed to have been joining up with Deja and his wife, Liseth, for a family day out at Disneyland. I promised Josh that Jaymie leaving wouldn't change our plans, and I told him to get some sleep and prepare for the day out. I went to my room, locked the door, and went on a wild coke binge, taking bumps between midnight and 6 a.m.

I showed up at Disneyland, having been picked up with Josh by our friend Gary, and Deja said he took one look at me and "knew that you were at the lowest point I had ever seen you."

"What the fuck happened?" he asked.

"She's left. I've lost her, dude."

"Tab, these drugs, this drink . . . it's making you unhappy, brother, so why you still doing this shit?" I now saw the sadness and disappointment in my best friend's face.

I felt like the loser in everyone's eyes. I saw Josh running off toward the park, and I wondered how much longer it would be before I lost him too.

Deja pulled me to one side at lunch and gave me one of his stern pep-talks. "Go home, get straight, pull yourself together, and call Jaymie," he said.

A couple of sober days passed and Jaymie arrived at the house, and she laid her cards on the table; stern but softly spoken. "Why do you do this?"

I had no answers so I just kept listening.

"You need to understand that I am here for you but only if you stop . . . because if you don't stop, it will ruin our relationship and there will be no more chances, Jimmy. So the bottom line is that if you don't stop drinking, I'm going to leave you."

It was November 21, 2006. I remember that date, as I remember all my blackest dates, because it was the day I stopped drinking, and I have not touched a drop since.

I stopped drinking on my own. I put my mind to something and I achieved it. I told myself I was going to do something and did it. I might have wrestled with it, but I never caved in because that would have cost me Jaymie.

Sounds too good to be true, doesn't it?

Well, it is true. I stopped *drinking*.

Because it is easier to stop when you have a stash of Kush, Ecstasy and cocaine tucked away in your bedside drawer. What you've got to understand is that this is what addicts do: they manipulate situations and make everything appear better. For a while.

On Valentine's Day 2007, I proposed to Jaymie.

After three months of going dry, it was an easy decision to make after everything we had been through. She had known me before the success and monetary gain. She had known me as a "broke-ass rapper" and "a loser alcoholic." She had been there for me and she had been there for Josh, and God knows how she had tolerated more than any woman should have to tolerate. She had shown me not just what love is but what love *means*—and she set the standard in being compassionate and spiritual, and being a better person. She was my best friend and chief ally and I couldn't imagine her being anyone else's partner or wife.

More than anything, she had stripped away all the layers of so-called status, finances and personas, and I knew that here was trust and faith, seeing me for everything I was not, but everything she hoped I would become.

Her words, not mine.

We had gone shopping in Beverly Hills and I steered us deliberately to-wards the counter of Neil Lane Jewelers, knowing she had been eyeing a particular ring from Tiffany's for some time now.

Inside the store, I made the well-rehearsed move.

"You know how you've been wanting that ring from Tiffany's?" I said. "Well, I don't want you to have a ring that someone else will be wearing. I want you to have your own ring. So we are here to design one."

I gave it a few seconds to settle in, and then asked her to marry me. She said yes, we got excited in front of everyone, and then set to work on the ring's platinum and diamond design—and starting a new future. Whatever mysterious force had connected us and kept us bonded through all the trials and tribulations, I had no doubt that I wanted to cement the connection and turn it into an eternal bond.

On these, my good days, I wanted nothing more.

I truly thought the worst was behind us.

THE EPIPHANY

You can ask me a thousand times and the answer will remain the same: I don't know why I did what I did on the morning of March 27, 2007. I don't know why I decided to gamble with my son's life.

Out of the litany of stupid actions, this day remains the most inexplicable, especially in light of everything that had gone on before. It was as if my self-destructive side had played dead, like the climax in a horror movie, only to leap up and grab my ankles at the exact moment when I thought we were done.

I had not touched a drink since that November day, and, apart from smoking weed and taking the occasional bump of cocaine, I hadn't partied hard at all (even if the people who know me will maintain that I still had that absent, vacant air about me). But, as I would learn in counseling, there is a huge difference between "going dry" for a spell and "being sober" for life. When you have not had brakes for so long, suddenly stopping isn't going to be as straightforward as I made it out to be.

On this day in March, a crazy impulse returned, took me over and I decided to do drugs harder than ever before—and I did it on the very morning when I knew I was driving Josh to school.

That is the most shocking aspect to me—that my recklessness didn't for one second consider my son's safety, let alone my own, and I would quiz my own conscience for weeks afterwards. But this ultimate self-destruct—the rock bottom moment—was always fast-approaching I guess, in whatever monstrous form.

Maybe that's what all addicts do in the end, unconsciously?

Maybe they *have to* do it to crack shit open.

They see the brick wall up ahead and speak about avoiding it, but all the time they are pressing the accelerator harder to the floor, driving right at it. Because, on some level, we are trying to control being *out of control*; that by engineering some ultimate crazy-ass act, we can pretend to have had the last word in the conflict between the self we have lost and the addiction we have become.

Whatever it was inside of me, it had been chasing the breaking point the previous night, when I called a neighbor, who could always get his hands on weed at short notice. Or so I thought.

With my supply running short, I called him up. "You got any weed?"

"Nah, I'm out—but I've got some Xanax bars."

It was the worst thing he could have said. I had never tried those before, and the same curiosity that had led me to Ecstasy and cocaine kicked in. "What do they do?" I asked.

"They are loopy, man—make you feel a real body high!" he said. "But you don't want to take too many."

The second worst thing he could have said.

There, once again, was that instruction that caused an immediate rise in me: the "don't do." Followed by my auto-response: *Don't do? You watch me.*

This guy lived nearby, so I told Jaymie I was going to get some weed, because it was the one substance she could handle me taking "in moderation."

At his front door, the neighbor handed me six Xanax. "Only take two at a time, Tab," he stressed.

C'mon son, you're talking to a veteran—I can handle them all.

"Two only," I said.

He didn't come FDA-approved. He didn't warn me about the intense high, and the dangers of mixing it with other drugs. He didn't tell me how heavy this shit was, but even if he had, it probably would not have made a difference.

I returned home and placed these curious-looking white bar-shaped tablets into the top drawer of my bedside table. I placed them alongside my last $400 supply of weed, and some red Ex tabs. I suddenly viewed this mini-collection like they were unwrapped gifts on Christmas Eve. Because I knew—I knew in that premeditated moment—that I was going to take them all the following morning.

Before taking Josh to school—Muscatel Junior High in Rosemead.

Jaymie was already asleep in bed beside me.

I turned out the light, rolled over, kissed her on the forehead and told myself that I couldn't wait for morning to arrive.

I lay awake in bed. The red digital lights on the alarm clock told me the time: 6:45 a.m. The California sun was not long from rising.

Within the next thirty minutes, Josh—now thirteen—would also wake and start his day. I looked over at Jaymie and she was still asleep. I swung my legs around, stood up, and quietly eased open the bedside drawer. I took out my Kush, two Ex pills and six Xanax and transferred this stash into the bathroom, shutting the door behind me.

I stood in front of the bathroom mirror, and washed down two Ex and two Xanax with a glass of water. I placed the four leftover Xanax in my wallet. I then rolled a blunt and went downstairs and out into the backyard for a smoke. This was my breakfast. I could not have felt more satisfied.

Josh got himself ready, and five minutes before leaving, I started to feel all the other shit kicking in, twenty minutes after seeping into my bloodstream. I was spacing out before I had even put the keys in the ignition.

I climbed inside my black Range Rover Sport and Josh jumped into the front passenger seat, switching on the radio like he always did. I placed both hands on the steering wheel and tried to get my bearings.

"You okay, Dad?" Josh asked.

"I'm good—just a little dizzy," I said.

The key turned, the engine started. I took a deep breath. The Xanax had induced this heavy feeling . . . like a ton of bricks being pushed against me. Yet, it was a good feeling; like some twisted joy splayed on my chest. As I drove, my speech started to slur, sounding—Josh said—like a tape cassette in playback when the batteries are dying.

With each new minute, I could tell my son was getting more and more freaked-out.

"Dad! What's up? What's happening?" he said, his voice ever distant.

I could sense him recoiling in his seat, but I couldn't verbally reassure him without freaking him out any more.

I was driving on autopilot, unaware of turns and signposts. I felt hot and clammy and then . . . BOOM! . . . the real shit started to hit me; this incredible, alienating, rocketing high. My body started to tremble and I was holding the steering wheel for dear life. The next thing I knew, we were outside the school.

Josh hurriedly opened the door and jumped out, like someone who has just gotten off a roller coaster that they didn't want to be on in the first place. He stood there, with the door still open, backing away but still looking at me. Confused. Scared.

"All right, Josh," I managed to say. "You have a good day."

He closed the door. I drove off. He still stood there.

Back on the 60 freeway heading home, the road—in my mind—started falling away to the left, then falling away to the right; a suspension bridge swaying in an earthquake.

I fought with myself to steer through these concrete waves.

I didn't once look in the rearview mirror. Had I done so, I would have seen the four cop cars tailing me, lights flashing.

I just wanted to get home; eyes fixed ahead.

But I got off at the wrong exit—Grand Avenue, not Fairway.

As I veered right and drove down the off-ramp, a white van came into view.

There was a jolt.

I hit it from behind, at a decelerating fifteen mph.

I looked at the digital clock on the dash-board. 7:55 a.m. Odd details in the obscurity.

"Fuck!"

I waved to this vehicle, pointing to a mini-mall just off the exit in the adjacent street, and both our cars crawled into empty parking spaces so we could exchange details. I wasn't even out of my vehicle when the police cars swept up, sirens screaming.

I laughed.

I'm being "Punk'd" again.

I stepped outside, uneasy on my feet.

Ashton Kutcher was hiding in a van somewhere.

I smiled, and the cop couldn't have looked more grave.

The first stupid words left my mouth: "Yo man, I'm the Black Eyed Peas . . . am I being 'Punk'd'?!"

"Please put your hands on top of your head, sir," he said.

I swayed left and right. "'Course dude!"

He gave me the sobriety test and asked me to follow his finger. All twelve of them.

My eyes were so dilated that I couldn't have followed a boulder had he rolled it in front of me.

"Have you been drinking? Taking drugs? You don't seem sober."

"Yes, my son was born in October," I replied, thinking that is what he asked—a warped response captured for posterity in the police report. Apparently, I kept on speaking gibberish and mentioning the group.

"I'm Black Eyed Peas—is there something you can do for me?"

"Sir, you just ran into the back of a lady," he said, cuffing me. "You're lucky you didn't kill anybody."

As I steadied myself against the side of the police car, he asked what I had taken.

I told him codeine, because of recent dental surgery.

He searched the Range Rover and found some left-over weed. "On this, too?"

He searched my wallet and found the other Xanax bars. "And these?"

I must have mentioned the Black Eyed Peas again because he told me he didn't care who I was, I was going to jail.

Just like St. Maartens all over again but with no get-out-of-jail card.

I was loaded into the back of the car, and I rested my head on the plastic shield dividing the front and rear seats. I don't remember the journey to the City of Industry police station. All I remember is standing inside the station with an officer holding me steady by my cuffed wrists. I was zoning in and zoning out, hearing muffled conversation about a urine test.

I didn't pee.

That much I do know.

I had been put in a holding cell with two gangster-looking guys; two *cholos*. Face to face with the past again, and this time in a heap of real trouble. I don't remember anything else until later that day, when the drugs wore off.

And I think that's where this book began . . .

I sit with my back against the stone-cold wall, aching and groaning.

This come-down feels like the steepest and darkest yet . . .

My head feels heavy and mechanical, my mouth is so dry that it feels like I've got a dozen cotton balls stuffed under my tongue . . .

I've got gray walls ahead, behind me, and to my left. On my right, there are floor-to-ceiling prison bars caging me off from the corridor leading to the sheriff's office.

Even being in my own skin feels claustrophobic, sweaty, unbearable.

I start pacing, my flip-flops shuffling and popping on the floor . . .

A police officer arrives at the door. He points at an empty cup and tells me they asked me to pee in it for a urine sample, but I was incapable.

I look behind him, down the corridor, and see a clock. It's 4 p.m.

He reminds me how he saved me from a beating.

"Oh," says the officer before leaving, "and you better know that the paparazzi are waiting for you outside."

I wait for management to post the $15,000 bail.

I had been arrested on suspicion of being in possession of narcotics and driving under the influence, but, without a urine test, there was not enough evidence, so I was released without charge while a file was sent to the DA's office.

What they *should* have done was give me a blood test but, for some blessed reason, they didn't and this technicality would later return to save my ass.

What the police did remember to do was take my mug shot, and I faced my first flashbulb moment within minutes of leaving the cell. It was the shittiest I have ever looked or felt and I was standing against this bare, white wall. All I thought was "*This is the photo that will end up on TMZ*"—and it was.

Irrational thoughts ran rampant because life with the Peas had taught me all about the power of an image; the everlasting visual was all about emitting the right message be it an album cover, a photo shoot, or a red carpet arrival. I started interpreting the message from the mug shot before it had even been printed.

It said "Busted." It said "Shame." It singled me out as the loser of the Black Eyed Peas. The black sheep. It said everything I had busted my balls to achieve now meant nothing. Look at me. Dream like me. Fuck it up like me. Here's your example of the had-it-all, threw-it-all-away guy. It said.

The officer told me to reclaim my belongings and pick up my vehicle, which meant taking a cab from the police station to the compound five minutes away. Outside, I faced more flashbulbs, with one paparazzi in front of me and one guy hanging from a tree for the elevated shot; two more images to freeze-frame the worst moment in my life.

When I got to the compound and the Range Rover, there was little damage, save for a scuff of white paint on the front bumper, so I walked over to the booth to sign for the keys. A woman was at her post, sitting there, head down, reading a magazine. I was standing at the other side of the counter, unnoticed, when life played one of its sick jokes.

On the wall behind her was our *Monkey Business* album poster and next to it was my arrest sheet hanging from a clipboard. It was as if God—or Nanny— had deliberately lined up the dream next to the shame as one final, stark reminder of choices made.

The woman looked up and her face immediately registered her as a Black Eyed Peas fan. My persona was derobed, unmasked, and stripped bare, leaving me—the idiot person—feeling nothing but exposed and embarrassed. Not that she noticed or cared. "Hey," she said, "before you leave, can you please sign my poster. I'm a huge fan."

I took her pen and scrawled my signature as I had a thousand times before, but on this occasion, I could not have felt more like a pretender.

The woman was gracious. She smiled and she told me I had made her day.

It must have been about 8 p.m. at night when I pulled into the driveway. I should have been home at 8:30 a.m. Walks of shame didn't get more depressing than this.

I turned the key and opened the door. Jaymie was already standing there, shaking her head, in the hallway. Josh was sitting on the stairs.

"I cannot believe you," said Jaymie, "I cannot believe you."

I didn't need to explain anything. Between Polo and Sean, she had received the full story, and Josh had clearly filled in the missing pieces about our drive to school. I hated myself for the worry I had put them both through. Jaymie

had been bombarding my cell with missed calls for hours until she received her first call from Polo.

"I'm sorry," I said.

"You're always sorry," she said, defeated, and she walked off into the kitchen.

Josh was now standing on the stairs, leaning against the rail.

"Dad, if you don't stop, I'm going to live with my mom," he said, and he ran upstairs to his room.

Hearing him say that killed me. A knife cutting through, right to the bone.

No woman or man could have made me feel what I felt when my child said—without ulterior motive—that he was prepared to leave me; that he loved me but he would feel better off living with Karish. Fathers leave sons, but sons don't leave fathers. Not under normal circumstances, anyhow. Tough love from a thirteen-year-old boy.

When people talk about clarity and incentives and willpower, I refer them to this moment. It arrived like a single shaft of light in the darkness, like a spotlight on stage that I suddenly stepped into.

I hadn't been home five minutes when the phone started ringing off the hook. First it was the attorney that had been hired, talking about all the legal shit, and then Seth Friedman, Sean Larkin, and Polo all giving me shit for pulling the final straw. I didn't hear from Will, Fergie, or Apl—and that silence, at the behest of management, was harsher than any words.

I knew what they would be thinking. I knew I had let them down.

Because everyone knew what I knew: that my arrest had put at risk the biggest multi-million dollar corporate deal we had ever been offered. Pepsi, in alliance with Doritos, had weeks earlier offered to sponsor and fund a new world tour for the fall of 2007. The ink was barely dry on the contract. It was another chance to tour in between albums, and there I was fucking it all up.

Both Sean and Polo reminded me of the painful truth: that under the contract's misconduct clause, Pepsi could cancel the deal if any one of the Peas brought the company into disrepute with his/her behavior, or if any one of us was convicted of a felony.

"You do understand what this means, Tab!?" said Polo over the phone, exasperated, "It means we could lose this deal because of you. Our *biggest deal to date*, brother!"

It seemed like a cruel consistency that everything felt out of control, and it all seemed too late. He mentioned that we "had the best attorney onboard" He said some shit about the media and how we needed to do damage control.

But all I could think about was what Josh had said.

Business manager Sean also laid it on the line: "Tab, you lack the tools to make this better by yourself. You need to understand that you have to get professional help from people with knowledge in this area. If you want to clean up, I can lead you to those people."

But all I could think about was what Josh had said.

Mom came over to the house that night. She had never interfered before, but not even a mother's biased love could stay quiet now. "Son, you are an addict and you need help. If you need me to come to the house every day after work, I will. I will be here. I will be your babysitter."

"Thanks, Mom," I said. I wanted to tell her what Josh had said but had I vocalized it, I think I would have crumbled, and, on this night, it was taking all my strength to hold it together. I felt weak enough already without falling to pieces in front of everyone.

Not much more was said that night. I was pretty much left alone, like the scolded kid given some serious thinking time. I lay down in the master bedroom, hearing muffled voices speak in concerned ways, and the phone never stopped. The house was filled downstairs with everyone I loved, and there was real concern for my welfare. I knew that, and it was an immense comfort.

I thought about what Sean had said, because it was no good just saying I wanted to get clean. I had *to want* to quit, *want* to get better—as much as I had wanted the dream as a kid.

I had to prepare to build a whole new being and retrain the mind, at the same time as flushing out the chemical dependency. This was not a case of giving up drinking and then keeping drugs in a side pocket; there was no room for any more sleight of hand. The water levels were reaching the ceiling and I had been given the smallest air pocket left to breathe. I was either going to give up, let go, and drown, or I was going to summon some strength from somewhere and push through the ceiling.

I thought about what Josh had said, and I lay there until exhaustion knocked me out.

The next day, I felt horrible.

I had the shakes. I had the sweats, and the guilt was crushing. I couldn't look Jaymie or Josh in the eye. I shuffled about like a stranger in my own house, wandering from room to room. All I could do was keep running the tapes over and over in my mind. 7:55 a.m. was when I crashed. 8 a.m. I was in handcuffs. 9 a.m. I was in the cell. 10 a.m. Jaymie was starting to go frantic . . . and so on and so forth.

But this VCR also started haunting me with the playback of how things could have turned out. In this what-if version of events, I was convicted and sent to jail and lost the dream, or I crashed with Josh still in the car and child services took him away; or I came home and Jaymie had left me a note, gone for good; or Will, Apl, and Fergie vowed never to speak to me again.

In my panic, the mind games were haunting.

Jaymie attempted to get me out of my head by getting me out of the house, and we went shopping at Target with Josh. It was as aimless as my day felt. I was sitting in the passenger seat, quivering with the sweats, and Josh was staying quiet in the back. All the way there, Jaymie—composed and strong—was talking to me gently, saying that the only way forward was to change. I could almost hear Josh listening.

"I'm here for you, babe . . . I want to help you but only if you want to help yourself," she said. She wasn't berating me as some wives might. She, once again, demonstrated gentle compassion, nudging me towards the higher path. She saw that her man was in trouble, and it must have been weird but *she* became the man in the relationship, taking charge, being the rock-solid support, being chief advisor.

All the way around Target, I kept repeating the same mantra in my head: "I am going to change my life . . . I am going to change my life . . . I am going to change my life."

I looked at Josh standing in one of the aisles, pretending to busy himself. *How did I ever put your life in danger?*

"'Scuse me," said this voice, and I turned around to be greeted by a girl, no older than fourteen. Around Josh's age.

"Can I have my picture taken with you?" she asked.

"Okay," I said.

I hugged her as her friend took one happy snapshot, and I forced a constipated smile. I looked at this kid, thinking, *You shouldn't be taking a picture with me . . . you'll be disgusted when the news breaks . . . I'm no hero. I'm zero . . .*

She walked away. So . . . happy. Yet oblivious. Two fans in two days had unwittingly made me feel like a fraud, unworthy of the position I occupied in their eyes.

You'll agree with me later, I thought, *when it all becomes clear.*

My arrest broke all over the media, the Internet, blackeyedpeas.com, and the TV entertainment shows.

People magazine: **"Taboo of Black Eyed Peas Arrested for DUI."** *USA Today:* **"'Black Eyed Peas' Taboo Arrested in Crash."** *NME:* **"Black Eyed Peas Singer Arrested for Drug-Driving."** It was an endless and necessary humiliation.

Deja called the cell. "Dude, what the fuck is going on? You're all over the Internet!"

In the blur, within all the calls, I hadn't told my best friend and he learned about it via the Web. Out of everyone, I think he was the least surprised. "C'mon, brother," he said. "This is the prime example of why you need to get a grip now. I'm coming over."

When I arrived home, everything caught up with me. There is only so long that you can outrun the avalanche.

"I don't feel good," I said to Jaymie, and I headed for the bathroom. I made it in time to throw up violently and all this water started coming out of me. This nausea seemed to arrive with every breath and I just kept throwing up, over and over, until I was empty. Jaymie heard the retching and came in to find me curled around the toilet leg.

"Babe . . ." she said, and that was it. I started wailing.

"I've fucked up . . . I've fucked up . . . I've fucked up."

She picked me off the floor like I was someone who had fallen out of a wheelchair, unable to help himself, and she stayed with me. Every mask, pretense, and front I had worn and swaggered around with just fell and shattered into pieces on that tiled floor, leaving me lying there as a raw bundle of nothingness. Because this is who I was without the stardom, the drink, the drugs, and the party-animal reputation. This was the nothingness that I had always been trying to hide.

I curled up into Jaymie's arms like a frightened child and I sobbed; the kind of sobbing that makes you howl and shake. The last time I had cried like that was after Nanny's death, but I can honestly say that this was the newest worst day of my life.

"I'm going to change . . . I'm going to change," I said.

"You need to call Sean," she said.

Once I had straightened myself out, I will.

I went upstairs to get myself together and I was sitting on the edge of the bed. I found myself opening the bedside drawer out of habit. I saw a clump of Kush, smelled it, and had that familiar craving.

I'm going to change. I'm going to change.

I kept looking at it, smelling it.

I want to get high right now. I need to get high right now.

Addiction doesn't give a fuck how low you are or how perilous a state you are in. It just taunts you. "Fuck jail. Fuck the career. Fuck change. Just get high"—it is like a voice implanted under your skin, urging you, pushing you.

Only this time, I got frightened.

I can't explain it, because that fear had never registered before, but I was suddenly cognizant of the fact that if I got high then and there, it would lead to me calling a supplier for more, and the vicious circle would repeat and I would lose the family and lose the career.

I grabbed the bag of weed like it was an enemy I was picking up by the throat.

"I'm not doing this shit no more," I said out loud. It was about reclaiming power.

I walked into the bathroom, flipped the toilet lid, threw in the remainder of my $400 bag of weed, and flushed it away. I then turned into the passageway

and opened the wardrobe door, knowing that was where I had last stored my glass bong. I took it out and smashed it against the bathroom wall.

That afternoon was the last time I would ever see or handle anything to do with weed. I returned to the bedroom, picked up the house phone, and made the best call of my life. "Sean? It's Tab. I need your help. I'll do whatever it takes."

Those first few steps into the recovery process felt like being an infant again. I felt small, inadequate, and helpless, needing to lean onto other adults to learn how to walk again and be the version of "me" that didn't need chemical enhancements to feel comfortable and confident in my own skin.

Those first few steps were taken on the eighth floor of an eight-story building in Sherman Oaks, Los Angeles, where Sean Larkin manages the business affairs of the Black Eyed Peas, and where a counselor named Dr. Betty Wyman was waiting for me.

Sean had hired her before for another client, and she is regarded in Hollywood as one of those therapy big guns, working out of the Promises rehabilitation center in Malibu.

I was a mess that first day: hesitant about what to expect, confused about how I felt, and nervous about confronting this lady because, before I knew her, it felt like a confrontation. As it turned out, she was nothing like the austere-looking therapist I expected. She was this casual-dressed, woman-next-door, in her forties, all natural with no makeup and wearing jeans and an untucked shirt. When she introduced herself firmly, she gave off one of those in-your-face vibes that said, "I'm just like you so let's cut the bullshit."

I was sitting next to her on this black suede couch, and Sean pulled up a chair to complete the triangle. All around us, on the walls, were the plaques commemorating platinum sales of our albums *Elephunk* and *Monkey Business*. The vista outside was an impressive view of the Hollywood Hills to the south and the San Fernando Valley to the north, both basking in streaming sunshine. I had been in this office before and felt on top of the world. Now, I needed a cup of tea between my hands to stop me from fidgeting.

Betty has seen people like me come and go over the years. I was just another bad repeat in Hollywood's legacy, and, as a result, she wasn't wasting time stroking egos. She doesn't honor any form of celebrity or care what you have achieved or where you have been. Those plaques on the wall meant shit. She is interested in straightening out the human being, not plumping reputations. I realized that when I started to cry as we spoke back and forth about my story and she checked me.

"You know what this is?" she said, unsympathetic. "Crying is the guilt and the shame you feel, and I am not here to share a pity party with you. I am here to assist you to help yourself and change."

Wow, this is the kind of tough lady I need.

I stopped crying, like a kid does once he has fallen over and realizes he's not getting the attention anymore.

"You're not a big thing in my world. You are the same as everyone else and if I invest my time in you, then you have to be fully committed and follow through," she said, all stern. She then broke it down: she wanted me to undergo a treatment called Pro-Meta, undergo therapy with a counselor, and attend AA meetings.

I didn't ask questions or wish to know what the treatment involved. All that concerned me was doing whatever it took to shake this disease from my system. If there was one thing I didn't doubt, it was my willpower to make shit happen. If I can rise up from East L.A. and become a Black Eyed Pea, then I can pick myself up from the bottom of the barrel and get myself back on track. That is what I told Betty.

"I've heard all the good intentions before," she said.

I sensed her doubt, and if there was one thing that has never changed about me it is the auto-response to hearing someone doubt me.

Oh, you don't think so? Well, you watch me!

It was probably the best piece of doubt I had ever heard.

Undergoing the Pro-Meta treatment program was like giving blood, and I only needed three thirty-minute sessions. "Three treatments covers you for the rest of your life, by taking away your cravings," I remember them saying.

It's fast-track route direct into the bloodstream, with an infusion of some colorless liquid, and it appealed far more than the conventional idea of getting locked away and confined within drug rehab. It cost $20,000, but that $20,000 would save my life.

I became an outpatient of Promises at its Santa Monica offices, not one of its residents in Malibu.

Basically, I lay on a bed, they found a vein, and this chemical shit jump-started the recovery process. After three blasts, I walked away with a month's supply of medications and a prescription—a Dr. Wyman demand—to attend Alcoholics Anonymous and undergo therapy. That is the point of Pro-Meta: it is designed to be integrated with medical and behavioral treatment. It is not some magic that works on its own, and it can only flush out the poison and work on the brain's chemical imbalances. It cannot sort out the mind's illness.

At first—between treatments—I battled temptation every single day. It was a starvation, and I got hungrier and hungrier, and it took all my willpower and a good two or three weeks before those pangs and the accompanying irritability calmed down. My insides were turned upside down and sent into a 360-degree spin on the chemical front, so I couldn't expect anything less, but it was tough. I couldn't have survived without Jaymie, Mom, Deja, and the AA meetings that I

attended religiously at a place called Windsor House in Glendale. Removed from the studio, music, and touring, my recovery and this haven became my all-consuming focus. I know that a lot of people say that "first-timers" dread stepping across that threshold, but I couldn't wait to dive in and grab its lifeline. I dreaded more the idea of *not* taking it. I just wanted to get better.

It was that mind-set that also meant I kept a distance from Will, Apl, Fergie, and the rest of the crew. Sean and Polo represented the only real contact that I had with the Peas for the first few weeks. Will and Fergie were conveniently wrapped up in their own solo projects anyway, which was fine with me. Ferg was promoting and gigging songs from her album *The Dutchess* and Will was pushing his own clothing line. We spoke on the phone and they sent messages of support, and I knew they were there if I needed them, but it was a blessing that they were not around, because I wanted to get my shit together before seeing them again. I didn't want to represent myself as this fragile, shattered guy who was recovering. They had only ever known me as the confident guy and I wanted some level of that confidence to have been rebuilt next time we met.

Meanwhile, the attorneys dealt with the legal formalities, and by May—in the absence of blood or urine samples from me—I was only charged with two misdemeanor offenses of possessing marijuana, and the case was dealt with in court in my absence. My punishment was a $200 fine. And because it was a misdemeanor, not a felony, there were no consequences to the Pepsi deal. Our biggest sponsorship deal—backing our Black Blue & You tour—would be unaffected and still go ahead that September.

Don't think for a second that I didn't understand how damn lucky I was. I was granted a second chance that most people don't get.

Think about it: a driver as wasted as I was under the influence usually crashes and either kills himself or others, but I got away with it. But I didn't just get away with my life, I got away with going to jail and I didn't lose the woman, the son, or the Pepsi deal. It is not even worth thinking about the repercussions and odds in another life. I crashed, I survived, and I was given leniency by a higher power to relive my life again through sobriety. That is why I had no problem throwing myself into the world of AA for the next six months, attending meetings three times a week and then attending therapy sessions in between. Betty Wyman demanded dedication and I gave her dedication.

It didn't matter that I had more of a drug problem than a drinking problem and was going to AA. As she explained, once an alcoholic, always an alcoholic, and an addiction is an addiction, and AA is full of drug addicts who have a drinking problem also. AA. NA. It's the same shit under a different sign.

I remember the reality check that came with my debut AA appearance.

In those early days of recovery, I still had some Hollywood shit going on, and I turned up wearing this full leather outfit, wearing a diamond earring, a diamond necklace, dope-ass sneakers, and sunglasses. I was shining. I looked like I was dressed to rock some premiere on Hollywood Boulevard, desperate to make a good first impression.

It was—I was—ridiculous.

In my own defense, I didn't know anything about AA and I had imagined that I was being sent to some rock star AA setup for other musicians and artists, and the room would be filled with some Ozzy Osbourne and Slash-type figures, not the ordinary man and woman in the street.

I found it hard to escape the mentality of hiding behind the mask of the performer and the performer's world.

I walked into this awkward silence inside a community center setting, with folding chairs laid out in a circle, and everyone was standing around dressed in casuals, sweatshirts and old tops, giving off the kind of vibe that they had already given up on life. All these eyes lifted off the floor and stared at me as if to say "Who the fuck is this joker?"

I had walked into a room with a group of people whose addictions and misery were more fucked up than mine, and one look from all of them made me feel like an idiot. My starlike pretense found its final frontier in a room which was anonymous by nature. I whisked off the sunglasses, took off the leather jacket, and took my seat, trying to blend in as best I could, but the shiny leather pants and dope-ass sneakers were something I could do little about.

As the "first-timer," and as the newly crowned idiot, it felt like everyone in the circle was looking at me and, without my sunglasses on, it was hell sitting there in that full-on gaze. The only way to warm up that room was to start getting real and honest. After some small talk went back and forth via the administrator, it was my turn to "share" and introduce myself.

I got to my feet and started speaking.

"Hi, my name is Jaime, and I am an alcoholic and drug user. I got arrested on March 27 . . ." and blah blah blah blah, I told my story: me pushing the extremes, me having drink binges, me acting like a loser, me crashing, me in a cell. Once I was talking, I couldn't stop. I found the unsuppressed story easy to tell. The release of that truth valve was liberating.

My story, if not my outfit, said that I was one of them, they accepted me.

It was a pretty beat-down bunch of fellow addicts sitting around me. There were about twelve of us in total. There was one pregnant lady who had her two children taken away from her until she cleaned up. There were two guys who had lost everything: job, wife, kids. There were some real down-and-out tales, and I belonged on the same stage as this sorry cast and felt comfortable without status, without having to be "someone." I had found a non-pressurized sanctuary where I could commune with people in equal trouble, and where I could share and listen and learn. People had fallen much deeper than me and they were summon-

ing the strength to get better, and that empowered me. More important, in seeing what others had lost, it made me grateful to leave a meeting and return home to Jaymie and Josh and a job. It was a gratitude that kept me focused.

At the end of each meeting we said the Serenity Prayer, which I know now as well as I know the lyrics to "Joints & Jam" or "I Gotta Feeling":

> *God, grant me the serenity*
> *To accept the things I cannot change;*
> *The courage to change the things I can;*
> *And the wisdom to know the difference.*

A prayer. A faith. A human understanding that I would never have received had I kept rummaging around the shallow end of Hollywood. In this AA commune, something new and spiritual opened up and realigned me with the kind of faith that Nanny had, and with the God that I had watched her speaking with in her armchair each morning, Bible in hand. I am not about to launch into some born-again mumbo-jumbo. Because it wasn't "born again," it was a second chance.

This was when I started to reconnect with what had always been part of Nanny's world; with something she had always tried to show me, at home or in church or by standing before Our Lady of Guadalupe at El Mercado and lighting a candle.

Nanny had instilled the importance of God in me, but I had lost Him because I had been chilling with the devil and we had been having drinks and smoking weed for too long. I got blinded by the whole stereotypical ways of the sex, the drugs, and the rock 'n' roll, until God held out His olive branch in that jail cell, and until I rediscovered a humbling faith in my AA meetings.

A faith in God. A faith in myself.

I carried that faith around me in the AA poker-style chips that were like medals handed out to mark the first day and then every thirty days of sobriety. In my eyes, instead of accumulating a stash of weed, I focused on building a small stack of chips. One day. Thirty days. Sixty days. Ninety days.

At the two-month stage, I felt strong enough to meet up with Will and Apl and we were kicking it, shooting the shit in the studio, talking about the Pepsi-Dorito tour, when Will asked: "Do you ever think you're going to drink again?"

"Nope," I said, confidently.

Apl laughed. "You'll be back!" he said, referring to my partying ways.

I didn't say nothing at the time, but it was a response that scared me because here was my brother and friend openly doubting my ability and mental strength to stay the course. I couldn't blame him after all he had seen, and all the false promises I had made before. But it was still a jolt, because it reminded me of how weak and hooked I must have been to warrant that cynicism.

"I won't," I said. "I won't be back."

Apl just laughed it off.

It stoked the old fires of doubt again; that rebel inside rose up once more having heard someone tell me that I wasn't able or capable. *Oh, you don't think so? Well, you watch me!*

It was the best thing Apl could have said in the circumstances, because he said it at a period when many addicts cave in: that two- or three-month danger period where a relapse stalks you the most intensely. Maybe that is why he said it? Some reverse psychology? Either way, I *knew* I wasn't turning back.

I remember reaching the three-month milestone and rushing home to tell Jaymie. "Yo, I've been sober for 90 days!"—and that felt like one of the biggest hurdles cleared.

The chips kept coming: one hundred twenty days. One hundred fifty days. One hundred eighty days. I still have them saved to this day. Like I said, they are my medals earned in the trenches. But I knew the acid test test would come when I returned to a life on the tour bus, went back on the road, and walked back into the dens of the music industry that had enticed me in the first place.

One way I coped and dealt with the public shame was by poking fun at myself, as conditioned by the Black Eyed Peas "fam-er-ree." During the first month, I had noticed on blackeyedpeas.com that chat forums were debating this and that surrounding my arrest: *Did you hear about Taboo? Was it for alcohol? I never thought Taboo was a druggie. What's that all about?*

I felt I had let these kids down as fans who looked up to me, and I responded by issuing a message: *We all make mistakes, but it is those who learn from their mistakes that come out on top. Thank you for all your love and support.*

But I didn't want to get too heavy and serious, so I thought, *You know what, I'm going to do a song and video about how ridiculous I am and turn it into a self-parody*. The rap and video were titled "March 27th" and it was my way of publicly addressing and owning the farce I had committed.

It was a rap-style commentary of the entire day's events, and I went into the vocal booth at Stewchia and free-styled that shit in one take. It flowed out of me in verse, and then we made the video to match: me driving along in the Range Rover, with a giant blunt in my hand—*"sliding it, colliding it/smoking that weed again"*—and then being cuffed while playing the clown with the cops. I had me in an orange jumpsuit, locked up in county jail, speaking with Josh through the visitor's phone at one of those shielded booths, and he was yelling at me—*"What was I doing? What the hell was I thinking?"*—and the whole video was me saying "Yeah, I fucked up and I understand the severity of it, but I'm getting better and, look, I'm poking fun at myself because I'm laughing at it—and it will not beat me."

Therapists encourage you to feel comfortable with, and own, your

"shadow side," and I used my darkest hour for a small outlet of creativity, issued via a viral video, so that the sober me could laugh—in public—at the under-influence me. I guess it was part of the necessary processing and it seemed to work. It made me feel better and the fans seemed to appreciate it. *"Cool video! Welcome back, Taboo!"*

Writing an autobiography should be part of the treatment program, because the writing process asks the same endless questions, digs up the buried past, and rakes over the same wounds. Spilling everything onto the page has reminded me of therapy sessions during the summer of 2007, and it is hard to name which is more laborious, painful, and exhausting: the emergency scrutiny of an outsider sitting in a chair and poking around in your issues or the self-examination that comes with the kind of reflection only time allows. Neither process is natural for me, and for someone who has never liked getting too deep, the search to make sense of it all seems to have taken up almost as much time as recording and touring. I didn't know what would come out when I first started writing this book in December 2009, and it was the same when I walked through the therapist's door: I was just open to the process.

I ended up going to the Santa Monica offices of Promises to meet with a woman named Dr. Poland, whose vibe felt like the snuggest fit the moment I walked through the door, accompanied by Jaymie. She had a more informal, non-office type space, with a couch for us and a leather chair opposite for her. Dr. Poland was a rock star: blond, perfect teeth, kind of hippie-looking, and she dressed real cool with these tie-dyed shirts and you could tell there was something of the flower child about her. And she wore some dope tennis shoes. I noticed them immediately.

Before she asked me any questions, she told me she had been in a band and she knew the scene. Now she was a therapist helping others. Here was someone who understood my world, and that insight and empathy meant we connected straightaway. Her chilled vibe made me feel comfortable on every level, and I felt I could tell this woman anything and everything, and over several months, with one session a week, my story came out; the bare-boned, hard-facts version of what you have been reading.

I started at the beginning, I worked through the middle, and I arrived at the end, step by step, always holding Jaymie's hand. It was more personal and more probing than the AA sessions, and one complemented the other in that respect: a balance between the general commune and deeply confessional.

I'm not going to start writing down the full complicated analysis. Anyhow, I have already mentioned the impacts of childhood events, my absent father, and my present stepfather. But Dr. Poland made me understand the bigger picture: that it was a gradual accumulation of *everything*—the childhood, the resulting low self-esteem, the suppressed guilt of not being there for Josh, the touring removing me from "normality," the handling of the Peas' explosion, the subtle music industry pressures—that had messed me up. The life I had been living was so far removed from any usual human experience that I drifted away and got lost in the process.

It took a lot for me to sit there with Jaymie, stripping myself away layer by layer, but she made me feel it was safe to do so. She took my vulnerability and never threatened to be turned off by it or run away with it, and I know that this process brought us closer together. It took me time to understand and accept the courage in truly communicating with the closest person to me.

Therapy, as it turned out, was as much about relationship counseling as it was about my own recovery. So when I say that Jaymie taught me about love—about intimacy, about who I am—I am not exaggerating.

During one session, Dr. Poland drew the blinds, turned out the lights, and told me and Jaymie we were doing an excercise. "You are going to lie down on the floor together, close your eyes, and breathe together," she said.

A few weeks earlier, prior to the arrest, the mere idea of doing such a thing would have brought out the "whatever" in me. But I was off the deep end now, and all I wanted to do was come back home to me. Dr. Poland could have said stand in a corner on one leg with your right index finger up your ass.

Will having my finger up my ass work? Yes! Okay, cool.

That was how much I was "trusting the process."

In the artificial darkness of daytime, I lay there with Jaymie, synchronizing our breathing. In. Out. In. Out.

I felt her life next to mine.

How many of us do that shit? Listen like that. I had lain in bed with her, feeling her physically, holding her, making love with her, but never this.

Appreciating her every breath, for endless minutes.

Holding each other's hands in the dark.

Jaymie has always been about "team" and "family." I had only ever been about myself.

Man is kidding himself if he thinks he can climb and conquer mountains alone. Without the base-camp of a home, a love, and a family to return to.

In that room with Dr. Poland, over many weeks and through a few tears, I glued back together all the pieces I had broken over the years, within me and within the relationship. In that room, I felt freed from so much of the shit from the past: eyes open now, aware, understanding better, learning patience, knowing compassion.

"You must come to our wedding," we told Dr. Poland.

"I wouldn't miss it for the world," she said.

THE HAPPY
EVER AFTER

Before walking down the aisle, I had to first prove to myself and others that I could stay on the right path.

I was six months into sobriety and it felt like the Pro-Meta was keeping its promise: there had been no cravings for more than half of that time. I felt good and strong, but I hadn't cleared the biggest hurdle: going back on the road.

The Black Blue & You world tour, sponsored by Pepsi—the very deal I had put at risk—was taking us to twenty countries that fall, including China, Russia, South Korea, Malaysia, Indonesia, Singapore, Nigeria, Thailand, Venezuela, and the Eastern bloc countries of Europe.

It didn't upset me when I heard that management needed to be certain that I would stick with the recovery and not buckle. If I am honest, I was certain of my intentions but not even I could guarantee what would happen once I was back in a tour setting. It was one thing walking, head down and focused, in a home environment surrounded by a support network: fiancée, best friends, counselor, and AA meetings. But the tour was a different story. It would bombard me all at once with the kind of tests that therapy wouldn't recommend: it would remove the stabilizers to see if I could ride on my own; it would whisk me into an orbit far removed from normality and without any hope of being settled in one place for any longer than forty-eight hours for a two-month period; and it would return me to the very social environment—the hotels, the tour buses and planes, the clubs where we were booked for appearances—that had led me astray in the first place. The acid test was only going to play itself out once I was face to face with the kind of boredom and crazy schedule that leads artists like me to view drinking and drugs as coping mechanisms.

That's why Dr. Betty Wyman designated me with a sober companion who knew what it took to reach a true level of recovery. He would stick to me like glue on the tour, management said, but don't worry, it will be no different than having a bodyguard.

I told Polo, Sean, and Betty the same thing. "I've come so far that I don't want to fall off so whatever it takes, let's do it."

My shadow was named Tim. His job was to guard me from the demon named "Relapse." Tim was this tall, nondescript white guy from Los Angeles who was chosen because he had been an effective sober companion to someone the camp knew, so it wasn't as if he was a stranger. We had seen this "shadow" before. I trusted him.

I trusted his journey, too. He was an alcoholic a few years into sobriety. He could walk alone without support—without hanging onto someone else's rope—and all I can think about when he comes to mind today is his sense of humor; this dry, sarcastic wit that meant he fit perfectly into the "fam-er-ree." He referred to his addict past as him being "a professional trashcan," whatever junk and shit was on offer, he took. It was hard for me to see that past in his face because he was now a solid watchtower of a man, eyes alive, fresh-faced. But I was looking at him in the future he once couldn't imagine, and that's what made him my example to follow.

He would hang with me, walk with me, share his stories with me, and listen to silence with me. We had meetings after every performance. I walked offstage, drenched in sweat and pumped with adrenaline, and straight into a compartmentalized mental zone with Tim; one-on-one time to bring me down and keep me focused.

I smelled weed in the air everywhere I went. There was the same free alcohol and the same easily available groupies seeking fame by association. Everything I had previously succumbed to was still around me.

"How are you feeling here? Talk to me," said Tim, keeping me focused.

"Disgusted. I feel disgusted by it all," I said. "And weakened," I added.

Kryptonite to my recovery.

When someone finds God or rediscovers a faith, they don't normally go and hang out with the devil some more. But I was still hanging out in the devil's den, because I had no other choice. The enabling environment of the music industry was my world. The stage was my home. The clubs and after parties were

my contractual obligations or paid-for appearances. I could not detach from this Siamese twin.

At first, I found it difficult seeing someone lighting up a blunt or pouring vodka into a glass as everyone laughed and had a good time. It paralyzed me. It was like I didn't know how to naturally hang out anymore.

Who am I in this environment if I cannot drink and smoke?

Will and Polo always encouraged me. "You don't have to drink. You just have to be here for an hour. It's work, Tab, view it as work," they said.

This is me working. Be professional.

But it was not always as easy as having a word with myself and falling back on Tim, because those one-hours sometimes felt a decade long and there were two or three occasions when I lasted only forty-five minutes and had to leave. Running away seemed better than dealing with it. Like a phobia. Scared of the life I might lose again.

It took me time to understand that I was reacting to the fear of something being pushed in front of me that I knew was bad for me. That understanding from Tim was indispensable on that tour, because the more he told me what was normal or routine in recovery, the more my awareness grew; the more my awareness grew, the more resilient I became. When you cannot see ahead and someone you trust tells you that you are heading in the right direction, it keeps you walking.

I was like the boxer coming off the back of a fierce round and getting a pep talk from my corner. And each city and concert and club represented one round, and each pep talk kept me off the ropes.

Keep fighting. Keep your guard up.

I poured all my thought and feelings into Tim at the end of each day, knowing I could express an experience, an emotion, confusion, worry, or doubt and he would have the answers. The best coach I could have.

Keep strong. Keep with me. You can do this. You can win this.

Our first date of Black Blue & You could not have been more accidentally appropriate, on September 9, 2007: Jerusalem.

We headlined the Jerusalem Rocks festival at the venue of Sultan's Pool, skipping the MTV Awards—where Fergie won Best Female Artist in her absence—for this non-profit festival celebrating peace and unity. From a personal perspective, what better location to be first tested than the city of the Holy Sanctuary.

It was the most spiritual venue we had ever played: performing in the outdoor pit of the ancient water reservoir with the walls of the old city climbing on one side to Mount Zion; on a stage built alongside the walls to create an amphitheater surrounded by bleacher-style green-seating. It was only an intimate venue, for about 6,000 people, but it felt unique stepping out there, within its crumbling stone and ancient history.

I had wondered how I would feel being back onstage, post-crisis and newly sober. *What if I cannot rock like before? What happens if I have lost something in recovery?*

I had felt so raw, guilty, and vulnerable for such a long time that I worried about how much of the performer I would be able to put out there. I felt shrunken somehow by the recovery and therapy, because the whole thing strips you bare, and I was still struggling with the guilt of my own actions. It would actually take me a good year before I started to stop blaming myself over my actions that had hurt Jaymie, and put Josh's life in danger.

This tour was only the beginning of me learning how to professionally function with all this extra weight on my back, and with the glued-back-together pieces still setting. It was a tour that determined if every moving part and natural instinct still worked as effectively. In hindsight, I can now see it was preparation for the E.N.D. tour that lay in the future.

In the dressing room in Jerusalem before going on stage, I talked to Tim and I talked to myself. But most of all I talked to God. If He was going to hear me best, it was here in the Holy Land. I looked at myself in the mirror. I no longer seemed haunted. I had color in my cheeks and my eyes didn't seem so dead. As an individual, I was in better shape. But the reflection of the performer and the reaction of the senses would only be known once onstage.

We got into our huddle pre-performance as the party-mad Israelis chanted our name. "Here we are in Jerusalem," said Will, always leading the pep talk. "The start of a new tour, a new beginning. Let's go out there and rock it. 1-2-3 . . . I appreciate all my friends around . . . white, black, and brown . . ."

No one fussed or made a big deal of this moment for me. That would have made me feel worse. But that huddle, and that all-inclusive pep-talk, made me realize that I was never alone with this fam-er-ree.

Our opening song, "Hey Mama," started up and we were on.

I remember picking up the mic and feeling weak. I remember busting some moves and not feeling the buzz. I told Tim that it felt like I was coming down with the flu and that all I could feel were aches and pains. It didn't matter that we rocked the show that night. It didn't matter that the crowd partied like Jerusalem had forgotten to party. I didn't feel *myself.*

For days afterward I had nightmares on the road that I was standing onstage, not knowing how to rap, dance, or perform, and the crowd was booing me. But this is where Tim stepped up as a mentor and brother, helping me understand that I was a new person now and I was growing into this new skin. Of course it would feel alien, he said.

So I viewed the rest of the Black Blue & You tour as physical therapy for

building myself up as this new person and getting stronger. Jerusalem represented so many things: the awakening, the realization of transition, the hope of being a more rounded person *and* performer—the city where I burrowed deep and relied on nothing but faith to pull me through.

Jerusalem was a monumental experience, because I returned home and actually had something important to say and share. It was no longer a vague memory through the haze of drinking, and it wasn't the same old story of "We did this venue, went to that club, and we did this venue and went to that club."

I floated in the Dead Sea. I visited the church in the Old City on a Sunday. I walked through Bethlehem, and visited the Wailing Wall, mesmerized by crowds of people of all ages standing and sitting before its great chunks of stone, placing prayer notes in between the cracks. Standing there in silent prayer, in its shadow. Just like Nanny used to stand before Our Lady of Guadalupe. It felt powerful being there, among them.

Maybe this is what Nanny felt when she prayed?

I said a silent prayer, imagining the Wailing Wall as El Mercado.

I had not really understood Nanny's morning prayer rituals, even though I had been fascinated by them, and yet in Jerusalem—of all places—this sense of spirituality hit me and made me better understand. It was as if I had asked God for help in that jail cell and this serendipity—the timing, the location, the realizations— was His answer.

We packed and prepared for the next tour date: Addis Ababa in Ethiopia.

I said goodbye to Jerusalem after just two days, but before leaving, I placed into my suitcase two souvenirs to take back for Jaymie: some sand from the Dead Sea and holy water from Bethlehem.

Something of substance and meaning to take back to my corner of Hollywood.

By the tour's end in October, I was returning to a new home that Jaymie was decorating and putting the finishing touches to. We had decided to leave the house in Walnut in the same hurry that the family left behind the house in *Poltergeist*. It was full of bad ghosts and negative energy and we needed a new start.

By May of 2007, two months after my arrest, we were out of there.

Sean Larkin, who was a real crutch throughout that entire period, knew we had been looking at homes in Pasadena, because that area was still close enough to Rosemead and a short drive into downtown. I thought we had already found a home when he called and made us think again. "I have found a house which I think you are going to love. Just view it before you decide anything else."

"Where is it?"

"Altadena," he said.

Altadena sits on higher ground to the north of Pasadena. It derives its name from the Spanish word for upper, *alta,* being attached to "dena." It is a place which feels more country than city, and is, for me, unlike anywhere else in Los Angeles. You don't see condos, apartments, or palm trees, and, because of its higher elevation and different temperatures, there is a sense of seasons—rare for L.A. In fall, the leaves on trees turn golden and the mountain air begins to feel wintry.

The trees here are unique: Altadena is home to a type of cedar tree that is normally found in the Himalayas—the deodar cedar—and it is these trees that make up Altadena's famous Christmas Tree Lane. Its scenic streets made us feel hopeful as we climbed one of the main roads toward the foothills in the distance.

When we pulled up outside the house that Sean had picked out, it was instantly breathtaking. It was standing, with its beige front and Mediterranean roof, all high, wide, and handsome on a hill set back from a quiet road. As soon as we climbed the steps to the front door and walked in, it felt right. We then went out back and the view sealed the deal: the backyard is the San Gabriel Mountains, which start to climb from the far end of the sloping garden.

This is home. This is Paradise.

I raced to the top of the garden, with my back to the mountains and my eyes looking down on this four-bedroom castle, and I was standing there absorbing it when I noticed the absence of Los Angeles sounds: no sirens, no traffic, no helicopters, no sense of hustle and bustle. Just silence, broken only by nature's frequency of the birds chirping and the trees whispering. All my eyes saw was luscious green. This place was beyond anything we had imagined.

I looked at the four-car garage and immediately started to envision taking out two spaces and building a studio (which, in 2010, became a reality). I looked at the dark-wood study and pictured an office from where I could run my affairs and hang all my plaques. Jaymie saw one room and pictured it as a nursery for the additional family we wanted to start.

And I saw one bedroom upstairs and pictured turning it into a shoe-room—designed just like a shoe store with a middle bench, pigeonhole shelving, and upward-tilting mirrors running alongside each side wall—to house my eight hundred pairs of sneakers. I am the Imelda Marcos of the Black Eyed Peas, having collected sneakers since being a teenager (and this room is also a reality today, painted red and black).

I painted those realities on that first day when I vowed that no one else was buying that house. I was in the backyard when I called Sean and said: "We love it, we want it, make an offer."

The beautiful irony is that we paid for it by using the slice of the money earned on the Pepsi tour. What I nearly squandered returned to me as a gift and provided us with a new home for fresh beginnings.

God, I made the right choice.

Lesson learned.

• • •

Having ditched one mask—that of the rock star party animal—in the process of learning how to be myself, it didn't take long for the life of show business to invite me to don another, even scarier mask: that of a Spanish ninja named Vega.

I guess Hollywood was always going to provide me with masks to wear. Thankfully, this was all in the name of progress for my acting career.

Prior to my arrest, I had attended an audition for the 20th Century Fox action adventure movie *Street Fighter: The Legend of Chun-Li,* and I thought nothing more about it in the dust storm I had kicked up.

Seven months passed and then Polo called. "Congratulations, you're going to be Vega!"

In the video game that inspired the movie, Vega is this masked warrior from Spain who wields a hand-claw that would give Freddie Krueger a run for his money if the two ever met during nightmares on Elm Street. He is half matador, half ninja, and he wears an expressionless silver mask because, as the legend goes, "he believes himself to be impossibly beautiful and is obsessively narcissistic." In other words, Vega had some Hollywood shit going on.

This would be my third acting role, having canned an indie movie called *Cosmic Radio* after doing *Dirty,* but it went straight to DVD. *Street Fighter* was in a different league, and when it was released in 2009, it went on wide release in a thousand theaters across America and grossed around $8 million at the box office.

I had been on my agent, Sarah Ramaker, saying that I was looking for a more challenging role that would better show my acting capabilities, and it seemed timely that this call-back came around as I was getting my head straight. Especially because my arrest had fucked up my chances of auditioning for *The Bucket List* which Sarah had also lined up. Second chances came in all shapes and sizes in 2007.

I was excited because Vega seemed tailor-made, allowing me to tap into my love of martial arts. I had long ago mastered the ninja-style form for the stage, but this screen opportunity allowed me, in my mind at least, to live some of the Bruce Lee action hero dream. It also meant going on location to film in Thailand for five weeks.

One of Vega's opposing numbers in the film is a character called Balrog, an African-American boxer raised in the ghettos, and this role was played by Michael Clarke Duncan, who was nominated for an Oscar for his role as John Coffey in *The Green Mile.* I will never forget Michael's kindness and professionalism, because he went out of his way to build a rapport before filming, and reached out to me at a time when my confidence was not where it should have been. He made a point of coming to a Black Eyed Peas show and hanging backstage, because, he said, "I wanted to see your moves and build a personal relationship going into the movie." That is what we had on set, and to this day I still regard him as a friend.

That kind of groundwork, and my talks with him about his experience as an actor, increased my confidence, and then I trained for two months with a fighter named Eddie Mills who was a K1 fighter and taught me kick-boxing and enhanced technique.

"You've done this before!" he said when he saw me in action.

"I learned in a garage many years ago as a kid!" I said.

I quietly thanked Antwon's dad for those sessions and bleeding knuckles while learning the basics of Jeet Kune Do.

When we arrived in Thailand, it felt strange, because it was the first time that I had traveled to Bangkok without the Peas, without the media attention.

I found myself removed from the comfort zone and transferred to a movie set, and I loved it, because, at a transitional time in my life, it showed I was standing on my own two feet.

The best bit about the Thailand trip was being able to take Jaymie on location and share the experience. On the days when I wasn't filming, I was able to feel like a tourist for the first time in my life. On previous visits, I was locked onto a conveyor belt from city to city, junket to junket but now I was able to taste the luxury of real downtime.

In walking around and exploring Bangkok, I will never forget the sight of a man walking a baby elephant through the street. I watched in awe as this unnatural scene played itself out before me. Within the bedlam of the city streets, this one Dumbo-sized elephant was walking on the roadside when he and his handler came to a stop sign.

The man said something and the elephant slowly heaved his ass onto the ground. When the lights turned green, the man said something else and the elephant rose and started to walk across the street. It was like the man was walking a dog . . . but this was a big-ass elephant.

I guess all beasts, no matter what they have been taught, can be re-trained to walk through life a different way.

Me and Jaymie were married on July 12, 2008, at St. Andrew's Church in Pasadena—two days before my thirty-third birthday.

Everyone except Dad and Eddie was there.

Will, Apl, Polo, Josh, and my brother-in-law Anthony were the groomsmen and Deja was best man on a day themed on the 1920s, inspired by *Harlem Nights*. The way they dressed in Al Capone's era was fresh, and Dolce & Gabbana tailored our suits to that fashion. It was one of those elaborate, no-expense-spared occasions to match the once-in-a-lifetime occasion. I wanted the day to be perfect.

That morning, waking up in the Westin Hotel in Pasadena, I felt pensive.

I didn't feel nerves stepping out in front of thousands of people on a stage, but now I felt a knot at the prospect of stepping out in front of one hundred fifty family members and friends.

As the hour arrived, I called Josh to my room.

He walked in wearing his suit, looking like a grown-up in his own right, and we were standing opposite one another—father and son, older brother, younger brother—face to face, saying nothing for a few seconds. He nudged his glasses up his nose, smiling.

"I want to give you something, son," I said.

In the palm of my hand, I held out two silver cufflinks with an ancient Mayan scripture on the front. They were a hand-me-down from someone in the family years ago; they didn't mean much back then, but they meant something now.

I weaved the links through his cuffs. "This is a symbol to say thank you," I said. "Thank you for being a part of my life . . . thank you for being with me . . . and I am honored to share this moment with you, my son, as I become a husband."

I might have failed in many departments with Josh. I learned late what it meant to be a father and he had kicked me up the ass at the time when I needed it the most. As he reads this, I hope he knows what I didn't say back then: that some accidental events in life prove to be the biggest blessings, and he, as my first son, is a gift I value beyond words.

Inside church, I was standing in front of the steps going up to the altar, with Josh and the groomsmen standing next to the altar to the right, and the bride's ladies to the left. "This is it . . . it's now or never," Deja had whispered to me.

I viewed that altar like a stage, and psyched myself up in my head. I wanted to keep my composure and not get all jittery.

Hold it together. Hold it together.

The organ piped up and the wedding march began. Ahead of me, at the far end of the aisle, Jaymie walked in on the arm of her mom, Vicky.

Hold it together. Hold it together.

I looked at these two women walking down the aisle in virtual slow-motion. Both of them have been rocks in my life. I saw Mom on the front pew, beaming. And somewhere, probably standing at the back tossing her walking stick to one side and wanting to dance, was Nanny. She was there. I felt her.

Jaymie passed the midway point—and there was my therapist Dr. Poland and the Black Eyed Peas fam-er-ree. All of them: the band, the crew, management. And Fergie, always looking like the superstar, standing beside her then-fiancé, Josh Duhamel. And they were probably all standing there, disbelieving that the day had arrived when I had done a complete 360 with my life.

Jaymie arrived at the bottom of the steps with me.

"Mrs. Gomez." That suits you, it suits us.

Forever impatient, always rushing ahead.

You need patience with all that Catholic shit going on . . . the rosary . . . the holy water . . . the lighting of the candles . . . the going on and on and on. We kneeled so long at the altar that I wondered if we were ever going to get up. The Catholic Church doesn't do brevity. I learned that lesson that day, too.

When it came to our vows, Jaymie broke with protocol. I had said to her, "Jaymie, do you take me, Jaime Gomez, to be your lawful wedded husband?" But when it came to her turn, she didn't want to use my name. Instead, she said "Babe."

"Babe, do you take me, Jaymie Dizon, to be your lawful wedded wife?"

That was Jaymie's way of telling me I was her babe no matter what, and I thought that was kind of classy. We slipped the wedding bands on our fingers and became husband and wife.

We had booked Boyz II Men and then Frankie J to perform at the reception at the Biltmore Hotel in downtown L.A. Boyz II Men sang "On Bended Knee," which had always been one of my and Jaymie's anthems, and Frankie J sang "More Than Words" for our first dance, on a night which saw us have a mariachi band representing my culture and traditional Filipino dancers representing Jaymie's.

But it was the speeches before the party that, for me, provided a special touch to the day.

Deja, my best man, stepped up—and killed it. I had seen "Encyclopedia Dave" earlier pacing the grounds, practicing with his sheets of paper and corrective pen, but when his moment had arrived, he ditched the paper and spoke from the heart. He gave some background as to how we met—him sitting in the library, me taking him under my wing—and the section of his speech that stayed with me the most went something like this:

"I was with Tab at the birth of Josh, I have been with him throughout his great professional success, and here is another milestone as he commits himself to Jaymie. Everyone in this room knows that it has not been an easy road getting here, but what strikes me the most is that Tab has had the character and courage to recognize his flaws and correct them where possible. Not many could have done it, but not many have his character or the love of a woman like Jaymie. Live each moment, and love, honor, and respect one another."

And he raised a toast to our happily ever after.

We both got a little choked up because we both appreciated where a friendship that began at school had taken us. Friends like Deja. Wives like Jaymie. Brothers and a sister like Will, Apl, and Fergie. A unit like the Black Eyed Peas. A band like Bucky Jonson. A fam-er-ree like we were blessed with. None of this is regular. So when I made a toast that afternoon to friends and family—especially

Mom, Julio, Celeste, and Nanny—I knew how lucky I was. Because, without their love, I don't just wonder where I would be today, I wonder if I would still be alive.

I was sitting down at the breakfast bar in the kitchen of our new house one morning in November, 2008, when Jaymie sneaked up from behind me. "I've got a surprise for you," she said.

From behind her back, she pulled out a pale-blue stick and handed me the result of one of those home pregnancy test-kits.

There was a "+" showing in its small window.

I looked up. Her eyes were beaming.

"Wooo—hoooo!!" I wailed. That is the only way I can express happiness at times.

When words don't work, "Wooo-hooooo!" says it all.

We were both ecstatic, jumping around. We had been planning this. Our first child and a brother for Josh, who was equally excited when we broke the news. We were going to be a family and a quartet of our own.

This was how it was meant to feel: planned, prepared and ready, mentally and financially. Not accidental, eighteen years old and without a job.

I had been through the shit and I was now a grown-up. I was clear-headed and everything felt right. I had been given the second chance to be a man. I was now being given the second chance to be a better father.

I vowed to be a better example in life.

DREAM WITHIN
A DREAM

There is no finish line in recovery and no prospect of being nominated for Best Recovery Artist of the Year. The sense of accomplishment in sobriety comes from looking back and seeing the distance I have put between my new self and the time of addiction. The bigger that distance, the greater the prospects of long-term recovery.

As of now, I am passing the three-year milestone, having not partaken of drugs since that day in March, 2007, and even longer for alcohol, since that day in November, 2006. I am now beyond that first two-year period, which they say is the most likely time for sinkholes to open up on the high road. I now know, with the same conviction I had to become a performer, that I am not going to touch drink or drugs or even smoke weed again. Nail that promise to the mast and hoist it high with the Mexican flag.

Today, among the Peas, I am no longer viewed as the fall-guy who gets bagged with the Eddie Murphy party song. I have two new nicknames now: "The Cardinal" or "The Christian." So when people ask how I am doing, that is how I am doing.

I can now sit in clubs and after parties as an observer and drink water, soft drinks, or green tea. I can be around alcohol and pour the vodka if you like. I can smell weed in the air and treat it like cigarette smoke—something inevitable but not for me. And I see the scene, appreciate its atmosphere and its fun, and I will always support Will and Apl when they DJ, but I now realize that I don't need substances to enjoy it. Because I feel confident enough in my own skin.

At the end of each concert or official appearance, my only thought is getting back home to my family. I have found the real substance in life, and it is this inner feeling—this certainty and sense of stability—that has become my true measure of recovery alongside the stack of AA chips.

In very different ways, each one of us—me, Will, Apl, and Fergie—have been through our own trials and tribulations. I have recounted mine. It is their choice as to whether they recount theirs. But we misfits have shared a dream and been on a journey since we began in 1995, and since Fergie joined us in 2003 before the main launch and lift-off.

That journey has tested our mettle as a group and as people, and taken us to different extremes, and we have all come through to the other side. It is as if life was seeing if we were capable of what it would present. For the time when we could justify a full-scale, monster world tour. When the world would download our music to record-breaking levels. When we would make the cover of *Rolling Stone* magazine, and it described our journey as "the science of global pop domination." When our dream would grow so big that we started calling it "the dream within the dream."

It was as if life was always preparing us for *The E.N.D.*

"Yo, we've got to be doing this shit!" announced Will, "Whoever cracks dance, wins the game! This shit is outta here!"

He returned to L.A. buzzed after being in Australia where he had filmed the movie *X-Men Origins: Wolverine*, in which he played the mutant John Wraith, and where he asked some locals in Sydney where the hottest hip-hop clubs were.

"Hip-hop?" the Aussies said to the American. "Hip-hop's not cool no more, mate. It's all about electro, mate."

Will explored, discovered, and was inspired. He came back raving about how these DJs were pumping out electro dance not just in Oz but all over the world. No rapping, just beats. It was this kind of sound we needed to capture, he said.

So, as the captain of our ship turned the wheel to steer a different course, all four of us found ourselves immersed in an electro-world, conducting our usual "research" by going to clubs on the East and West Coasts of America. We met with the likes of the Crookers, an Italian DJ duo, and Boyz Noize, a German electronic music producer, and both Will and Apl advanced from being MCs to beat-makers, learning how to DJ, tapping into the pulse of the youth, riding this electro vibe.

We were being conducted into the DJ-led culture which had once risen in the 90s in America before returning to the underground again. But it is today's re-emergence of dance music that provided Will with the foundations for our new sound.

At first, I was standing on the edges feeling hesitant because my tastes were not in the same lane. It took me a minute or two to grasp Will's thinking.

What is this? Why are we changing a winning formula?

"Trust me, Tab, trust me," he said. "This is the shit that is going to take us to places we have never been."

He cast my mind back to the underground scene of the early 90s, when hip-hop was dance-oriented. "It is just like then—the new shit everyone is doing, but with harder beats, no lyrics," he said, "We've all got to understand that this sound is going to do big things, so we need to listen to it, learn it, study it, believe it—and become it," he said. Without Will, there would be no Black Eyed Peas. He has been the visionary who has always paved the way, so when he compels you with passion to think outside the box, you do it.

We continued the evolution by borrowing, interpreting, and expanding electro sounds and building them into songs. I might not have had as many words and it is harder to rap over electro beats, but the more beats we made, the more I started to feel it. We took electro music as our inspiration and added the Peas signature, increased the BPMs (beats per minute), and simplified lyrics and live instrumentation.

It was a musical twist we named "electric-static funk."

The end result was, as Will once put it, "an album that was about escapism—light on gray matter but heavy on good-time vibes."

Its title, *The E.N.D.*, came about partly because we decided to enjoy some mischief at the media's expense. Since 2004, it had excitably convinced itself on a couple of occasions that we were splitting up because Fergie and Will had launched solo projects.

"The End—that would cause some controversy huh?" said Will.

As we played around with the word, we agreed on the acronym *E.N.D*—Energy Never Dies—to represent our friendship and our music, and to cause a little bit of an eye-catching stir.

The majority of the album came together at Will's house where we now recorded, but we had to take one week of studio time in London, because Fergie was filming her role in the Rob Marshall movie *Nine*. We returned to Metropolis Studios where we had recorded *Monkey Business* and we packed in the majority of Fergie's vocals on her days off. There was no real downtime to enjoy in our second home of London. We arrived with a factory mentality: strict work, clock on, clock off, and leave.

We finished up the album in L.A. and we had our usual collection of about fifty songs to choose from. When Will took the final cut of fifteen songs to Inter-

scope, they loved it. The label could not have been happier. Its verdict was that it was ahead of its time and sounded like a different Black Eyed Peas.

The sound was not the only difference. The imagery was all futuristic and robotic as a concept, built on the idea that we were moving from 2008 to 3008 in a post-apocalyptic vibe that would set the tone for our fashion, sound, and videos.

As performers, we all presented new images in different ways, some more visible than others. Will and Apl were no longer sporting long dreds, Fergie went from blonde to black and my Indian-length hair became shorter, now dropping to the shoulder, not the back. But the main difference with me was the invisible one—this was the first album I would be sober.

In every possible way, the album represented the future. A new sound and a new look for a new time. The only unknown quantity was what the fans would make of it.

In a club on the Mediterranean island of Ibiza, Will was tapping into the latest electro-beats coming out of Paris and London, when some guy offered him the mic to do a spot of rapping. Will couldn't exactly see who it was in the dark who offered him the stage but he stepped up, did his thing, and didn't think anything more about it.

It was only after leaving the club that the cell of the guy he was with rang out and his boy goes: "Do you want to speak with David Guetta?"—the Godfather DJ of Europe and one of the biggest taste-makers on the electro scene.

Will got on the phone, and David told him he was glad he took the mic and thanked him for free-styling.

That is how Will and David Guetta first met in 2008, and that spontaneous meet in Ibiza led to Will calling David a few months later, asking him to collaborate on our fifth album (and he would also work with us on *The Beginning*).

David is this fun, great soul, an angular-looking Frenchman who had been on the European music scene since the 90s. As a DJ, he was in the vanguard of the DJ-as-an-artist future that is just starting to happen in America; the culture where a DJ and his laptop is the same as one man and his traveling band. It was presumably from that laptop that David sent via email the main beat for "I Gotta Feeling."

The moment Will received the beat, he set to work. In the same way that inspiration arrived on a bullet train in Tokyo, it arrived in his studio near the Hollywood Hills—and the song started to grow there and then.

"Da-da-da-DUH! Da-da-da-DUH!" he started mumbling, "Da-da-da-DUH/ Tonight's da-duh/da-da-da-DUH!"

He kept on repeating it over and over.

Until it became a line: *"Tonight's the night/Let's live it up . . ."*

The song came together in a little over an hour.

The first time I heard the beat and the hook, the immediate emotion was to start jumping around. It was one of those energizing, party anthems and I was like "Wow—this is going to be a big college anthem."

A college anthem, but no bigger than that.

No one ever truly knows what is going to take off. This game is about instincts, not guarantees, but the truth is that none of us were jumping around listening to "I Gotta Feeling" and saying "This is a world smash!" It was, to our ears, just another club joint representing one-fifteenth of an album that we felt was strong from start to finish.

The *E.N.D.* album was officially released in June, 2009, but before then, a curse from the past returned to haunt us: the curse of the leaked song.

Somehow—and subsequent inquiries didn't get to the bottom of it—an unfinished version of our lyrically sparse club beat, "Boom Boom Pow," found its way onto the Internet. It was so rough that Apl's verse had not even been added.

The first we knew was when a fan on blackeyedpeas.com posted a comment in a forum and said: "Have you heard the new song? It's dope!"

Sure enough, "Boom Boom Pow" was out on YouTube. Will was furious that we had been breached a second time, but instead of being defeated by it, he decided to run with it. "Fuck this shit—we're putting it out!"

It was not exactly the start we had in mind. With virtually no chorus, its fusion of Miami bass, its boom-boom punch, hard synths, and Auto-Tune vocals, it wasn't a radio song and was never intended as our first release. But events had forced our hand, and, in the second week of March, it was released to radio before being launched via iTunes.

We might as well have dropped an accidental match in a California national park. The song we considered "radio unfriendly" started receiving humongous airplay and went #54 in the *Billboard* Hot 100. By week two, it went #39 and, in its fourth week, it shot to #1, selling 465,000 downloads in its first week of digital release. Our disbelief continued as we remained #1 for twelve consecutive weeks. A song we regarded as a club joint had become our first #1 single in the U.S. *Billboard* Hot 100.

It became a running joke that office workers, teachers, and kids in the street started using "Boom Boom Pow" as a catchphrase.

It confirmed what Will had been saying all along: we were living in a different day and age compared to our last monster hit, "Where Is the Love?," which had only been a Top 40 Mainstream #1 based on airplay. Instead of socially conscious, politically leaning lyrics, we now had a song with three beats and the lyric "boom" repeated one hundred sixty-eight times.

And people loved it.

In May, it became our second UK #1 and the news kept coming in, with

long-running #1's in Australia, Canada and Belgium. In total, we sold over 4.25 million digital downloads and it became our fastest-selling, highest-selling song in the U.S. It wouldn't get bigger than this, we told ourselves.

But that was the thing about 2009–2010—it would keep on surprising us.

When my second son, Jimmy Jalen Gomez, arrived into the world on July 19, 2009, the moment of becoming a father again was a whole new experience compared to the fainting nausea I went through as a teenage dad.

I saw this little man scooped up into the doctor's arms, some mucus was removed from his nose and mouth, and then . . . he let the air out of his lungs!

I could download the sound of him crying until it broke all download records. *This is how it is supposed to feel*, I said to myself: *soul-bursting joy.*

We named him Jimmy in honor of Nanny but we use his middle name: Jalen.

I couldn't wait to get him home and start his life with us and Josh.

This tiny being in my arms—blind and innocent to everything that had gone before his arrival—looked up at me with a God-given right for me to look after, protect and be there for him, and I was more ready than I could ever be.

We released our second single on June 16, 2009, with "Boom Boom Pow" still at #1. We had tested "I Gotta Feeling" ahead of time in the clubs because we were intrigued to see how people reacted. What was clear about its reception was that it brought instant positive energy and people were like "What's this track?"

So we thought, cool, it's a feel-good summer song. Upbeat. Lively. A party anthem. Something to play on a Friday night as you are getting ready.

But the moment it was released, we knew something crazy was happening because it vaulted straight to #2 in the Billboard Hot 100, tucked in behind "Boom Boom Pow."

How often will that *not* happen in our careers.

Having a back-to-back 1–2 felt incredible. More to the point, it was the first time in five years that a group had achieved it; one of only eleven groups ever.

"You have just made *Billboard* history." Polo said.

But the momentum had only just started.

"I Gotta Feeling" then swapped places with "Boom Boom Pow" and stayed at #1 for the following eight weeks—making us the first group to ever top the *Billboard* Hot 100 for twenty consecutive weeks.

"You have just made music industry history," Polo said.

When shit that big happens, it is hard to take in. It happens. It registers. And then before you know it, this whirlwind of activity and media is sucking you up so fast that the news never seems to have the time to sink in and hit home. But I won't lie—a part of me wanted to raise a fist in the air to all the doubters who ever accused us of selling out. Because if this was selling out—selling records, breaking records—then cool, because this is why each one of us entered the music industry with a dream: to make music that sold.

"You've earned this!" said Jimmy Iovine. "I'm proud of you guys—now get out there and enjoy it."

Interscope had said they needed another big album, but this ride was going beyond anyone's expectations. For if "Boom Boom Pow" was the monster hit, "I Gotta Feeling" was its superhero sibling. The moment it was born, it started breathing for itself and took on a life and form of its own.

I have heard the argument that the seminal moment for "I Gotta Feeling" was the day it was showcased as the opening song for the kickoff party for the twenty-fourth season of the *Oprah Winfrey Show*. There is no disguising the fact that "the Oprah factor" applied jet engines to the momentum. But here's the thing. We recorded Oprah on September 8. We had released the single on June 16—and it went to #1 on its own steam. I think those dates speak for themselves.

If anything, this song built its own momentum on the back of "Boom Boom Pow," not on the back of Oprah. But that takes nothing away from the experience we shared with Oprah, and we *shared* it because we, like her, had no idea about the scale of what went down that day when we recorded the show.

More than four million people have watched the YouTube footage of the "I Gotta Feeling" flash mob dance on Michigan Avenue, Chicago, and it was an event and spectacle that will live with me for the rest of my life: 20,000 ordinary men, women, and teenagers coming together as one and erupting into dance in a burst of perfect synchronicity.

If you haven't seen it, watch it because my words can't do it justice. If you were one of the thousands who took part, you will know what that thrill felt like when humanity united and danced and shut down the Magnificent Mile.

That event first came across our radar when the people at Harpo Productions started talking to BEP management about ways to mark Oprah's twenty-fourth season. Oprah is a big friend of Will's and has always been there for the Black Eyed Peas, so we wanted to be a part of whatever was going down.

The brief was to "plan something memorable that would surprise Oprah and make great television." For our part, we tweaked the song for a daytime show, starting the hook with *"Today's gonna be a good day . . ."*

After that, we pretty much left it to the choreographers and producers. All we knew going into the day was that there was going to be some kind of "special dance." We expected about twelve to fifteen dancers doing something rare. Beyond that, we were as much in the dark as Oprah was.

What management had kept from us was the fact that two hundred

choreographers had each spent time with one hundred–strong pockets of ordinary people in halls and community centers and then on the streets, teaching them every basic dance move: the jumps, the bobs, the sways, the waves.

On the day, as we were introduced and the music started, I was standing to the right of the open-air stage. I looked out and saw people as far as the eye could see, all clustered in and around the city buildings. Then the beat started up and one woman dressed in black started dancing at the front. Alone.

One woman dancing like a crazy fan. 19,999 other people standing still.

To our right, Oprah—wearing yellow for summer—had her camera phone out, capturing the gig from her backstage perspective.

About six people around the lone woman at the front of the stage then started breaking into dance; six synchronized swimmers. And then twenty others joined in—all in step, all dancing in unison.

Cool, it's catching on! I thought.

But it kept growing; this energy and dance spread out and back like a rolling wave. One hundred people dancing. Then the entire front section. Then the crowd one block away. Two blocks back. Until every one of the twenty thousand people who filled Michigan Avenue were dancing like the street was one big-ass set for a musical.

That is when I *stopped* dancing. I leaned forward and looked left, and Oprah was bouncing on the spot with excitement, still holding her camera phone, screaming, "OH WOW! OH WOW!"

It was the first time I have ever stopped dancing mid-performance. It was a sight to behold and I don't think any of us could understand the scale of that thing, and we couldn't wipe the smiles from our faces. Oprah had tears in her eyes at the end of the song. She was jumping up and down like an excited kid.

"That is so cool! That is so cool! THAT IS THE COOLEST THING EVER!! How did you guys do that?" she screamed.

Ask me what the biggest moment is with "I Gotta Feeling," and I won't tell you that it was when we were nominated for Song of the Year at the World Music Awards or for Record of the Year at the Grammys. I won't tell you it is when we performed it at the Super Bowl XLIV weekend in Miami or at the Grammy Nominations Live Concert. It wasn't even when the single passed the six million mark in 2010 for digital downloads.

As amazing as those experiences were, I will tell you the biggest moment was when we staged a party in a street and pulled off the craziest flash mob dance. For one of our fans.

Every time we dared think that an experience had just peaked all experiences, life pulled another white rabbit from its hat. Not long after leaving Chicago behind, we received the call that booked us as the support act to open for U2 at the Rose Bowl. What made this extra-special was the fact the stadium in Pasadena is virtually down the road from my house. It felt like we were opening for Bono in my backyard.

At rehearsals the day before, the scale of what we were walking into blew us away. It wasn't the vastness of the stadium. I knew that space all too well. It was the scale of the setup—it dwarfed anything we had seen with the Rolling Stones.

We ants stepped out onto a circular stage at the center of the field; a 360-degree view for U2's 360 tour to promote its album *No Line on the Horizon*. It was our first taste of performing inside a stadium, and just being out there, even minus a crowd, brought out the goose bumps. I looked directly above me into the underbelly of a one hundred fifty feet rocket ship named the "Claw," with its four outward curving legs planted around the circle, holding in place a giant video screen. It looked like a remake of *War of the Worlds.*

I was standing at the center, turning and taking in the 360-degree view, remembering the magnitude of the events that had been held here: the Super Bowl, the 1984 Olympics, the 1994 World Cup, and then the rock concerts, from the Stones to Pink Floyd, from Guns N' Roses to Kiss. And now U2—supported by the Black Eyed Peas.

My spirit swelled and I suddenly felt twenty feet tall.

There was a time when Bono was standing in this same position, I told myself. When he also dreamed of moments like this—and then he made it happen.

I had read about his childhood that same year. It was an article a friend showed me from a cover story in the *Sunday Times* magazine of London, and it said how "his father told him never to have dreams because he didn't want him to be disappointed—and that made him dream even bigger."

An Irishman with the same *Oh, you don't think so? Well, you watch me.*

A crowd of 96,000 people came to watch him that night, and most of them were in place as we ramped up the energy to fill that stadium with a set from *The E.N.D.* This was a warm-up for the world tour of our album, which had already become our most successful yet.

It had debuted at #1 in the *Billboard* Hot 200, shifting more than 300,000 copies in its first week. It has now sold more than seven million worldwide. *Rolling Stone* magazine said it was the best thing we had ever recorded. We couldn't wait to take the album on the road.

The Rose Bowl also gave us the platform to showcase our third single—"Meet Me Halfway"—which went #7 in the U.S. Hot 100 but became another #1 in both the U.K. and Australia. In the song's video, I orbited the sun in a space-suit, spinning around in a different galaxy. Which was a fair metaphor for our U2 experience.

Bono is the ultimate example of the ultimate performer, and he is artist,

humanitarian, and activist rolled into one; someone who has made a difference with his music and his voice. He stirs the soul of audiences. He pricks the conscience of governments. His tireless work—using his platform to campaign against Third World debt and to shout for Africa's causes and welfare—is an example of an artist using his celebrity in the way it should be used: as a guiding light and a mover of mountains.

U2 also stands as an example as a group—each one of them defines "brotherhood." I was impressed to see that they still share one dressing room after all these years. The sense of camaraderie, playfulness, and silliness was obvious the moment we met. Unlike our Rolling Stones experience, there was no separateness between headliners and support act. No them and us.

Bono went out of his way to bring us into his fold.

"Hey, Peas!" he said, breezing into our dressing room with his Irish charm. "What's up, guys? We're so glad you are here with us on this tour." After some warm man-hugs, he was then gathering both groups into one circle with his camera.

"Let's do one big U2–Black Eyed Peas picture!" he said.

He wanted a picture to remember the occasion.

Think about that: Bono wanted a picture to remember this moment. Humble. Down to earth. Making us feel included. In the time we spent with U2—we did a handful of dates with them—a recurring theme cropped up for me in the conversations: the importance of a band's chemistry and its friendship; the growing, failing, and succeeding together; and how longevity can strengthen the collective creativity. Because there is more than just a togetherness, there is a synergy. Wisdom from the master.

These occasions are not just about supporting a massive headliner, they are about watching and learning, too. Onstage, when you have seen someone like Bono put some place like the Rose Bowl in the palm of his hand and sing to it, you have witnessed magic. From the flamboyance of Busta Rhymes to the finesse of Bono: these are the peers who have inspired me throughout my journey.

Offstage, there is experience and insight to collect from the greats.

As Bono told Will: "It is the music we produce that gets closer to people than we can ever be. You are in their ears. You are in their head. That is the power of music."

We were invited to fly with Bono and his boys aboard what I referred to as "Air Force U2." We spent a whole night flying somewhere. I have got on and off so many planes that I can't remember the exact destination, but I remember Bono cracking open the Irish whiskey and I commemorated the occasion with water. If raising a toast with this icon at 25,000 feet in a private plane isn't going to make me want to drink, I think my sobriety is pretty safe.

The best thing that impressed me was that the group's parents, wives, and families were also along for the ride. This is what it is all about, he said—sharing it with family.

My new nickname "The Cardinal" suddenly sounded very rock 'n' roll.

On the night of June 25, 2009, we were attending our record release party in Paris to celebrate *The E.N.D.* We had just performed and were inside the VIP Room club just down from the Champs-Elysées, and Will was doing a spot of DJ-ing. We were buzzed that night because we had earlier performed "Meet Me Halfway" live for the first time and it had gotten a great reception.

I was on the side of the stage watching Will rocking this venue when he picked up his cell and checked his text messages. He came over and shouted out that he's got text messages saying Michael Jackson is dead.

At first, we all thought it was one of those texted pranks. Will had a personal relationship with Michael and good noises had been coming out of rehearsals for his AEG This Is It tour. The guy was two weeks away from kicking off his comeback in London. There is no way he could be dead.

I stepped outside and called Jaymie in L.A. She hadn't heard anything, but then again, the TV wasn't on. I asked her to check the Internet. "Oh my God, I don't believe it . . ." she said. At the same time, Will had sent a text to Quincy Jones in Moscow. The reply confirmed that Michael Jackson had suffered a fatal cardiac arrest.

I was walking back inside the club when Will stopped the music, and, in the uncharacteristic silence, he announced the news we had all just learned. The place was devastated. The party was over. I saw French clubbers, men and women, in tears as the lights came up. I don't think I've seen one event so deeply impact so many people all at once.

Outside the club, the rest of Paris seemed oblivious. It was already into its next day. I was standing in the Champs-Elysées. I was passing the Arc de Triomphe in the car. I was watching the news on CNN in my hotel room. I was calling Deja back in California, trying to connect with the long-distance reality. As teenagers, we spent hours at his house watching Michael Jackson concert videos on his VCR.

In the false storm of tabloid headlines surrounding his private life and unproved allegations, people far too easily forgot his musical genius. He was, simply, the greatest performer to have ever set foot on a stage. He set the bar so high—in terms of music, fashion, entertainment, songwriting, and production—that he will never be rivaled. If there is one justice in his premature death, it is the fact that his music has achieved what he always wanted it to achieve—it has had the final word.

The one thing none of us could have known in the immediate time after

his death was that the Black Eyed Peas would be picking up the touring baton left behind with AEG Live, the promoter behind This Is It.

Michael Jackson's passing left a massive hole in AEG's schedule and it started looking at ways of filling the void—and it offered us the opening. This was not about filling MJ's shoes: that was an impossibility. It was more about inheriting the scope of a tour and the gravitas of AEG. It was offering us touring support we had once only dreamed about. We could now go big and spectacular for the first time. Create a true "Black Eyed Peas experience."

We would be embarking on the one hundred-date AEG E.N.D. tour in 2010, and we had a feeling it was going to be special.

As great minds went to work on creating something ambitious for what became the BlackBerry E.N.D. world tour, we first took the album to Australia, New Zealand, and Japan with Frontier Touring, performing in cities like Tokyo, Osaka, and Nagoya, and Sydney, Brisbane, and Adelaide. But the highlight of that tour wasn't what happened on the ground, it is what happened when we joined the mile-high club.

The Black Eyed Peas Karaoke Mile-High Club.

We had started to acquire a taste for record-breaking so we had this crazy idea to break the record for the highest-altitude gig, previously held by Jamiroquai in 2007.

When the record-breaking day arrived on October 9, we arrived on the airport tarmac in Melbourne and Richard Branson's boys at Virgin Atlantic had pulled out all the stops. Because there, standing in front of us, was a 737 Virgin Blue jet with our faces plastered across each side of the fuselage.

We were speechless. Suddenly, it felt like we had traveled back in time and become members of Led Zeppelin.

At the height of their career, they had commandeered a tour plane called The Starship—a former United Airlines jet—for North America tour dates between 1973–75, and it was famously described as "a fucking flying gin palace." It flew them through the skies in another gas-guzzling, drink-guzzling rock 'n' roll era long before Gulfstreams and private jets became commonplace in the music industry.

But this October day in 2009 still felt like a magical throwback—and Led Zeppelin, to the best of my knowledge, only had the group logo on the fuselage. We had our own Black Eyed Peas wrap with 120-foot-high versions of our faces staring back at us.

We stood there for about five minutes taking photos and video, reconstructing the great Led Zeppelin pose in front of their own plane, not really believing that it was happening.

Fergie, who is a big Zeppelin fan, was in her element.

"Wow—this is IN-SANE!" I said. I looked at Apl and we were both thinking the same thing: from Roach Motel and riding buses in East L.A. to this?!

I remembered the time when the tour bus rolled up at the Warped tour wrapped in our album cover, and we thought *that* was the height of decadence.

"This is cray-zeeee!" said Apl, and we cracked up laughing.

On board, there was no water bed, shag carpeting, bar salon, or club room with leather couches. We couldn't have everything that Led Zeppelin enjoyed. We had a more makeshift version as Virgin gutted the business-class section and set up the DJ-deck and karaoke machine. The rest of the middle and back row seating remained for takeoff and landing, but once we were cruising, we enjoyed the space up front and turned it into one big jam session in the air.

The fun we had made it the funniest flight we had ever had on tour. Dante Santiago kicked off the karaoke by singing "Kiss" by Prince, Fergie ripped into Led Zeppelin's "Black Dog," and me and Apl sang "All the Small Things" by Blink-182. During mine and Apl's questionable performance, Will decided to do some crowd-surfing, and people—including thirty VIP guests who had won a charity auction—stood down the aisle, passing him all the way to the back, above their heads, and across the seats.

He then walked to the front and chose his own number—Barry Manilow's "Copacabana." I don't think any of us saw that one coming.

Somewhere over western Australia, between Melbourne and Perth, we performed the gig and played a couple of our songs including an acoustic version of "I Gotta Feeling." The captain came on the intercom and announced that we had reached 41,000 feet and just flown into the *Guinness Book of World Records.* The gods were woken by a rocking and cheering airplane, probably for the first time since the 1970s.

In the big dreams that we painted as kids, me and Deja always said that we would one day run together. In our days with the crew, United Soul Children, the one thing we'd always say out loud was: "We're going to be on tour one day."

I had never forgotten that, and neither had he. And the day he was standing beside me as best man at my wedding was the day when I knew I was going to be dishing the ball to this brother. I like to use that NBA metaphor because it is all about making assists, and I was now in a position—mentally and financially—to assist the one boy who has been by my side through everything.

Deja had left Activision and was working as a project leader at Electronic Arts, but I knew he was seeking a fresh challenge in life, and I was seeking a leader with a brain, an intellect, and organizational skills. So I called him up and reminded him about the dream we once had.

"So I think it's about time we made it happen and went on tour together,"

I said. I offered him a job and put an offer on the table that expressed my gratitude. "For real?" he said.

"Yessirr," I said.

Just in time for the start of the E.N.D. tour, I found the missing piece in my setup and installed Deja as my right-hand man, day-to-day manager and new addition to the BEP "fam-er-ree." Like Bono said, it's all about the brotherhood.

When the stage was built for the BlackBerry E.N.D. world tour, and we saw the full bells and whistles production roll out and light up for its first dry run in January 2010, we knew we had reached our dream destination.

It might not have been a planet-sized U2 setup, but it was still the ambitious monster we had always visualized seated inside Jimmy Iovine's office in 1997, when we held out for touring support as part of our first contract. Thirteen years later, we had what we wished for: a full-scale world tour complete with band risers, a giant wall of LED screens, illuminated decks, lasers, pyrotechnics, special effects, and cool mechanical gadgetry.

We had never had this scale of professional production before, and the man behind it all, Tim Miller, is the crème de la crème of the industry. He worked with our creative director Fatima Robinson and production designer Bruce Rodgers to create a set that matched the cybertron theme of the album. As Bruce says, what we ended up with "was a cross between a monster alien insect and a futuristic time machine."

We had twenty-feet-high steps leading down from a curved bandstand and a sixty-foot-long runway extending into the audience, and we had eagle-ramps shooting out from the left and right sides of the stage. The postage-stamp stages of L.A.'s clubs and London's Jazz Cafe seemed a different world away.

Beneath the stage, there was an underworld lit with Christmas lights to show the way to our individual mini–dressing rooms for the wardrobe changes we had to get used to. There were toaster-like elevators that catapulted us onto stage for the opener; the same air-assisted "spring-boards" that Michael Jackson was going to use for his concert.

Mine was always pod number 4, and me and Will started a competition in rehearsal to see who could be launched the highest, and we took that competitiveness around the world. The referee was always Bobby Grant. As soon as we landed, we'd take a sly look to the left and there was the wild-haired one, in his airport-style ear-muffs, pointing out the winner. I think my personal best going into 2011 was fifteen feet, according to Bobby. Bobby now had a one hundred fifty–strong operation behind him. Not sixty. Not eleven. But an army. I walked into rehearsals—and every venue—and couldn't believe how many people we now had traveling with us.

I remember the story Bobby brought back from London when we were recording the *Monkey Business* album and James Brown, during a break between sessions, sat him down and presented him with a pearl of wisdom.

"You are someone who works his ass off, Bobby," Mr. Brown told him, "and you can't wait for the pat on the back because you're moving too fast for a pat on the back. We are the stars. We get the pats on the back. But remember this, Bobby—a star ain't no star without no sky—and you is the sky!"

We had one hundred fifty different versions of Bobby, and I was grateful to each and every one of them for making us shine.

In a previous incarnation, we didn't need production on tour. We had ourselves, the band, and our spontaneity. But now we had a moving world, a framework, a specific set list, wardrobe changes, down-to-the-second timings . . . and dancers. Six female talents: Marlyn Ortiz, Julianne Waters, Jessica Castro, Niki Delecia, Brandee Stephens, and Nina Kripas.

The idea of incorporating choreography was foreign to us, but I was eager to learn. The challenge it posed was like my early days of b-boying. I was hungry to learn every minor detail. Each Pea worked with a dancer, and we spent good hours mastering little sections of choreography in repetitive bursts. Break it down. Keep it repetitive. Easier to learn that way, they said.

My guide was an Austrian bundle of energy, Nina Kripas. I nicknamed her "The Coach"—always smiling, positive, and patient. Under her guidance, I reverted back to being the kid with the video camera in the backyard, using my flip-cam to record different moves and then analyze them at home. As Nina says: "All you would ask is how am I doing? Does my arm go there? Is this right? You wanted to nail it 100 percent."

The perfectionist within me is the one thing that will never change.

The girls would sit on the stage, shouting out tips, making observations, especially when it came to mastering the harness and bungee work for aerial work which Marlyn and Jessica made look effortless. That shit *wasn't* effortless, and those bungees almost busted my balls, with back-flips and air-ninja spins. But I practiced like someone possessed, and when I nailed it, the girls were seated on the edge of the stage applauding and cheering.

Dance, monkey. Perform, monkey. Get ready for your biggest stage yet, monkey.

THE E.N.D.

Los Angeles: March 30, 2010:

I hear it before feeling it.

I am crouched down in pod number four beneath the stage, adrenaline racing. There is no one to to my left, but Fergie is to my right, head down, tucked into her own glass box in our secret "underworld." To her right, in these pods side by side, are Will and Apl.

We resemble four athletes on their marks, waiting for the starting gun. In a cave.

We have just got ourselves into position and it is pitch black.

It is even darker in my world—I have my sunglasses on.

The lights have faded front of house and everyone out there is in mild darkness.

And then . . . that unmistakable but unnameable sound.

It arrives like a stiff breeze, a growing murmur from the crowd. Expectant. My eyes are closed. I am trying to savor every moment. I have never felt this alert, this alive. It feels different this time. When sober. On this scale. It feels like my debut again.

That sound builds and whips up loud, gathering pace until the crowd's roar is an approaching tornado, sweeping the stage, passing over us. I feel the vibration. Under my feet. Against the elevator glass.

Then the chant: *"BLACK EYED PEAS . . . BLACK EYED PEAS . . . BLACK EYED PEAS!"*

Here comes the ride.

My muscles tense and I re-balance myself. My feet are installed in the springs that are about to catapult me into the air. I cannot wait to get out there and rock this shit.

The crowd starts screaming. They have seen shadowy figures appear on stage. I now know that the band, Bucky Jonson, is in place.

A robot speaks in a deep booming voice, like a spaceship announcing its invasion: "WELCOME . . . TO THE END!"

I hear the scream rising. I now know the lasers are swirling on stage, circling, starting to create four green pools of light.

And then the space-like countdown begins.

10-9-8-7-6 . . .

I think of Jaymie, Josh, and Jalen. I thank God for this and every moment.

5-4-3-2-1 . . .

And I am in the air, front of stage, flying beneath a blinding gaze of light.

I had forgotten how good it felt: performance mode.

I had been caught up in the party for too long, and stopped being true to my dream. I ran through it, pissed on it, shitted on it, threw up on it, fucked it, smoked it, drank it, and I don't like to know how close I came to killing it.

We had kicked off the tour in Atlanta at the Philips Arena on February 4, 2010, and that feeling—that transmission of energy and that wall of sound of the people echoing our songs back to us—is the best kind of high there is: sex, drugs, and rock 'n' roll rolled into one.

For the year-long tour that took us into 2011 and sent us north, south, east, and west across North America, Canada, Europe, and South America, I woke up each morning with that certainty of knowing that this high was guaranteed at the end of each show day.

And then, during the in-between times, I had my family time. Even when away on the road, there was Skype, allowing me to see Jalen growing up remotely. I was tasting what I had never appreciated before: the real sense of substance and fulfilment in being a father.

In the abnormal life of a performer and the normal life of a father, there was no emptiness to fill. No need to find holes and fill them with alcohol, drugs, and girls, and all that artificial shit that ultimately made me miserable.

Today, I have learned to leave the masks in the dressing room. I have learned how to leave the day job, switch off, and become the family man I always wanted to be.

■　■　■

Our feet didn't seem to touch the floor for most of 2010 and, as demanding as the schedule was, it turned into our most successful and profitable tour. We sold out wherever we went and when you can say that at the end of one hundred dates, you know you have hit a home run, capable of playing in the big league.

We had already had the highs of the record-breaking sales, opening for U2, the Oprah flash mob dance and the Karaoke Mile High, and 2010 carried on in the same mad vein.

We were nominated for six Grammys, and added to our untelevised-victory collection with three Grammys for Best Pop Vocal Album, Best Performance by a Duo or Group ("I Gotta Feeling") and Best Short Form Video ("Boom Boom Pow").

A month later, we shut down Times Square with "a surprise concert" to launch Samsung's new 3D TV. New York City safety regulations meant we couldn't promote the outdoor gig until fifteen minutes before its start, but even then, thanks to the speed of social media and Twitter, ten thousand still showed up and Times Square came to a standstill. That's gone down as "the day we stopped time in Times Square" in the "fam-er-ree" scrapbook.

There was the maddest European festival circuit we had ever done, headlining seven cities in eleven days: Lille, Barcelona, Venice, Athens, Dublin, Edinburgh, and Brussels. Then came Canada and the Festival d'été de Québec where 120,000 people crammed onto the Plains of Abraham at night. We had seen a vast crowd before—on Ipanema Beach—but Québec was an intense experience; a mass of people front, back, and sides, each holding red lights in the darkness, jumping, bouncing, pumping, going crazy. When we played the encore of "I Gotta Feeling," that atmosphere built for me the eighth wonder of the world.

I looked forward to that encore wherever we went. The chill people tell me they get when that song comes on is the same chill I get performing. It has become one of those rare smashes that will never get old, and there was nothing more empowering than going from continent to continent and city to city and seeing that song bring out the same reaction in people, regardless of age, creed, race, or religion.

I remember the moment when we performed the *Good Morning America* Summer Concert Series in Central Park after a night of traveling and no sleep. We were groggy to say the least for the 7 a.m. sound check. Then that inner switch flicked and we were "on." We performed three songs on live television and played out to "I Gotta Feeling," and that was when I saw middle-aged women and grandmas dancing and bobbing, singing the words. What we thought was a college anthem had turned into a world anthem. We realized that much when we were invited to play at the Kick-Off Celebration Concert to launch the FIFA World Cup in South Africa in June: my personal highlight of 2010.

It wasn't special just because we got to perform before a worldwide audience of two billion people at the world's biggest event, which was mind-blowing in itself. It was also because I would get to perform twice: once with the group, once by myself.

A phone call had come out of the blue in the run-up to the tournament.

"What are your thoughts about performing *without* the Peas?" Deja asked.

"Are you for real?"

"Yes sir," said Deja. "Juanes wants you to perform with him. Just you, brother."

"What song does he want me to do?"

"La Paga," said Deja.

In English, "The Payback."

I had never before had an appreciation of soccer until arriving in Johannesburg for the World Cup, and Soweto for the concert. Give me a basketball or a baseball bat and I'm all about it, but soccer? It made me yawn.

I had not even paid attention to the tournament before. I thought world events got no bigger than the Oscars or the Grammys. But then we got there and BOOM—this beautiful reality hit me between the eyes. South Africa was holding the world's biggest party, and me, the dumb American, had just walked into the room, wondering what all the fuss was about.

There were flags of different nationalities everywhere, being waved without antagonism and every second car seemed to be flying the South African colors. It was a carnival atmosphere and different races of people mingled, hugged and high-fived one another.

I saw Mexico jerseys and flags, the Stars & Stripes and the St. George's flag of England. We had come here in 2004 and saw only one race—white people—enjoying our concert; and here we were six years later witnessing black and white people from all backgrounds united. Planet Football seemed like the coolest place on earth, and the concert was one of the biggest occasions we had been part of, shared with Shakira, John Legend, and Alicia Keys.

The atmosphere on stage inside the Pirates Stadium was electrifying and I remember performing "I Gotta Feeling" before a packed stadium with the Peas and thinking the whole stadium was shaking. It was that song, we found out, that the Portuguese team used as a pre-match anthem to motivate them during the tournament's qualifying stages the previous year.

It was a privilege to be a part of the World Cup vibe, and it was a double privilege to then be asked to perform with Juanes, one of Latin America's best-selling musicians. I couldn't believe that I first represented with my group and then got to come back on stage and represent for the Latinos. There I was, this

American artist coming from a Latino background known for English-style music, stepping into the Spanish market with the Colombian master on the world stage in South Africa. Opportunities don't feel anymore international than that.

The night before, I had done a sound check and I couldn't nail the part. I had only been given ten days to reacquaint myself with a song I had recorded as a remix for Juanes in 2003, and it hadn't gone well at rehearsals. It probably didn't help that I knew all those seats would be filled the next day and two billion people would be on the other side of the TV cameras for this. Doing it alone—my first "live" performance outside of the Black Eyed Peas—kind of threw me for a loop.

On the day, after the Peas had done their segment, I had about thirty minutes to prepare myself before I was invited into Juanes' set. I took myself to the restroom to snatch a private moment. In my head, an NBA coach was psyching me up, telling me he was about to bring me off the bench and put me in the game. My chance to sink a three-pointer in front of the world.

When the time came, I was standing in the wings, feeling pumped. I was wearing all white—white pants and a white leather jacket with the proud word "MEXICO" embossed on the back. I looked out and saw the same crowd I had just performed to with the Peas.

It's no different, I told myself. *It's all in your head.*

I call on Nanny. *Way to go Jim. Way to go . . .*

Then I hear Juanes announce my name: "TABOOOOOOOOO!"

I race on, and it feels instantly strange not to have Will, Apl, and Fergie around me, but I didn't feel lost either, not with my comrade Juanes beside me. As we launched into "La Paga," I fed off his energy and brought my own weapon to the stage, and the Latin American crowd went crazy.

It was beyond special. I looked out and saw all these South African flags being waved. Then the blue of Italy. The yellow of Brazil. Then the green, white, and red of Mexico. One to the left. One mid-center. At the end of my first verse, I shouted out to my people: "VIVA MEXICO!"

This massive cheer bounced back to me, and more Mexican flags were held high and proud. I could almost hear the delayed response: "Wait. The scary-looking Asian dude is from MEXICO?! He's one of us?"

As we came off the back of the last verse, I took out a folded green, white, and red *Bandera de Mexico,* unfurled it, held it aloft, and then raised my fist in salute.

It was a powerful moment for me, my culture, and the importance I recognized in having a voice as a Mexican-American. I had a voice at an event broadcast to the world and where sport had brought North Korea onto the same level playing field as the U.S.A., in a country where Nelson Mandela had sacrificed his liberty to overturn racial discrimination.

And yet in America, in a country which stands as a model of fair democracy, there was an injustice being perpetrated against Latinos, and I couldn't wait to get back to use my voice, stand up, and make some noise.

Each time I reenter the U.S.—and especially at its borders with Canada—the name "Gomez" always attracts interest from Customs. There is always a long list of questions, and, sometimes, I have been pulled into an office because of the activities of other Jaime Gomezes out there. At airports and borders, I understand why a matching name throws up a red flag.

What I don't get and can't accept is the idea that someone can be pulled over in the street, at random, as he or she goes about his or her daily business, in a U.S. state, just because they *look illegal*. By "looking illegal," I mean someone of Latin descent.

Because that was the reality of a new immigrant enforcement law that was passed and signed by Arizona in the summer of 2010. Its Gestapo will say that Bill 1070 does not target Latinos but *anyone* "who arouses reasonable suspicion." But that is bullshit political speak. The reality is that Arizona is viewed as an illegal gateway for border crossers, and those breaches nearly always involve Latinos. So the moment you place some new hunt-seek-and-deport law into the hands of police officers *untrained* in immigration, there is only one likely outcome: racial profiling.

We were in Berlin touring Europe in the middle of May—two weeks before the World Cup—when it came up in conversation with Deja and Will. My first reaction was to get on Twitter and start speaking out against it.

The more I thought about it, the more angry I became. Imagine the uproar if Arizona's Gestapo suddenly started pulling people over because they had pale skin, looked British, and *that* constituted grounds for suspicion, I said.

It hit a nerve because I remembered Nanny's stories about how she was racially profiled as a kid in Jerome, and it got me wondering what Nanny would say now. "We've got to do something about this," Deja said. "You're a Latino with a platform."

"Ask yourself this, Tab," said Will. "Look in the mirror and ask yourself 'Do you look illegal?' "

I had never felt so moved to do something and speak out, but I wasn't articulate enough to stand at a podium and make the point. I wanted to do what we had historically done as the Black Eyed Peas, and use music as the medium . . . but stand alone, as a Latino. This wasn't about being a celebrity with a cause. It was about using my voice to speak up for those who didn't have one.

Latinos are a proud people, and all they want to do is earn a living and provide for their families by doing the farm work, cleaning the houses, and picking the strawberries. They give their blood, sweat, and toil for America—and then

Arizona points its finger at them and makes them vulnerable to arbitrary detention. Treating them like the enemy, not a workforce.

It was on the European leg of the tour that we had the support act of solo talent Cheryl Cole, this petite British singer who is massive in London and is just counting down until she blows up in America. Will has always believed in her talent, and I got to meet her for the first time in Europe. This girl is a superstar in the U.K., and I couldn't believe the amount of press attention she got on a daily basis, and so it was impressive to see how unaffected and down-to-earth she was. It almost felt like she was in awe to be on the Black Eyed Peas tour—that she almost didn't believe it herself—and I liked that humility in her. I was also blown away by the way she kept her team tight and together—the band, the singers, her assistant Lily—and when I heard the voices of her backing singers Kristen and Sarah, I was like "Damn, you two should have your own record deal!"

It was during one of the Peas' Bacardi after-parties—it was either Paris or Prague—when I was sitting around with our drummer and music producer Keith Harris talking about doing a solo project against Bill 1070. That is when I looked across the VIP room, saw Cheryl's dynamic duo, and an idea formed. We already had the beat. What we needed next was lyrics, and Kristen and Sarah said they were singer-songwriters.

When we were back in London at the end of May, we played them the beat and they started feeling the topic, and began writing. I had only ever seen Will work faster. Suddenly, they started writing down *"One heart, one beat . . ."*

As I worried about how I was going to pop a hook, their lyric then inspired me to write *". . . it takes one to fight for y'all, one man to stand up tall . . ."*

Then there was Mooky, the other third of Atban Klann and our old friend, who was still tight with us all and still doing what he does best: producing and writing songs. Me and Mook have a lot in common: we had kids at an early age, we have both been a part of Will and Apl's life, and we have both had our struggles. Today, we are tighter than we have ever been, and he read a passage at my wedding. He is today an integral part of my team and, back in L.A., he came up with the line: *"We're marching, we're marching . . . justice must be served."*

Suddenly, this song started forming and started building momentum.

At the World Cup, I spoke with Juanes. "I'm all about it, Tab . . . you have my backing."

I spoke with Shakira. She was "behind me every step of the way."

Once back in America, I went to Eva Longoria's house to call on her support. I visited Oscar de la Hoya at a fight—and they backed me all the way. Each one of them provided a brief video clip and message that said "I oppose Bill 1070." I recorded them with the Flip Video that Cheryl Cole had given each Pea as a thank-you present.

But the real coup and honor was enlisting the support of Dolores Huerta, one of the most powerful figures and activists in the Latino community. She had been an active force with JFK, Martin Luther King, and Cesar Chavez. She had stood alongside Bobby Kennedy at his podium at the Ambassador Hotel in L.A. on June 5, 1968, in the moments before he was assassinated. This was a woman whose power to lobby was soaked in history.

She is an eighty-year-old woman who still has the passion of a student campaigner when it comes to representing the Latino people, so when she agreed to not only back my song but appear in its video, it personally felt like I had recruited a Mother Teresa or a Gandhi.

We had met three years earlier during the Cesar Chavez March in L.A., representing the farm-workers in 2007. She knew where my heart was, and we both knew the power of this song's message. I released "One Heart, One Beat"—thanks to director Fernando Diaz—virally, via YouTube and Twitter, in July, 2010, just as a judge announced a temporary injunction that suspended the Arizona law. Common sense held the prevailing wind, but the state said it would keep on fighting. As we must.

We are one world, one tribe, one people, and somewhere along the way we have lost compassion for humanity. But then there are people like Dolores Huerta. Nelson Mandela. Bono. Voices of reason. In the great examples life continued to show me, it taught me that it only takes one person to speak up and to keep knocking gently. One voice can grow into millions of voices, in the same way one song can get downloaded six million times. If we keep that in mind, places like Arizona might wake up. I like to think that God gives even states a second chance when they fuck up.

2010 seemed to be a year when I found my wings. First, the opportunity with Juanes. Then "One Heart, One Beat." And then, in August, the new release of my own shoe line. The theme of "a dream within a dream" kept continuing.

Ever since being twelve years old, I have collected sneakers. Hence the need for a shoe room at the house. I am a self-confessed "sneaker pimp" who has OCD when it comes to both my and other people's footwear. I am always looking at the style, the make, and dissecting the look and color someone has chosen. I'm not a people watcher. I am a shoe watcher.

I never dreamed the day would come when I would be lucky enough to step into the fashion game and put my stamp on my own sneaker. Not until New York Fashion Week 2008 when I was shopping in Bloomingdale's. I pulled a Jump sneaker off the rack and started raving about its style to the man standing next to me.

"Are you from the Black Eyed Peas?" this guy asked, and I said yes, thinking he wanted an autograph. But then he introduced himself.

"Hello, I'm Victor Hsu, marketing director of Jump Corp. footwear. I'm

glad you like the shoe so much," he said. I told him what I liked about it. I told him about my OCD. I told him what I liked to wear onstage. He said he would send me some free shit. Then I told him that we needed to collaborate on some shit.

"Sure," he said.

As Victor would soon find out, that was all I needed to hear. I kept on at him for weeks, saying I wanted to work with him. Guided by one of those powerful gut instincts, I couldn't let it go. The moment I started even imagining a footwear deal, it became a dream on the same level as shooting for a record deal.

I started going to bed, visualizing my own line on the racks in Bloomingdale's. "I'm going to make it happen," I kept telling Deja, "you watch me."

Then, one day, the phone rang, and it was Victor. "We've got a new range coming out called the Zeto," he said, "so I thought we could mix fashion with music and do our first collaboration."

Long story short, they laid out plans for this high-end sneaker packaged in satin bags and drawer boxes, priced at $300 and called the Taboo X-Jump.

"Where are you going to be stocking it?" I asked.

"Bloomingdale's," said Victor, "and Saks Fifth Avenue." I felt like running up and down the length of Manhattan. And then I felt like going to China. I wanted to see how they were made, who made them, and what conditions they were made in.

I'm a musical artist—I like to shake the hand of the producer.

I didn't want to be just another name adding my name to a product. I wanted to get to know it intimately and get under its leather skin. So I found myself in China, and met the one hundred people whose hands the sneaker passed through before it reached the rack. I watched them choose the leather, cut it, nail it, stitch it, make it perfect. Manufacturing a personal dream on the factory floor. It was incredible being on the assembly line, seeing these rows of people sitting at sewing machines in blue overalls, applying an intense focus to their handiwork. I got the bug to do more in China.

"Let's not stop here." I said. "Let's design a more affordable sneaker," I said.

And guess what? In August 2010, at a Foot Locker store in New York, I launched the Taboo Deltah, making a sneaker for the masses. I like to think the end product is a bit like this book—it gives you a chance to walk in my shoes.

There was a joke on the American leg of the E.N.D. tour that I used to go to clubs and be stumbling around or falling over, bouncing from person to person. Now, all the "fam-er-ree" sees me doing is sitting around sipping green tea, interchanging from this person to that person showing them cell-video footage of Jalen: his first time in a shopping cart, his first time sitting in a high chair in a restaurant, his first time in the swing in the garden, his first time in his play-pen.

I missed out on the vivid memories of so many "firsts" with Josh—and in the first half of my career—that I don't want to miss a moment second time around.

Jalen is the kind of kid who just exudes happiness. His face tells the whole story. His face makes my day. I could be—I have been—in the shittiest of moods, and all I need to is look at his smile. That might sound chunky-cheesy but the truth can sometimes be chunky-cheesy.

That has become the hardest thing about touring: the leaving home and leaving behind the family. I am in the zone on the stage, but, in Australia and Japan, I found my mind wandering to Jaymie, Josh, and Jalen, wondering what they were doing.

I didn't want to keep imagining Jalen's face on tour. I wanted it with me. I wanted to carry around his smile and "firsts" like a pocket book of memories and have it with me on the plane and tour bus, and backstage and back at the hotel.

On the day before leaving for the AEG marathon, as Jaymie was arranging some clothes and helping me pack, I was carrying Jalen, sitting up high, in my left arm. I backed out of the bedroom, moved down the hallway, and went into the bathroom, locking the door.

I wanted a father-and-son moment.

I looked at us both in the mirror: him curious at his own reflection, his fingers in his gums, his mouth opening like a fish. I reached into my pocket with my right hand, brought out my cell, and held up the video to the mirror. Recording us as if the lens was somebody else's eyes.

I started speaking quietly to his reflection, in my head.

I wanted to tell him what he meant to me and what a difference he had made; that he will read this story one day and understand how I became his dad.

I am stronger now that you are here.

I want you to know how much I love you, that I'll never leave you and I'll be there for you through life. You have my heart. I have your back.

I was standing there for about two minutes, observing me and him together until I heard Jaymie calling me. I pressed "stop" and the footage was saved.

I kept playing that moment back on my screen, over and over on tour. I watched it play back and noticed the things I missed in the moment: the way he paws my hand; the way he rests his head against my shoulder; the way he depends on me; and the way I could burst with pride.

I show the flight attendant. I show the bellman at the hotel. I show the bodyguards. I show anyone who will watch and listen.

In London, I show Cheryl's backup singers, Kristen and Sarah. We had been writing up "One Heart, One Beat" when, as we watched the Jalen footage, I said something on impulse: "What I really want to do is write a song for my son."

I told them the story I have just told you: about stealing a moment and

telling him what he meant to me, but I wanted more than just words. I wanted it to become a song.

Kristen pulled aside Cheryl's guitarist and, together, they wrote the hook. Over the coming weeks, it built into a song we would call "Innocence."

It is a song with a universal pull for any proud dad who understands his legacy. I hope it is released one day soon.

Without music, without the beat, it doesn't carry the same force, but there is one section of the lyrics that the team wrote, and I share them here because they do justice to what I feel more than anything else I could express:

> *Is it the love in your eyes, or the way that you glow*
> *The music in your voice that speaks to my soul*
> *Your innocence reminds me of how we once shined*
> *It's been a hard climb, but today's now our time*
> *Your laugh is enough to make the world seem so free*
> *You're worth every moment that I fought to believe*
> *Forever in my heart*
> *Together we are one*
> *You'll be my guiding light*
> *I'll be your shining sun . . .*

Jalen came into my life when everything had been lined up perfectly: the marriage, the success, the financial stability, the recovery. When the party life went, a new life began, and grace brought that new life in the form of Jalen.

As for Josh, he is a young man now and provides me with equal pride. He is growing into a real go-getter, and his togetherness exceeds anything that I had ever taught him. At eleven, he started learning how to rap. At fourteen, he became classically trained on the piano. Self-taught. He bought a book called *Teach Yourself Piano* and his musical instincts did the rest. And today, he is emulating Will, Apl, and David Guetta. He is a DJ—a cool beat-maker—who is already booking gigs and parties around Los Angeles.

Los Angeles: March 30, 2010:

I am beneath the stage, straddling a motorbike straight from the set of Tron, all wide, black, and bad-ass with white neon trims glowing in the dark.

I am leaning forward, arms out wide on the low-lying handle-bars, legs pushed back. Sleek in black leather. The bike rests on a slow-rising elevator beneath center stage. There are four wires suspending the bike, front and rear. I trust their durability. I have to—they are about to lift me forty feet in the air, above the stage, and carry me out across the audience.

We are just awaiting the signal.

Above me, out of sight, cheers and whistles are dying down. Which means Apl's solo segment has just ended with his song "Mare."

The lights front of house dim. Then there is loud buzzing and electric static. A frequency changing. I now know that the audience is seeing my name flashing up in big Tron letters on the video wall as wide as the stage. Then different black and white photos on six video screens. I hear that sound building again.

This is my biggest rush of the night.

But tonight is not just about fans inside this arena. It is about an audience across America. We are being beamed in 3D in a live simulcast into four hundred fifty sold out Regal Theaters.

It is a first for a concert. We are breaking another record.

My song, "Rockin' to the Beat," starts up.

I am rising. I sit up, eyes now level with the stage. The roar rises with me. I am rising high, hoisted in slow motion, and this packed crowd falls away to my right.

At forty feet, my bike turns head on—and I am moving forward, above a sea of heads. Rapping. Soaring. I couldn't care less if I was singing "Baa Baa Black Sheep." Neither could the crowd. They are cheering the spectacle. I am riding the energy.

I am on top of the world.

Out of all the one hundred dates, it was always this concert at the Staples Center that we were looking forward to the most. We have been on the road for almost eight weeks, and this is our "homecoming concert."

We have just finished "Where Is the Love?"—the song that leads us into the encore set.

But Will is on the mic talking about how special this night has been. It is the beginning of a monologue that could only ever have meaning in Los Angeles.

He is dripping in sweat, but he's beaming. We all are. There are cardboard banners being held up high in the crowd: "EAST L.A." and "BOYLE HEIGHTS!" I see one saying "VIVA MEXICO TABOO!" I raise a fist in the air.

Apl waves to a girl shouting out for the Philippines. We are surrounded by homies, not just fans.

Out there, somewhere, is my old homie Eclipse—the man who gave me a leg up into this dream. The first person in the world to believe that I had something. He's here with his two kids, telling them how it all started in school gymnasium halls.

In a separate section, there is Miss Moran and Mr. Musgrave, my language arts teacher from Rosemead High and my math teacher from Muscatel Junior; both here to say how proud and pleased they are. But there is no Mr.

Callaham, my English teacher, so I'm not sure what he makes of my story—my beginning, middle, and end.

Backstage, there is Deja and Mooky waiting in the wings. Ever-present.

But the biggest joy for me tonight is learning that Boogaloo Shrimp is here with his manager Jim White. Standing in the same row as Eclipse. We had both grown up being inspired by this dancer. As had Michael Jackson. And there I am, being watched by this pioneer of b-boying, who inspired me to dream big.

Life turning full circle.

All these significant figures are adding to the emotion that everyone is feeling, and Will is explaining to the fans why it means so much, and he is speaking for us all.

We are locals, he says, just like you. We had a dream, he says, just like you.

And tonight we look back on our journey and cannot believe we are here, performing inside the Staples Center down the road from where it all began. We could not have done it without your support. It is you who helped us make the dream possible.

Thank you. Thank you!

It's the end of the encore after "Boom Boom Pow." The sex moment of the concert—and the Staples is rocking.

It seems that every one of the 18,000 people are on their feet and bouncing. Across the floor and packed around the runway. In the tiered seating and outside the suites. The whole place is pulsing in tandem with the light show.

Bucky Jonson cues in our last song of the night. The place erupts.

Six spaceship-sized lights arched above the stage flash on full beam, flooding the arena in white light. Then fade.

I'm skipping down the blue-lit runway, wearing a red leather jacket and black pants.

Will, all silver-jacketed, bounces in front: "Clap your hands, y'all . . . Clap your hands, y'all . . . Clap your hands, yerr-all," he chants.

Fergie and Apl are behind us, halfway down the runway, nearer the stage.

Together, we sing: "I Gotta Feeling. . . ."

As one, the crowd steps up: "WUH-HOOOO!"

"That tonight's gonna be a good night . . . That tonight's gonna be a good night . . ."

Whatever that feeling is, capture it, bottle it, live it.

Dream it.

Keep it on the positive.

ACKNOWLEDGMENTS

Somewhere between *The E.N.D.* and *The Beginning* I decided to write this book, and so, while traveling the world on tour, I found myself simultaneously traveling back through my life, pouring everything out, trying to make sense of the journey so far.

In the year's time between December 2009 and December 2010, I probably spent as much time speaking into a tape recorder as I did singing into a microphone, and the production of a book is just like the creation of a single, an album, or a tour—it's a collaborative effort.

As with the Black Eyed Peas dream, I couldn't have done it without the best team of people around me, so my gratitude goes to a cast of family members, friends, and publishing professionals:

First and foremost, thank you to my wife, Jaymie, who has been there since the beginning, when I had nothing but a dream. You took care of me through thick and thin, believed in me, supported me, and recognized the potential of the man that I could become. I am so blessed to have you in my life, and that we have remained in love and dedicated to each other. You, your love, your friendship, and your strength are truly appreciated every single day.

Joshua Gomez—we have almost grown up together, and you have taught me so much about life. I am honored to have been blessed with you as my first-born son. You are a wonderful and beautiful old soul whose vast knowledge of music and the arts continues to inspire me. You're the next one in line. Get um J/1der! I love you with all my heart, son.

Jalen "Kung Fu" Gomez—you are a dream come true. Your light shines bright within all our lives and you are a true joy to be around. I look at you and feel the love, and cannot believe the joy you've brought. OMG. You are such a blessing to your mother and I, and I'm so excited to watch you grow and become whatever you want to be. Go get um Bam Bam! I love you.

I certainly wouldn't be anywhere if it were not for my "brothers" Will and Apl. You both have taught me everything I know about music, dance, production, and style, and I owe a great deal of my career to you guys, for seeing something in me as a performer that has allowed me to live out my wildest dreams. Thank you. And then there is Fergie, whom I want to thank for being such a wonderful "sister" and a positive influence. You have shown me a great deal of what a superstar is capable of accomplishing within our group, and independently. I love you, Ferg!

Polo Molina, *gracias carnal.* You saw something in me at age fourteen and told me that you would "make me famous." Look at us now! Thank you for your belief, guidance, and unstinting support.

And then Mom, Julio, and Celeste—I know times were often rough, but without those growing pains, I would never have become the person that I am today. I have your love to thank for that. You were there when I needed you the most, and I don't know if I ever expressed my gratitude, but it means the world to me. I pray that you will grow to show that same love to the rest of my family, who are natural extensions of me.

Special thanks must go to David "Deja" Lara. You are the true meaning of a childhood friend, brother, and confidant. I'm grateful that you came into my life, and I am honored that you are now a part of the Tab Magnetic team. I know big things await us in the future, and I look forward to growing our empire. Let's shake up the world. Long live the Montezuma Project!

Those are the people behind my life. Now for the people behind this book, who helped shape that life into a story, and the great team within the Simon & Schuster publishing house. My immense gratitude goes to:

Publishing impresario Stacy Creamer who, from the moment we met, impressed me with her vision and infectious passion for this project. I wouldn't have wanted to have done this with anyone else. She led me, with an expert hand, through unknown territory, and toward a product I am proud about. It's been some ride!

My cowriter and partner in crime, Steve Dennis. "How many chapters are we doing, Steve?!" Thank you for your patience, honesty, and talent, "mate." You made this book "a smasher," and I enjoyed (most) of our time together, on the road and in L.A.

Then, literary agent Alan Nevins for believing in this story together with

ACHNOWLEDGMENTS

ACKNOWLEDGMENTS

H. Yu Esq., and making this book happen; George Pajon, Printz Board, Keith Harris, Nick Lauher, and Bobby Grant for being my distant memory in the compiling of events. It's also George's camera lens that has expertly captured many of the on-the-road, backstage photographs in this book—providing a nostalgia that transports us back to where it all started.

And the rest of the team at Simon & Schuster: Stacy Creamer's right-hand woman Lauren Spiegel for being such a crucial linchpin; copy editor Patricia Morrison for your thoroughness and expert eye; and Cherlynne Li for creating such an impressive, standout book jacket. Thanks also to in-house counsel Emily Remes, interior designer Ruth Lee-Mui, production editor Josh Karpf, production managers George Turianski and Mike Kwan, associate publisher David Falk, marketing manager Meredith Kernan, publicity director Marcia Burch, publicity manager Shida Carr, and managing editor Kevin McCahill. Thanks also to other dear friends and family: Fernando Diaz, for your stunning work with the book cover photographs, and for being such a brother; Julio Godina for being an integral part of the same team; then, my mother-in-law Vicky; and Roger; my sister-in-law Leslie and Rolly Bayaca; and my brother-in-law Anthony Dizon; and Cathy Dizon, for all your love and support. Not forgetting the hospitality of the staff at our restaurant writing bases: Teresita's in East L.A., and Canali in Venice Beach.

I'd also like to thank the fans who have supported me, and the readers who have taken the time to read my story. I hope it gives hope to anyone who faces the walls of "can't do" or "that's impossible" I hope my story serves to remind any dreamer to walk the positive path, and do what's in your heart.

Finally, I have saved the biggest thank-you till last because she deserves special mention: Nanny—you have been the greatest support system in my life. Even in your absence, you continue to shape and inspire me. You shine your light from the heavens so I can still follow the right path. I love you with all my heart and I know there will never be anyone like you again. You are truly one of a kind. Your Jim is definitely "going to get um." Thank you for simply believing in my dream.

Jaime Gomez